PUBLIC SECTOR ECONOMICS

Public Sector Economics

RANDALL G. HOLCOMBE

Auburn University

Wadsworth Publishing Company
Belmont, California
A Division of Wadsworth, Inc.

ECONOMICS EDITORS:
Kristine M. Clerkin and Stephanie Surfus

EDITORIAL ASSISTANT:
Cindy Haus

PRODUCTION EDITOR:
Jerilyn Emori

PRINT BUYERS:
Barbara Britton and Ruth Cole

DESIGNER:
Andrew H. Ogus

COPY EDITOR:
Tom Briggs

TECHNICAL ILLUSTRATOR:
Joan Carol

COVER:
Andrew H. Ogus

Cover photographs of the Lincoln Memorial in Washington, D.C., courtesy of the National Capital Parks, U.S. Department of the Interior

Printed in the United States of America 19

1 2 3 4 5 6 7 8 9 10 --- 92 91 90 89 88

Library of Congress Cataloging-in-Publication Data

Holcombe, Randall G.
  Public sector economics.

  Includes index.
  1. Finance, Public.   2. Economic policy.   I. Title.
HJ141.H58   1987   338.9   87-13344
ISBN 0-534-08190-8

To Lora

Brief Contents

PART FOUR: TAXATION

PART FIVE: REDISTRIBUTION

PART SIX: ECONOMIC ACTIVITIES OF GOVERNMENT

Detailed Contents

APPENDIX TO CHAPTER ONE: INDIFFERENCE CURVE ANALYSIS
Page 18

CHAPTER TWO: PRINCIPLES FOR ANALYZING GOVERNMENT
Page 28

Part Two: Economic Efficiency

CHAPTER THREE: ECONOMIC EFFICIENCY AND THE ALLOCATION OF RESOURCES
Page 46

CHAPTER FOUR: PROPERTY RIGHTS AND ECONOMIC EFFICIENCY
Page 69

Part Three: An Economic Analysis of Democracy

CHAPTER FIVE: VOLUNTARY AGREEMENT: A THEORY OF COLLECTIVE ACTION
Page 86

APPENDIX TO CHAPTER SIX: DEMAND REVELATION WITH A CONTINUOUS DECISION
Page 117

CHAPTER SEVEN: PUBLIC SECTOR DEMAND
Page 120

Part Four: Taxation

CHAPTER NINE: POSITIVE PRINCIPLES
OF TAXATION
Page 158

Part Six: Economic Activities of Government

CHAPTER SIXTEEN: BORROWING
AND MONEY CREATION
Page 314

CHAPTER SEVENTEEN: THE GOVERNMENT
BUDGETING PROCESS
Page 334

CHAPTER EIGHTEEN: REGULATION
Page 351

CHAPTER NINETEEN: THE FEDERAL SYSTEM OF GOVERNMENT
Page 370

CHAPTER TWENTY: ALTERNATIVES
TO GOVERNMENT PRODUCTION
Page 390

Preface

The subject matter of public sector economics has evolved a great deal over the past few decades. In conjunction with traditional material on taxation, advances in expenditure theory and the theory of collective decision making have greatly enhanced the economist's understanding of the public sector. My primary goal in this book is to coherently organize both the traditional public finance material and the recent advances in public sector economics. The book begins by discussing expenditure theory to explain why government activity can enhance resource allocation. Next, the economic theory of public sector decision making is explored. Finally, more traditional areas of public finance, including taxation, the government's budgeting process, and fiscal federalism, are covered. Throughout the book I have attempted to build the analysis on the foundation of the democratic decision-making process that has produced our taxing and spending institutions.

The unifying theme—that government activity is a result of a democratic decision-making process—should be evident throughout the book. This theme is significant for two reasons. First, one's understanding of the public sector will be incomplete unless one understands the process by which democratic decision making has created the existing public sector institutions. Second, unlike the invisible hand of the market that is the result of human action but not of human design, the public sector of the economy is consciously designed, so that every voter plays a part in the process. The better the process is understood, the more likely we are to design public sector institutions that behave as their designers intended.

This theme manifests itself throughout the book. For example, the tax system is examined not only in terms of traditional equity and efficiency criteria but also as a product of a collective decision-making process. The analysis of redistribution also relies heavily on a public choice foundation. A traditional analysis of redistributive programs and their effects is undertaken, but again, the programs can best be understood within the context of the democratic decision-making process that produces them. Likewise, government regulation is the product of a democratic decision-making process and so is analyzed in the same way.

To provide a foundation for understanding the public sector as a product of a democratic decision-making process, one of the book's six parts is devoted specifically to an economic analysis of democracy. This section begins by analyzing the nature of collective decisions, both in voluntary settings and in government, and then explains some basic voting models and develops an economic model of the public sector supply process. My goal was to use this public choice foundation to present public sector economics as a unified body of knowledge rather than a collection of different models.

Teaching from This Book

The order of the chapters in the book was chosen for two reasons. First, it represents a logical structuring of the ideas in public sector economics. Second, the chapters that discuss fundamental principles appear earlier in the book, and chapters built on these fundamentals appear subsequently. Thus, an instructor can cover the earlier chapters in order and then omit or rearrange later chapters as individual courses warrant.

The first three parts of the book deal with expenditure theory, broadly defined. Part One describes the public sector and introduces concepts for evaluating public sector performance; Part Two discusses efficiency reasons for governmental activity; and Part Three analyzes the public sector decision-making process. Because a distinguishing feature of this book is its emphasis on the public sector decision-making process, Part Three serves as a springboard to subsequent material. With this in mind, most users will probably be comfortable covering the first three parts in the order that they occur without omitting any chapters.

Part Four, on taxation, discusses traditional public finance material that, again, is probably best covered in order without omitting chapters. But from there, chapters are written so that they can easily be covered in various orders, or omitted if they hold less interest in particular situations.

For example, borrowing and money creation, examined in Chapter 16, represent methods of public finance as well as taxation, so this chapter can logically follow Chapter 13, the final taxation chapter. Chapter 18, on regulation, is written from a public choice perspective and can be covered between Chapters 8 and 9 without loss of continuity. It can be omitted altogether by teachers who do not want to devote a chapter to regulation in a course on public sector economics. Chapter 19, on federalism, is an important element of public sector economics and can easily be covered after the tax chapters rather than at the end of the book for someone so inclined.

Studying from This Book

My overall goal in writing for students of public sector economics was to unify the material into a single body of knowledge rather than present it as a collection of theories. I tried to do this in several ways. First, I do not overwhelm the reader with complicated technical explanations of concepts when simple explanations can convey a principle just as well. Second, I explicitly note related concepts at the time that a concept is presented, which means sometimes referring ahead to material not yet covered and other times referring back to material previously covered. Finally, the unifying principle of the public sector as a product of a democratic decision-making process underlies all of the material.

As an aid to comprehension, all of the figures in the book are accompanied by brief explanations. Although the figures are explained fully in the text, the brief explanations serve both to help focus on the key idea illustrated and to facilitate review.

The conclusions to each chapter provide summaries of the important points in the chapter. These conclusions not only review the key material in the chapter but also help reinforce how that material is related to other topics.

The questions at the end of the chapters are also intended to aid in review. Sometimes the questions ask the reader to restate an argument made in the chapter, and other times they ask the reader's opinion on a subject for which there are arguments on both sides.

Sometimes a question is used to try to draw together ideas that at first may not appear to be related. As such, some questions have specific "correct" answers, while others are meant to stimulate thought rather than to suggest one answer.

The book contains two appendixes. The Appendix to Chapter 1 reviews indifference curve analysis, which traditionally is taught as a part of microeconomic theory. The appendix provides enough information to get a student started, but someone wanting a more thorough understanding should consult a microeconomic theory textbook; several are listed in the appendix. The appendix can serve as a convenient review that can be referred back to as material applying indifference curve analysis appears in later chapters.

The Appendix to Chapter 6 describes a method of demand revelation that is outlined in that chapter. The concept of demand revelation provides interesting insights into incentives for honest voting and for efficient public sector resource allocation. Because this material is more involved than is necessary to understand the fundamentals, it is placed in an appendix, making it easy either to exclude or to cover.

Acknowledgments

I have accumulated many debts, both general and specific, while writing this book. The general approach that I have used in analyzing the public sector will reveal, to those who know the subject, my indebtedness to James Buchanan and Gordon Tullock, who have done much to change the way that economists think about the public sector. A number of other individuals have commented on my approach to the subject, have read and critiqued parts of the manuscript, or have offered helpful comments and information. Any list is sure to leave someone out, but a partial list includes Andy Barnett, Robert Ekelund, Bradford Holcombe, Lora Holcombe, James Long, and Robert Tollison. Stephanie Surfus, formerly the economics editor at Wadsworth, has also provided a great deal of help, encouragement, and support. She left the position shortly after the book went into production, but deserves much credit for the final product.

In addition, a number of outside reviewers provided many useful comments. The reviewers of the manuscript were: Aniruddha Banerjee, Pennsylvania State University; Joseph J. Cordes, George Washington University; J. Fred Giertz, University of Illinois; Robert P. Inman, University of Pennsylvania; Sharon B. Megdal, University of Arizona; Ruth Shen, San Francisco State University; and James M. Suarez, Manhattan College. Although I did not always follow every piece of advice from the reviewers, they all had valuable insights to offer.

My largest debt is to my wife Lora, to whom this book is dedicated. In addition to her patience and support as my wife, she is also an economist and one of my colleagues. Her input, both as a family member and as a colleague, has done a great deal to shape the final product.

PUBLIC SECTOR ECONOMICS

PART ONE

Introduction

CHAPTER ONE

The Public Sector

*P*ublic sector economics analyzes, from an economic standpoint, the activities of government. The United States economy is primarily a market economy, but despite the fact that most of our resources are allocated through the market, a significant proportion are allocated through the government—the public sector of the economy. One goal of this book is to explain how the government allocates resources. Another goal is to establish a framework for analyzing what economic activities the government should undertake.

Questions about what the government should do are less easily answered than questions about what it actually does, but such questions are especially important to a study of the public sector of the economy. After all, people choose what the government does and how it goes about doing it. Because governmental activities are a matter of choice, it makes sense to try to understand as much as possible about how the government actually operates, and about how it could operate. It also makes sense to establish some criteria for determining what activities the government should undertake. If there are alternative ways that a government might deal with a problem, or if there is the possibility for the market to deal with a problem in addition to—

or instead of—the government, then this provides additional motivation for understanding and being able to evaluate governmental activity.

There are several good reasons for studying public sector economics. First, one might simply be interested in understanding how the government works. But on another level, an understanding of the principles of public sector economics can help us as a nation to create a more effective government. In a representative democracy some responsibility for government extends to each citizen, and the more informed we are about the operation of the public sector of the economy, the better our collective choices will be.

In order to fully understand the public sector, we must not only understand how the government might allocate resources but how the political decisions of voters and their elected representatives will tend to be translated into public policies. Our study of the public sector will build on an analysis of the public sector decision-making process. By understanding the theory of how public sector decisions are made, we can better comprehend what the government does, and why. We will also be in a better position to understand what activities should be undertaken by government and what activities are better left to the market.

This chapter begins by discussing, in very general terms, the types of activities that will be examined throughout the text and the types of analysis that will be used. Then we present a more detailed, part-by-part over-view of the contents of the text. Finally, we take a brief look at the history of public sector spending in both the United States and other developed economies to get some idea of how much the government spends and what it buys.

Introduction

The economic analysis of the public sector can be divided into two main categories. First, there are questions about what types of goods the government tends to produce and what types of goods the government should pro-duce. Private markets do a good job of pro-ducing many goods and services, but other goods and services, such as police protection, national defense, schools, and roads, tend to be produced by the government. Why? Are there characteristics associated with those goods that make it difficult for the private sec-tor to supply them effectively or that make it more desirable for the government to produce them? How is it determined when government activity is desirable? Until we un-derstand what the government can do in cer-tain situations and what the limits on its activities are, we cannot fully assess what it should do.

The first part of the text examines the activ-ities of government from both of these per-spectives. It looks at situations in which government activity might be desirable, and it looks at how the government makes its deci-sions about what goods and services, and how much of them, to produce. This area of public sector economics has a number of interesting aspects. In the market sector of the economy, output is regulated by the laws of supply and demand, whereas in the public sector the de-mands of individuals are registered through the ballot box. Our elected officials then de-termine the goods and services that will be produced in the public sector. Because this process is much more involved than the sup-ply and demand process in the market, one of our goals is to explain how the votes of indi-viduals eventually are translated into the pro-duction of government goods and services.

The second part of the book examines the three basic ways the government finances its activities—taxation, borrowing, and money creation—with the emphasis on taxation.[1] Government borrowing and money creation are important issues, to be sure, but they over-lap other branches of economics, such as

---

[1] A fourth source of revenue is the sale of government output. The differences between the sale of govern-ment output and the income tax will be discussed in the chapters on taxation. For the purposes of this discus-sion, however, revenues from government enterprises will be included in the category of taxation. For exam-ple, the postal service sells its output, tolls are used to finance bridges, and user fees are charged at parks. The government often forces consumers to buy its ser-vices whether they want to or not (garbage collection), grants itself monopolies (first-class mail, toll bridges), or covers only a part of its costs by the user fee (public parks). And taxes intended to substitute for user fees (gasoline taxes to finance roads, social security taxes) fur-ther obscure the difference between revenues from gov-ernment sales and taxes.

macroeconomics and money and banking, whereas taxation traditionally is associated with the study of public sector economics. But before exploring the theory of public sector economics, the next section charts the course of the text in more detailed terms.

Overview

Even in a market-oriented economy such as the United States, the government allocates a major proportion of the nation's resources. This fact alone should be reason enough to analyze the government's spending activities. In a very real sense, when individuals go to the polls and vote, they are making the choices that determine how resources will be allocated in the public sector in the same way that private sector spending decisions determine the private sector's allocation of resources. The purpose of this text, which is divided into six parts, is to explain how the choices of voters are translated into public sector output and what the economic effects of those choices are.

Introduction

Part One includes this chapter and Chapter 2. Chapter 1 provides a brief introduction to the public sector. By examining some facts and figures about the government's economic activities, the reader should obtain a basic idea about what the government does and how the role of the government has changed in the twentieth century.

Chapter 2 explains some principles that can be used to evaluate governmental activity. In many areas of economics it is sufficient simply to recognize how the economic system works. After understanding economic cause and effect, an individual may form opinions about economic activities, but these opinions take on greater importance in public sector economics because we, as a group, choose the activities of government. In general terms, the government should undertake desirable activities and refrain from pursuing undesirable ones. Chapter 2 looks at specific criteria that might be used to judge public sector activity.

Economic Efficiency

Part Two discusses the concept of economic efficiency. The first thing to recognize is that the market generally does a good job of allocating resources. The economic efficiency of an ideally competitive market is explained to provide a standard against which inefficient markets can be measured—many forces in the real world could cause a real world situation to be less efficient than the ideal competitive market.

For example, inefficiency in the market can arise if some people are able to impose costs on others without their consent. Air pollution, water pollution, and noise pollution are all examples of this type of cost, also known as a negative externality. The problem is that people who produce negative externalities do not have an incentive to take into account the costs they impose on others, which leads to an inefficient allocation of resources in the market.

A similar problem arises when individuals produce benefits that can be enjoyed by others without the consent of the producer. At first, this hardly seems to be a problem. But if goods produce benefits that can be consumed without the consent of their producer, the producer will not have enough incentive to produce the goods, and they will be underproduced in the market. Inefficiency results because too little of this type of good is produced.

Inefficiencies might arise for other reasons as well, but the point is that even though the market allocates resources efficiently, market allocation is not perfect. When the market fails to allocate resources perfectly, government involvement may be desirable. The word *may* should be emphasized, because there is no guarantee that the government will allocate resources perfectly either.

Problems of inefficient allocation of resources can be traced to high transactions costs or poorly defined property rights. If property rights to a scarce and valuable resource are not clearly defined, then there is not an owner who has an incentive to maximize the value of the resource. The simple solution is to define clearly the ownership rights to all scarce and valuable resources, but sometimes this is not possible. For example, even though air pollution may be a problem, it is hard to imagine how rights to the use of air might be assigned such that they could be traded in the market like, say, soft drinks. Even though it might be possible for the government to establish marketable pollution rights, it is not the same as allowing an individual to purchase a certain amount of clean air to breathe.

These property rights problems are discussed in some detail in Chapter 4, which focuses on the role of transactions costs in establishing property rights. A significant impediment to the perfectly efficient allocation of resources is that often the bargains that would have to be struck for the resources to be allocated efficiently are too complex to be feasible in the real world. This suggests the possibility that the government could become involved, allocating the resources in a way that maximizes the benefits to all. However, because the government may not allocate resources perfectly either, it is important to understand the economic theory behind political decisions.

An Economic Analysis of Democracy

Part Three looks at the way in which our government makes its decisions. First, the government is viewed as a collective organization—much like a club—where citizens band together to produce goods and services that cannot be produced efficiently in the market. People join swimming clubs, tennis clubs, and golf clubs all the time. It should be easy to understand, then, why governments might also produce services for their citizens. Highway systems, police protection, and national defense are commodities that citizens desire as a group, and the government represents a collective organization that everyone joins in order to produce such goods.

In real terms, however, the government is not a club. For one thing, the government forces people to join, to obey its rules, and to pay dues. Unlike club dues, the taxes used to pay for public sector output are not voluntary contributions. Why not operate the government as a voluntary club and rely on contributions to run the government? One potential problem is that some individuals would "free ride" off of the contributions of others. For example, if everybody else were paying for national defense, an individual would be relatively safe from attack and therefore would have an incentive not to contribute voluntarily. Because everyone would have the same incentive, some valuable goods and services that almost everyone wanted produced would be underproduced, or not produced at all. One solution would be to force people to contribute to programs that furthered the common good.

In democratic countries governmental decisions are made by majority rule. Sometimes the decisions are made directly, but more often they are made by elected representatives. For example, the U.S. government spends over one-third of *GNP*, so somehow individual votes must be translated into the demand for public sector output, and the public sector must supply output in response to this demand. In light of the government's significance to the economy, the process by which individual votes eventually are transformed into public sector output should be examined. Chapter 7, on public sector demand, explains how individual demands for public sector output are aggregated into the collective demand for output; Chapter 8, on public sector supply, explains how suppliers respond to this demand in their production of public sector output.

Taxation

Somehow the government must pay for the goods and services it produces, and taxation is the main source of revenue. Part Four discusses some general principles of taxation and then compares particular taxes to the general principles. The main objective here is to understand the effects of the various tax sources used to finance the government.

Most of the chapters in Part Four deal with several types of taxes, but Chapter 12 focuses on the personal income tax. Tax reform has been a controversial issue in the 1980s, and the personal income tax, in addition to receiving the most publicity, is also the largest source of tax revenue. There are, however, limits to the benefits of analyzing taxes in isolation. Indeed, the tax system must be analyzed as a whole system, because the effects of one type of tax will depend on how that tax interacts with the provisions of other types of taxes.

Redistribution

One of government's primary functions is the redistribution of revenue. In 1980 over half

of the federal government's budget went to human services, which means taxing income from some people and transferring it to others. Sometimes the transfers consist of direct cash payments; other times they consist of goods and services. In either case the expenditure programs are significant.

The tax system forms a part of the government's redistributive activity. The progressive income tax has long been viewed as a tool for taking a greater-than-proportional share of income from those who can most afford it to pay for redistributive government programs. Regardless of government spending programs, the fact that higher income people are asked to pay a larger share of the cost of government constitutes redistribution. Considering the role of the tax system, the discussion of redistribution in Part Five follows logically from the discussion of taxation in Part Four.

The largest redistributive program the government runs is social security, which is examined in Chapter 15. Established in 1936, the social security program has grown rapidly, and ever-increasing taxes have been levied to pay for it. Social security represents the largest government program that has its own separate earmarked tax source. A payroll tax shared by employers and employees finances the program, which in itself makes the program worthy of note. As the costs of social security have escalated, there has been increasing doubt as to whether the program can continue to pay the benefits it has promised to those now contributing to the system. The potential problems with the social security system will be analyzed, and some suggested reforms will be discussed.

Economic Activities of Government

Part Six looks at some economic activities of government not covered elsewhere. Chapters 16 and 17 examine some aspects of public finance, which is considered, in its narrowest sense, as the way in which the government finances its expenditures. The government can obtain revenue in three ways: it can tax, it can borrow, and it can print new money. Chapter 16, which deals with the latter two methods of public finance, is linked closely to the economic analysis of democracy provided earlier in the text. Government borrowing and money creation have economic and political effects, and these effects are studied within the context of the incentives facing the individuals who determine policy. Economic analysis is based on the premise that people respond to incentives, and politicians are people just like anyone else. What incentives do politicians have to manipulate monetary and fiscal policy, and what are the likely results of such manipulation? These are some of the significant issues to be considered in the chapter on borrowing and money creation.

Chapter 17 looks at the government budgeting process to see how the government budget is determined and how the level of funding for government programs is determined. Here, the public finance process is closely scrutinized both in terms of the steps that lead toward the production of the federal government budget and the techniques for evaluating the merits of public programs.

Chapter 18 is devoted to regulation, a major activity of government, and considers the ideal goals of government regulation as well as the political aspects of the regulatory process. The chapter also demonstrates the parallel between taxation and regulation and suggests that regulation can be viewed as a form of taxation. The government could undertake programs by taxing and then paying for certain output. For example, the government could raise tax revenues in order to finance the reclaiming of land that was strip-mined. Or the government could pass a regulation requiring strip miners to reclaim their mined land. This would have the same result as the taxing and spending program, but because the activity was required by regulation, it would not show up in the government's budget.

Government regulations require individuals and businesses to undertake certain activities, thus forestalling the need for government spending to undertake the activities. Because regulation can be viewed as a method of taxation, it is a natural extension of any discussion of public finance. Furthermore, regulation causes the economic influence of the government to be larger than figures showing government spending as a fraction of *GNP* would indicate.

Although the principles of public sector economics apply to state and local governments as well as the federal government, a separate chapter is devoted to the federal system of government and the role that state and local governments play in the allocation of resources. Note that different activities of government are more appropriate to different levels of government. By using many small governments instead of one large one whenever possible, more variety in the types of public sector output will be available for consumption. Just as individuals prefer to drink different types of beverages and drive different types of cars, so there is diversity in the demand for government output. In addition, the existence of many governments will tend to foster some degree of intergovernmental competition, which can aid the efficient production of resources.

For some goods and services, such as defense, a national or even international level of government (for instance, NATO) is most appropriate, but there are benefits to be reaped from producing output at the lowest level of government possible. The governments, however, may want to shelter themselves from intergovernmental competition by forming what amounts to a cartel of smaller governments. Chapter 19 discusses this phenomenon as well.

Finally, Chapter 20 looks at alternatives to government production. Government production may be desirable, and even necessary, for some goods and services, but other potential sources of production should be examined before drawing a conclusion about any particular good or service. The most obvious choice is simply to have the good financed and produced in the private sector, but intermediate alternatives exist, too. For example, almost all defense hardware is produced by private sector firms under contract to the government, whereas defense is financed through, and decisions about what to produce made in, the public sector.

Another alternative is to finance a good in the public sector but allow the private sector to both design and produce it. For example, the government could build low-income housing, but it could also supply housing grants to individuals and allow them to choose their own housing. Another much-discussed proposal is for a voucher system for financing education. Each student would be granted an education voucher by the government, and the voucher could be spent by the student at the school of his or her choice. Chapter 20 examines the relative advantages and disadvantages of such alternatives.

Each chapter is followed by several questions for thought, discussion, and review. Some of the questions are based directly on material in the chapter; others require an application of the material; still others are more oriented toward thinking about concepts and may not have a specific "correct" answer. In all cases, however, the questions are intended to cover the main points in the chapter, so that a comprehensive chapter review is provided.

The Activities of Government

An examination of the government budget over the past several decades should provide an overview of what the government actually does, and how its priorities have changed over time. In the United States the institution that we refer to as the "government" is actually comprised of thousands of governmental units. The United States was originally created as a federation of state governments, with the federal government maintaining jurisdiction over the fifty individual states. Each state contains counties, cities, townships, or similar local governments within its boundaries. In addition, a large number of special districts—of which school districts are the most common—in some cases have the power to raise tax revenues, and they spend governmental funds to produce public sector output.

For convenience, the governmental units in the United States can be divided into the federal, state, and local governments.

Federal, State, and Local Governments

Table 1.1 lists revenues and expenditures for all levels of government for the 1982 fiscal year, a total in excess of a trillion dollars. Total government revenues of $1,145 billion are less than the sum of federal, state, and local because of intergovernmental transactions. For example, some state and local government revenue comes from the federal government.

To give a rough idea of the relative economic importance of the different levels of government, Table 1.1 also lists the percentage of the total revenues and expenditures for

Table 1.1 Government Revenues and Expenditures by Level of Government, 1982*

	ALL GOVERNMENT	FEDERAL		STATE		LOCAL	
	Billion $	Billion $	Percent	Billion $	Percent	Billion $	Percent
Revenues	1,145	688	51.7	331	24.9	313	23.5
Expenditures	1,231	796	56.2	310	21.9	311	22.0
Surplus or (deficit)		(108)		21		2	
S or (D) as percent of expenditures		(13.6)		6.8		0.6	

*Total revenue and total expenditures are less than the sum of federal, state, and local because of intergovernmental transactions. Percents are calculated as a proportion of the sum of federal, state, and local.

Source: *Statistical Abstract of the United States*, 1985 edition, Table 438.

which each level of government is responsible. For example, the federal government accounts for slightly more than half of total government spending, while states and localities are each responsible for a little less than a fourth.

Finally, Table 1.1 lists the budget surplus or deficit for each level of government and the percentage of total revenue each figure represents. For example, in 1982 the federal government had a deficit of $108 billion, or about 13.6 percent of total federal expenditures. In 1960 the federal budget showed a slight surplus but since then has operated with a deficit every year except 1969; furthermore, the deficits have been growing as a percentage of the budget. By contrast, state and local governments typically have balanced budgets, and combined they show a slight surplus.

The Federal Budget

Federal government expenses account for over half of the money spent in the public sector, and federal spending combined with government regulations and related activities makes the federal government the major governmental force in the economy.

Table 1.2 lists the major areas of federal government spending for 1960 and 1980, illustrating how the emphasis of federal spending has changed over those two decades. 1960 and 1980 might be regarded as transitional years from a political standpoint. President Kennedy, elected to replace President Eisenhower in 1960, viewed government as an institution that should actively engage in programs to help people. President Reagan's election in 1980 reversed that philosophy— Reagan believed that the government could best serve people by reducing its presence in their lives.

Assuming that the government budget indicates the nation's priorities, a comparison of the two budgets can be very revealing.[2] Note that Table 1.2 divides federal spending into

[2]Every year the Brookings Institution publishes a book about the annual budget, called *Setting National Priorities*. The premise behind the book, as its title suggests, is that one can determine the priorities of a government by examining how it spends its money.

Table 1.2 Federal Budget Outlays by Function, 1960 and 1980

Function	1960		1980	
	Billion $	Percent	Billion $	Percent
National defense	48.1	52.2	134.0	23.2
Human resources	26.2	28.4	312.1	54.1
Income security	7.4	8.0	86.4	15.0
Health	.8	.9	23.1	4.0
Veterans' benefits	5.4	5.9	21.2	3.7
Education, training, and employment	1.0	1.0	30.8	5.3
Social Security and Medicare	11.6	12.6	150.6	26.1
Other nondefense	17.9	18.2	130.6	22.7
Commerce and housing credit	1.6	1.8	7.8	1.4
Transportation	4.1	4.5	21.1	3.7
Natural resources and environment	1.6	1.7	13.8	2.4
Energy	.5	.5	6.3	1.1
Community and regional development	.2	.2	10.1	1.8
Agriculture	2.6	2.8	4.8	0.8
Net interest	6.9	7.5	52.5	9.1
Revenue sharing	.2	.2	8.6	1.5
International affairs	3.0	3.2	10.9	1.9
General science, space, and technology	.6	.6	5.7	1.0
General government	1.0	1.1	4.1	0.7
Administration of justice	.4	.4	4.6	0.8
Undistributed offsetting receipts	−4.8	−5.2	−19.9	−3.5
	92.2	100.0	576.7	100.0

Source: *Statistical Abstract of the United States*, 1985 edition, Table 492.

three categories: national defense, human resources, and other nondefense spending. In 1980 over half of federal spending (54.1 percent) was for human resources, with slightly less than a quarter of the budget (23.2 percent) going for national defense. By contrast, in 1960 these percentages were roughly reversed—over half of the federal budget (52.2 percent) went for national defense, and slightly more than a quarter (28.4 percent) went for human resources. Other nondefense spending as a percentage of the budget changed less between those years. Clearly, the shift in national priorities from 1960 to 1980 is reflected in these figures. The percentage of government revenue spent on national de-

fense was far less in 1980 than it was in 1960.

Table 1.2 lists several subcategories of human resources. Note that veterans' benefits is the only budget outlay that has decreased as a percentage of total expenditures since 1960; in the other categories budget outlays have increased by about two to four times.[3] For example, income security, which includes such transfer programs as Aid to Families with Dependent Children and unemployment compensation, approximately doubled as a

[3]One might argue that veterans' benefits would be more appropriately placed under national defense. The taxonomy here is the same as is used in the *Statistical Abstract*.

percentage of the federal budget, from 8 percent in 1960 to 15 percent in 1980. New programs have been created, and more benefits have been paid under old programs, accounting for the increase. Health expenditures have had the largest percentage increase, approximately quadrupling, although they still are a relatively small percentage of the total budget. Keep in mind that Medicare is not included in this category. Education, training, and employment programs have tripled as a percentage of the federal budget.

By far the largest subcategory under human services is social security and Medicare, for which outlays have more than doubled, from 12.6 percent of the federal budget in 1960 to 26.1 percent in 1980. Like defense, this area of the government budget has been a source of heated debate recently, and the growth in the program suggests why. Social security is an important enough program that a separate chapter is devoted to it later in the book.

The figures in the other nondefense category are largely self-explanatory, but some items deserve mention. For example, revenue sharing as a percentage of the federal budget increased from 0.2 percent in 1960 to 2.2 percent in 1975, then decreased to 1.5 percent in 1980. Some people argue that because the federal government runs a consistent deficit while state and local governments balance their budgets, the federal government should not share its revenues with lower levels of government. Other people argue that because revenue sharing accounts for such a small percentage of the total federal budget and finances such useful programs, it should be retained.

Net interest payments—the revenue needed to finance the federal debt—increased from 7.5 percent of the 1960 budget to 9.1 percent of the 1980 budget. Note that this revenue could be used for other purposes and that the current deficit increases future

interest payments. This issue will be considered in more detail in Chapter 16, on borrowing and money creation.

Table 1.3 lists similar categories of federal spending as Table 1.2, but for the years 1980, 1985, and 1987. Where the figures in Table 1.2 reflected the significant change in political philosophies in 1960 and 1980, the figures in Table 1.3 indicate how government spending has changed through the 1980s. As Table 1.3 shows, President Reagan had increased defense spending from 22.7 percent of the federal budget in 1980 to 28.7 percent in 1987.[4] At the same time, although general purpose fiscal assistance (federal payments to state and local governments) has continued to increase, as has spending on energy, the environment, housing, and social services, it has declined as a percentage of total spending.

Interest payments on the growing federal debt and social security and Medicare outlays have also increased as a percentage of federal spending, which becomes significant because these three items comprise such a large share of the federal budget. The budget deficit has been a source of political and economic debate for decades, and the figures in Table 1.3 suggest that little can be done to bring the budget into balance without reducing expenditures on national defense, social security, and interest payments, which account for almost 65 percent of federal spending by themselves. The method by which the nation makes decisions on these issues, and the

---

[4]Note that the total level of government spending for 1980 differs in Tables 1.2 and 1.3. The difference is that off-budget items such as the Postal Service are included in Table 1.3 but not in Table 1.2. The use of off-budget items will be discussed in Chapter 17 on government budgeting, but it is interesting to note here how government statistics showing the same thing (the government budget) can vary depending on how the counting is done. This suggests the value of examining the source of summary statistics rather than just accepting them as fact.

Table 1.3 Budgetary Outlays by Function, 1980 and 1985, and Estimates for 1987

Function	1980		1985		1987	
	Billion $	Percent	Billion $	Percent	Billion $	Percent
National defense	134.0	22.7	252.7	26.7	282.2	28.4
International affairs	12.7	2.2	16.2	1.7	18.6	1.9
General science, space, and technology	5.8	1.0	8.6	0.9	9.2	0.9
Energy	10.2	1.7	5.7	0.6	4.0	0.4
Natural resources and environment	13.9	2.4	13.4	1.4	12.0	1.2
Agriculture	8.8	1.5	25.6	2.7	19.5	2.0
Commerce and housing credit	9.4	1.6	4.2	0.4	1.4	0.1
Transportation	21.3	3.6	25.8	2.7	25.5	2.6
Community and regional development	11.3	1.9	7.7	0.8	6.5	0.7
Education, training, employment, and social services	31.8	5.4	29.3	3.1	27.4	2.8
Health	23.2	3.9	33.5	3.5	35.0	3.5
Medicare	32.1	5.4	65.8	7.0	70.2	7.1
Income security	86.5	14.6	128.2	13.6	118.4	11.9
Social security	118.5	20.1	188.6	19.9	212.2	21.4
Veterans' benefits and services	21.2	3.6	26.4	2.8	26.4	2.7
Administration of justice	4.6	0.8	6.3	0.7	6.9	0.7
General government	4.4	0.7	5.2	0.6	6.1	0.6
General purpose fiscal assistance	8.6	1.5	6.4	0.7	1.7	0.2
Net interest	52.5	8.9	129.4	13.7	148.0	14.9
Undistributed offsetting receipts	−19.9	−3.4	−32.8	−3.5	−38.1	−3.8
	590.9	100.0	946.3	100.0	994.0	100.0

Source: *Economic Report of the President*, February 1986, pp. 340–341.

economic criteria behind these decisions, will be an important part of this book.

Table 1.4 lists federal budget receipts for 1960, 1980, and 1985. As with spending, note the shift in emphasis in government revenue generation for the three years. For example, individual income taxes went up as a percentage of federal revenues from 1960 to 1980, but due to a significant tax cut passed in 1981, income tax revenues were down to about the same percentage of total federal revenues in 1985 as they were in 1960. The largest increase as a share of federal revenues is social insurance revenues, which include social security, unemployment compensation, and

several other programs. This seems logical in light of the large increase in social security expenditures previously noted. Note also the tremendous decline in corporate income tax collections as a percentage of total revenues raised. The other categories of revenue generation are relatively insignificant.

The Growth of Government in the Twentieth Century

The figures in Tables 1.1 through 1.4 suggest how the role of the government has changed over the past twenty-five years. Table 1.5, which lists government spending in dollar

Table 1.4 Federal Budget Receipts by Source, 1960, 1980, and 1985*

Source	1960 Billion $	1960 Percent	1980 Billion $	1980 Percent	1985 Billion $	1985 Percent
Individual income taxes	40.7	44.0	244.1	47.2	329.7	44.7
Social insurance revenues	14.7	15.9	157.8	30.5	268.4	36.4
Corporation income taxes	21.5	23.2	64.6	12.5	66.4	9.0
Excise taxes	11.7	12.6	24.3	4.7	37.0	5.0
Estate and gift taxes	1.6	1.7	6.4	1.2	5.6	0.8
Customs duties	1.1	1.2	7.2	1.4	11.8	1.6
Miscellaneous receipts	1.2	1.3	12.7	2.5	18.0	2.4
	92.5	100.0	517.1	100.0	736.9	100.0

*Figures for 1985 are estimates.

Source: *Statistical Abstract of the United States*, 1985 edition, Table 488.

Table 1.5 Government Expenditures in the United States for Selected Years

Year	ALL GOVERNMENTS Million $	ALL GOVERNMENTS Percent of GNP	FEDERAL GOVERNMENT Million $	FEDERAL GOVERNMENT Percent of GNP
1980	932,200	35.4	576,700	21.9
1970	332,985	34.0	208,190	21.3
1960	151,288	30.0	97,284	19.3
1950	70,334	24.7	44,800	15.7
1940	20,417	20.5	10,061	10.1
1932	12,437	21.4	4,266	7.4
1922	9,297	12.6	3,763	5.1
1913	3,215	8.1	970	2.5
1902	1,660	7.7	572	2.7

Sources: *Historical Statistics of the United States*, Part 1 (Washington, D.C., 1975), p. 1119–1123 and *Statistical Abstract*, 1986 edition, p. 262.

terms and as a percentage of *GNP* for selected years throughout this century, provides an even broader perspective of the changing role of government in the United States. For ex- ample, note the tremendous growth of government at all levels since the beginning of the 1900s. In 1902 all levels of government in the United States spent about 7.7 percent of *GNP*, and the federal government spent 2.7 percent. Whereas in recent years federal spending has comprised over half of total government spending, in 1902 federal spending was only 35 percent. At the turn of the century, government represented only a small part of the total economy.

By 1932 the federal government was spending 7.4 percent of *GNP*, or about the same percentage as federal, state, and local governments combined in 1902. Total government spending in 1932 was 21.4 percent, meaning the federal government was still spending significantly less than half of the amount spent by all governments. But by 1940 the federal government was responsible for about half of total government spending. By 1960 the federal government was spending nearly two-thirds of the amount spent by all governments, but the growth in federal government spending over the following two decades was relatively mild compared to the growth in state and local government spending.

Clearly, government has grown enormously in the United States in the twentieth century. At the turn of the century, when the government was small, it could be analyzed primarily from a political standpoint, but today the government represents over a third of the American economy, which means an understanding of the economics of public sector activity is vital to an understanding of the overall economy.

Foreign Governments

Before moving on, it might be interesting to compare government spending in the United States with government spending in other economies throughout the world. Table 1.6 lists total government spending plus lending, minus repayments of loans, for selected countries in 1972 and 1982. Surprisingly, Table 1.6 indicates that although government in the United States has grown substantially throughout the twentieth century, government spending as a percentage of *GDP* (gross domestic product) is relatively low compared to other countries. From 1972 to 1982, total government spending in the United States rose from 32.8 percent of *GDP* to 38.3 percent, an increase of 16.8 percent. Meanwhile, in such countries as France, West Germany, Kuwait, and Ireland, the government spends over half of *GDP*, and Sweden allocates 71.2 percent of *GDP* through its government. Furthermore, the data in Table 1.6 also indicates that the growth rate in the percentage of spending allocated through the government has actually been lower in the United States than in most other countries. In Kuwait and Mexico, for example, government spending as a percentage of *GDP* more than doubled in the ten-year time period. In short, the recent growth in government in the United States is not unique but rather reflects a world-wide phenomenon.

Politics and Economics

Historically, the study of politics and the study of economics have been closely associated. Until the late nineteenth century economics and politics were studied together as the combined discipline of political economy. By the end of the century, economics and political science had gone their separate ways, and while economists have continued to make policy recommendations, only in the second half of the twentieth century have economists be-

**Table 1.6 Government Expenditures and Lending Minus Repayments
as a Percentage of GNP for Selected Countries, 1972 and 1982**

COUNTRY	1972	1982	PERCENT CHANGE
United States	32.8	38.3	16.8
United Kingdom	42.6	49.8	16.9
France	37.7	51.2	35.8
West Germany	41.0	51.0	24.4
Sweden	51.7	71.2	37.7
Switzerland	28.8	37.4	29.9
Ireland	39.9	61.7	54.6
Australia	32.3	37.6	16.4
Mexico	17.5	36.7	109.7
Brazil	28.9	35.9	24.2
Kuwait	28.5	57.3	101.1
Singapore	19.8	27.7	39.9

Source: International Monetary Fund, *Government Finance Statistics Yearbook*, Volume 8 (1984), p. 72.

gun to consider political institutions in the same way that they consider economic institutions.[5] Rather than merely examining the private sector of the economy and then recommending government action, economists are becoming increasingly interested in studying the way in which economic resources are allocated through political decision making.

Economics and politics are intrinsically linked. On the one hand, economic activities influence political decisions. The antitrust activities of government provide one example of this, the government's energy policies provide another. During the 1970s price controls, government allocations of petroleum, and the windfall profits tax on oil companies were important political issues. Furthermore, the performance of the economy, which is influenced by such factors as inflation, unemployment, and interest rates, often plays a significant role in elections and in the platforms of political candidates.

Just as economics influences politics, so do political decisions influence the economy. For one thing, government ownership of industry—Amtrak in the United States, the steel, health care, petroleum, and broadcasting industries in Britain, and virtually all industry in the Soviet Union—is quite common. For another, government influence in the form of tax policy, the national debt, and regulation of private business clearly represents areas of current policy interest where politics influences the economy.

A full understanding of public sector economics requires an awareness not only of how political decisions influence the economy but also of how the economy influences political decisions—and even how political decisions are made. How are the votes of citizens on election day translated into the votes of our

---
[5]This theme is explored in James M. Buchanan, "Public Finance and Public Choice," *National Tax Journal* 28 (Dec. 1975), pp. 383–394.

representatives in the legislature, which then are translated into public policy? Although economists understand much more about resource allocation through the private sector, we have made impressive advances in the past several decades in our understanding of how resources are allocated through the public sector. There is still much to learn. But the recent advances, and the challenges for the future, make public sector economics an interesting area for study.

Conclusion

The goal of this book is to provide the reader with an understanding of the economic activities of government, both how the government does work and how the government ideally should work. The overview in this chapter provided a logical outline for accomplishing this goal. This chapter also discussed, in very general terms, what the government does, how significant its influence on the economy is, and how it has changed in the twentieth century.

The facts and figures presented in the chapter indicate that government spending exceeds one-third of *GNP*. From this alone it is clear that one must understand the economic activities of government before the broader economic picture can be fully appreciated. This is even more true because government regulations, the government's tax structure, and government spending programs themselves have such a significant influence on private sector economic activity. Chapter 2 discusses some criteria for evaluating government activity and then introduces the concept of economic efficiency to provide an indication of when government activity might be warranted.

Questions

1. What share of *GNP* is spent by governments in the United States? How is this divided among federal, state, and local governments?

2. Trace the history of government spending in the United States in the twentieth century. How do you account for the large increase in the size of the government? Do you view this growth as desirable or undesirable? Why?

3. What are the major activities undertaken by the federal government? How have these activities changed since 1960? Does this indicate a conscious shift in the priorities of government? Do you view these changes as desirable or undesirable? Does the government's budget accurately reflect the priorities of government?

4. In a democracy the government's decisions are made by majority rule. Is majority rule a good method for allocating resources? What are the advantages and disadvantages of allocating resources by majority rule? When would majority rule allocation of resources be most appropriate, and when least appropriate?

5. What activities should the government undertake? Schools? Defense? Highways? Medical care? Housing programs? Why?

Appendix to Chapter One
Indifference Curve Analysis

Some of the analysis in this book is graphically illustrated with indifference curves. This appendix serves as an overview to indifference curve analysis for readers unfamiliar with it and as a review for others. The appendix illustrates the concept of indifference curves and budget constraints and shows how consumers will maximize utility subject to a constraint. The effects of changes in price and income are demonstrated, and an illustration of a two-person model within an Edgeworth box diagram is provided. This appendix does not provide a complete exposition of indifference curve analysis, and readers unfamiliar with the concepts would probably benefit from additional study. Readers who are comfortable with this material can safely skip the appendix. Readers interested in a more detailed exposition can find one in most microeconomics textbooks.[1]

Indifference Curves

Indifference curves depict the level of well-being a consumer experiences in consuming different combinations of goods and services; the higher the indifference curve, the greater the consumer's welfare. For example, in Figure 1A.1 a consumer can consume two goods, X and Y. At point A the individual consumes X_1 of X and Y_1 of Y and experiences a certain level of well-being. The consumer's level of well-being is sometimes referred to as utility, so a higher level of well-being means greater utility.

Assuming that individuals prefer more

---

[1]Some examples are Donald N. McCloskey, *The Applied Theory of Price*, 2d ed. (New York: Macmillan, 1985), Jack Hirshleifer, *Price Theory and Applications*, 3d ed. (Englewood Cliffs, N.J.: Prentice-Hall, 1984), and Steven T. Call and William L. Holahan, *Microeconomics*, 2d ed. (Belmont, Calif.: Wadsworth, 1983).

Figure 1A.1 Indifference Curves Indifference curves have this general shape. Curves further from the origin represent higher levels of well-being. They are convex from the origin to depict diminishing marginal rates of substitution between goods.

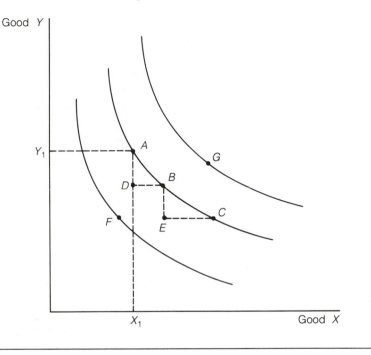

goods to less, the consumer in Figure 1A.1 would be just as well off with less *Y* only if compensated by being able to consume more *X*. If the individual's consumption of *Y* were reduced and the consumption of *X* increased such that the additional *X* compensated the individual for the reduced *Y*, then the individual would be indifferent between the two consumption bundles. Therefore, those two consumption bundles would be on the same indifference curve.

For example, in Figure 1A.1 points *A*, *B*, and *C* are on the same indifference curve, meaning that the individual would be indifferent between the various combinations of *X*

and *Y* at each point on that curve. Thus, if the individual's consumption of *Y* fell by amount *AD*, some amount of additional *X*—in this case, *DB* additional *X*—would leave the individual as well off at point *B* as at point *A*. The indifference curve containing points *A* and *B* signifies that the individual is equally well off with any combination of *X* and *Y* represented by points on that curve.

Note that indifference curves must be downward-sloping. Again assuming more goods are preferable to less, an individual could only be indifferent between consuming more of one good and less of another good if a reduction in consumption of one good was compensated for by an increase in consumption of the other.

Consumers are also assumed to have diminishing marginal rates of substitution between goods. This means that as an individual's consumption of a good is reduced by a constant increment, the individual must receive increasing amounts of the other good to be completely compensated. For example, an individual with lots of peanut butter but only a little jelly would be willing to give up a certain amount of peanut butter to get more jelly. The less peanut butter and more jelly the individual has, the more jelly the individual would need to compensate for the loss of a given amount of peanut butter and still remain indifferent between the two bundles.

This concept, called a diminishing marginal rate of substitution, is depicted in Figure 1A.1. From point A, the individual has less Y but more X at B but is indifferent between the two bundles of goods—the gain of DB of X just compensates for the loss of AD of Y. From point B, if amount BE, equal to AD, of Y is taken from the individual, the individual would have to be compensated by more than amount DB of X to remain indifferent. Point C is on the same indifference curve as A and B, and AD equals BE. Even though the individual gives up the same amount of Y in moving from A to B as in moving from B to C, the amount of X needed to keep the individual indifferent increases. Because for constant reductions in Y the amount of X must increase at an increasing rate to remain on the same indifference curve, an indifference curve must have the convex shape illustrated in Figure 1A.1.

The indifference curve with points A, B, and C on it is but one of an infinite number of possible indifference curves. Some indifference curve must pass through every point on the diagram, and Figure 1A.1 has only three

of the infinite number of possible curves. At any point on indifference curve ABC, the individual would be indifferent between that combination of X and Y and the combination represented by point A, B, or C.

The indifference curve that passes through point G is farther from the origin than curve ABC and thus represents consumption possibilities that would make the individual better off than at point A. Again, the individual is indifferent between the combination of X and Y at point G and any other point on that same indifference curve. But because G is on a higher indifference curve, the consumer would rather have the combination of X and Y at G than any combination on the lower indifference curve ABC. Likewise, point F is on a lower indifference curve than point A, so the individual would be better off at any point on indifference curve ABC than at point F.

The farther an indifference curve is from the origin, the higher the level of well-being it represents. Thus, the individual would prefer to be at C than at F and would prefer to be at G rather than C. But the indifference curves can never cross; that would result in a contradiction. For example, if indifference curve S crossed indifference curve T, that would mean that S was preferred to T when S was farther from the origin, but T was preferred to S when T was farther from the origin. Because the individual is indifferent among all points on curve S and all points on curve T, it would make no sense to say that sometimes T is preferred to S and at others S is preferred to T.

All of the individual's possible indifference curves taken together are called the individual's utility function. An individual will want to maximize his or her well-being, or utility, which simply means consuming at the highest possible indifference curve.

Figure 1A.2 The Budget Constraint The budget constraint shows the maximum amount that an individual can consume. A parallel shift of a budget constraint shows a change in income, whereas a change in the slope of a budget constraint shows a change in relative prices of goods.

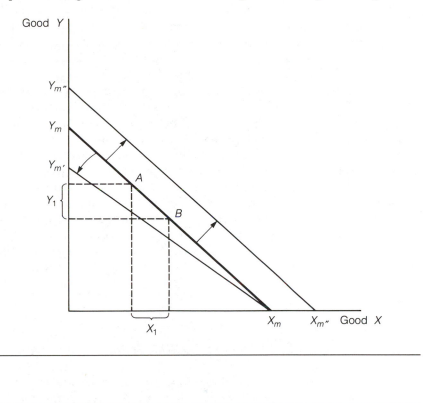

The Budget Constraint

The individual's budget constraint is the maximum amount of one good the individual can consume with a given level of consumption of other goods. In Figure 1A.2 the heavy line represents the budget constraint for goods X and Y; the end points of the budget constraint, X_m and Y_m, represent the maximum amounts of a good that the individual could consume if all income were devoted to the consumption of one good. In other words, whereas indifference curves show the individ-

ual's preferences, the budget constraint shows the individual's opportunities. As will be discussed later, what an individual does depends on both preferences and opportunities.

Because the budget constraint shows the maximum amount of consumption the consumer can enjoy, given the consumer's income level, only one budget constraint can exist at any given time. The consumer will allocate all income by consuming at some point on the line, but the consumer cannot consume amounts represented by points farther from the origin than the budget constraint.

The slope of the budget constraint indicates the relative prices of the two goods. For example, in Figure 1A.2 assume that the individual is now consuming the amounts of X and Y represented by point A and could consume more X only by giving up a certain amount of Y. The budget constraint shows that Y_1 would have to be given up in order to obtain X_1 and end up at B, so the ratio Y_1/X_1 is the relative price of X in terms of Y.

If the price of Y rises, then if all income were spent on only one good, less Y—but the same amount of X—could be consumed with the same income. Thus, if the maximum amount of Y that could have been consumed at the original prices was Y_m, an increase in the price of Y would reduce the maximum amount that could be consumed to Y_m'. For a price increase the budget constraint would rotate inward on the axis for the good that had the increase. With an increased price for Y, the new budget constraint would be the line connecting X_m and Y_m'. A price decrease would cause a rotation in the other direction. Note that with a higher price the individual's consumption opportunities are reduced unless the individual consumes none of the good that had the price increase.

An increase in income is depicted by a parallel shift outward in the budget constraint. The prices of goods are represented by the slope of the budget constraint, and because prices do not change due to an income change, the slope of the budget constraint remains the same during a change in income. The outward shift of the budget constraint simply means the consumer can now consume more of both goods due to the higher income; conversely, a decrease in income would shift the budget constraint inward.

Utility Maximization

The consumer wants to choose the available combination of goods that will make him or her as well off as possible. This is what is meant by utility maximization. In Figure 1A.3 the straight line represents the individual's budget constraint, and the individual will maximize utility at the point on the budget constraint that is tangent to the highest indifference curve. For example, the individual could consume Y_1 and X_1 at point A but could move down the budget constraint to point B and be better off, because the indifference curve at point B is farther from the origin than the one at point A.

It should be clear from Figure 1A.3 that if an indifference curve is not tangent to the budget constraint, like the indifference curve at point A, then it must extend below the budget constraint. Because of the shape of indifference curves, only one indifference curve can be tangent to the budget constraint, and that point of tangency is the point at which the consumer's well-being is maximized, given the consumer's income and the prices of the goods. In Figure 1A.3 the utility-maximizing consumption bundle is X_2 amount of X and Y_2 amount of Y. If the budget constraint shifted due to changes in income or changes in the prices of goods, as in Figure 1A.2, the utility-maximizing individual would locate on the point of tangency on the new budget constraint.

Figure 1A.3 Utility Maximization The individual maximizes utility by consuming at the point where the utility function is tangent to the budget constraint, point B in the figure.

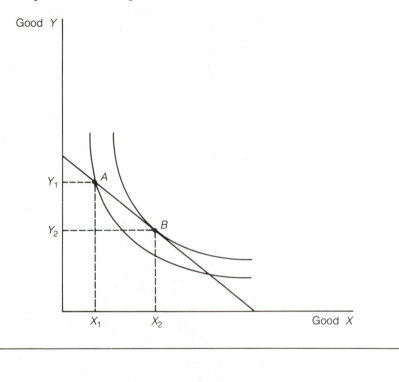

Income and Substitution Effects

If an individual's budget constraint shifts, the changes in the consumption activities of that individual can be broken down into two components: income effects and substitution effects. Income effects result from individuals altering their behavior because of a change in income available; substitution effects result from individuals substituting a relatively cheaper good for a relatively more expensive one because the relative price of the goods has changed. When isolating the substitution effect, the real income of the individual is held constant. These concepts can be shown more clearly with the assistance of indifference curves.

In Figure 1A.4, which illustrates an income effect, an individual begins at the utility-maximizing point A, on the indifference curve and budget constraint tangent to that point. When the individual suffers a decline in income, the budget constraint shifts leftward, parallel to the original budget constraint, putting the individual at point B. At point B the individual has a lower level of

Figure 1A.4 Income Effects An income effect depicts the change in the consumption of a good that is due only to a change in income. Because the two budget constraints in this figure are parallel, the individual's income has changed. Therefore, the changes in the consumption of goods *X* and *Y* are due only to income effects.

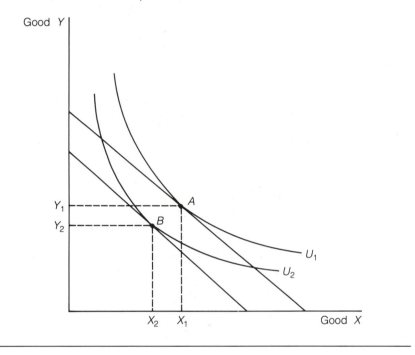

utility and consumes less of both goods *X* and *Y*. Because relative prices are given by the slope of the budget constraint, and because the slope of the budget constraint at *A* is the same as the slope of the budget constraint at *B*, no substitution effect (which would be caused by a change in relative prices) has taken place. The entire change in the individual's behavior in moving from point *A* to point *B* is due to an income effect.

Figure 1A.5 depicts both an income and a substitution effect. In this figure an individual maximizes utility at point *A*, subject to the budget constraint *LL*, consuming Y_1 of good

Y. But when the price of good *Y* rises, the budget constraint rotates in to *L'L*, and the individual consumes only Y_3 of good *Y*. There are two reasons for this. First, because *Y* is now relatively more expensive than *X*, the individual substitutes into the relatively cheaper good. That is the substitution effect. Second, the higher price of one good effectively leaves the individual with less overall income, so the individual will consume less. This is the income effect that was depicted in Figure 1A.4.

The two effects can be isolated in Figure 1A.5 as follows. If the relative price of *Y* has risen but the individual is left with the same

Figure 1A.5 Income and Substitution Effects When the budget constraint rotates from *LL* to *LL'*, the individual consumes less *Y* for two reasons. The reduction from Y_1 to Y_2 is due to the substitution effect, and the reduction from Y_2 to Y_3 is due to the income effect.

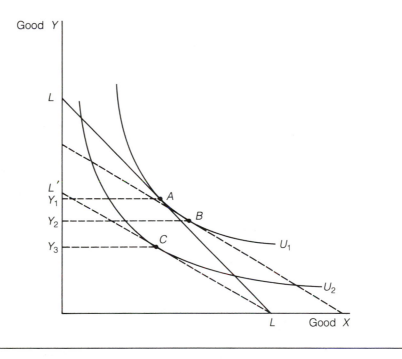

level of utility as before the price increase, the individual will move to point *B*. The individual is just as well off at point *B* as at point *A* because both points are on the same indifference curve, but because the dashed budget constraint at point *B* has the same slope as budget constraint *L'L*, the individual must pay the same relative prices at point *B* as at point *C*. By changing the relative prices but leaving the individual with the same level of real income (or utility), the movement from point *A* to point *B* is a pure substitution effect.

From point *B* to point *C*, however, the budget constraint shifts in a parallel fashion,

a pure income effect. Therefore, the increase in the price of *Y* that causes consumption of *Y* to drop from Y_1 to Y_3 can be divided into two separate effects. The movement from *A* to *B* is due to the substitution effect; the movement from *B* to *C* is due to the income effect. In other words, of the total reduction in the amount of *Y* consumed, the reduction from Y_1 to Y_2 results from the individual substituting out of the relatively more expensive *Y* into the relatively less expensive *X*, and the reduction from Y_2 to Y_3 results from the reduction in overall purchasing power due to the price increase.

Figure 1A.6 Indifference Curves of Two Individuals The indifference curves of two individuals are shown here, with the indifference curve diagram for individual 2 rotated 180 degrees. The next figure shows how they can be connected to form an Edgeworth box diagram.

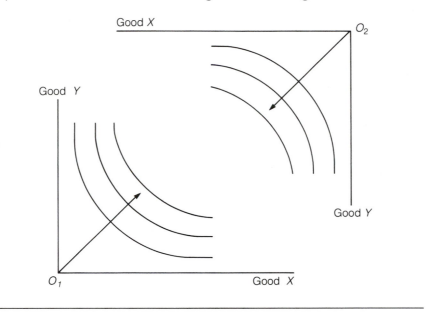

For goods on which a relatively small portion of income is expended, income effects will be small compared to substitution effects. But for goods on which a significant portion of income is expended, income effects as well as substitution effects become very important. The distinction between the two effects becomes crucial when examining major government taxing and spending programs.

The Edgeworth Box Diagram

An Edgeworth box diagram is made by combining the utility functions of two individuals. Figure 1A.6 depicts the utility function of individual 1, with origin marked O_1 in the lower left corner. Individual 2's utility function is rotated around so that the origin is in the upper right corner, meaning individual 2 will re-ceive higher levels of utility the farther to the lower left he or she can move in the diagram. The arrows pointing from the origins for individuals 1 and 2 point toward higher levels of utility.

The Edgeworth box contains a fixed amount of goods X and Y, and individual 2's

Figure 1A.7 The Edgeworth Box Diagram The two indifference curve diagrams from the previous figure are combined such that the length of the side of the box labeled Good X measures the entire amount of X available and the side labeled Good Y measures the entire amount of Y. Any point within the diagram represents a distribution of X and Y between the two individuals.

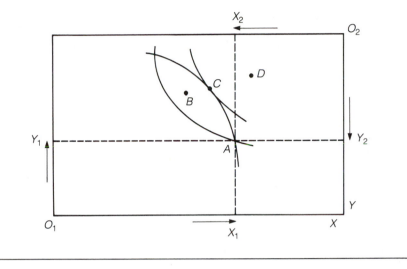

utility function is moved toward individual 1's utility function until the axes of each intersect at the levels of X and Y available for consumption. This is shown in Figure 1A.7, where the X-axis extends to the length of the maximum amount of X and the Y-axis extends to the maximum amount of Y available to both consumers. A point in the box will indicate how X and Y are distributed between the two individuals. For example, at point A individual 1 will consume X_1 of X and Y_1 of Y, while individual 2 will consume X_2 of X and Y_2 of Y. The arrows on the axes show how the consumption of each individual is measured. Note the $X_1 + X_2$ equals the total amount of X available; the same holds for Y.

The indifference curves that pass through point A for individuals 1 and 2 are also depicted in Figure 1A.7. Note that they intersect at point A and produce a lens-shaped area to the upper left of A. At any point within that lens-shaped area, for example point B, both individuals will be on higher indifference curves. Thus, a move from point A to point B could benefit both individuals. At point C individual 1 is on a higher indifference curve compared to A, but individual 2 remains on the same indifference curve. Therefore, a move from A to B makes individual 1 better off, but individual 2 is indifferent between the two points. At point D individual 1 is made better off, but individual 2 is worse off.

CHAPTER TWO

Principles for Analyzing Government

*O*ne of the most important lessons that economics has to offer is that the unfettered market system does an exceptionally good job of allocating economic resources. This lesson is hardly new; over 200 years ago Adam Smith noted that in a market economy, individuals pursuing their own self-interests are led as if by an invisible hand to pursue the best interests of the society. The market system is based on the principle of voluntary exchange, which means two people will not make an exchange unless they both view the trade as beneficial. It follows that the society in which such a mutually beneficial trade takes place must also be made better off, because everybody who is affected by the trade is made better off. In a market economy people have an incentive to produce goods or services they think others will want if the value of what they expect to get in return can be obtained more cheaply than what they produce. In essence, a market economy provides everyone with the incentive to produce the most valuable output possible so that they can trade it for the most valuable possible output of others.

This chapter begins by discussing the efficiency of a competitive market economy, noting that under ideal circumstances the market allocates resources in the most efficient possible manner. One might then wonder why we should even have a government. First, government protection of individual rights enables individuals to engage in market transactions. Second, the government can be viewed as an institution that acts in the public interest, but because the concept of public interest is difficult to define precisely, several definitions are considered in this chapter. Ultimately, one's definition of the public interest becomes a value judgment. The distinction between fact and value judgment will also be discussed in this chapter.

The Market Economy

We tend to take the productivity of the market economy for granted. But imagine that instead of trading for the goods you consume, you had to make them yourself—grow your own food, make your own clothes (including the cloth), build your own living quarters, make your own automobile (including manufacturing the steel, glass, and plastic; pumping and refining gas; and so on) build your own stereo, make your own watch . . . well, you get the idea. Because of the cooperation involved in the market economy, each of us consumes far more than we could produce individually. By specializing in one economic activity, our productivity is enhanced, which is reflected in the increased value of the goods we exchange. In short, specialization and gains from trade are the key elements in the productivity of the market economy.

In a market economy people are entitled to exchange the output they produce for output of equal value produced by others. The value of one person's output is determined by how much others are willing to pay for it, so the market assesses the value of everybody's contribution and rewards them accordingly—the more highly valued an individual's output, the greater the income from it. The market economy depends on two characteristics to make it so productive. First, the process of voluntary exchange encourages specialization and gains from trade. Second, the right of people to receive the value of their output as determined by the market provides the incentive to produce output that others consider valuable. The amazing economic progress of the past two centuries is a tribute to how well the market system works in allocating resources.

Economic Efficiency and the Competitive Market

The efficiency of a competitive market can be illustrated graphically with the supply and demand diagram in Figure 2.1. The demand curve represents the value of the output produced in the market, according to the consumers of the output, because it shows how much consumers are willing to pay for the output. The supply curve represents the opportunity cost of producing the output, because it shows how much producers must be paid in order to agree to produce the output. As long as the value of additional units of output, measured on the demand curve, exceeds the opportunity cost of the output, measured on the supply curve, then additional output will be more valuable than the cost of producing it. In other words, when the demand curve lies above the supply curve, more output should be produced because more value can be obtained, but when the supply curve lies above the demand curve, the cost of producing the output exceeds its value, so the output should not be produced.

Thus, in Figure 2.1 the level of output that will maximize the value of output to the economy is Q^*. If less than Q^* is produced, the demand curve lies above the supply curve, meaning that demanders place a higher value on consuming additional units of the good than it costs producers to provide additional units. Therefore, a potentially profitable trade can be made between suppliers and demanders. Conversely, when the supply curve lies above the demand curve, to the right of Q^*, suppliers require more compensation to produce additional units than demanders are

Figure 2.1 Resource Allocation in a Competitive Market A competitive
equilibrium produces the optimal amount of output. If less than *Q** were
produced, then the demand curve would be above the supply curve,
meaning that additional output would be worth more to consumers than
its opportunity cost and more should be produced. But output beyond
Q* would cost more than the value of the output, which means *Q** is the
optimal amount of output.

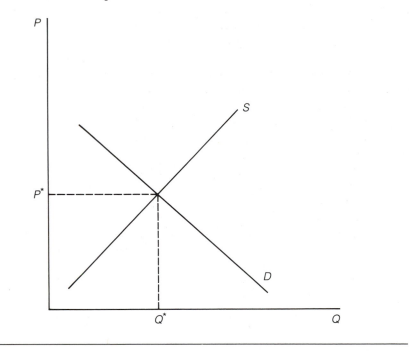

willing to pay. Because the cost of producing
the units exceeds the benefits of the units, it is
inefficient to produce output beyond *Q**.

Reflect on this a little further. The value of
the output to the purchaser is the amount that
the purchaser is willing to pay for the output;
this can be read directly from the demand
curve. The value of the output to the seller is
the amount the seller would be willing to sell
for; this can be read directly from the supply
curve. It follows that if the demand curve lies
above the supply curve, the value of the output to the potential purchasers is greater than

the value of the output to the potential sellers,
and an exchange would increase the well-
being of the society. Exchange is beneficial as
long as the demand curve lies above the supply curve, but it is detrimental when the supply curve lies above the demand curve.

This should be familiar to anyone who has
studied economics before. The level of output
that maximizes the value of an economy's output is found at the intersection of the supply
and demand curves and will be the level produced by a competitive market. Thus, in a
competitive market economy each individual,

in pursuing his own self-interest, is led as if by an invisible hand to further the best interests of society. Note that certain forces can interfere with the efficiency of the market. Perhaps something prevents a trade from taking place, so that output less than Q^* is produced; or inefficient trades might cause output greater than Q^* to be produced. These situations will be discussed in detail throughout the book. For now it is important to see how the "invisible hand" of the market leads individuals in the economy to be as productive as possible.

The Role of Government

These voluntary exchanges that occur in the market economy comprise what is known as the private sector of the economy. The public sector of the economy consists of government activity and has a different economic character. Typically, government activity is financed by mandatory taxes. After citizens pay their taxes, they can choose to consume some public sector output, such as roads and highways, without additional charges, but they must avail themselves of some output, such as national defense, whether they like it or not. Furthermore, they are obligated to live under the government's rules or face the penalties imposed by society and enforced by the police and court systems. But if the market economy works so well, why is a government even necessary?

There are a number of ways to address this question. One possible answer is that the government makes its citizens better off by undertaking activities that are in the public interest. Because presumably we all benefit from public parks, police protection, and national defense, we all share in paying for these services through our tax dollars. But this raises a whole new set of questions. How do we know that we all benefit from the government's programs? Should someone who never uses a park be forced to pay for it? If these things really benefit us, why do we have to be forced to pay for them? These are the types

of questions that will be addressed throughout the text as we analyze the activities of government within the context of the economic system in which the government exists.

The government's activities can be analyzed within the framework of two general categories. The first category concerns the scope of governmental activities—what types of activities the government *does* undertake, and why it chooses those activities. A related question concerns what types of activities, and how much of each type, the government *should* undertake. Should the government provide a police force? Parks? Highways? Dams? If so, how much of a police force? How many roads? How many dams? Clearly, what the government should do is related to what the government does do, but it is just as clear that the two are not necessarily the same.

The second category concerns how the government finances the activities it is involved in. Briefly, the government can raise revenues through taxation, the issuance of debt, or the creation of new money, all of which will be discussed in turn.

Earlier, the activities of a government were justified by saying that the government can act in the public interest. Considering the efficiency of a market economy, one still might wonder why a government must act in the public interest when the invisible hand of the market guides us so well. There are two possible reasons. First, the market might not function at all without certain government activities. Second, the government can do some things better than the market and so should be used in those cases. These alternatives will be considered now.

The Market System and Individual Rights

As noted already, the market system is able to allocate resources efficiently because all individuals have the right to exchange the output they produce for output produced by others. This presupposes that individuals have the right to the output they produce. The rights of individuals are protected by police, national defense, and a court system. Police protection safeguards individuals from having their rights violated by other members of the society. National defense protects individuals from aggression by foreign countries. The court system settles the legitimate disputes that will arise between individuals.

Without government protection of individual rights, people would have to find ways to protect their own rights, which would greatly reduce the efficiency of an economy. Nobody would have the incentive to produce any more than he or she could individually protect. And even though the strongest and most ruthless individuals in a society would have the ability to take what they wanted from others, such a society would not even benefit them particularly, because there would not be that much produced for them to take. Think of all the things that people own and leave unattended every day: homes, cars, boats, businesses. If this property were not protected in the absence of the owner, nobody would have an incentive to produce it, and the society would be very poor as a result. Nobody would have an incentive to produce goods that would only be stolen from them.

The Government as Protector of Rights

The operation of a market economy depends on the protection of individual rights, which is the primary function of all governments. Without such protection, any economy would of necessity be very poor. In a feudal society, for instance, the king guaranteed protection to the peasants in exchange for some of their output, thus providing an incentive for the less powerful to be productive. In a socialist society, even though the structure and function of the government, and what it asks from its citizens in return, differ from a market economy, the government still provides police protection, national defense, and a court system for its citizens. Indeed, any government is the protector of its citizens' rights, even though the rights that the government protects and the duties it expects in return will vary. The simple fact is that an orderly society is not possible otherwise.[1]

But how much protection a government should provide is open to debate. The simple

---

[1]These issues are discussed from an economic and philosophical standpoint in James M. Buchanan, *The Limits of Liberty: Between Anarchy and Leviathan* (Chicago: University of Chicago Press, 1975), Robert Nozick, *Anarchy, State, and Utopia* (New York: Basic Books, 1974), and John Rawls, *A Theory of Justice* (Cambridge, Mass.: Belknap, 1971). An interesting commentary on these three works is given in Scott Gordon, "The New Contractarians," *Journal of Political Economy* 84, no. 3 (June 1976), pp. 573–590.

answer is that the government should provide enough to protect the rights of its citizens, but this is not very instructive because it does not consider how much protection is necessary. For example, a change in the size of the police force can make the streets more or less safe. And individuals can take measures to protect their own rights. They can stay off the streets at night, they can buy locks for their doors, they can install burglar alarms, and they can hire private security guards. Further analysis is needed to determine how much the government actually should do.[2]

The same is true of courts and national defense. Individuals can use private arbitration or agreements to supplement the court system. Military force can serve strictly as protection for a nation's borders, or it can be used to protect a nation's interests around the world. An orderly society depends on the protection of individual rights, but more order can be purchased by spending more on police, courts, and defense. How much is the right amount? This is one of the questions that will be discussed later in the text.

The Public Interest

In theory, the minimal government acts only to protect the rights of its citizens and does nothing more; however, in reality, all governments do more than this. Furthermore, a government is not an entity in itself, independent of the people who run it and the people who are governed by it. Rather, the government's activities result from the choices made by those who run the government. In a democratic government every voter has at least some input into the governing process, so it becomes especially relevant to ask what activities people in a democratic society would like the government to undertake. Earlier, the simple answer was that the government

should act in the public interest; now it is time to try to identify the public interest, a question that has been debated by philosophers for centuries.

The Greatest Good for the Greatest Number

Over two centuries ago Jeremy Bentham suggested that the public interest would be served by policies that produced the greatest good for the greatest number. Although this idea is intuitively appealing, in practical terms it is difficult to apply. Using Bentham's criterion, a policy that benefited everybody would obviously be desirable, but what about a policy that benefited some people while imposing costs on others? Presumably, a policy that provided large benefits for most people and imposed small costs on a few would conform to Bentham's formula, but some gray areas begin to appear. For example, some method must be devised to measure the benefits to some against the costs to others. Otherwise, it

---

[2]We should note that not everybody agrees that a government is necessary to protect individual rights. For example, Murray Rothbard, *For a New Liberty* (New York: Macmillan, 1973), argues that the market will be more efficient at providing this type of protection than the government. Rothbard's book provides a very readable defense of the virtues of eliminating all government.

would be impossible to tell whether a policy that benefited some but harmed others actually did produce the greatest good for the greatest number.

Bentham's method of considering the public interest is sometimes referred to as *utilitarianism*, because it attempts to take account of the relative satisfaction, or utility, of everyone in a society. If a policy were to cause some individuals to be worse off—to lose utility—this loss could be offset by a gain in utility by others. Although Bentham's concept of the greatest good for the greatest number is a bit imprecise, social scientists have subsequently narrowed the meaning of the term.

Utilitarianism

In the latter half of the nineteenth century, some utilitarians—John Stuart Mill, for one—considered the amount of satisfaction, or utility, an individual received from consuming goods or services to be a measurable quantity, at least in theory. One way to measure the public interest was to add up the total utility of all the individuals in a society; any policy that increased the total social utility would then be in the public interest. Some of the earliest applications of the utilitarian framework applied to the distribution of income. A rich person, it was reasoned, would lose less utility from a dollar less in income than a poor person would gain from an additional dollar of income. Therefore, the public interest would be served by taxing income away from the rich and redistributing it to the poor.

The use of utilitarianism to decide what policies are in the public interest has several drawbacks. First, there is no valid way to compare the utility, or measure of satisfaction obtained, of one person with the utility of another. For example, if a dollar were taken from one person and given to another, how would the utility lost by the first person be compared with the utility gained by the second? Reflect on this for a moment. If a dollar is taken from you and given to your neighbor, is there any way to tell whether your neighbor's gain is greater than your loss? If a bridge is built with tax dollars, is there any way to tell whether the gain to the bridge users is greater than the loss to the taxpayers? Economists simply do not see any way to make interpersonal utility comparisons of this type.

Second, taken to its logical consequences, utilitarianism implies social arrangements that most people would find objectionable. Using utilitarianism as the criterion for judging the public interest, one person could be forced to do something for another person as long as the decline in the first person's utility was less than the utility gain for the second person. For example, if it was determined that one person would gain more utility from having a slave than another person would lose from being a slave, a utilitarian would have to recommend slavery as being in the public interest.[3] Indeed, one must be careful about the logical complications of utilitarianism as a measure of the public interest.

Although most people would consider slavery to be objectionable, something akin to slavery occurs when the government uses the tax system to redistribute income. In essence, the government forces some people to give their earnings to others whether they want to or not. For example, do welfare programs paid for by tax dollars actually serve the public interest? This is the type of question that must be raised when evaluating whether policies are in the public interest.

Contemporary utilitarians argue that in the

---

[3]This argument is made within the framework used in the optimal tax literature by Martin Ricketts, "Tax Theory and Tax Policy," in Alan Peacock and Francesco Forte, eds., *The Political Economy of Taxation* (New York: St. Martin's Press, 1981).

real world the only way to make policy recommendations is to weigh in an impartial manner the benefits to some against the losses of others. No conceivable real world policy can benefit everyone—someone will always be worse off. One can cloak one's value judgments in scientific-sounding jargon, but ultimately every policy recommendation must weigh the benefits to some people against the costs borne by others.[4] There are alternatives to utilitarianism, however, that should be considered.

The Pareto Criteria

Economist and sociologist Vilfredo Pareto (1848–1923) developed two criteria, now known as *Pareto optimality* and *Pareto superiority*, for judging the public interest. Pareto reasoned that because it is not possible to compare the utilities of two individuals, the only way one can be sure that a change will increase the social welfare is if at least one person is made better off by the change, but nobody is made worse off. Such a change would be called a Pareto superior move. Conversely, a proposed change that makes some people better off but others worse off cannot be said with certainty to be in the public interest, because there is no way to compare the welfare loss of those harmed with the welfare gain of those who benefit.

Whereas Pareto superiority is used to compare two possible situations, Pareto optimality is applied to a single situation. According to Pareto, a situation is optimal if nobody can be made better off without making someone else worse off. It follows logically that if a situation is not Pareto optimal, at least one person's welfare could be improved without harming anyone else. In other words, if a situation is not Pareto optimal, it would be possible to make a Pareto superior move, but if a situation is Pareto optimal, no Pareto superior moves would be possible. Note that Pareto optimality refers to a state of the world—a situation either is or is not Pareto optimal—whereas Pareto superiority compares two states of the world.

These concepts can be further clarified by referring to the Edgeworth box diagram in Figure 2.2, in which indifference curves for apple and orange consumption for Steve and Judy are depicted. Steve's origin is in the lower left corner of the box, and Judy's origin is in the upper right. The line from Steve's origin to Judy's is the contract curve—the locus of points where Steve's indifference curves are tangent to Judy's. Thus, Steve's indifference curves (one is marked *US*) are bowed away from his origin, as indifference curves would normally be depicted; because Judy's origin is in the upper right, her indifference curves (one is marked *UJ*) are also bowed away from her origin. The total amount of each good is given by the length of the good's axis. Steve's apples are measured on the bottom axis, and Judy's apples are measured on the top. Whatever apples Steve does not consume, Judy consumes. Thus, if Steve has *AS* apples, measured from Steve's origin, then Judy will have the rest of the apples—*AJ* apples, measured from Judy's origin. The same is true for oranges, so if Steve

---

[4]For a defense of utilitarianism, see Leland B. Yeager, "Rights, Contract, and Utility in Policy Espousal," *Cato Journal* 5, no. 1 (Summer 1985), pp. 259–294.

Figure 2.2 The Pareto Criteria Pareto optimal points are all points at which the indifference curves of Steve and Judy are tangent. These points are on the contract curve that goes from Steve's origin to Judy's origin. Pareto superior moves, such as from point *A* to point *D* and from point *D* to point *B*, place at least one individual on a higher indifference curve without placing the other on a lower indifference curve.

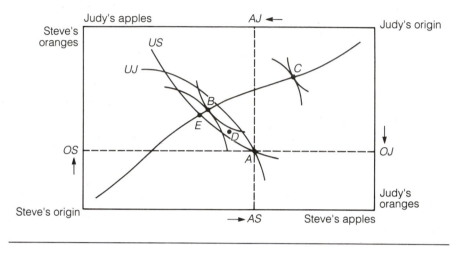

has *OS* oranges, Judy will have *OJ*, and they will be at point *A* in the diagram.

Starting from point *A*, Judy is on indifference curve *UJ* and Steve is on indifference curve *US*. Each will be better off if they can move to higher indifference curves, or indifference curves farther away from their own origins. For example, in moving from point *A* to point *B*, both Steve and Judy will be made better off, because both have moved to a higher indifference curve. This represents a Pareto superior move, meaning at least one person is made better off but nobody is made worse off. Point *B* is Pareto superior to point *A*. Note that it would not make sense simply to say that point *B* is a Pareto superior point; the point must be compared to something. But point *B* is Pareto optimal. Steve and Judy's indifference curves are tangent at that point, so it would not be possible for one of them to move to a higher indifference curve without the other one moving to a lower indifference curve. Point *A* is not Pareto optimal, because it would be possible to make at least one person better off without making anyone else worse off, as in the move from *A* to *B*. Points *C* and *E*, and every other point on the contract curve, are also Pareto optimal points, because from those points it would not be possible to make one person better off without making the other person worse off.

The concept of Pareto optimality is the same as the concept of economic efficiency; if a situation is not Pareto optimal, the existing resources are not being used efficiently to produce the highest possible level of satisfaction for the society. For example, at point *A* Steve could trade some of his apples for some of Judy's oranges, and both would consider themselves better off. In other words, at point *A* the existing resources (apples and oranges) could be used more efficiently to produce a greater level of satisfaction for both Steve and Judy.

Would a move from point *A* to point *C* be in the public interest? Using the Pareto criteria, there is no way to say. The move is from a point that is not Pareto optimal to a point that is Pareto optimal, meaning efficiency is increased, but the move makes Steve better off and Judy worse off. Because there is no way to compare the utility lost by Judy to the utility gained by Steve, the Pareto criteria do not offer a way to compare *A* and *C*. We cannot say that the change is in the public interest because we have no way of knowing whether the benefit to Steve is greater than the cost to Judy.

This is one of the drawbacks of the Pareto criteria. It can compare some points to some other points, but it cannot compare all points to all other points. Thus, for proposed changes that benefit some at the expense of others, the Pareto criteria offer no insight into whether the changes are in the public interest or not.

A move from *A* to *B* would be Pareto superior and in the public interest; a move from *B* to *A* would be Pareto inferior and not in the public interest. A move from *A* to *D* would also be Pareto superior, even though *D* is not Pareto optimal. At point *D* both Steve and Judy are better off, so the move is Pareto superior, but there is still the possibility of further Pareto superior moves. In short, a move to any point in the lens-shaped area formed by Judy's and Steve's indifference curves would be a Pareto superior move, because at least one of them would be better off without harm to the other.

Market Exchange and the Pareto Criteria

Unless people not involved in the exchange are harmed, every market exchange is a Pareto superior move—people will not agree to an exchange if it is not to their benefit. According to utilitarians, any market exchange is in the public interest because nobody suffers a loss in utility and some people gain. But market exchange also satisfies the more exclusive test of Pareto superiority. The Pareto criteria become especially relevant in evaluating governmental activities that could also be undertaken in the private sector. For example, when comparing public and private schools, the choice of going to a private school involves a Pareto superior move, but the same cannot be said of public schools, because some people (most notably, taxpayers) may not be in voluntary agreement about paying taxes.

Limitations of the Pareto Criteria

The Pareto criteria can be useful indicators of the public interest, but they have some drawbacks as well. For one thing, a Pareto improvement in social welfare requires that the proposed change benefit some people but not harm anyone. Unfortunately, in a complex society comprised of millions of people, any proposed policy is almost sure to make someone worse off. Few changes could fulfill to the letter the conditions that must be met for it to be a Pareto improvement. In practical terms it may not be possible to take any action in the public sector if the strict conditions of the Pareto criteria are adhered to. One might argue that the Pareto concepts are not meant to be applied literally, but if this is the case then the problem remains one of comparing the gains of the gainers against the losses of the losers. To have meaning, it would seem that the Pareto criteria must be taken literally.[5]

[5] However, Knut Wicksell, "A New Theory of Just Taxation," reprinted in Richard A. Musgrave and Alan T. Peacock, eds., *Classics in the Theory of Public Finance* (New York: St. Martin's Press, 1967), pp. 72–118, argues for an approximate unanimity in public sector decisions that might be thought of as approximating a Pareto superior move.

A second problem with the Pareto criteria is that they lend legitimacy to the status quo. Because any change must improve the welfare of at least one person but not harm anyone to be a Pareto superior move, the status quo enjoys a position that may not be justified if that position was obtained through illegitimate or unfair means. Where there are no complaints about the status quo, this is not a problem. However, where the status quo is viewed as unfair, people might be tempted to improve the social welfare by changes that make some people worse off.

Consider, for example, slavery in the pre–Civil War American South and the apartheid system in South Africa. Although freeing the slaves imposed an economic loss on the former slave owners, many people viewed slavery as an objectionable system and felt that the social welfare would be improved if the slaves were freed. That view was not unanimous, obviously, but those who favored the abolishing of slavery in effect were rejecting the pure Pareto criteria as a measure of social welfare.

A third problem with the Pareto criteria is that they do not rank all possible states of the world. A change that makes everyone better off is a Pareto improvement, but what about a change that makes some people better off and others worse off? The change may not represent an improvement in welfare, but it is not necessarily a reduction in social welfare either. The Pareto criteria do not provide for interpersonal comparisons of utility, so when some people are made better off while others are made worse off, there is no way to say whether, on balance, social welfare has been improved or reduced.

Other Measures of the Public Interest

Accepting that most changes will benefit some people and harm others, various methods might be used to assess whether a proposed policy change is in the public interest. One method evaluates the compensation that gainers from a policy might pay to losers to make the change Pareto superior. Another method uses an explicit social welfare function.

Potential Compensation

According to this method, if a proposed change benefits some people enough that they potentially could pay the losers, then if the compensation were paid, nobody would be made worse off by the change. This does not mean that the compensation actually has to be paid—if it were paid, the change would be a Pareto superior move. Rather, the criterion here is whether the gains to the gainers are greater than the losses to the losers. But whereas nobody is harmed by a Pareto improvement, in this case it may be little consolation to someone who is made worse off by a change that the gainer could have provided compensation.

However, there is some justification for favoring public policies that would have been Pareto superior moves if the gainers had compensated the losers. Any compensation scheme would be both costly and difficult to administer, but on the average individuals are compensated for those occasions when they are made worse off by other policies that make them better off. The government is constantly undertaking new policies, and under each of the policies some people gain while others lose. But different people will gain and lose from different policies, so over the course of a large number of policy decisions, people should enjoy a net gain if the test of potential compensation is used.

The Social Welfare Function

A social welfare function can be thought of as a set of indifference curves that depict the welfare of the entire society rather than just one individual. Critics of the social welfare function charge that it makes interpersonal utility comparisons that in fact cannot be made. In this sense, the social welfare function is really a type of utilitarianism. Supporters of the social welfare function argue that in the real world such comparisons must be made constantly for purposes of public policy and are better made explicitly rather than obscured by devices such as potential compensation. In fact, economists who accept the principle of the social welfare function often use it in a manner similar to the utilitarians of the nineteenth century. For example, they frequently apply it to income distribution problems to determine the optimal amount of redistribution through the tax system. By contrast, the Pareto criteria are not well suited to distributional issues because redistribution, by its very nature, benefits those who receive income but not those who lose it.[6]

Benefit-Cost Analysis

In actual practice a frequently used method to determine whether public sector projects are in the public interest is benefit-cost analysis. In a benefit-cost analysis a dollar value is placed on all of the costs and all of the benefits associated with a particular project. Quite simply, if the benefits are greater than the costs, then the project is deemed to be in the public interest. However, the benefit-cost analysis method of assessing the public interest is not without problems.

The main difficulty arises in trying to place an accurate dollar value on all of the benefits and costs of a particular project. For example, consider a benefit-cost analysis of whether the government should build a dam in a particular area. If some people do not want to move from the land on which the lake will form, how should the cost to them be weighed? If the probability of flooding is reduced downstream, how should this be weighed? If boating will be possible on the new lake, how should the recreational benefits be translated into dollar figures? And how can a dollar value be placed on the environmental impact, particularly because some aspects of the environment may be improved, whereas others will deteriorate. Ultimately, a benefit-cost analysis must rely on one of the previously discussed methods for assessing whether a project is in the public interest. Chapter 17 discusses the use of benefit-cost analysis in more detail.

Positive and Normative Economics

The distinction between positive economics and normative economics is an important one, especially as it relates to the public sector. Positive economics examines the real world to discover what it is like and how it works. Within the realm of positive economics, there is no concept of the public interest, nor of what the

---

[6]However, Harold M. Hochman and James D. Rogers, "Pareto Optimal Redistribution," *American Economic Review* 59 (Sept. 1969), pp. 542–557, argue that redistributional programs may satisfy the Pareto criteria if the redistribution is of a type of collective consumption good. Collective consumption goods are discussed in Chapter 3.

world ideally should be like. Normative economics makes value judgments as to how the world *should* be. Normative analysis assesses the desirability of the facts determined through positive analysis.

Because positive analysis makes no value judgments, conclusions arrived at through positive analysis will be either right or wrong. Of course, the real world is a complex place, and it may not always be easy to tell whether positive conclusions are correct. But even if disagreements arise over the facts, the facts themselves cannot support both sides of the disagreement. For example, one might argue that the minimum wage law causes unemployment. By holding the wages of some people at a rate higher than the market equilibrium, employers (the demanders of labor) will want to hire fewer low-skilled workers than if the minimum wage rate did not exist. Meanwhile, the higher wages produced by the minimum wage law will cause more low-skilled workers (suppliers of labor) to want to work. With more workers looking for jobs, but fewer jobs available, the result is that the minimum wage law has caused unemployment.

This is an example of positive analysis—we have simply analyzed the facts of the world and determined that the minimum wage law causes unemployment. That conclusion is either correct or it is incorrect, in that either the reasoning accounts for the facts of the real world or it does not.

The argument might continue that because unemployment is an undesirable result, the minimum wage law itself is undesirable. Now the argument has shifted from positive analysis to normative analysis, from simply describing the facts of the real world—the minimum wage law causes unemployment—to making a value judgment that the consequences of the minimum wage law are undesirable.

A counter argument to this normative analysis can be made. Certainly the minimum wage law causes unemployment, but it is unfair to allow employers to exploit workers and force them to work for less than the minimum wage. If a person cannot earn more than the minimum wage, then the most humane alternative is for society to care for the person through some type of welfare program.

It is impossible to say which of these normative arguments is correct. The first argument places a high value on reducing unemployment and allowing everyone to work, whereas the second places a high value on making sure that everyone receives a sufficient wage so that they are not exploited by the economic system. Because no scientific evidence exists that one person's values are any better than another's, there is no way to conclude that one person's normative argument is any more correct than anyone else's.

Compare that to a situation in which two people disagree not about why the minimum wage law is undesirable but about whether the minimum wage law actually causes unemployment. The difference is no longer one of normative conclusions. Because the two people disagree about the facts, the disagreement is positive; this positive disagreement has led them to different normative conclusions. When people disagree about facts in the real world, at most one of them can be right. But when they agree on the facts but come to different normative conclusions because they make different value judgments, there is no way to say that one person is any more right than another.

The distinction between positive and normative applies any time a value judgment is made, in economics or anywhere else. For example, one person might assert that Franklin Roosevelt was a great president, and another person might disagree. They could concur about the facts of his presidency and the consequences of his policies, but where a political liberal is likely to interpret those consequences favorably, a conservative is not. And there is no scientific way to resolve a normative disagreement such as this one.

As another example, one person might look out the window, see that it is raining, and say that the weather is bad; another person, who wants rain for his garden, would argue that the weather is good. They agree that it is raining, yet they evaluate that fact differently. In economics, as elsewhere, there is no way to determine whether one person's values are more correct than another's; thus, there may be no resolution to normative disagreements.

The distinction between positive and normative is crucial to public sector economics. In a course on microeconomic theory, for instance, one is interested mainly in how the economy works in the real world, not in attaching any value judgments to it, so the analysis is essentially positive (although once the facts are understood, it would certainly be possible to make value judgments). With public sector economics, on the other hand, normative elements necessarily enter into the picture because the government's activities are voluntarily chosen by the individuals in a society. In a democracy the choices extend to every voter, each of whom has some input into the decision-making process. One can use positive analysis to evaluate the potential effects of a particular governmental policy, but because policies can be chosen through the political process, it is a short step indeed from analyzing the effects of governmental actions to evaluating their desirability. Furthermore, whether those actions are viewed as desirable or not will have an impact on how likely they are to be implemented.

Although normative questions have no easy answers, some possible criteria for shaping those answers, or at least framing the questions, were discussed earlier in the chapter. Bentham's dictum of the greatest good for the greatest number has intuitive appeal, even though it is not always clear when this criterion is met. The Pareto criteria are especially appealing because they find change to be desirable only when nobody is hurt by it. Recall, though, that many changes benefit some people but at a cost to others; the Pareto criteria offer little help in resolving such cases. Determining what is in the public interest is a normative problem for which no single, easy answer exists. All of the methods discussed—the Pareto and utilitarian criteria, the concept of a social welfare function, and the possibilities of benefit-cost analysis—address the issue to varying degrees, but which offers the most guidance?

When looking at possible criteria for evaluating the public interest, the Pareto criteria stand out from the others because they do not require interpersonal utility comparisons. Something furthers the public interest, according to Pareto, only when someone benefits but nobody is harmed. Thus, there is no need to weigh the benefits of some people against the costs of others. Because there is no good way to make interpersonal utility comparisons, we can state with more confidence that the public interest is being served when a change is Pareto superior. Furthermore, Pareto optimality means the same thing as economic efficiency—resources are not being inefficiently used because no change in resource allocation can be made that will not leave someone worse off. But again, the fact that most proposed changes will help some people but harm others means the Pareto criteria have limited practical applications; their real value is in allowing the public interest to be judged without resorting to interpersonal utility comparisons.

Conclusion

The market system of economic organization has been responsible for a tremendous amount of economic progress over the past several centuries. In general, the market allocates resources quite effectively, but there are times when the economy benefits from government activity as well. The primary function of the government is to protect the individual rights of its citizens—no economy can expect to operate at any more than a subsistence level without the order provided by the protection of these rights.

Furthermore, as a society we expect the government to carry on other activities that are in the public interest. However, defining the public interest ultimately depends on normative analysis, from which no single, scientifically proven solutions can be obtained. Nevertheless, the government does make choices in order to try to further the public interest, and because every voter in a democratic country is a part of the public choice process, we should at least have some idea of what might generally be considered the public interest. For example, a change that would benefit at least one person and harm nobody, according to the criterion of Pareto superiority, would be in the public interest.

If it functioned perfectly, we could leave all economic activity to the market. We would require a minimal government providing only police protection, national defense, and a court system. In reality, the market does not always work perfectly, in which case governmental activity to improve on the shortcomings of the market might become necessary. However, it is not enough merely to show a problem with the market; one must also show that the government could do better than the market. This requires a two-step process. First, problems with the market have to be identified. Second, the effects of the government intervention have to be identified. Only then can the market's shortcomings be compared with governmental policies designed to deal with those shortcomings.

This process of analysis points the direction for the next few chapters of the text. Chapter 3 examines reasons why the market may be inefficient in performing certain functions or producing certain types of goods. In these cases government intervention can improve the situation. Subsequent chapters analyze how the government makes its decisions and evaluate the characteristics of public sector output.

Questions

1. Using a graph, explain why in a competitive market each individual, in pursuing his or her own self-interest, is led as if by an invisible hand to pursue the best interest of the entire society. Is your explanation positive or normative?

2. Why does the operation of a market system presuppose that individual rights are protected? What would an economy in which individual

rights were not protected be like? What institutions of government protect individual rights, and how do these institutions work?

3. What is utilitarianism? What are the advantages and disadvantages of using utilitarianism to determine the public interest? Is some form of utilitarianism currently used to measure the public interest? Should some form of utilitarianism be used?

4. Explain the concepts of Pareto optimality and Pareto superiority. How do the two concepts differ? Would the Pareto criteria or utilitarianism provide a more effective measure of the public interest?

5. Relate the notion of potential compensation to the concept of Pareto superiority. If the beneficiaries of a change could potentially compensate the losers, is the change in the public interest? Are there some conditions under which potential compensation would suffice and others under which actual compensation would be preferred?

6. What is a benefit-cost analysis? What problems might arise in trying to carry out such an analysis? Is a benefit-cost analysis more similar to utilitarianism or to the Pareto criteria? Given the necessity of determining what is in the public interest, is a benefit-cost analysis a reasonable method to employ? What additional criteria could be used to supplement a benefit-cost analysis?

7. What is the distinction between positive and normative economics? Why is this distinction especially relevant to the study of public sector economics?

PART TWO

Economic Efficiency

CHAPTER THREE

Economic Efficiency
and the Allocation
of Resources

*I*n Chapter 2 we argued that the market is a very good allocator of economic resources. The market system is built on the principle of voluntary exchange in which both participants in the exchange benefit, so that when individuals trade, they are making Pareto superior moves that further the public interest. If all potentially mutually profitable exchanges were made, the market economy would make Pareto superior moves until reaching a Pareto optimum. In short, the process of exchange leads naturally toward an efficient allocation of resources.

However, two types of problems can interfere with the efficiency of the market process. First, some exchanges might not actually be Pareto superior moves, because someone other than the parties involved in the exchange might be adversely affected by the exchange. For example, you might hire someone to cut down a tree in your yard, which would benefit both you and the tree cutter, but if the noise from the chain saw disturbed

your neighbor, your neighbor would be made worse off by the transaction. Although most transactions affect only the traders directly involved in the exchange, in cases such as this where someone not party to the transaction is harmed, a *negative externality* has been created. The efficiency of the market is affected, and the trade is no longer a Pareto superior move.

A second type of problem occurs when potentially profitable trades are not made because, for one reason or another, the market does not provide the right incentives to make the trades. Resources are not being used as efficiently as if the potentially profitable trades were actually made, so the economy is not at a Pareto optimum. Economists have identified a number of potential circumstances in which this might occur, including collective consumption goods, nonexcludable goods, positive externalities, and economic instability. The exact meanings of these terms will be discussed in detail later; for now note simply that in some cases the potential to make a Pareto superior move exists, but for one reason or another the market system does not provide the incentive for the move to occur.

The market is sometimes accused of another type of shortcoming. Some people argue that the market does not produce an equitable distribution of income and that the government should actively engage in income redistribution on equity grounds. Equity issues are certainly important, and they will be discussed in detail in later chapters. Equity issues require some type of interpersonal utility comparison, whereas this chapter focuses on issues of economic efficiency. Furthermore, if the economy can be made to utilize resources more efficiently, some people will be better off without making anyone worse off, which will alleviate the need to compare the utilities of individuals to see that the overall social welfare has improved.

Negative Externalities

Recall that a negative externality is a cost imposed on a person by the actions of others, without the consent of the person who bears the cost. In the tree-cutting example the two people who engaged in an exchange to have a tree cut down were both made better off, but a third person disturbed by the noise had to bear a cost of the exchange because of the disturbance, even though that person had nothing to do with the transaction. The cost imposed on the third person is the externality.

Another example of an externality is air pollution. In industrial areas factories frequently will produce air pollution as a by-product of their marketable output, and people in the surrounding areas must suffer the cost of breathing polluted air even though they have nothing to do with producing the pollution. Clearly, the exchanges made by, say, a steel manufacturer and the firm's customer will benefit both parties to the exchange. But the exchange is not Pareto superior—while some people (the traders) gain, others (nearby residents) lose.

A closer look at the characteristics of a negative externality illuminates the inefficiencies of this transaction. The steel mill uses a variety of inputs to produce steel, including labor, for which it pays wages; land, for which it pays rent;[1] and capital equipment, coal, and iron ore, which it must purchase. The steel mill must pay the opportunity costs of all of these valuable resources, but it pays nothing for the valuable resource of clean air, which it turns into dirty air. All of the other resources are paid for by transactions internal to the market system, but the use of clean air is external to the market system, thus giving rise to the name externality.

The problem here is that when a firm does not have to pay for a resource, it will tend to use too much of that resource. For example, labor is a scarce and valuable resource, for which a firm must pay a wage of X dollars per hour. The firm must take account of the opportunity cost of labor and will use labor as long as the value of each laborer's output exceeds X dollars per hour. But if the firm could

---

[1] The firm may own the land, in which case it in effect rents the land to itself. The opportunity cost of the land will be the same in either case, because the firm could rent the land to someone else if it were not using it as a steel mill site.

Figure 3.1 Negative Externality Usually, the supply curve includes the entire opportunity cost of production, so the optimal amount of output is determined by the intersection of the supply and demand curves. When a negative externality exists, there is an additional cost that must be added to the costs in the supply curve to find the optimal level of production. Including the cost of the externality, the optimal level of output is Q^*. An optimal tax is one designed to make the producers in the market take account of the cost of the externality, so the optimal tax equals the cost of the externality.

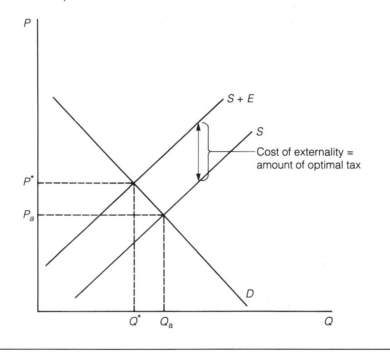

get all the labor it wanted for free, it would use additional laborers as long as the value of their output was greater than zero. As a result, the firm would use too much labor.

The same is true of clean air. When a firm does not have to pay a price to use up clean air, it tends to use too much of it; the result is air pollution. One obvious solution is to have the firm pay a price for polluting the air equal to the opportunity cost of the pollution.

Economic agents must take account of the opportunity costs of their actions in order for them to have the incentive to allocate resources efficiently. The price system enforces this accountability by requiring economic agents to pay the opportunity costs of the resources they use. Because most resources are allocated internally to the market, the market price generally reflects the opportunity cost. But in cases such as the pollution example, the allocation of clean air is external to the market, and the opportunity cost is not taken into account.

The concepts of negative externality can be illustrated graphically. Figure 3.1 depicts the supply and demand curves for a competitive industry that generates some external cost. Without taking into account the cost of the externality, the industry will produce output Q_a at a price P_a. But if the firms in the industry had to pay the cost of the externality in addition to their other costs, the industry supply curve would become $S+E$—the total opportunity cost of production—and the industry would produce Q^* at price P^*. The firms in the industry have been using one of their inputs at no charge, so they have used too much of the input and have produced too much output, at too low a price. The optimal amount for the industry to produce would be Q^*, but because they do not pay for one of their inputs, they end up producing Q_a.

Private Exchange to Correct an Externality

If only a few people are affected by an externality, then a private exchange might correct the problem. For example, assume your neighbor causes air pollution by burning leaves that produce smoke in your yard. If your neighbor is courteous, then whenever she imposes this cost on you, she might invite you over to lunch. Because there is no such thing as a free lunch, this imposes a cost on your neighbor any time she wants to burn leaves, which causes her to take account of the cost of the externality. Thus, a private transaction can correct the externality.

What if your neighbor is not so courteous? If the smoke bothers you, you might be inclined to bear a cost to keep your neighbor from burning the leaves. For example, you

might agree to dispose of your neighbor's leaves for her in exchange for her refraining from burning them. This imposes a cost on you, to be sure, but once again, somebody (this time you) takes account of the cost of the externality.

A private exchange of this type is sometimes possible, as will be discussed in detail in Chapter 4. But when large numbers of people are affected by the externality, such as when air pollution blankets an entire city, such an exchange ceases to be feasible. The remainder of this chapter assumes that private trades to internalize an externality are not a viable option, so that if the government does not pursue some type of policy to control the externality, it will continue to be produced unchecked.

Corrective Taxation of an Externality

In theory, taxation represents a relatively simple, straightforward solution to the externality problem when private exchanges to internalize the externality are not feasible. If the firms in the industry are charged for the amount of pollution that they produce, and if the price is exactly equal to the cost of the externality, then an economically efficient level of output will result. In Figure 3.1 output Q^* would sell at price P^* to reflect the additional cost.

In practice, it is not always easy to charge firms for the costs of the externalities that they produce. Again using the air pollution example, the first problem is measuring the cost of the externality. One method might be to take a poll of all the people affected by the air pollution to see how much they would be willing to pay to eliminate it. The first person polled might be willing to pay $10 per year for clean rather than dirty air; the second person polled might be willing to pay $1000 for clean air; the third person polled might not mind the pollution at all and be unwilling to contribute anything. The poll would require responses from everyone affected by the pollution, keeping in mind the pervasive effects of the pollution, such as environmental damage to wildlife, corrosive effects on painted objects, and so on. Although in Figure 3.1 we simply drew in a graph that showed the costs of the externality, in the real world it is obviously much more difficult to estimate accurately the total external cost.

The next problem is to decide who is responsible for the cost and to charge them accordingly. Again, obtaining an accurate measurement is difficult, not only because factories pollute in different amounts but also because they produce different kinds of pollutants, some more harmful than others. The problem is compounded in a place such as Los Angeles, where much of the pollution is caused by automobiles. How could it be determined how much each polluter contributed to the total problem so that each polluter could be charged accordingly? It would not suffice simply to charge a certain amount per car, or even per gallon of gas used. The tax should be placed directly on the source of the pollution to give people an incentive to keep their catalytic converters working properly and their cars tuned up to reduce pollution.[2]

Taxation Versus Regulation

Because it is so difficult to apply a pollution tax in the real world, governments typically pass regulations requiring that certain steps be taken to reduce the externality. Perhaps

people would voluntarily use catalytic converters on their cars if they were charged for the pollution they caused, but because charging is not practical, the government simply requires that cars meet certain emission standards, which mandates the use of pollution control devices on automobiles. Likewise, other polluters, such as steel mills and electricity generators, are required to use certain pollution control devices. Such regulations seek to force polluters to reduce their pollution using the same methods they would if they had to pay a price for the amount of the externality for which they were responsible.

In some cases there might be no way directly to reduce the amount of pollution per unit of production. The optimal tax described previously would cause firms to produce less, which would reduce the overall amount of the externality to the optimal level even though the externality per unit of production would not change. Ideally, as depicted in Figure 3.1, a tax equal to the cost of the externality would reduce output from Q_a to Q^* and effectively limit the damage from the externality. But in many cases a tax on the externality is not feasible, perhaps because of problems in measuring the externality. If it were cost-effective, the firms in the industry would employ resources to reduce the amount of the externality per unit of production, but assume for now that the only way to reduce external damage is to reduce output to Q^*. In the short run, a quota might work, but in the long run the results from a quota on output and a corrective tax will differ.

This is illustrated in Figure 3.2, which depicts the cost curves of a representative firm in the industry depicted in Figure 3.1. In the short run, when a tax is placed on the industry, output declines to Q^* and the price rises to P^*. The amount of the tax is shown by the entire shaded area in Figure 3.2, and as a re-

[2]An excellent discussion of corrective taxes for negative externalities is presented in William J. Baumol, "On Taxation and Control of Externalities," *American Economic Review* 62, no. 3 (June 1972), pp. 307–322.

Figure 3.2 Taxation Versus Regulation of an Externality A tax and a regulation that each have the effect in the short run of reducing output to Q^* will have different effects in the long run. The regulation creates profits equal to the entire shaded area and encourages entry in the long run, whereas the optimal tax creates losses equal to the darkly shaded area and encourages firms to leave the industry.

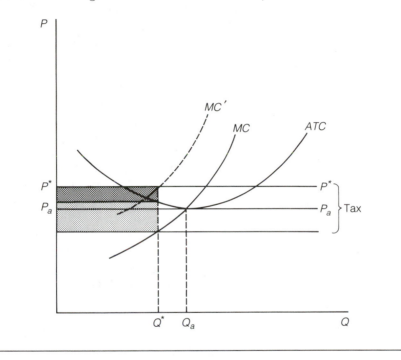

sult of the tax, the firms in the industry are taking losses. The marginal cost of producing will rise to MC' when the tax is included in the cost of production. But if each individual firm in the industry is required to restrict output to Q^*, the firms produce the same amount of output as if they were being taxed, but they are making above-normal profits, represented by the heavily shaded area. Obviously, the firms in the industry prefer output restrictions to taxation because the tax creates losses to the firms whereas the output restriction

creates profits. Because firms have some influence over regulatory policy, it is not hard to imagine them lobbying for output restrictions rather than a corrective tax as the solution to the externality.[3]

Note also the difference in the long-run implications of the tax versus the quota. The

---

[3]See James M. Buchanan and Gordon Tullock, "Polluters' Profits and Political Response: Direct Controls Versus Taxes," *American Economic Review* 65, no. 1 (March 1975), pp. 139–147, for a discussion of this idea.

losses caused by taxation will encourage an exodus of firms from the industry until, after taking account of the cost of the externality, it achieves a new long-run equilibrium. Here, firms will be producing at their minimum average total cost. By contrast, quantity restriction means firms will not be producing at the minimum average total cost, and the profits in the industry will provide an incentive for new firms to enter and for existing firms to produce more. In this case regulators would have to monitor the output of firms to prevent overproduction and devise a method for keeping new firms from entering the industry. In summary, the short-run similarities between the effects of a corrective tax and a quantity restriction do not hold up in the long run.

A similar distinction applies for regulation requiring the use of some type of pollution control device that would be optimal if a tax were also applied. For example, assume that regulators decide that if a corrective tax can be applied, firms in the industry will use smokestack scrubbers, so the regulators require the installation of smokestack scrubbers in lieu of the corrective tax. Obviously, the firms in the industry are better off, because under the tax plan the firms would have to buy the smokestack scrubber and are also liable for the tax, whereas with regulation alone the firms avoid the cost of the tax.

In conclusion, from the externality-generating industry's point of view, regulation is preferable to corrective taxes as a means of controlling the externality, but from the taxpayers' point of view, the tax is preferable. Tax revenue raised from the corrective tax can be used to reduce other taxes or to buy additional public sector output. However, industry representatives typically have more political clout than the general public, so from a political standpoint there is a bias in favor of regulation rather than corrective taxation in response to an externality.

Public Policy Toward Externalities

Would it be desirable to eliminate all pollution? Although we would all rather live in a pollution-free world, if one weighs the benefits against the costs, the answer is no. One by-product of production is pollution, and as with anything else, the benefits of pollution reduction are achieved only at a cost. Certainly it is worthwhile to try to reduce automobile emissions in the Los Angeles area, but in some places the costs of trying to reduce pollution may outweigh the limited negative effects of the pollution. For example, Auburn, Alabama, where this book was written, is a small college town without much manufacturing and with little pollution. Nevertheless, its residents pay hundreds of extra dollars to buy cars with pollution control devices. Furthermore, most of these cars run on unleaded gas, which costs more than leaded gas, so the town's residents again pay to reduce pollution. On top of that, cars with pollution control devices get lower gas mileage than cars without those devices, so the residents pay yet again. In short, the residents of Auburn pay a large amount to achieve a barely noticeable reduction in pollution.

If one were really serious about eliminating all pollution, farm tractors could be required to have catalytic converters, or better yet, farmers could be required to give up tractors in favor of mules and oxen. Certainly this is going to extremes. The point here is that while pollution reduction is desirable, one must weigh the benefits against the costs—it is desirable to eliminate pollution as long as the marginal benefits of doing so exceed the marginal costs.

The existence of negative externalities is

frequently cited as a reason for the government to get involved in the economy. Air and water pollution, acid rain, strip mining of coal, and offshore oil drilling are all areas in which the economic activities of some impose costs on others. Unfortunately, those who impose the costs frequently have no incentive to take account of those costs when making their decisions. And it is much easier to see that an externality exists than it is to determine who is responsible, and for what part of the total cost. As a result, government regulation is frequently used to require those who generate externalities to take some action to try to limit their costs.

Positive Externalities

In contrast to a negative externality, a positive externality is a *benefit* received by a person as a result of the actions of others. Although a positive externality certainly seems preferable to a negative externality, a problem arises here as well. If the activities of some people produce benefits for others that the others do not have to pay for, then the true value of the activity will not be reflected in the market demand for the activity, and too little of the activity will take place.

This can be illustrated in Figure 3.3, which depicts the supply and demand curves in a competitive market in which a positive externality exists. Because the generator of the externality produces a benefit that others are able to take advantage of without paying for, the demand curve no longer reflects the total social value of the output in this market. Rather, some benefits are produced external to the market. Adding the external benefits to the benefits received by demanders in the market produces curve $D+E$, where the value of the positive externality is added to the value placed on the output by the demanders in the market. When the entire social benefit, $D+E$, is accounted for, the optimal output in the market is Q^* rather than Q_a that would be produced in the market with the externality.

For example, in fixing up their house, a family makes the whole neighborhood a nicer place to live, which constitutes an external benefit. The benefit may result simply from the enjoyment of living in a nicer neighborhood, but the neighbors might also profit financially from the externality if they were to sell their house, because a house in a nice neighborhood is worth more than a house in a poor neighborhood.

However, as Figure 3.3 indicates, a problem arises when too little of the activity that generates the positive externality is undertaken. It would seem that in a run-down neighborhood a family would be willing to fix up its house if the other families would, but nobody wants to invest a lot of money in fixing up a house in a poor neighborhood. Those who want nicer homes tend to move rather than renovate, and eventually the whole neighborhood deteriorates. The possibility that too few resources will be used to fix up the run-down neighborhood is evident; what the government can do to solve such problems is less clear.

One solution has been urban renewal projects and other types of housing subsidies, which in effect represent negative taxes that correct for positive externalities. Rather than

Figure 3.3 Positive Externality A positive externality produces benefits not captured in the demand curve for the good. When those benefits are added in, the optimal amount of output of the good is shown to be Q^* rather than the amount Q_a that would be produced in a competitive market.

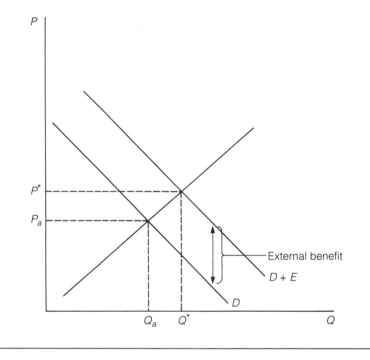

charging an individual a certain amount, the government pays the individual generating the externality a subsidy equal to the external benefit. However, as with taxation for negative externalities, the government can have trouble in calculating the appropriate subsidy. In subsequent chapters we will examine other ways that the government might become involved in solving this type of problem; at this point, note simply that the market can work less than perfectly in allocating too few resources to a market that exhibits positive externalities.

Positive externalities are frequently used to try to justify government subsidization of various activities. For example, people have argued that because a well-educated population provides benefits to everyone, the government should subsidize education. Similar arguments have been made about the external benefits generated by symphony orchestras, opera and ballet, art, museums, and libraries. But consider what benefits orchestras, libraries, and so on actually provide to people other than their patrons. Perhaps there are some, but the positive externality argument is often used by opera buffs, symphony fans, and so on, as a way of trying to get the government to pay for the activities these individuals enjoy.

Additional Externalities Concepts

A number of more complex issues arise in an examination of externalities and their control. This section deals with two of those issues by distinguishing between technological and pecuniary externalities and between marginal and inframarginal externalities. These distinctions may appear subtle at first, but they do have some significant implications for public policy toward externalities.

Technological and Pecuniary Externalities

There is an important distinction between an externality that directly affects a firm's production function or an individual's utility function and an externality that affects the supply and demand conditions that the individual faces in the market. An externality that influences production or utility functions is called a *technological externality*; an externality that influences market supply and demand conditions is called a *pecuniary externality*.

Thus far, the discussion in this chapter has focused on technological externalities, which public policy tries to control. A classic example of a technological externality is a factory whose smoke soils the clothes that a neighboring laundry hangs out to dry. This directly affects the laundry's production function by increasing their costs. The factory also makes it less pleasant to live in the polluted area, thereby influencing the utility functions of the factory's neighbors.

By contrast, a pecuniary externality does not involve inefficient allocation of resources, so there is no need for public policy to address the issue. Although a pecuniary externality is external to the individual's behavior, it is not external to the market. For example, if a Burger King opens next door to a McDonald's, the demand for McDonald's hamburgers will decline due to the increased competition. Strictly speaking, this constitutes a negative externality—McDonald's is harmed by Burger King's actions—but the harm results from a change in demand (and the resulting effects on prices and quantities), so while it is external to McDonald's actions, it is internal to the market. Because the market accounts for all of the costs and benefits, a pecuniary externality does not result in a misallocation of resources.

Consider another example. An increase in automobile sales causes an increase in the demand for steel, which results in an increase in the price of steel not only for automobile manufacturers but also for refrigerator manufacturers. Clearly, refrigerator manufacturers are made worse off by the change in supply, but as in the Burger King example, the effects are internal to the market, and there is no reason to interfere with the market. These examples have dealt with negative externalities, but the same logic applies to pecuniary positive externalities as well. For example, decline in the price of air conditioning since World War II has increased the value of land in Southern states, but this is a pecuniary benefit to landowners. It does not involve a misallocation of resources because the resources are allocated within the market system rather than external to it.

In short, when someone is made worse off by a pecuniary externality, the individual is worse off only because of changes in supply and demand conditions. A pecuniary externality does not produce an inefficiency, because all costs and benefits are reflected in market prices. Throughout the text in discussions of externalities, we will be referring to technological externalities unless otherwise specified.

Marginal and Inframarginal Externalities

It would seem that almost anything anyone does would have some effect on others, thus creating an externality. Does this suggest that there is a major role for public policy in correcting for the problems of externalities? Note that many externalities are *inframarginal externalities*, which means that individuals would not change their behavior even if they bore the full costs or received the full benefits of the externalities. Inframarginal externalities do not necessarily imply an inefficient allocation of resources.

For example, an educated population creates a positive externality to the population as a whole. The ability to read, write, and do arithmetic helps banks because they can rely on the customers to write checks, maintain their account balances, and so on. Retail stores benefit because customers can read signs and understand prices. Indeed, an advanced economy requires a literate population. Should the government subsidize education because it creates a positive externality?

Regardless of the positive externality individuals also have private incentives to receive an education. A college education, for example, is probably not necessary to produce the social benefits of an educated population—almost all of the benefits of a college education will accrue directly to the individual who is being educated. Because individuals have a private incentive to receive enough education to enable them to function in society, the positive externality derived from an educated population does not constitute a reason to subsidize education. In other words, the marginal units of education do not confer the externality; rather, it is the inframarginal units that individuals have a private incentive to obtain anyway. An inframarginal externality does not require any policy actions on efficiency grounds.

Consider another example, of an industry that pollutes a lake and kills the fish that live there. The industry creates a negative externality, but it might be that even if the industry created only half as much pollution, the lake would still be too polluted to support fish. Assuming the pollution caused no other damage, its marginal cost would be zero. It would cause inframarginal costs, but if the firm increased or decreased its amount of pollution by a small amount, the cost of the externality would not be affected.

This concept is illustrated in Figure 3.4, which, like Figure 3.1, depicts a negative externality. But in this case the externality does not cause any marginal damage when Q^* is produced. Because the optimal corrective tax is set equal to the marginal cost of the externality, the optimal tax is zero, and Q^* remains the optimal amount to be produced. Note that if the demand for the good in question were less, as would be the case with demand curve D', then the externality would be a marginal externality and would have a marginal cost associated with it.

The point is that some activities can create externalities that are not relevant at the margin, in which case the optimal amount of output in the market is not affected by the inframarginal externality. But it is also possible for the cost of the externality to be so high that the optimal output of the good is zero. For the polluted-lake example the optimal amount of output was Q^* in Figure 3.4 if the externality was inframarginal, but if the lake was more valuable for fishing than for industry, the optimal output of the industry would be zero. In reality, however, such comparisons are difficult to make. The fundamental idea to remember is that when an externality exists, the market does not take account of the full

Figure 3.4 Inframarginal Externality The inframarginal external cost depicted here does not impose a cost at the margin, so there is no reason to impose a tax that will marginally affect the generation of the externality. If the demand in the market were D', then the externality would be relevant at the margin.

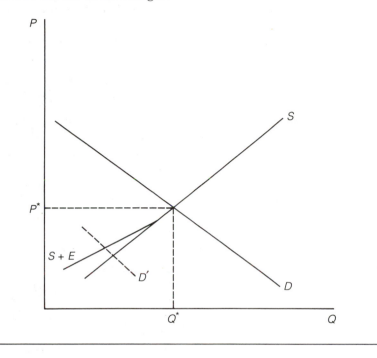

costs or benefits of some activities. Ultimately, the goal of public policy toward externalities is to try to create incentives for economic agents to take account of those costs and benefits.

Collective Consumption Goods

A *collective consumption good* is a good for which consumption by a consumer will not reduce the consumption of any other consumer. This definition does not apply to most goods; for example, for each additional hamburger you eat, one less hamburger is available for everyone else; for each additional record album you purchase, one less is available for everyone else. A good example of a collective consumption good is a television broadcast signal.

If you turn on your set to watch a program, no other viewer will have to watch any less. Note that the television set itself is not a collective consumption good, but the broadcast signal is, because additional consumers can consume the good without reducing the amount available for anyone else.

Because of the characteristics of a collective consumption good, if the good is produced for one person, it does not cost any more to make the same amount of the good available to every other person in the society. For this reason economists sometimes call a collective consumption good a public good, though the term *public good* may be somewhat misleading.[4] As the example of a television broadcast signal indicates, the good does not necessarily need to be produced in the public sector of the economy.

The Argument
for Public Sector Production

In arguing for public sector production, assume that the good is produced in the private sector and that a private sector firm charges each consumer for the good. A good example is the privately produced cable movie services that can be purchased by those with cable television. Once the cable is installed in a person's house, the movie channels are normally scrambled and can only be received if the subscriber pays extra. The cable company must pay for the movie channels, but once the service is extended to some subscribers, it could be extended to all subscribers at no additional cost. Assume that the cable company charges $10 a month to receive a movie channel. If a subscriber is willing to pay only $5 a month and the cable company charges $10, the subscriber will not get the movie channel, even though the service could be extended to the subscriber at no cost. The cable company in the private sector cannot do so, of course, because it uses the revenues from subscribers to maintain the cable and pay for the programming, and to provide the service in the first place.

By not allowing the subscriber who is willing to pay $5 per month to receive the programming, the possible social value of the cable service is reduced by $5. The cable company could receive an additional $5 in revenue without incurring any cost, and both the company and the subscriber could be made better off. The same argument applies for someone willing to pay only $1 for the service. Because the marginal cost to the cable company of adding an additional consumer is zero, the social value of the good will be maximized when everybody to whom the good is worth anything is allowed to consume it. Thus, in order to maximize the social value, it is argued that the good should be paid for by tax dollars and then given to anyone who wants it.

Several aspects of this argument merit special consideration. First, the inefficiency generated by a collective consumption good whenever it is not given away free to all consumers who want it represents a potential Pareto superior move that could be made but is not. When a charge is made for the collective consumption good, the consumer willing to buy the good for less than the going rate will not consume the good, even though both the consumer and the seller of the good could be made better off. The sale will not take place because the seller, who has no way of measuring the relative value each consumer places on the good, must charge the same price to each

[4]This terminology is attributed to Paul Samuelson in two pioneering articles, "The Pure Theory of Public Expenditure," *Review of Economics and Statistics* 36 (Nov. 1954), pp. 387–389, and "A Diagrammatic Exposition of a Theory of Public Expenditure," *Review of Economics and Statistics* 37 (Nov. 1955), pp. 350–356.

consumer, thereby excluding some consumers who value the good but not enough to pay the higher price. Although it is inefficient to exclude these consumers, the market has no good way of allocating the good to every consumer who places a value on it. In this sense, the market is inefficient in allocating resources to collective consumption goods, and it is inefficient in distributing the goods to potential consumers.

Note that the market sometimes does make an effort. For example, a movie theatre that has empty seats is a collective consumption good, because an additional consumer could consume the good without reducing the consumption of anyone else. Movie theatres charge different prices for adults and children, even though children take up just as many seats (some would argue that they take up more seats). Furthermore, some theatres have afternoon matinees at reduced prices to try to separate the working audience that would have to attend after work from the nonworking audience that might not be willing, or able, to pay as much. Nevertheless, some consumers willing to pay for the good will still be excluded because even the bargain price is more than they are willing to pay. Again, such an inefficiency might be reduced if the government produced collective consumption goods and allowed anyone to consume at no charge.

The Argument for Private Sector Production

There are compelling arguments against public sector production of collective consumption goods as well. The movie theatre may have the characteristics of a collective consumption good when it is not congested, but as it fills up it takes on more of the characteristics of a private consumption good. The same can be said for such goods as swimming pools and highways. If they are not crowded, an additional consumer can consume without interfering with the consumption of anyone else, but as they get more crowded, they lose their collective consumption characteristics. In each case there is a marginal cost associated with additional consumers. Highways and swimming pools that have no tolls or admission fees must be built larger to accommodate everyone who wants to use them without paying, which represents the marginal cost of additional consumers.

Other collective consumption goods, such as the television broadcast signal, are less prone to congestion, though. The cost paid by consumers indicates to suppliers the relative value consumers place on the product and thus provides a market signal for efficiently allocating resources. For example, consumers can choose from several cable movie channels as well as other specialized channels that show, music, weather, sports, and so on. If these services were all given away free, producers would have no idea of the value of each service. Thus, even though it may be inefficient to exclude some consumers, the payment for the service provides a market signal of the value of the service to those who do consume it and thus provides an indication of which services should be expanded and which are less worthwhile.[5] In a static sense resources might be best allocated by charging nothing to consume them, but unless a charge is levied to indicate the relative worth of the good, it may not be clear how many resources should be allocated to the future production of the good.

---

[5]A good exposition of this principle is given in Jora A. Minasian, "Television Pricing and the Theory of Public Goods," *Journal of Law & Economics* 7 (Oct. 1964), pp. 71–80. Also of interest is Paul Samuelson's article, "Public Goods and Subscription TV: A Correction of the Record," *Journal of Law & Economics* 7 (Oct. 1964), pp. 81–83.

The Optimal Output of a Collective Consumption Good

Given the special characteristics of a collective consumption good, how much of the good should be produced? For a private good production occurs up to the point where the marginal benefits of production equal the marginal cost. The same general principle holds for collective consumption goods, although some specific differences result from the differences in the two types of goods.

Vertical Summation of Individual Demand Curves

For private consumption goods such as hamburgers and soft drinks, the market demand for the good is found by horizontally summing all of the individual demand curves to get the market demand curve. For a collective consumption good market demand is found by vertically summing all of the individual demand curves. In Figure 3.5, D_1, D_2, and D_3 represent demand curves for three individuals for a collective consumption good. For any quantity of the good, such as Q^*, individual D_1 is willing to pay price T_1 per unit, individual D_2 is willing to pay T_2, and individual D_3 is willing to pay T_3. Because once the good is produced it will be available to every consumer, the total social value of producing Q^* can be found by adding T_1, T_2, and T_3 at Q^*. The sum of all the demand curves, added vertically, is curve ΣD, which is the market demand curve for the three individuals. The demand curves are summed vertically because, for each unit produced, every consumer can consume every unit, so that the value of each unit is the sum of the values placed on the unit by each consumer in the market.

If the marginal cost of producing this good is given by *MC*, then the optimal amount of the good that should be produced is determined by the point at which the marginal social cost of production equals the marginal social value of the output. The marginal social value is given by ΣD, so the intersection of ΣD and *MC* is the optimal level of output, Q^*. Note that the good is so expensive to produce that no one person would be willing to purchase even one unit individually, but if all individuals share in the expense, they all can benefit. For example, if the good is a swimming pool, and no one would be willing to buy a pool individually, but together the individuals could form a swimming club in order to enjoy collectively the benefits of the pool. However, if the price for D_1 were set at T_2, the average price for each individual, individual D_1 would not be willing to join, even though there would be potential social benefits from admitting D_1 as a member.

Frequently, different consumers of collective consumption goods pay different prices for the goods, especially when the goods are produced in the public sector and paid for by tax dollars. For example, public schools typically are financed through a property tax, which means that the people who have the most valuable property end up paying a higher price for public schools than those who have less valuable property.

Lindahl Pricing

If each individual pays a marginal price equal to the marginal benefit he or she receives from the good, that price is called a *Lindahl price*, named after economist Erik Lindahl.

Figure 3.5 Collective Consumption Good The market demand for a collective consumption good is found by vertically summing the individual demand curves. The optimal level of output is the level at which the marginal cost equals the sum of the demands. T_1, T_2, and T_3 are the Lindahl tax shares for the three individuals whose demands are depicted in the diagram.

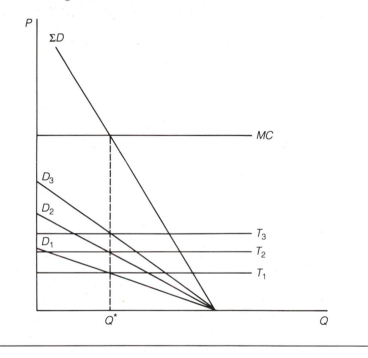

Lindahl prices are depicted in Figure 3.5. At quantity Q^* the marginal value of the good to consumer D_1 is T_1, T_2 to consumer D_2, and T_3 to consumer D_3. If those prices are charged to the individual demanders, then each individual is paying a marginal price equal to the consumer's marginal value of the good, which is a Lindahl price.[6]

Note that Lindahl prices are not necessary for the efficient output of a collective consumption good. The optimal level of output, at Q^*, is determined by the intersection of the ΣD and MC curves, no matter who pays what share of the cost. One might even imagine a case in which Lindahl prices could be considered unfair. Assume that a television broadcast antenna is arbitrarily located in an area. Those who live near the antenna and receive a clear signal will place a relatively low marginal value on additional wattage, but those who live some distance away and do not get a clear signal will place a higher marginal value

---

[6]Erik Lindahl's original exposition of this idea can be found in his "Just Taxation—A Positive Solution," in Richard A. Musgrave and Alan T. Peacock, eds., *Classics in the Theory of Public Finance* (New York: St. Martin's Press, 1967), pp. 168–176.

on additional wattage to improve the signal. Because the transmitter was located arbitrarily in the first place, it seems unfair to charge Lindahl prices, which require those receiving the weakest signal to pay the most for the transmitter output.[7]

The main advantage of Lindahl prices is that when they are charged, every individual prefers the same level of output of the good.

This is an advantage because in the real world, public sector output is determined through the political process, and if there is unanimous agreement on what the public sector should produce, public sector decisions are both more easily made and more likely to be efficient. In subsequent chapters the public sector decision-making process will be analyzed in more detail.

Pure and Impure Collective Consumption Goods

The conditions for the optimal level of output of a collective consumption good (in Figure 3.5, $\Sigma D = MC$) were developed for the extreme case of a collective consumption good where the marginal cost of adding an additional consumer is zero. In the real world many goods can accommodate additional consumers at low cost, but not necessarily at no cost. For example, as mentioned earlier, an interstate highway often will have the characteristics of a collective consumption good. When the highway is not crowded, an additional driver can use it at no additional cost, but under conditions of extreme congestion, an additional car might not be able to enter the highway until another car already on the highway exits.

Another example discussed previously was a movie theatre. In an uncrowded theatre an additional consumer can watch the movie at no marginal cost, but in a fuller theatre an additional viewer might partially obstruct someone's view, thus incurring some cost. If the theatre is full, then an additional viewer can watch only if an existing viewer gives up

his or her seat, in which case the theatre will more closely resemble a private consumption good. The point is that the physical characteristics of a good do not necessarily indicate whether it is a collective consumption good, because under different circumstances the same good may be either a collective consumption good or a private consumption good.

Though the optimality conditions for the examples discussed in the previous section were derived for the extreme case of a pure collective consumption good, they can generally be applied at any time when the amount of the good consumed by one consumer is a function of the total amount of the good produced. This is obviously the case with a pure collective consumption good such as broadcast signals or national defense—whatever is produced for one person is exactly what is available for everyone else. Consider, however, the deliberately extreme example of a pure private good for which each consumer's level of consumption is a function of the total amount produced.

Assume that a law is passed requiring that the same number of pairs of shoes be produced for every individual in the nation. If one pair is produced for you, one pair will be produced for everyone else; if five pairs are

[7]This idea is explored in Arthur T. Denzau and Robert J. Mackay, "Benefit Shares and Majority Voting," *American Economic Review* 66 (March 1976), pp. 69–76.

produced for you, five will be produced for everyone else. In this case your consumption is a function of the total amount produced even though the good is a private consumption good. Referring back to Figure 3.4, the number of units of output produced for everybody is measured on the quantity axis; for example, Q* equals two pairs of shoes for everyone. Note that shoes could be more efficiently allocated if it were possible to give different quantities to different consumers, but given the restriction that each person's consumption is a function of the total amount produced, Q* is the optimal level of output.[8]

This type of situation arises frequently in the public sector. Education is a good example. People can choose to send their children to private schools, but the same public school system is produced for all taxpayers, and the share of the output that they receive is given by the number of children that they have. Although education is not a pure collective consumption good—the amount that one consumer receives is a function of the total amount produced—the optimality conditions derived in the previous section apply to this case of an impure collective consumption good as well.

This is an important point because it illustrates the generality of the optimality condition described for collective consumption goods. The optimality condition applies any time a specific individual's consumption is a function of the amount produced for the entire group; it does not require that the good be a pure, or even an impure, collective consumption good. The optimality condition also applies to private goods if one person's consumption is a function of the total amount produced.

To review, recall that collective consumption goods are goods that an additional consumer can consume without reducing the consumption of any other consumer. Such goods are not produced completely efficiently in the market because some consumers who place a positive value on the good are excluded from consuming it, even though it costs nothing to add consumers. But drawbacks exist if the government provides the good and allows everybody to consume at no cost. Because producers receive no clear signals about the value of their good, many valuable goods may not be produced. In addition, the taxes necessary to pay for pure collective consumption goods entail a different type of cost. Finally, some goods that exhibit collective consumption characteristics may come to resemble private consumption goods as more people consume them. Thus, arguments can be made both for and against producing collective consumption goods in the public sector. Some, such as parks and roads, are commonly produced in the public sector, whereas others, such as television signals and movies, are typically produced in the private sector. Still others, such as swimming pools, are frequently produced in both the public and private sectors.

[8]This idea is developed in R. G. Holcombe, *Public Finance and the Political Process* (Carbondale: Southern Illinois University Press, 1983), ch. 2.

Nonexcludability

Goods can also be difficult to produce in the private sector if they are nonexcludable, that is, if, once produced, it is difficult to exclude people from consuming them. Nonexcludability tends to be a matter of degree, reflecting how costly it would be to keep people from

Figure 3.6 The Prisoners' Dilemma Ralph's potential prison sentence is represented by the number in the upper right portion of each box, and Jake's is in the lower left portion. Note that no matter what Jake does, Ralph has an incentive to confess, and the same is true with Jake. But although their narrow self-interests would lead them both to confess and serve 10-year sentences, they both would be better off if neither confessed and they served only 3-year sentences.

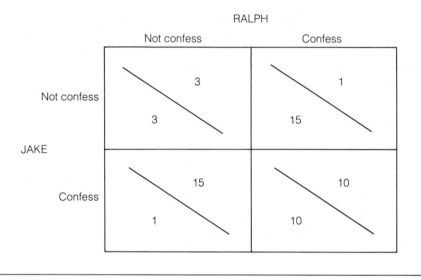

consuming a good once it is produced, and can pose certain problems for the market.

Perhaps the best example of a nonexcludable good is national defense. Once some people in a certain area are being defended from foreign aggressors, it is virtually impossible to prevent others in the same area from being protected as well. As a result, once the good is being provided to some people, others in the area have no incentive to pay for the good. Instead, they become "free riders," benefiting from the goods that others produce but not paying for their share. An even more serious problem is that because everyone has the same incentive, nobody really has an incentive to produce the good; rather, everyone will tend to wait for others to produce the good.

Ultimately, the good may not be produced at all, even though everyone places a high value on it.

Nonexcludability and the Prisoners' Dilemma

This type of situation is sometimes called a *prisoners' dilemma* after the example illustrated in Figure 3.6. In the prisoners' dilemma two dangerous criminals, Ralph and Jake, are caught for a petty crime. The sheriff believes that they are guilty of a more serious crime, but he needs a confession in order to have a good case against them. To get a confession, the sheriff employs a rather cunning strategy. He places Ralph and Jake in separate rooms, where they have no possibility of communicating with each other. Then he tells Ralph that if neither he nor Jake confesses, the best he can do is to put them in jail for 3 years each for the petty crime. But if Ralph will confess to the bigger crime, and if Jake does not confess, he will let Ralph off with a light 1-year sentence. However, if Jake confesses and Ralph does not, then Ralph will have to serve a 15-year sentence. And if both confess, they will both serve 10-year sentences. The sheriff makes the same offer to Jake.

The alternatives are summarized in Figure 3.6. If neither confesses, the sentences will be 3 years; if both confess, the sentences will be 10 years; and if only one confesses, the confessor gets 1 year while the nonconfessor gets 15. Because they are separated, Ralph cannot know what Jake will do. Ralph will reason that if Jake does not confess, then Ralph could confess and get 1 year or not confess and get 3. But if Jake does confess, then Ralph could confess and get 10 years or not confess and get 15. No matter what Jake does, Ralph will get the lighter sentence by confessing, so Ralph has an incentive to confess. The same applies to Jake. Thus, motivated by self-interest, each will confess and get 10 years, whereas if they could have cooperated, they need not have confessed and could have gotten off with 3 years.

How is this related to nonexcludability? Assume that Ralph and Jake are neighbors who share a common driveway. They wake up in the morning and find that it has snowed, and each wants the driveway shoveled so he can get his car out. But both Ralph and Jake may be waiting for the other to shovel the drive, because once it is shoveled, the person who shoveled the drive cannot exclude the other one from using it. Ralph and Jake might be able to make a deal to cooperate, but for large numbers of people, cooperation becomes far more problematic as everyone waits for someone else to shovel the roads. The same is true for national defense, and for other nonexcludable goods. If national defense were produced by voluntary contributions, everyone would have an incentive not to cooperate and would contribute less than the true value of the good, preferring to free ride off the contributions of others. The obvious solution is to force everyone to pay through taxation and then provide the good at no additional charge to everyone in the economy.

Exclusion Costs and Public Sector Production

Nonexcludability is often a matter of degree, as consumers can be excluded from consuming most goods, but only at a very high cost. For example, although television and radio broadcast signals are frequently made available without exclusion, the signals can also be scrambled so that only those who pay for a descrambler can consume the service. Likewise, access to roads can be limited, and tolls can be charged for road usage. Tolls on highways and bridges that people use to travel long distances are relatively common, and the cost involved in collecting the tolls is comparatively small. By contrast, it would be far more costly to exclude nonpaying customers from city streets. Where exclusion becomes too costly, it can be argued that the government must produce the good because the private sector doesn't have a sufficient incentive.

Nonexcludability and Collective Consumption

Collective consumption goods, such as national defense, highways, and broadcast signals, tend to share some of the characteristics of nonexcludable goods as well. As the broadcast signal example suggests, it is possible to produce these goods in the private sector;

nevertheless, the inefficiencies caused by the joint problems of collective consumption characteristics and nonexcludability implies that these goods might better be produced in the public sector.

Economists often argue that goods having both characteristics of collective consumption and nonexcludability should indeed be produced in the public sector. Yet technological innovations in the twentieth century have generated several goods of this type, such as television and radio broadcasts, that are produced quite efficiently in the private sector. Another good example that has emerged only recently is computer software. Before the use of personal computers were widespread, program authors could control the distribution of their programs by leasing them to the owners of mainframe computers. Because relatively few mainframe computers were in operation, it was not difficult to monitor and enforce the leasing agreements. But now, programs are distributed on easily copied diskettes. Once a program is created, it can be easily copied, which makes the program a nonexcludable good. At the same time, no former user has to give up use of the program, which makes the program a collective consumption good. Thus, computer software is a perfect example of a nonexcludable collective consumption good produced in the private sector.

Program authors complain about unauthorized copying, of course, and some try to use copy protection devices to keep the software from being copied, but the private sector still seems quite capable of producing this nonexcludable collective consumption good. Because the market is relatively new, legal and economic developments will undoubtedly change it significantly. Over the next few years the ever-increasing supply of programs relative to the demand will shift the supply curve outward and lower the price, making it more attractive to buy the software package in order to get an original copy of the manual. And over time, the nonexcludability problem should be less of a factor in the market. The market for personal computer software is relatively new and thus provides a good opportunity to apply economic analysis to real world markets.

Monopoly and Economic Instability

The market is sometimes accused of allocating resources inefficiently where monopolies exist and also where economic instability occurs. (These problems will be discussed more thoroughly later in the text.) The problem with a monopoly is that the monopolist has an incentive to reduce output below the optimal level in order to charge a higher price for the product. As a result, too few resources are allocated to the production of the monopolized product. One solution is to use antitrust laws to break monopolistic producers up into smaller, competing firms. Where this is not feasible, however, government regulation is necessary to try to get the monopolist to produce as if the monopolist is a competitive industry. Chapter 18 will discuss how this might be done, as well as some of the problems involved. At this point note merely that monopolies are inefficient because, in raising their prices and producing too little output in order to maximize profit, they are not making potential Pareto superior moves.

Economic instability, which became a major concern after the Great Depression, causes problems because in such times resources tend not to be fully utilized. Because the economy produces at less than full capacity, it is inefficient. The proper role of the government in these cases is not at all clear; some economists argue that the government itself is a major cause of economic instability. The issue of the proper role of government will not be debated here; it is sufficient to observe that once again there are possible Pareto superior moves that are not being made.

Indeed, in most problem areas of the market, the economy, for one reason or another, fails to make Pareto superior moves that could be made. These areas include not only monopoly and economic instability but also nonexcludability, collective consumption goods, and positive externalities. In each case a Pareto optimum is not reached because the necessary Pareto superior moves are not made. By contrast, with a negative externality a non-Pareto superior move is made.

Conclusion

In most instances the market allocates resources very efficiently. However, some problems may arise with market allocation that keep the market from being as efficient as theoretically possible. Most of these problems result from potential Pareto superior moves that are not made because the market does not provide the proper incentives for such potentially profitable trades. Positive externalities, collective consumption goods, nonexcludability, monopoly, and economic instability all represent situations in which the market does not provide the incentive for possible Pareto superior moves.

With negative externalities the problem is that an exchange is made that adversely affects a third party, resulting in a non-Pareto superior move. Here, the result is also ineffi-
cient, but there may be some reason to treat this case differently from the market problems previously discussed. In viewing the government primarily as the protector of individual rights, the society may want to guarantee that the activities of some people do not harm others. Because the negative externality does in fact cause harm to some, it differs from the situations in which, although some potential for benefit is left unexploited, people are not actually harmed.

This theme of individual rights is relevant not only to negative externalities but also to many of the problems of the market discussed in this chapter. The next chapter picks up where this one leaves off by examining in more detail the relationship between individual rights and the efficiency of the market.

Questions

1. What is a negative externality? Using a graph, explain how a tax could correct the externality in an ideal setting. What impediments are there to using corrective taxes in the real world?

2. Would it be desirable to eliminate all pollution? Explain.

3. Explain why a positive externality results in a misallocation of resources. How can a subsidy correct for the positive externality? Does this imply that subsidies should be paid when positive externalities exist? (Keep in mind that someone must be taxed to raise the revenue to grant a subsidy.)

4. What is a collective consumption good? Explain the argument that the private sector will produce too little of a collective consumption good, even in cases in which the good is produced in the private sector.

5. What are Lindahl prices? Are they necessary for the efficient output of a public good? Why might they be desirable considering the political setting within which the government makes decisions?

6. Explain the conditions for determining the optimal level of a collective consumption good. This condition applies more generally than just to collective consumption goods. Explain the condition(s) that must be satisfied for the optimality condition to apply to a good.

7. What are the problems associated with nonexcludability? Why can some nonexcludable goods be produced in the private sector whereas other nonexcludable goods cannot?

8. List some problems of resource allocation in the private market. Which of these problems involve cases where a non–Pareto superior move is made, and which are cases where a potential Pareto superior move is not made? Should these cases be treated differently?

9. National defense and personal computer software share the characteristics of nonexcludable collective consumption goods. Why is national defense produced in the public sector and computer software produced in the private sector?

10. Explain the difference between technological and pecuniary externalities. What differences should exist with regard to public policies toward the two types of externality?

11. Explain the difference between marginal and inframarginal externalities. How is the difference significant for purposes of public policy toward externalities?

CHAPTER FOUR

Property Rights and Economic Efficiency

*I*n Chapter 2 we discussed in some detail the role of government in protecting individual rights. We argued that the efficiency of the market system rests on the foundation of individual rights that allows market participants to engage in voluntary exchanges. Trades cannot take place unless the traders are in some way viewed as having the right to own the goods that are being traded. Furthermore, if these rights did not exist, there would be no incentive for trade, nor would anyone produce any more than he or she could protect from predation. A system of property rights is indispensable to an efficient market economy; problems with economic efficiency can arise when trying to define, protect, or exchange those rights. Chapter 4 begins with a general discussion of property rights and then reexamines the issues discussed in Chapter 3 from a property rights prospective.

Property Rights

The term *property rights* conjures up an image of a piece of property that a person owns and can do with as he or she pleases. In reality, people cannot do anything they please with most property. Rather, a property right represents a set of rights to engage in specific activities if the owner chooses, and the rights may entail a set of responsibilities as well. Consider, for example, a person who owns a home in a residential neighborhood of a city. That person has the right to live in the home, to play a stereo at a reasonable volume at reasonable hours of the day, to invite visitors to the home, and so on. However, the homeowner's activities typically are constrained by zoning laws as well as many other laws that restrict how the person can use the property. In many areas the homeowner will not be allowed to burn trash in the yard, to have excessively loud rock and roll bands play in the driveway, or to discharge firearms on the property. Frequently, zoning laws will prevent the homeowner in a residential neighborhood from tearing down the house and building a gas station in its place, or even dividing a single-family home into apartments.

Such restrictions will vary depending on local laws, of course; the point is that owning a piece of property does not confer on the owner the right to do anything he or she wants with it. The owner does have the right to do certain things, but the owner also assumes certain responsibilities, such as paying taxes and maintaining the property in a certain condition—if it is not maintained, then the government may have the right to condemn it. In short, property rights are really just the rights to do certain things with the property, and not anything that the owner desires.

The automobile is another example of how property rights are restricted rather than absolute. The owner has the right to drive an automobile certain places, but the automobile must be maintained to certain standards, the owner must pay taxes on the auto, and driving laws must be observed. The owner of a car has a right to drive it at 55 miles per hour on the interstate highway but not to drive without brake lights or to park on the highway median. Similarly, the owner of a house has the right to live there, but not the right to open a store in the house if the house is in a residentially zoned area. Again, property rights should be viewed as rights to engage only in certain types of behavior. In this sense they are no different from any other types of rights; the right to free speech, the right to bear arms, and so forth also limit individuals to certain types of behavior.

A government may grant certain rights to all citizens, as in the United States, where all citizens have the right to free speech and the right to bear arms, but it is conceivable that these rights may be granted to nobody or that they could be sold to only a few people. But even the right to free speech, for example, is not unconditional—one may not yell "FIRE!" in a crowded theatre. Note that free speech has the characteristics of a collective consumption good and can be granted to everyone simultaneously. Other rights, such as the right to live in the house at 231 Oak Drive, obviously cannot be granted to everybody. Somehow, these types of rights must be assigned to some subset of the population, as if they were private consumption goods.

In a market economy most rights are assigned to individuals, but the rights can then be traded or sold, so that if the right is more valuable to someone other than its present owner, the present owner can exchange it for something the present owner values more. For example, if the right to live at 231 Oak Drive is more valuable to someone other than the current resident, the other person can offer the current resident an exchange. Suppose the current resident values $50,000 more than the right to live at 231 Oak Drive, while someone else values the right to live at 231 Oak Drive more than $50,000. By exchanging $50,000 for the right to live at the house, both will be better off. Such an exchange is a Pareto superior move; recall that if all possible Pareto superior moves are made, the economy will end up at a Pareto optimum, allocating its resources completely efficiently. The key to reaching a Pareto optimum is establishing property rights for all valuable resources, so that all resources can be traded in mutually beneficial exchanges. Where property rights are not clearly defined, the market will not be able to allocate resources efficiently.

Poorly Defined Property Rights

The key to economic efficiency rests in the right of a person who produces something to exchange that production for the valuable resources owned by others. If property rights are not well defined, then individuals may be able to use valuable resources without paying for them, which leads to problems with resource allocation. A review of some of the examples discussed in Chapter 3 will illustrate this point.

Property Rights and Externalities

Consider the negative externality generated by the smoke-producing factory. The problem is that although clean air is a scarce and valuable resource, nobody really has property rights to it. Because nobody is in a position to charge the factory for using the clean air, the factory uses too much. In this sense the problem is one of poorly defined property rights. If someone held property rights to the air, then the factory would purchase the rights to pollute the air only as long as the additional benefits to the polluter exceeded the additional costs. But because nobody owns the air, the factory has the incentive to emit pollution as long as it receives any benefits at all from emitting pollution. With no mechanism to ration its use, the clean air, a scarce and valuable resource, is overused.

The key in this case is to establish clear property rights. If the ownership of air were clearly defined, and if the rights to the air could be bought and sold in the market, as the rights to labor, land, and other scarce resources are, then there would be an incentive for the rights to the resource to be traded to the individuals who valued it most highly. But no market for air exists because the property rights to air are not clearly defined, so every individual has an incentive to use air without regard to the cost. The resource should be used up to the point at which the marginal benefit from use equals the marginal cost, but poorly defined property rights mean the resource will be used as long as the marginal benefits are greater than zero. Ultimately, the resource is overused because there is no incentive to conserve on the use of a resource obtained at no cost.[1] This type of problem will arise any time that the property rights for a scarce resource are not clearly defined.

Overutilization of Resources

Consider another example. In the 1800s buffalo were hunted in the American West almost to the point of extinction while the cattle population steadily increased, even though Americans were consuming more cattle than buffalo. How can this be explained?

The answer becomes clear once the different types of property rights systems governing buffalo and cattle are understood. Buffalo freely roamed the ranges, and nobody owned a buffalo until the buffalo was killed, at which time the hunter could claim ownership rights. This gave hunters the incentive to kill every buffalo possible. In passing up the opportunity to kill a buffalo, a hunter, in effect, was giving up the rights of ownership over the

---

[1] Harold Demsetz has made an important contribution to the economic analysis of property rights; see, for example, "The Exchange and Enforcement of Property Rights," *Journal of Law & Economics* 7 (Oct. 1964), pp. 11–26, and "Toward a Theory of Property Rights," *American Economic Review* 57, no. 2 (May 1967), pp. 347–359.

buffalo, because a buffalo not killed by one hunter would probably be killed by another. Thus, every individual hunter had the incentive to kill as many buffalo as possible, without consideration to maintaining the size of the buffalo herd.

By contrast, herds of cattle were owned by individuals, so that property rights to cattle were always well defined. As a result, the cattle owner had an incentive to maximize the value of the herd of cattle. By keeping cattle alive in order to maintain a breeding stock, the owner would have cattle to sell in the future as well as in the present. Thus, live cattle were a valuable asset to the owner, whereas with buffalo nobody had an incentive to maintain a breeding stock. Like the air in the earlier example, the scarce resource of buffalo was overused because the property rights to buffalo were poorly defined.

Recently, some concern has been voiced that excessive hunting of whales will cause some species to become extinct. With the buffalo example in mind, it is easy to see that in this case too the problem is one of poorly defined property rights. If individual whales could be owned, then hunters would have an incentive to maintain the stock of whales, but because property rights to whales are not well defined and the only way that ownership can be claimed is to kill the whales, the incentive is to overuse that resource.

The problems caused by positive externalities and nonexcludability can be analyzed in similar terms. In these cases someone produces a valuable good or service that people consume at no cost, which means the producer does not have enough of an incentive to produce the good. Where the producer has a clearly defined property right over the good such that nobody can benefit from the production without paying the producer, then the producer has the proper incentive to produce the good. This is the case for most goods.

For example, the producer of a soft drink provides the benefit of the drink only to those who pay for it. However, when benefits are produced that can be consumed by others at no charge, there is not the proper incentive to produce the output, so too little will be produced. Again, the problem is one of poorly defined property rights.[2]

In Chapter 2 it was argued that an economy cannot utilize resources efficiently without protecting individual rights. Here we expanded the argument by illustrating how property rights are no different from any other types of rights; property rights simply allow the individual to engage in certain activities. If these rights are protected and well defined, then exchange through the market system can channel resources to their most highly valued uses. However, when property rights are not clearly defined, resources are not channeled to their most highly valued uses, but tend rather to be overutilized, whereas output over which the producer does not have a clearly defined property right will tend to be underproduced.

---

[2]Steven N. S. Cheung, "The Structure of a Contract and the Theory of a Non-exclusive Resource," *Journal of Law & Economics* 13, no. 1 (April 1970), pp. 49–70, argues that externalities and related problems can be understood much more readily within a property rights framework than within a traditional presentation.

The Coase Theorem

The Coase theorem, named after economist Ronald Coase, seeks to explain the types of situations examined in this and previous chapters, but from the standpoint of the incentives that exist for individual exchange.[3] The *Coase theorem* states that in the absence of transactions costs, the allocation of resources will be independent of the assignment of property rights. This means that when there is nothing to stop a potentially profitable trade from taking place, the trade will take place, and scarce resources will be allocated to their most highly valued uses. In the case of externalities, this implies that when it is feasible for the generator of an externality and the victim of an externality to bargain, the inefficiency caused by the externality should be eliminated through a trade by the parties. To illuminate this concept, consider the following example, which actually occurred, and which is taken from Coase's article.

A confectioner had been using mortars and pestles in his business for several decades. When a doctor moved in next to the confectioner, no problem arose until, after eight years, the doctor added a consulting room built right next to the confectioner's kitchen. The noise and vibration caused by the confectioner's equipment made it difficult for the doctor to use his new room, particularly when listening through his stethoscope. Ultimately, the doctor brought suit against the confectioner to try to get him to stop the disturbing vibrations.

In analyzing this case, the first point to be made is that the confectioner is generating a negative externality. From the standpoint of

protecting the doctor from the negative effects of the externality, we might decide in favor of the doctor. In fact, this is what the court did. Note, however, that courts do not always protect victims from the negative effects of externalities. For example, it is unlikely that a suit trying to stop people from driving their automobiles in Los Angeles would be decided in favor of the victims of the air pollution. Thus, on economic grounds, the case merits further examination.

Assume that the court has only two options in the case: either to allow the confectioner to continue with the activities that he has engaged in for decades without complaint from anyone or to order the confectioner to cease creating the externality. Solely in terms of economic efficiency, if the doctor's output is more highly valued than the confectioner's, it is preferable for the doctor to use the office. In this case the court made the correct decision. But what if the confectioner's services are more highly valued than the doctor's? Coase provided an insightful answer to this question. In this case, Coase observed, if a right is given to the doctor that is actually more valuable to the confectioner, the confectioner can purchase the right from the doctor. That is, if the court gives the right of silence to the doctor, the confectioner can offer to pay the doctor (or rent the doctor's new room) in order to obtain the right to use the mortars and pestles that were responsible for generating the externality. But if the court gives the confectioner the right to generate the externality but the right of silence is more valuable to the doctor, the doctor can pay the confectioner in exchange for silence.

To illustrate this principle, consider some simple numerical examples. Assume that the doctor can earn $100 in additional revenue

---

[3]Ronald Coase, "The Problem of Social Cost," *Journal of Law & Economics* (Oct. 1960), pp. 1–44.

every day by using the consulting room, whereas the confectioner can earn only $80 in additional income from using the vibrating machinery. In this case the market reveals that the doctor's use of the room is more valuable than the confectioner's use of the vibration-causing equipment. Therefore, by awarding the right to the doctor, the court acted to promote the efficient use of a scarce resource.

Suppose, however, that the confectioner can earn $100 a day using the vibration-causing equipment but that the doctor's use of the room generates only $80 in additional revenues. In this case, if the property right were awarded to the doctor, the confectioner could make a profitable exchange with the doctor. For example, the confectioner could offer to pay the doctor $90 per day in return for being allowed to use the equipment. In this scenario both the doctor and the confectioner would be $10 per day better off than if the doctor did not sell the court-awarded right.

Thus, Coase concluded, it does not matter to whom the right is given. The person to whom the right is most valuable will be willing to purchase that right, and the exchange can be made if the cost of entering into the transaction to buy the right is low. That is, individuals will find it feasible to enter into exchanges to purchase property rights from others when they value those rights more than the current owners do. In short, the resource will go to its most highly valued use, regardless of who originally holds the right to it.

The Implications of the Coase Theorem

Coase also recognized the reciprocal nature of any negative externality. For example, the problem between the doctor and the confectioner is reciprocal, because if the confectioner continues to use his equipment, the doctor will be harmed as a result of the externality, but if the doctor has the right to silence, then the confectioner will be harmed when he produces silence for the doctor. The question becomes whether to give the right to the doctor, which benefits the doctor but harms the confectioner, or to the confectioner, which harms the doctor but benefits the confectioner. Essentially, the doctor's right to silence and the confectioner's right to use his equipment represent two sides of the same right, and to give the right to one of them harms the other. This is true for the smoke-producing factory as well. The factory's smoke harms the surrounding residents, but to give the residents the right to breathe smoke-free air would harm the factory owners.

The Coase theorem states that if transactions costs are low, resources will be allocated the same way regardless of the assignment of property rights, but note that the assignment of rights will still make a difference to the participants involved. In the doctor-confectioner example assume that the right is more valuable to the doctor. If the court assigns the right to the doctor, then the doctor can have the quiet room without paying for it, but if the right is assigned to the confectioner, the doctor will have to pay the confectioner for the right. These rights, just like any property rights, are valuable, and people will always prefer to own rather than have to buy those rights.

In summary, the Coase theorem states that in the absence of substantial transactions costs, the allocation of resources will be independent of the assignment of property rights. This means that when rights can be easily bought and sold, valuable rights will be bought by the individual to whom they are worth the most. There is a reciprocal nature to the negative externality problem, because to assign the right to one party harms the other, and vice versa. Furthermore, because property rights are so valuable, an individual is always better off owning the right and selling it, if desired, to someone who values it more.

Small Numbers and Large Numbers

If one is concerned solely with economic efficiency, then the key aspect of the Coase theorem is the stipulation that the theorem works only in the absence of transactions costs. Recall that a transactions cost is anything that makes a potential Pareto superior move difficult to implement; a transaction cost might be something as simple as a lack of information about the potential trade. However, in considering resource allocation problems for which public sector involvement may be necessary, the most important transactions costs arise when large numbers of people are needed for the potential trade to take place. This can be illustrated with two examples, one with small numbers of people and the other with large numbers.[4]

Small Numbers Means Low Transactions Costs

Consider a situation in which you are having a picnic in your backyard when your neighbor begins burning leaves, thus interfering with your picnic. It should be relatively easy for you to strike a bargain with your neighbor. You could ask your neighbor to wait until tomorrow to burn the leaves, you could invite your neighbor over to your picnic in exchange for waiting until tomorrow to burn the leaves, or you could even offer to pay your neighbor cash in exchange for waiting. At any rate, if it is worth more to you to have a smoke-free picnic than it is worth to your neighbor to burn the leaves at that moment, you should be able to arrange an exchange with your

neighbor. In a small-numbers situation transactions costs will be relatively low, so it will be relatively easy to internalize the externality.

Large Numbers Means High Transactions Costs

Now consider a smoke-producing industry in an urban area, where thousands of residents may be affected by the smoke. In one sense this example closely resembles the picnic example previously discussed. The difference is that whereas in the picnic example only one individual was generating the externality and only one individual was harmed, in this case many individuals are generating the externality and many individuals are harmed. Although there is a potential Pareto superior move to be made that will reduce the level of the externality, the chances of getting literally thousands of individuals to participate, to say nothing of finding an exchange that they can all agree to, is highly unlikely. Therefore, nothing will be done voluntarily. In a small-number situation individual exchanges can take place to internalize externalities, but in a large-number situation such exchanges become virtually impossible because of the high transactions costs involved, which is why the government has to get involved.

Transactions Costs and Property Rights

In the large-numbers case, the government must also consider economic efficiency in the assignment of property rights. When small numbers are involved, transactions among those affected can, as the Coase theorem suggests, lead to efficient allocation of resources. In the picnic example exchange between neighbors is likely to produce a smoke-free picnic if that is more valuable than the burning of the

---

[4]The distinction between small numbers and large numbers in collective action is emphasized in Mancur Olson's insightful book, *The Logic of Collective Action* (New York: Schocken Books, 1965).

leaves, and is likely to produce the leaf burning if that is more valuable than a smoke-free picnic. But in large-numbers cases such transactions are not feasible, and whoever is assigned the rights will likely not be able to trade them away. If the industry is given the right to produce smoke, it is doubtful that the residents will be able to devise a trade in order to pay the industry to reduce the pollution, even if pollution-free air is more valuable to the residents. Likewise, if the residents are given the right to clean air, it is unlikely that the firms in the industry will be able to pay the residents in exchange for the right to produce some pollution, even if the right is more valuable to the firm. Thus, in the large-numbers case the allocation of resources depends on

the assignment of property rights because, in violation of the Coase theorem, substantial transactions costs are involved.

We have come across this small number–large number distinction previously, in Chapter 3. Recall the example of two individuals with a common driveway reaching an agreement to share in the shoveling of the driveway when it snowed. Though such an agreement would be relatively easy to achieve between these two individuals, think how difficult it would be to get everyone in a city to agree to pitch in and help shovel the city streets after a snowfall. In the large-number situation we are more likely to rely on the government to solve the problem simply because of the high transactions costs involved.

The Common Pool Problem

In the discussion of property rights issues, it was argued that when the market fails to allocate resources as efficiently as possible, the problem can be viewed as one of poorly defined property rights. The Coase theorem suggests that the allocation of resources is independent of the assignment of property rights in the absence of transactions costs, but problems can arise in trying to exchange rights when no clearly identifiable owner exists. This represents a type of transactions cost, because every possible user of the common resource could agree to sell it to the user who places the highest value on it. Indeed, this is not an uncommon problem.

Common Ownership and Overuse

Resources can be either privately owned or owned in common; the latter are subject to the

common pool problem. The origin of the term *common pool problem* is perhaps best explained with an example. Assume that an underground pool of oil extends below the land of four landowners. Each rancher is fortunate to have an underground store of wealth in the form of oil, but each must decide how rapidly to pump the oil. If a single person owned all four ranches, the oil could be extracted at a profit-maximizing rate, but because the pool of oil extends under the property of four individuals, each individual has an incentive to extract the oil as rapidly as possible, so as to prevent the other three from pumping it first.

If the common pool problem sounds familiar, it should—it is exactly the same problem as the overhunting of buffalo and whales discussed earlier in the chapter. The solution, when possible, is to allocate the resource to a private owner, but sometimes this is difficult to do.

Solutions to the Common Pool Problem

One solution is to divide the common property into individual parcels. For example, several centuries ago in Europe it was not unusual for villages to have common grazing grounds to which anyone could bring his or her animals. Because the grazing land was available to anyone and grass not eaten by one person's animal would be eaten by someone else's, the land was overgrazed and ended up being poor grazing land for everyone. The solution was the closure movement, which allowed common lands to be fenced and grazed by only one individual. When a single individual had property rights over a piece of grazing land, the owner had an incentive to make sure that pasture quality was maintained.

Although this solution does not appear to be applicable to the common oil pool problem, other possible solutions exist. All of the ranchers might lease their oil rights to a single oil producer; indeed, this is often done not only for oil rights but also for mineral rights. The ranchers would continue to do their ranching on the land and would be paid royalties by the oil producer for the oil that was pumped. Such a contract to pump oil at a slower rate would make the pool more valuable, and the additional profits would provide an incentive to coordinate the use of the common pool. The Coase theorem applies here just as readily as with other property rights problems.[5]

In general, where property is owned in common, people do not have an incentive to maintain the value of the common property, which leads to overuse of the resource. If transactions costs are low, one would expect contracts to be written that would allocate rights to scarce resources to individual owners. But in cases where individual contracts are difficult to write, public policy should be cognizant of the common pool problem. International agreements limiting the hunting of whales are an example of intergovernmental cooperation that seeks to limit the problems that arise when resources are not individually owned.

Government Versus Private Ownership

Ownership of resources by the government is not the same thing as common ownership. With common ownership there are no restrictions on the use of resources by individuals, so the resources tend to be overused. But with government ownership access to resources is limited, so the resources tend not to be overutilized. For example, the use of motor vehicles within national parks is restricted to certain areas, under certain conditions. And the appropriation of government-owned natural resources such as oil and timber is also limited, though not completely eliminated. Therefore, the common pool problem that exists with commonly held resources does not exist with government-owned resources, although it is, of course, possible that the government's policies might allow individuals to overutilize such resources.

---

[5]See Steven N. S. Cheung, "The Structure of a Contract and the Theory of a Non-exclusive Resource," *Journal of Law & Economics* 13, no. 1 (April 1970), pp. 49–70.

Government Ownership and Resource Allocation

The previous sentence raises a provocative issue. How is it determined what the best use is for government-owned scarce resources? For example, oil companies would like to lease oil rights in national parks, and they claim that the oil can be extracted without environmental damage. Naturally, environmentalists are opposed to the leasing of mineral rights, but they have little incentive to consider the benefits, which will go primarily to other people. The problem of how such resources should be allocated can be illuminated by comparing government ownership to private ownership.

Assume that the national parks were not owned by the government but by environmental groups who wanted to preserve the environment. By not allowing the leasing of mineral rights on their land, these groups would be foregoing income that could be used either to purchase more land or to aid other environmental causes, such as saving the whales. Because of the opportunity cost involved, environmental groups would have an incentive to consider seriously any proposal to lease mineral rights if the lessee could provide reasonable assurance that the environment would not be damaged.

Compare that hypothetical situation to the reality of government ownership of the parks. Environmental groups will not profit from the leasing of mineral rights, so they have no incentive to measure the benefits of the leasing against the costs. But they do have every incentive to oppose the leases, even when the potential social benefits are significant and the potential for environmental damage is small. Under private ownership an owner will weigh the marginal costs against the marginal benefits and favor any proposal that promises benefits greater than costs. Under public ownership a proposal that will produce public profits but may impose private costs will be opposed by various groups because the profits will accrue to the general public rather than to the groups that bear the costs.

The problem with government ownership of property rights is that individuals will consider the private costs and benefits but won't have the incentive to weigh the public costs and benefits, which will be dispensed to the population as a whole. This is evident not only in the example of public lands just discussed but in many other aspects of government ownership as well.

Communal Ownership in Centrally Planned Economies

Consider communal farming, which is practiced in many parts of the world, including the Soviet Union and China. The Soviet Union has a population about equal to that of the United States, but a larger land area and an abundance of fertile land. In the United States less than 5 percent of the population is engaged in agriculture, yet the United States produces enough agricultural output to be a net exporter of food, whereas in the Soviet Union about 25 percent of the population is engaged in agriculture, yet the Soviet Union must import food. One reason for this disparity is that the U.S. farmer has much more capital to work with. Another, and perhaps more important, reason has to do with property rights. Private farmers in the United States have an incentive to be as productive as possible because they reap the benefits from the agricultural products that they sell. Communal farmers in the Soviet Union turn their production over to the government and do not directly profit from it, which takes away much of the incentive to be productive.

Soviet farmers do have private plots that they can work for themselves, keeping or selling the output as they see fit. It is interesting to note that these private plots are much more productive than the communal plots that make up the bulk of Soviet agriculture. This suggests an easy solution to the Soviet agricultural problem. Simply turn over the communal farms to private owners and productivity will increase in much the same way as the closure movement in Europe increased the efficiency of resource allocation for grazing land. The property rights problem in the Soviet Union is that the farmers consider the private costs of farming for themselves but not the public benefits of communally produced food.

The Incentives of Government Managers

The same types of problems exist for any publicly owned enterprise. Public managers have an incentive to consider their private benefits and costs rather than the public benefits and costs.[6] By contrast, the owners of a private firm have the right to sell the firm (or shares of stock in the firm, if it is a publicly held private firm). This right provides an important incentive for the managers of the firm to maximize the value of the firm. For one thing, their compensation may depend on the value of the firm, but more importantly, if some other individual or group thinks that they can manage the firm more effectively and make it more valuable, they can buy the firm. Thus, poorly managed firms that do not efficiently use the resources at their disposal will tend to

be bought out (if they do not go out of business altogether), which means the resources that they control will be available on the market to be used more efficiently. Furthermore, private enterprises have a distinct advantage over publicly owned firms in that the market continually provides an assessment of how well resources are being allocated.

For a government-owned firm there is no way for a dissatisfied taxpayer to sell his or her shares in the firm. This eliminates the possibility of the market passing judgment on the effectiveness of the public enterprise in using the resources available to it. It also eliminates an important mechanism whereby managers are accountable to the owners of the firm. As a result, government enterprises in general tend to resemble communal farms, which, after all, are an example of a government enterprise.

This is certainly not an argument against all government ownership. Many goods and services would be difficult to produce in the private sector, if they could be produced at all. Poorly defined property rights give rise to externalities and collective consumption goods, and where the transactions costs needed to rectify these problems would be prohibitive, government ownership may be the best alternative for efficient production. We must recognize, however, the problems involved in government ownership.

Zoning Laws: An Application of Property Rights Theory

At the beginning of the chapter, property rights were examined within the context of the ownership of a home. There, it was noted that ownership does not confer on one the right to do whatever one wants with the home; rather, one is limited to certain activities and

also has certain obligations, such as the payment of taxes. In this sense ownership, like

---

[6]See Armen Alchian, "Some Economics of Property Rights," *Economic Forces at Work* (Indianapolis: Liberty Press, 1977), ch. 5, for an elaboration of this theme.

any right, represents the right to engage in certain types of behavior, perhaps in exchange for certain responsibilities. In fact, there is not as much difference between, say, property rights and free speech rights as there might initially seem to be.

The Justification for Zoning Laws

Some of the restrictions that are placed on the use of property come from zoning laws. Not all property is subject to such laws, but most towns and cities do have zoning requirements that specify what the property can and cannot be used for, thereby defining some of the rights and restrictions associated with ownership of the property. Zoning laws are often justified as a method of internalizing potential externalities that could arise due to incompatible use of land. For example, few people in a residential neighborhood want to see a gas station built next door, so areas are designated as residential, commercial, and so on to prevent the externalities that might be generated. Likewise, residents of single-family dwellings generally do not want apartments next door, so zones are further subdivided into single- and multiple-family dwellings, and restrictions may be placed on the density of housing or number of stories allowed on buildings as well. Furthermore, industry may be offensive not only to residential dwellers but also to commercial businesses, so industrial areas typically are zoned separately from commercial areas.

The justification for zoning seems fairly straightforward, but recall that according to the Coase theorem, resources will be allocated to their most highly valued uses without government interference as long as transactions costs are low. Does land use fall into this category, or must the government be involved to ensure the efficient use of land?

Houston, Texas, provides an interesting case study of this issue because there are no zoning laws in Houston.[7] Without zoning laws individuals are relatively free to use land in any manner that they see fit. Surprisingly, the types of incompatibilities in land use that were just mentioned do not seem to be a problem in Houston. Separate residential, commercial, and industrial areas have evolved without the aid of zoning laws, and apartments do not tend to be built in residential neighborhoods alongside single-family dwellings. Indeed, land use in Houston strongly resembles that in other cities where zoning laws are in effect.

When you think about it, land-use patterns like those found in Houston make sense. A gas station, for example, is unlikely to locate in a residential neighborhood because residential streets tend to be relatively uncrowded. Instead, a gas station or other commercial enterprise is much more likely to locate on a major thoroughfare, on the type of property that would probably be zoned for commercial use in another city. Commercial enterprises tend to group together both because they seek similar locations (in easily accessible and well-traveled areas) and because commercial enterprises profit from having other commercial enterprises nearby. If this were not so, businesses would not choose to pay premium prices to locate in shopping centers as they now do.

Apartment complexes are likely to locate near major thoroughfares, unlike neighborhoods with single-family homes, which are more likely to have limited access. Industrial users seek property that is convenient to suppliers, perhaps near rail lines, rivers, or interstate highways. In short, land use seems to segregate naturally, without the influence of zoning laws.

---

[7] Information in this section comes from Bernard H. Siegan, "Nonzoning in Houston," *Journal of Law & Economics* 13, no. 1 (April 1979), pp. 71–147.

Restrictive Covenants

Although the market will do much to eliminate incompatible uses of land, the owners of property in Houston are able to limit incompatible uses of land by another method—the restrictive covenant. A *restrictive covenant* is a contract agreed to by all of the owners of land in a particular area that specifies uses to which that land may or may not be put. Typically, a restrictive covenant is written to cover a tract of land before any of the individual lots are built on, and the developer sells the land with the covenants in force. The restrictive covenant remains in force unless a majority of the landowners covered by the covenant vote to remove it, although the covenant could also be ruled invalid if it were poorly drafted or if it had a history of not being enforced.

The city of Houston has estimated that there may be as many as 10,000 individual subdivisions affected by restrictive covenants. Their terms can cover items normally included in zoning laws, specifying, for example, minimum lot sizes, minimum house sizes, distance that structures must be from the lot boundaries, and so on. The covenants might also have other provisions, such as not allowing commercial vehicles to be parked on the street or even specifying allowable exterior colors of homes.

Restrictive covenants can provide the security of zoning laws, but they are more easily changed if the land covered by a covenant would now have a more highly valued use. For example, if a single-family neighborhood becomes more highly valued as a site for a shopping center, the owners can vote to eliminate the covenant and sell their homes to the shopping center developer. The city need never become involved with a zoning change. Of course, some residents may not like the change, but where zoning laws in other cities change as well, it tends to be in response to political pressure more often than directly

through economic forces. And often in areas covered by zoning laws, those laws are unresponsive to the best economic uses of land, allowing residential neighborhoods to decay rather than rezoning them for more profitable commercial or industrial use.

One could argue the merits and demerits of zoning, but that is not the point here. Rather, note that without zoning land can still be developed in an orderly way and, more significantly, that contracts in the private market can be written that serve the same function as government regulation—if the owners want that regulation. Where owners desire restrictions on land use, restrictive covenants can be employed to provide those restrictions without the government becoming involved. This is a good example of the Coase theorem in action, where private contracts are written to ensure that resources are devoted to their highest valued uses and that externalities among neighbors are minimized.

This discussion of zoning is directly related to several of the main themes of this chapter. Zoning is a method whereby property rights are established and property owners can be protected from some potential externalities created by other property owners. But whereas zoning is a method by which this protection can be provided by the government, private contracts—restrictive covenants—can be written that serve the same purpose. When transactions costs are low enough, private bargains can be struck to allocate resources efficiently without government intervention. These restrictive covenants are a good example of the application of the Coase theorem, and they illustrate how institutional arrangements can evolve to allocate resources efficiently through voluntary agreement.

Conclusion

Chapter 4 argues that no real difference exists between property rights and any other types of rights. Rights of any type grant the holder the right to engage in certain activities. For example, someone who owns a house has the right to live there and to invite friends over, but not the right to make loud noises that disturb the neighbors, nor the right to build a convenience store on property zoned for residential use. Owning something confers on the owner the right to do certain things, and these rights typically can be bought and sold in the market.

Many of the problems examined in Chapter 3, such as externalities and nonexcludability, result from poorly defined property rights. If property rights were all clearly defined, then scarce resources would not be overused, because property owners would have an incentive to produce output only to the point at which marginal costs equaled marginal benefits. In this sense the problems of resource misallocation in the market can be viewed as property rights problems.

Where there are no impediments to the exchange of these rights, the rights will tend to be bought by the individuals who place the highest value on them. The result is that resources are allocated efficiently regardless of the assignment of property rights—this is the conclusion of the Coase theorem. However, in cases where property rights are not clearly established, transactions costs can be too high for the resources to be allocated efficiently. This usually occurs when large numbers of people must be party to the exchange, because an optimal agreement involving many people is more difficult to achieve than one involving only a few people.

This leads us directly into Chapter 5. Often, voluntary agreement may be possible with large numbers of people, and even when it is not, understanding the principles of voluntary agreement will help to illuminate the cases in which the government must get involved.

Questions

1. Discuss the similarities and differences between rights such as the right to free speech and the right to own a home or a business. How would the right to an education or the right to be free from hunger fit into your categorization of rights?

2. During the 1800s in the American West, cattle were being consumed in larger quantities than buffalo, yet buffalo were hunted to near extinction while the population of cattle grew. Explain how these facts can be reconciled.

3. What is the Coase theorem? Under what conditions does the Coase theorem apply?

4. Why are transactions costs important in assessing the appropriate public policy for dealing with an externality? Exactly what is meant by transactions cost in this context? What factors will affect the level of transactions costs?

5. Describe the common pool problem. Give some examples, and suggest how solutions might be worked out to allocate resources more efficiently.

6. What is the difference between common ownership and government ownership of resources? What resource allocation problems exist in each case? How can resource allocation problems be solved in each case?

7. Explain the differences between public ownership and private ownership. Why is it significant that the owners of a private firm can sell the firm, whereas the public firm cannot be sold?

8. Explain the difference between communal ownership and government ownership. What property rights problems are unique to each type of ownership?

9. Zoning laws are enacted to ensure that land in an area is not put to incompatible uses. Explain how Houston, which has no zoning laws, is able to allocate land use in an orderly manner.

PART THREE

An Economic Analysis of Democracy

CHAPTER FIVE

Voluntary Agreement: A Theory of Collective Action

The profitable trades that frequently take place with only two parties to the transaction make up the bulk of our economic system. But sometimes, potentially profitable exchanges require more than two parties. Just as two people engage in a market exchange for their mutual benefit, a club might be viewed as a larger group of people getting together for the mutual benefit of all. The analogy can be extended—though only imperfectly—to the activities of governments. In this sense a government can be viewed as an organization of all of its citizens that undertakes activities for their mutual benefit. Of course, an important distinction between a club and a government is that a club allows its members to leave the club, thus escaping from its rules, whereas a government requires everyone to participate whether they want to or not. But by the same token, contracts in the private sector may require participation (for example, the restrictive covenants discussed in the previous chapter), and one can in a sense quit a government by moving out of the government's jurisdiction.

Collective Action

This chapter will explore the similarities and differences between clubs and governments and examine the many common principles that can shed light on their organization and activities. We are not so much concerned here with the activities of governments as with decisions that are made by groups of people rather than by individuals in conventional market exchanges. The discussion focuses on voluntary agreement and on the types of decisions that a group of people might make collectively. In the sense that we are dealing with people who voluntarily join together into group decision-making processes, this chapter is really dealing with a theory of collective action. This type of voluntary association for the purpose of collective action might best be thought of as a club.

Although individual motivations may vary, people join together to form clubs for economic purposes mainly because greater economic benefits are available to individuals acting collectively than when they act alone or in pairs. People might form a group to try to control a negative externality that affects them all, or they might want to work together to produce a collective consumption good, a nonexcludable good, or a good that produces positive externalities.

A few examples can illustrate the point. In a neighborhood plagued by mosquitos, it does little good for one family to try to control the problem on its property, because the mosquitos can easily migrate from one person's property to another's. One possible course of action is for everyone in the neighborhood to form some type of club or voluntary organization to solve the problem. Or a group of people in a neighborhood might like to have neighborhood tennis courts (or a swimming pool, or both), but no one family wants them enough to buy them individually. Because each family would only use the good a small part of the time, the good would tend not to be congested and thus would have the characteristics of a collective consumption good. This is depicted graphically in Figure 3.5, where the marginal cost of the good is so high that no individual family will demand it, but collectively the three families can chip in and produce Q^*.

Charitable organizations, theatre groups, symphonies, and philanthropic groups are often run by voluntary organizations that elect officers, require dues, and make collective decisions. The fact that membership in such organizations is voluntary suggests that members must derive some benefits from joining. But unlike the market, where two individuals voluntarily exchange, groups typically make decisions according to majority rule. Therefore, we need to examine the characteristics of collective decision making from the standpoint of economic efficiency.

The Pareto Principle and the Rule of Unanimity

Recall that market exchanges are efficient because they are voluntary—everybody benefits from the exchange (except, of course, when negative externalities are present). Thus, market exchanges represent Pareto superior moves. In the absence of transactions costs that might hinder Pareto superior moves from being made, the market continues to make Pareto superior moves until reaching a Pareto optimum. The market system allocates resources by making a succession of Pareto superior moves.

By contrast, most public sector resource allocation decisions are not Pareto superior moves. In a democracy political decisions are usually made by majority rule, which means that while the majority who voted for a policy will benefit from it, the minority who voted against will be made worse off. Because some people benefit but others lose, a Pareto superior move is not made. Decisions made by majority rule have, in effect, a built-in externality. A negative externality exists when the actions of some impose costs on others, as when the decisions of a majority are imposed on a minority. According to the definition in Chapter 3, this is a negative externality.[1]

The public sector equivalent to market exchange, which is built on the principle of voluntary agreement, is unanimous agreement. With unanimity rule, as opposed to majority rule or some other less inclusive rule, everyone agrees to the change, so everyone signals that the change improves their welfare. When unanimous agreement for political decisions is required, everyone is made better off by every decision, which means that only Pareto superior moves are made.

The implication here is that in order to ensure that no inefficient political decisions are made, all decisions should be made according to the political rule of unanimity. If decisions are made according to majority rule, then the majority can impose costs on the minority. Therefore, to ensure that the decision will be in the public interest, there must be some way to weigh the benefits to some against the costs to others. Obviously, not all political decisions are in fact in the public interest, but we can hope that most are, because as a society we choose what the government does.

Optimal Departures from Unanimity

Does this mean that unanimity rule is the optimal political decision rule? In most cases the answer is no. Recall from the previous chapter the problems involved in trying to get large numbers of people to agree to a transaction. Similar problems arise in trying to get large numbers of people to agree to any political decision. As a result of the costs securing unanimous agreement, the optimal decision-making rule in most circumstances is less than unanimity.

Consider a situation in which it would be necessary to select a decision rule. Perhaps a group of people all want access to a swimming pool, but no member of the group considers the option valuable enough to build a private pool. An alternative is to form a swimming club, in which all individuals act together as a group to build a pool, to collect dues, and to

maintain and manage the enterprise. Everyone in the club benefits from having access to a pool.

In order to make sure that every decision of the swimming club benefits every club member, the club can choose to make all of its decisions with the unanimous approval of its members. Although the club would never be able to make a decision against the best interests of its members, it would impose another type of cost on the members, because it would be relatively hard to get everyone in a group to agree to everything. For example, it could take years to decide how big the pool should be, what type of pool furniture should be available, how lifeguards should be selected, and so on. In fact, the club might not be able to agree to anything. Readers should recall from their own experiences as members of clubs, student organizations, sororities, and fraternities how difficult it would be for those groups to reach agreement on anything if every one of the group's decisions had to be approved unanimously. In view of these

---

[1]This idea is the theme of James M. Buchanan, "Politics, Policy, and the Pigouvian Margins," *Economica*, n.s., 29 (Feb. 1962), pp. 17–28.

Figure 5.1 The Optimal Decision Rule The costs of arriving at a collective agreement can be divided into two distinct costs: decision-making costs *(D)* and external costs *(E)*. The optimal decision rule minimizes the sum of these two costs.

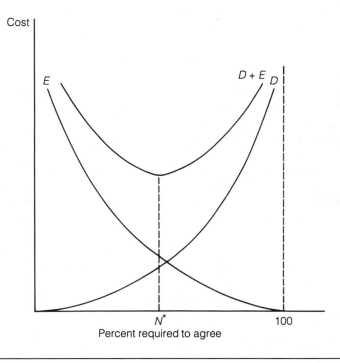

decision-making costs, the optimal decision-making rule is less than unanimity.

Decision-Making Costs

Two types of costs must be considered when selecting the optimal decision rule—decision-making costs and external costs—each of which can be considered from the standpoint of a representative member of the decision-making group.[2] The concept of decision-making costs is depicted in Figure 5.1. The decision-making cost curve *D* shows the relationship of this cost to the proportion of the group that must agree for any particular decision to be implemented. The horizontal axis measures the percentage of the group that must agree for the group to take action; the vertical axis measures the expected cost from one of the group's decisions. The decision-making costs include only the costs of trying to reach some type of group agreement, not the costs to the individual members of the group trying to make up their own minds. Therefore, if one person is empowered to act for the group, no group decision-making costs will be incurred. But as the number of

---

[2]This framework is developed in James M. Buchanan and Gordon Tullock, *The Calculus of Consent* (Ann Arbor: University of Michigan Press, 1962), ch. 6.

people needed to reach an agreement increases, it becomes more difficult to find proposals acceptable to all, meaning the decision-making costs increase.

As the proportion of people required to agree approaches 100 percent, the decision-making costs will be very high, because it is so hard to find anything that everybody in a group of even moderate size will unanimously approve. This may be true when people honestly vote their preferences, but there is also the possibility of strategic voting when the decision rule approaches unanimity. For example, an individual might vote against a proposal that will benefit the individual in the hope that another proposal will be made that will benefit the individual even more. The difficulty of reaching agreement is amplified when the possibilities for strategic voting are recognized, but it is not necessarily any easier to find proposals that would be unanimously approved even when people vote honestly on their preferences. These factors explain the shape of the decision-making cost curve D.

External Costs

As noted earlier, any time a decision is made with less than unanimous approval, an externality is generated, because the majority is imposing its choice on a minority. This cost incurred by the minority represents the external cost of a decision, curve E in Figure 5.1. The external cost curve shows the expected external costs that an individual will bear from a decision made by the group that is against the wishes of the individual. Before the decision is made, the individual does not know whether the decision will be in agreement with his or her wishes or not, but the smaller the percentage required to agree, the more likely it is that the group will make decisions that are against the desires of the particular individual.

If 100 percent of the people are required to agree—that is, with a decision rule of unanimity—no external costs will be generated. A unanimous decision cannot be made without the approval of everybody, which guarantees that every such decision will be a Pareto superior move. Because there are no external costs with a unanimous decision rule, curve E meets the horizontal axis at 100 percent.

As fewer people are required to agree with the decision in order for it to be approved, the likelihood that the group will make a decision that the individual does not agree with increases. If 90 percent of the group is required to agree, then there is some chance that the group will make a decision not approved of by the individual, giving rise to an external cost. If 51 percent are required to agree, there is an even greater chance that the group will make a decision that the individual does not agree with, thus increasing the expected external costs of the decision rule. In short, the smaller the percentage required to agree, the more likely it is that the group will make decisions that are against the desires on the individual, and the larger the expected external costs will be. This is what gives the external cost curve its downward slope.

The Optimal Decision Rule

In order to find the optimal decision rule, both the decision-making costs and the external costs must be considered. In Figure 5.1 curve $D+E$ represents the sum of the decision-making and external curves, thus indicating the combined cost of any decision rule. The decision rule that confers the least cost on the individuals in the group is the rule with the lowest combined cost, or N^*. Generally, the optimal decision rule is less than unanimity. But whatever decision rule the group uses, the individual is better off as a member of the group as long as the combined decision-making and external costs are less than the benefits of being a member of the group.

Consider a case in which a particular group begins its existence with a decision rule of unanimity. It is possible (and even likely) that all members of the group will unanimously agree to adopt a decision rule of less than unanimity for future decisions. In this case the less-than-unanimous rule is Pareto superior to the unanimous rule. Some of the group's particular decisions might not be in the best interest of each individual, but overall the individuals are better off having some decisions go against them in exchange for the lower decision-making costs. This explains why it may be optimal to have a decision rule of less than unanimity.

Sometimes, groups will even choose decision rules of less than majority rule. For example, a group of people who work in a particular office might form a coffee club with, say, twenty members who all pay dues to buy the coffee. However, the group might decide that if any three individuals want coffee, then they have the right to make a pot for the club. In this case only 15 percent of the group is required to agree in order to take action for the group. Note that a different decision rule is used to decide to make coffee from the one used to decide not to make coffee. Only 15 percent of the members of the coffee club need to agree for coffee to be made, which means that over 85 percent of the group must vote against it to stop coffee from being made.

The most commonly used decision rule is majority rule. Majority rule is likely to be the best choice when there is no way for the group to estimate which side of an issue is more intensely preferred. If everybody's opinion is weighed equally, then the preferences of the majority constitute the optimal decision for the issue in question. The coffee club example indicates that a less-than-majority rule can be used when the external costs are expected to be relatively low; by contrast, a jury requires unanimous consent because of the high external cost of convicting an innocent person. Likewise, Congress usually makes decisions by majority rule but chooses a more inclusive two-thirds majority to impeach a president or to override a presidential veto.

Optimal Club Output and Club Size

Many different types of collective organizations exist in an economy, from relatively small groups such as bridge clubs, to larger groups such as country clubs, to cities, and on up to the national government. The reason for this is that different goods have different characteristics that make them amenable to different-sized sharing groups.[3] Consider the collective consumption good discussed in Chapter 3. The definition of collective consumption good implies that no marginal cost is associated with additional consumers, so that an additional consumer can consume at no social cost. This is true for many goods, in many circumstances. For example, a swimming pool with few people in it can be used by additional swimmers without detracting from the use of any other swimmers. However, when the pool gets congested, the collective consumption good takes on some of the characteristics of a private consumption good, because a potential consumer cannot use the good until a current consumer ceases using it.

---

[3] The material in this section is drawn from James M. Buchanan, "An Economic Theory of Clubs," *Economica* (Feb. 1965), pp. 1–14.

Thus, given the amount of the good produced, or in this case the size of the pool, there is an optimal size of the sharing group that can use the good.

If additional consumers are to consume the good, the optimal amount of the good produced will increase. This can be seen in Figure 3.5, where market demand ΣD is found by vertically adding the individual demand curves. Clearly, if another demand curve is added, the ΣD curve will shift outward, and output Q^*, determined at the intersection of the ΣD and MC curves, will increase. With more people in the sharing group, the optimal level of output for pure collective consumption goods increases. However, the marginal cost curve remains constant only when the addition of another consumer will not detract from a current consumer's level of consumption. In a good that can become congested, such as a swimming pool or a highway, this is not the case. Therefore, the best solution is not to continue expanding the size of the swimming pool but to build a second pool.

Indeed, for any given good there is an optimal sharing group. This is true even when congestion is not a factor, as with the television broadcast signal. Any viewer in the broadcast area can receive the signal without reducing the consumption of another viewer, so congestion is not a problem. Nevertheless, a signal of given strength will reach only a certain number of viewers; after that point, additional viewers can only be added by increasing the power of the broadcast signal. One way to achieve that would be to erect a giant broadcast tower in the center of the country and broadcast a signal strong enough to reach everyone. However, it is cheaper to divide the country into areas and broadcast less powerful signals to those areas. Thus, the optimal sharing group in this instance is not the entire nation, even though congestion is not a factor.

Sometimes, though, the entire nation will be the appropriate sharing group. With the increasing use of satellite technology, it is only a matter of time before everyone in the nation receives broadcasts from a single source, though it will be a satellite rather than a tall tower. National defense is another example of an optimal-sized sharing group comprising the entire nation. Perhaps the boundaries of optimal defense extend even beyond national borders, to other nations that perceive the same threats—organizations such as NATO provide defense as a collective consumption good to many nations.

As a result of the different characteristics of various goods, the size of the optimal sharing group depends on the particular good being considered. For private consumption goods the size of the optimal sharing group is one person. The optimal-sized tennis club is larger but still encompasses fewer people than the optimal city, which provides such collective consumption goods as roads, parks, and streetlights to make the area more desirable. For such goods as national defense, the sharing group may extend to national boundaries, and beyond.

The implications for a society's social structure can be seen in the various types of groups that compose a society. Governments as well as clubs and organizations can vary in size and can produce different types of collective consumption goods. Optimal sharing arrangements vary from one good to another, and different-sized sharing groups are the result. In this light it is easy to see why, based on economic efficiency considerations, it is preferable to have many different levels of government, from local to state to national, rather than just one level, to provide all public sector output.

Representative Democracy

Up to this point, groups organized for collective action have been analyzed as if every member in the group had an equal input into the group's activities. In reality, for all but the smallest groups this is not likely to be the case. Usually, members of the group elect representatives or officers, who take on more of the responsibilities for making the group's decisions. There are two reasons why an individual might rather belong to an organization run by a representative governing board rather than an organization run by all of its members collectively. First, lower decision-making costs are incurred when fewer people are involved in making a group's decisions. Second, as with any activity, benefits are gained from specialization.

The problems of group decision making when large numbers of people are involved have already been discussed at some length. Recall that one way to reduce decision-making costs is to use a less inclusive voting rule. Another way is to reduce the number of people involved in the decision-making process by having a representative body make the group's decisions. Imagine, for example, how complex the debates in the U.S. Congress could become if every American citizen were encouraged to submit bills for review and to actively engage in debate. By electing representatives, the decision-making process is greatly simplified because fewer people are involved directly. This system of representation works so well to lower decision-making costs that even when groups are small enough that every member can attend meetings, the groups still rely on elected officers for direction.

The other factor that makes a representative type of government desirable is the gains from specialization. As the activities of groups become more complex, more specialized knowledge is required in order to efficiently run them. Even a country club employs many full-time workers, and governments are obviously far more complex. It makes sense to have selected representatives oversee the collective activities rather than to entrust this task to the group as a whole; indeed, specialization and gains from trade are at the foundation of any economic system.

Keep in mind the economic orientation of this discussion. A group of people will find it in their best interest to act collectively to produce certain benefits, whether the benefits are access to a golf course or national defense. Given these common economic interests, the individuals act collectively, but due to decision-making costs and the benefits of specialization, the group elects representatives to form a decision-making body for the collective organization. Viewed this way, the purpose of a representative government becomes the reduction of the expected costs of engaging in specific types of collective action.

Representative democracy makes a great deal of sense from an economic point of view. The virtues of a representative government in general were just discussed; the virtues of the periodic selection of representatives by majority rule lie mainly in the fact that it is relatively easy for dissatisfied voters to replace elected officials. Thus, the government is both representative—to lower the decision-making costs of the group and to benefit from specialization—and democratic—to provide a mechanism for replacing representatives.[4]

---

[4]This idea is discussed at greater length in R. G. Holcombe, *An Economic Analysis of Democracy* (Carbondale: Southern Illinois University Press, 1985), ch. 2.

The Economic Model of Democracy

People often regard the primary mandate of a representative democracy such as the United States as the furthering of the will of the majority. Note how different this is from the economic model of representative democracy, in which the government has certain well-defined tasks. Given the scope of government activity, it is evident that a representative democracy is the best means for undertaking these specific tasks. The representative democracy allows for specialization and for lower decision-making costs and provides a mechanism for regular evaluation—and possible replacement—of elected officials. But the key to the economic model is that the tasks that the government undertakes are specified in advance. The government's job, quite simply, is to carry out these tasks, not to further the will of the majority. Majority rule is simply a means toward the predefined ends of government.

An examination of the Constitution shows that the U.S. government actually was structured more along the lines of the economic model of government than along the lines of a system to further the will of the majority.

The Constitution enumerates the areas of governmental responsibility, but then the Bill of Rights states that any powers not specifically granted to the federal government belong to the states or to the individual citizens of the nation. Clearly, the government has carefully delineated areas of responsibility for collective action. Accepting the desire to undertake these activities collectively, the economic model of government suggests a representative democracy as an efficient governing mechanism. But, to emphasize, the representative democracy is simply a means to a carefully stated end rather than a way to further the will of the majority.

From an economic standpoint the establishment of a government to further the will of the majority does not make much sense, because in such a system the majority could simply produce benefits for themselves at the expense of a minority. As previously noted, this automatically creates an externality, because some people's actions impose costs on others. For this reason alone it makes good economic sense to limit the powers of a government. Otherwise, an unrestrained majority could exploit a minority just as effectively as a dictatorship could.

The Clubs and Governments

The answer to the question of how a club actually differs from a government is more elusive than it first appears. It should be pointed out that clubs and governments occupy opposite ends of a continuum of collective organizations but share many of the same characteristics. Although here we try to identify the dividing line between the two, the reader may want to think carefully about the issue rather than merely accepting the answer given here.

Clubs

Consider first a bridge club, which occupies the club end of the continuum. The game of bridge, like so many endeavors, is necessarily a collective undertaking—it takes four people to play the game. The simplest bridge club might be made up of four people who agree to meet once a week, rotating the meeting place from one player's house to the next, so that each person hosts a meeting every four weeks. The person at whose house the meeting takes place is responsible for providing refreshments to the entire group.

Obviously, the benefits of playing bridge cannot be enjoyed alone. Collective action becomes necessary in order to provide this benefit, but it encompasses certain obligations as well. First, each individual has the responsibility to attend the meetings of the club, because the game cannot be played with only three people. Second, once every four weeks each individual has the responsibility of providing a meeting place and refreshments. In effect, this amounts to a tax (or, perhaps, dues) that must be paid by the members of the club in exchange for the benefits provided by the collective organization.

The provision of refreshments is analogous to a tax imposed by a government, and the requirement that the members attend each meeting (which is necessary for the good to be produced) is analogous to the laws that citizens of a government must obey. The club might also have penalties for disobeying the laws. For example, it could be agreed on that if a member misses two meetings in a row, the club will replace that member. Frequently, bridge clubs are much larger, in which case they may have a regular meeting place, elected officers, and mandatory dues. Thus, though they are still at opposite ends of the continuum, the bridge club and a government can share many characteristics. Tennis clubs and swimming clubs may be arranged the same way, so that members enjoy the collective benefits at lower cost and with less effort than if these benefits were produced individually.

Collective Facilities

Consider another case. When new subdivisions are being developed, the developer may include swimming pools and tennis courts in the development in order to attract buyers for the homes. Often, the ownership of the collective facilities will go to the collective group of homeowners. In addition, the homeowners elect officers to oversee the facilities. Each homeowner must participate in the collective activities as a part of the responsibility of buying a house in that neighborhood. Indeed, the developer requires that the buyer of a home also buy a share of the common facilities, which is then bought and sold along with the home. According to the contract, every homeowner has the right to vote for officers and use the facilities but also the obligation to pay dues.

Here the line between a club and a government begins to blur. This club is set up in the private sector and is independent of any government organization. And yet, just by virtue of owning property in a particular area, the resident is obligated (by contract) to pay dues, which now seem to more closely resemble taxes, in exchange for the right to use the common facilities. How, then, does this arrangement differ from a government?

Governments

By comparison, one can choose to live in a small town like Auburn, Alabama, pay taxes to the city, and use the municipal pool and tennis courts as well as other collective services. If a person does not want to participate in the Auburn city government, that person can relocate in another nearby city and simply work in Auburn. And if a person does not want to live under any city government, it is certainly feasible to live outside the city limits and commute to work. Thus, as in the subdivision just described, a person can live in a geographical area, pay dues or taxes, and participate in the collective benefits produced. But it is also possible in both cases to live outside the boundaries of either city or subdivision, thus avoiding the taxes but foregoing the benefits. In either case, because one can choose whether to live there, participation is essentially voluntary.

Now compare the city government to the state government. Again, taxes must be paid, and a person has an option to live in one state as opposed to another. But though one can elect not to live in a city, one must live in a state, and it is more difficult to choose one's state than to choose one's city. The federal government is even more encompassing. One can move to a different country, but this may not represent a meaningful choice for most people. Thus, one must ultimately abide by the rules of the federal government and pay taxes in exchange for benefits received.

The Characteristics of Government

We have already noted the element of compulsion in every club or government, though admittedly it is easier to escape a tyrannical bridge club than a tyrannical national government. Both club and government provide some type of collective benefits but expect some type of payment in return. In the continuum from club to government, what characteristics enable us to identify one organization as a club and another as a government?

One frequently used definition classifies the government as that organization that has a monopoly on the legal use of force.[5] The element of compulsion is certainly present in government, but it is also present, to a degree, in any club—either obey the rules or leave the club. Likewise, one who does not want to obey city governments can escape by moving away. The definition also does not readily admit to the multiple layers of government. For example, city, county, state, and federal governments can all have jurisdiction over an area. It makes no sense to say that all four have a monopoly over the same thing.

In this text government is defined as an organization that has the ability to finance its activities by compulsory contributions from individuals in a given geographic area. The difference between a swimming club and a municipal pool, for example, is that individuals in a given geographic area (the municipality) are forced to pay for the municipal pool, whereas only club members pay for the club pool, and the club members might live anywhere.

Note that the key point in this definition is how the financing for the organization's activities are generated. Individuals in the United States pay for the U.S. government, but the U.S. government's activities can extend beyond its boundaries to, for example, Vietnam or Lebanon or even the moon. Note also that not all of the individuals in the area must make compulsory contributions; some individuals might be exempt from taxes. The contributions might also come in some other form, perhaps as a compulsory contribution of labor in a military draft.

The reader will want to consider this definition carefully before accepting it, for it does include some organizations not normally thought of as governments. For example, both the subdivision with the communal pool and condominium associations would qualify as governments under this definition. The point is that these organizations are in fact governments, even though they may not call themselves that, because they have the power to force contributions for their activities from individuals within their geographic boundaries.

---

[5] This echoes the definition of popular writer Ayn Rand. See, for example, her essay, "The Nature of Government," in *The Virtue of Selfishness* (New York: New American Library, 1961). See also Robert Nozick, *Anarchy, State, and Utopia* (New York: Basic Books, 1974), for a philosopher's views on the subject.

Conclusion

Some type of collective organization can usually produce the benefits that people desire more efficiently than two individuals in a market exchange can. Collective organizations—clubs and governments—can be formed in order to allow the collective activities to take place. Market exchange tends to allocate resources efficiently because, by its very nature, it ensures that every exchange is a Pareto superior move. The analogous decision-making rule in a collective organization is the rule of unanimity.

Although a unanimous decision-making rule will ensure that all collective decisions are Pareto superior moves, the unanimity rule often generates such high decision-making costs that a rule of less than unanimity becomes more feasible in collective decision making. As a result, collective decisions made under less than unanimity rule can produce non-Pareto superior moves and potentially inefficient resource allocation as well. Nevertheless, considering both decision-making and external costs, the less-inclusive decision-making rule is generally optimal.

Collective organizations vary in size from just a few people to millions of people due to the fact that the optimal size of the sharing group for a good will depend on the good in question. Therefore, many different types and sizes of groups provide collective consumption goods. In a sense there is no clear division between the smallest club and the largest government, but rather a continuum from one to the other. As groups get larger and more inclusive, there are fewer alternatives to being a member. Though one can choose not to be a member of a swimming club or a city, there is little in the way of a practical alternative to being subject to some national government. This degree of compulsion is a characteristic for identifying the presence of government, but governments also are geographic in nature. A definition of government that encompasses both of these characteristics is the following: Government is an organization that has the ability to finance its activities by compulsory contributions from individuals in a given geographic area.

Clubs are based on the idea of voluntary agreement, whereas governments require the participation of their citizens. The material in this chapter is really applicable to either clubs or governments, but in the next chapter we focus on governments in examining the factors that make voluntary agreement for the production of some goods infeasible. Recall that representative democracies reduce decision-making costs and produce benefits by allowing the group's representatives to specialize in the production of the collective output. If the key characteristic of government is its ability to force citizens to contribute to its support, then one might wonder how these compulsory contributions can be justified. This is the central issue of the next chapter.

Questions

1. Explain the relationships among market exchange, majority rule, and unanimity rule. Why can it be said that unanimity rule in the public sector is analogous to market exchange in the private sector?

2. If unanimity rule requires that Pareto superior moves be the result of any decision while majority rule allows the possibility of non-Pareto superior moves, explain why a group might still rather use majority rule than unanimity rule to make its decisions.

3. Explain the theory behind the calculation of an optimal decision-making rule. Relate this theory to some decision-making rules in the real world.

4. In the United States there are many different levels of government, including local, state, and federal. Why does this arrangement make sense from a strictly economic point of view.

5. Give two reasons why individuals might prefer to belong to a group that allows group representatives to make decisions for the group rather than have everyone in the group participate in the decision-making process.

6. What are the similarities and differences between a club and a government? What determines the dividing line between them?

CHAPTER SIX

The Free Rider Problem
and the Role of Government

Many types of activities are performed more efficiently through collective organizations than through individual effort or bilateral exchange. Indeed, this has been a dominant theme in the text thus far. In general, the aim of an economic system is to improve the economic well-being of those living under the system. Every time individuals engage in a market exchange, a Pareto superior move is made. When collective groups engage in economic activities Pareto superior moves again are made, but in these cases the trades involve groups of people instead of two individuals, with each individual in the group benefiting from the group's activities.

In Chapter 5, in drawing parallels between their activities, we concluded that governments and clubs lie at opposite ends of the same continuum. Certainly, they share characteristics, but an important distinction between a club and a government is the element of coercion involved in government. The dividing line between some private sector collective organizations and governments in the public sector may be a fine one, but the degree

of coercion present in an organization probably indicates where the organization falls on the continuum between club and government. Indeed, as the example in the last chapter of the homeowners' collective group that required individuals to belong to the swimming and tennis club suggests, one reason that the organization so closely resembled a government is that the contract binding the homeowner to the club was written in such a way that the government would enforce the contract in court. Could such an agreement exist without the government's courts and police to back it up? Note that in the bridge club, by contrast, one could simply say "I quit" and exit the club.

Having thus far emphasized the virtues of voluntary agreement to improve the welfare of individuals in an economy, we have good reason to examine carefully the nature of the coercion. In the case of voluntary agreements among individuals, whether the agreement encompasses two individuals or a larger group, positive analysis of the agreement is usually sufficient. But government activities tend to involve an element of coercion, which implies that a normative evaluation is necessary, because as citizens of a democratic country, we have some power to choose the types of activities that our government will pursue. To make any judgments about what governmental activities are in our best interests, we must engage in normative analysis. For one thing, we must ask ourselves how we can justify governmental activity that forces some individuals to participate whether they want to or not. Because we are in the realm of normative analysis, answers are less clear-cut; nevertheless, some generally accepted principles of public sector economics merit discussion. One principle that was touched on in Chapter 3 is the free rider problem. After reviewing some aspects of the free rider problem, this chapter will extend the analysis and examine some of its implications for governmental activity.

The Free Rider Problem

Recall from Chapter 3 the example of the two individuals who shared a common driveway. After a snowfall, each waited for the other to shovel the driveway, with the result that although both would have liked to use the driveway, neither did because each was hoping the other would provide the collective consumption good of a shoveled drive. Clearly, they would have been better off if they had agreed beforehand that after a snowfall, they both would participate in clearing the driveway.

Free Riding and Shirking

Such an agreement is likely to be made between the two individuals in the small-numbers setting. However, in a large-numbers setting, perhaps a whole town, the possibility of an agreement is more remote. Consider a situation in which everyone in a town agrees to participate in clearing the town streets after it snows. Of course, infirm and ill persons cannot be expected to help out, but this gives people who have only a small illness (or a large imagination) the incentive to allow others to clear the roads. Those who really can help but prefer to take advantage of the work of others are *free riders*.

Even the individuals who actually are helping will have an incentive not to work as hard in the group. If they are working alone, hard work will get the job done sooner, but with many other people working, each individual has the incentive to allow others to carry most of the burden. The problem is known as the free rider problem because everybody has an incentive to allow others to do the work, or produce the goods, and then free ride off the efforts of others. And no matter who does the work, everybody benefits.

This situation is analogous to the prisoners' dilemma situation, discussed in Chapter 3, in which each prisoner, acting in his own self-interest, ended up acting against the best interest of the group. The same is true of the snow shovelers. The good being produced—snow-free streets—is a collective consumption good that has high costs of exclusion, and because people can take advantage of the work of others, the incentive structure is not conducive to the efficient allocation of resources. The resource misallocation occurs because everybody has the same incentive to be a free rider; the goods therefore are underproduced. The results may range from inconvenient, as when everyone must try to navigate on snow-covered streets, to clearly unacceptable, as would be the case if everyone tried to free ride on the national defense produced by others.

National Defense

National defense may provide the best example of the possible perils of the free rider problem. Presumably, almost everyone wants to be protected from invasion by foreign governments, but the possibility of free riding on national defense is strong. If national defense is provided for some people in an area, it also defends the other people in the area whether they want it to or not. But what if people are asked to contribute voluntarily to national defense? They will figure that if everyone else contributes, then the area will be well defended, and also that their individual contribution will make little difference to the overall level of defense. Thus, if others provide defense, they will see little reason why they should contribute to the effort. Furthermore if they see that nobody else is contributing,

they will figure that their individual defense effort will make little difference—one person cannot defend against a foreign army. Like the individuals in the prisoners' dilemma who find it in their self-interest to confess no matter what the other person does, here each individual finds it in his or her self-interest not to contribute to the national defense effort, no matter what anyone else does. Even those who might want to contribute something have an incentive to contribute less than the true amount that the good is worth to them, so they will undercontribute or not contribute at all.

The result of all this is that less than the optimal amount of national defense will be produced with voluntary contributions. People will have different demands for national defense, and some pacifists may actually demand none at all. However, nobody will know what another person's actual demand is, so every person will have an incentive to understate his or her true demand. Therefore, it is argued, the government must not only produce the good but also require that people pay for their share. This argument will be examined in more detail after similar problems are discussed.

The Holdout Problem

The holdout problem can arise whenever unanimous approval is required for some Pareto superior move to occur. For example, assume that an individual decides to build a highway to connect two locations. To put the example in explicitly economic terms, the highway will be a toll road, and the individual expects to be able to make a profit on the road if it is built. The proposed road will run over property owned by ten different individuals,

each of whom, without knowledge of the toll road, is willing to sell his or her property for $10,000. The individual building the highway calculates that if all ten pieces of property are obtained for the highway, their combined value would be $150,000. The holdout problem exists because the builder of the road needs all ten pieces of property to complete the road. But if the individual owners find out about the road project and can estimate the value of the road to the builder, they will have an incentive to hold out for a price not only higher than they were originally willing to sell for but also higher than the builder could pay.

Consider the following case. Assume that the builder of the road has already bought nine of the ten pieces of land, paying $10,000 each for a total of $90,000. All ten parcels put together are worth $150,000, so the value of the remaining parcel to the builder is $60,000. As a result, the remaining landowner has an incentive to hold out and demand $60,000 for the property, even though he would have been willing to sell for $10,000 if he had not known about the road.

The problem is this. Before the builder of the road buys any land at all, each landowner is potentially a holdout. Realizing that the last parcel of land will be worth $60,000, each landowner has an incentive to hold out and ask as much as $60,000 for the property, in which case the potential developer will find it almost impossible to assemble the tract. Building the road would be a potential Pareto superior move, but because each existing landowner has an incentive to hold out, the developer may not even try to complete the project. This type of problem is likely to arise any time someone wants to assemble a large parcel of land currently owned by a large number of people, as, for example, when a utility company or railroad tries to buy a right of way for power lines, pipelines or railroad tracks, or when a developer tries to build a shopping center.

Solutions to the Holdout Problem

One way to avoid the holdout problem, when the alternative exists, is to assemble the property from fewer rather than more individual tracts. A shopping center can be developed outside of a heavily developed area on farmland owned by one individual, rather than as-

sembled from property owned by many individuals. Another solution may be simply to have alternatives to present to prospective sellers. A shopping center may require ten pieces of land, but if an alternative site exists, holdouts may be enticed to sell. Contingency contracts can also be used. The buyer may agree to purchase one of the tracts of land contingent upon being able to buy the rest. Thus, if a holdout problem develops, the buyer is released from the obligation, reducing the incentive of the seller to hold out.

The government frequently finds itself involved in these types of situations through laws of eminent domain. Under eminent domain laws the government has the right to order a piece of property sold at its fair market value if the property is to be used in the public interest. Eminent domain has been used to buy land for highways, railroad rights of way, power lines, and even urban development projects. Typically, the government and the property owner will try to reach an agreement on a fair sale price for the property, but if an agreement cannot be reached, then eminent domain laws are applied.

The key to the holdout problem is that everyone in a group must agree on an exchange for it to be a Pareto superior move; recall that the Pareto superior move, by its very nature, produces net benefits for the group. But the holdout hopes to capture a larger individual share of the benefits. And because everyone has the potential to be a holdout, agreement can be difficult to reach. Clearly, the holdout problem will exist if unanimous approval is required in a voting situation as well. In a group using a unanimity rule, a proposal can benefit everybody, and yet some people might vote against the proposal in the hope of gaining a larger share of the collective benefits through another proposal.

Consent and Coercion

The problems posed by the free rider and the holdout exist when an action that would benefit everyone in a group is not taken because each individual in the group has an incentive not to cooperate with the group but rather to reap the potentially greater personal gains from not cooperating, regardless of what anyone else does. In such a situation all individuals have an incentive to minimize their cooperative behavior. The result may be that the government coerces people to cooperate with the group, as when people are forced to pay taxes for national defense or to sell property under the government's right of eminent domain.

Up to this point, collective action has been framed in terms of group agreements that are Pareto superior moves. For example, as discussed in Chapter 5, people can agree to a less-than-unanimous decision-making rule because of the decision-making cost involved in reaching a unanimous decision; with clubs this is certainly possible. But in terms of society as a whole, the Paretian framework is being strained, because the government forces people to pay taxes and abide by laws and does not allow people to exclude themselves if they are not in agreement. This raises the hypothetical question—and we must emphasize the word *hypothetical*—of whether people can agree to be coerced.

The argument that people can agree to be coerced goes as follows. For many goods, such as snow removal and national defense, people generally desire for the goods to be produced, but they have an incentive to free ride if others are willing to produce them. In recognizing the free rider problem, individuals can volunteer to contribute to the production of the good as long as everyone else is willing to contribute as well. This solution resembles the contingency contract often drawn up when assembling a large plot of land—an individual agrees to cooperate under the condition that all others likewise agree.

In effect, individuals are saying that they will agree to be forced to participate in the collective action as long as everyone else is forced to participate. People are agreeing to be coerced for the benefit of everyone. In this way the Paretian framework can be extended even to government activities that force people to contribute whether they agree or not, according to the logic that individuals have an incentive not to agree—to be free riders—but that each individual is better off if all individuals are forced to participate. In this sense there is no contradiction in saying that individuals can agree to be coerced.

The reader must be wary of this argument, however, for it has been extended from one in which people actually agree to one in which it is possible that people could agree. The agreement does not actually take place; we are only supposing that it could. We are saying that although people are coerced to pay their taxes for national defense, they are actually better off by being forced to agree. Because individuals have an incentive to free ride and to say they will not agree, even if it will benefit them to do so, they must be coerced, regardless of whether they agree.

The problem with the argument in favor of consent to be coerced is that there is no way to know whether it is true or not. Although we hope that the government makes Pareto superior moves, we might use the supporting argument to state that a Pareto superior move is being made when in reality it is not. In fact, such an argument might be used to justify virtually any type of governmental activity; one could simply state that there is a free rider problem, but that individuals could agree to be coerced.

Perhaps the most extreme example of governmental coercion is when the government takes money from some people and gives it to others. Yet such governmental activities have been justified in the following terms. People care about the well-being of those less fortunate than themselves—the existence of voluntary charity attests to this fact. Yet when one person behaves charitably and helps less fortunate individuals, other people benefit by having the well-being of the less fortunate individuals improved. Thus, some people free ride off of the charitable activities of others. Therefore, a Pareto superior move can be made by collecting taxes from people who are better off and redistributing the money to those who are worse off.[1] Unfortunately, there is no way to tell whether this argument is right or wrong. If taking money from some to give to others can be justified by arguing that individuals could agree to be coerced, then any governmental activity could be justified the same way.

The argument here is based on such problems as the positive externality and the collective consumption good. In both of these cases,

individuals have an incentive to free ride and consume the benefits produced by others without paying for them, which results in too little of these types of goods being produced. But the solution to these problems of less-than-ideal allocation of resources is not as clear. Perhaps people could agree to be coerced, but this does strain the Paretian framework a great deal.

In fact, if one wants to remain strictly within the Paretian framework to justify public sector activity, it is unlikely that any public sector activity can be justified on the basis that individuals agree to be coerced. Although almost everyone may agree on certain things, it is highly unlikely that absolutely every one of millions of citizens will agree to any one government activity. And even if there is only one dissenter, then the government activity does not constitute a Pareto superior move.

Perhaps a framework to find the optimal decision rule, such as was discussed in Chapter 5, could be invoked at this point. Individuals do not agree to every decision, but they agree that the decision-making process is optimal and that on net they benefit from government activity.[2] This is the social contract theory of state, which we will discuss now.

The Social Contract Theory of the State

The *social contract theory of the state* is not new; it dates back at least to Locke and Rousseau.[3] According to the social contract theory of the state, the state can be thought of as a con-

tract that binds its citizens and that is agreed to by those governed by it. Of course, the citizens of a country do not actually agree to the nation's government, so the social contract theory must rely on some notion of conceptual agreement.

[1] This argument has been made in Harold M. Hochman and James D. Rogers, "Pareto Optimal Redistribution," *American Economic Review* 59 (Sept. 1969), pp. 542–547.

[2] This idea is developed in James M. Buchanan and Gordon Tullock, *The Calculus of Consent* (Ann Arbor: University of Michigan Press, 1962), ch. 6.

[3] Sir Ernest Barker, *The Social Contract* (New York and London: Oxford University Press, 1960), traces the origin of the social contract theory as far back as Plato.

One of the most significant recent contributions to the social contract theory of the state was made by philosopher John Rawls.[4] He argued that all individuals have to agree in concept on the role of government, including its taxing and spending policies, for there to be a social contract, but that the conceptual agreement occurs behind a "veil of ignorance" about one's specific conditions in life. To illuminate this view, imagine a society in which everyone must agree about what the government's policies are to be, but they must agree before they know their positions in life. That is, they have no idea as to what their race, sex, appearance, intelligence, or abilities will be. From behind this veil of ignorance, they have to agree on what type of society they want to have; this choice is the social contract.

Rawls is not arguing that the rules of our current society—or any real world society—were actually established that way. Rather, he is arguing for this procedure as a method of establishing whether the existing rules are just, whether, in the absence of individual characteristics and biases, the existing rules could be agreed on. For example, in assessing the fairness of the progressive income tax, which forcibly collects money from some people and then redistributes it to others, one would be asking whether such a plan could be agreed on behind a veil of ignorance. If so, then the policy can be justified as fair. The disadvantage of this criterion is that people in the real world might disagree on what could be agreed on behind the veil of ignorance. Nevertheless, it does provide some basis for considering the question of justice.

James Buchanan views the social contract theory along much the same lines as Rawls, but he relies on another device to determine agreement with the social contract.[5]

Buchanan suggests that people consider how well off they would be if the existing government were eliminated and a social contract drawn up to produce a new government. If the likely range of new governments includes a government like the existing one, then the individual agrees conceptually with the existing government. In other words individuals would think it likely that a social contract could have produced a government like the existing one even though the existing government was not in fact produced by a social contract.

In the social contract theory of the state government is viewed as a type of a club. One could certainly ask the kinds of questions that Rawls or Buchanan raised about the existing government. Could the terms of our government be agreed upon behind a veil of ignorance? If we started over again, would it be likely that we would end up agreeing to a government like the one we have today? If the answer to such questions was yes, then according to the social contract theory the provisions of the current government would be fair.[6]

Criticisms of the Social Contract Theory

Three fundamental criticisms of the social contract theory of the state should be noted. First, the notion of the contract is hypothetical—everyone did not actually agree to the social contract, but rather was born into a society and had to accept the rules of the society whether they wanted to or not. This is, of course, the problem that modern contractarians such as Rawls and Buchanan have tried to address through such concepts as the veil of

---

[4]John Rawls, *A Theory of Justice* (Cambridge: Belknap, 1971).

[5]James M. Buchanan, *The Limits of Liberty: Between Anarchy and Leviathan* (Chicago: University of Chicago Press, 1975).

[6]See Scott Gordon, "The New Contractarians," *Journal of Political Economy* 84, no. 3 (June 1976), pp. 573–590, for a discussion of the social contract theory of the state.

ignorance and renegotiation of the contract. Still, the social contract represents a hypothetical, not an actual, contract.[7]

The second criticism follows from the first. Because the agreement with the contract is conceptual rather than factual, there is no way to state with certainty that features of the real world would be approved by the social contract or to identify what the world would be like if an actual social contract existed. That is, individuals might agree on the validity of the contractarian framework but disagree about what features of actual governments would be approved as terms of the contract.

Third, the social contract theory of the state gives the illusion of agreement with the government and its institutions and minimizes the coercive nature of government. Earlier, we argued that the coercive power of government—and particularly the ability to force citizens to contribute to its support—are crucial characteristics of government. Citizens of free countries must remain vigilant to try to control the coercive power of the state, yet in the social contract theory of the state the government is viewed as an organization everyone has agreed to rather than an organization that has the power to force compliance on those who do not agree.

Certainly these criticisms have merit; if nothing else they suggest that the social contract theory of the state cannot be taken as a literal description of the nature of government. Nevertheless, the social contract theory does provide a framework within which one can analyze the activities of government. For example, the establishment (or abolishment) of a certain government program may not be a Pareto superior move, but if one believes that the change would be approved from behind Rawls's veil of ignorance, then from a contractarian standpoint there is reason to argue for the change.

Rules and Outcomes: A Procedural Theory of Justice

The social contract theory of the state contains a procedural theory of justice that is generally applicable in measuring economic performance. A procedural theory judges an outcome by the procedure used to generate the outcome rather than by the outcome itself. For example, one might observe that two people within a society have vastly different incomes—one person receives $10,000 a year, the other receives $100,000. Is this fair? Initially, it is tempting to regard such disparity in income as unfair, but what if the higher-income person works hard ten hours a day, whereas the lower-income person, who is capable of doing the same work, prefers to work only one hour a day? In the real world an unequal distribution of income can be caused by some people working harder than others, by some people saving while others consume, by differences in natural talents and abilities, by discrimination, or even by luck. Although some of the reasons for an unequal distribution of income might be viewed as more fair than others, if the procedure that generates the income is fair, then the outcome can be viewed as fair.

According to the procedural theory a fair outcome is an outcome that is generated by fair rules; there is no need to look at the out-

---

[7]This criticism and others are considered in Leland B. Yeager, "Rights, Contract, and Utility in Policy Espousal," *Cato Journal* 5, no. 1 (Summer 1985), pp. 259–294.

come directly to judge its fairness. If someone told you that the final score of a football game was 35–7, would you consider this to be a fair game? To judge the fairness of a football game, you probably would not look at the score (outcome) at all. Instead, you would probably say that if the two teams played under the same rules and if the officiating was unbiased, then the outcome of the game is fair regardless of the score.

The distinction between judging a procedure and an outcome is relevant to many areas of public policy. For example, the government, citing the antitrust laws, might accuse a group of firms of forming a cartel to attempt to extract monopoly prices from their customers. One way to make a determination in a case like this is to examine the outcome. Because restricted output levels and higher prices result from monopoly power, it would be appropriate to ask, Are prices in the industry higher than they would be without collusion? Is the industry output lower than would be expected in a free market? Another way to judge whether the firms have formed a cartel is to question the procedures by which the prices and output are determined. Are there barriers to entry in the industry? Have the firms established a method of allocating output, such as dividing the market into exclusive geographic areas? If so, then the procedures used within the market will produce a lower level of output and higher prices. Note that there is no need to look at the actual levels of output or price directly; rather, the outcome is judged by the procedure that produces it. In short, whether in antitrust matters or in football games, one can judge the appropriateness of the outcome by looking at the procedure that produces the outcome.

The term *justice* is typically associated with criminal activity, and here, too, a procedural theory of justice is routinely applied. If one person kills another person in self-defense or accidentally, then the killer might be judged innocent of wrongdoing. But in a holdup of a convenience store, the robber who kills the clerk is likely to be judged far more harshly. Again, the fairness of the outcome (the penalty placed upon the killer) is determined by the circumstances that produced the outcome—the procedure—rather than solely by the outcome.

The social contract theory of the state discussed in the previous section is a procedural theory because it concludes that if a real world outcome is determined by a procedure that is a part of the social contract, then the real world outcome is fair. Although the procedural part of the theory should be evident, a number of questions relating to how one decides what the terms of the contract are need to be answered. Is the distribution of income fair? It is if it has been determined by a fair procedure. Is it fair that some people are elected to public office while others who want the positions cannot get them? It is if those elected are chosen by a fair procedure.

The Evolution of Cooperation

This chapter has focused thus far on the problems that might arise in a society when individuals pursue their narrow self-interests instead of acting in the general public interest. Often in the real world people are confronted with prisoners'-dilemma-type situations, in which the procedure of following individual self-interest leads to a result that is less than optimal from a social standpoint. Recall that individuals have an incentive to be free riders rather than act in the public interest. If a government doesn't force people to cooperate, the results can be inconvenience, as when snow is not shoveled off the roads, or they can be potentially disastrous, as would likely be the case if the private sector was responsible for national defense. Clearly, few people would want to risk a private sector national defense; in this sense it is easy to visualize individuals being better off agreeing to be coerced by the government to cooperate with others.

Axelrod's Tournament

Nevertheless, one should be careful in observing the potential for the free rider problem and jumping to the conclusion that resources will not be used optimally unless the government gets involved. Without government society would not necessarily deteriorate into a Hobbesian state of anarchy in which life was nasty, brutish, and short. Indeed, Robert Axelrod argues persuasively that cooperation can emerge naturally among individuals without any outside institutions (such as government) forcing them to.[8]

Axelrod's arguments come from the results of a computer tournament that he set up where entrants submitted computer programs to play a prisoners' dilemma game with each other. Each entrant played against each other entrant a large number of times (over 100), and each entrant could remember its playing history with the other programs in the tournament.

The payoff matrix for the game is given in Figure 6.1. At each play a program could either cooperate or not cooperate with the other player. If both programs chose to cooperate, each received a payoff of 3 points. If one cooperated while the other defected, the defecting player received 5 points while the cooperating one received nothing. If neither program cooperated, each of the defectors earned 1 point. The winner of the tournament was the program that received the most points.

Axelrod had fifteen programs in the first tournament, and the winning strategy was TIT FOR TAT, a program that cooperated with each of the other players the first time they met and then on subsequent meetings did whatever the other player did the previous time. For example, if TIT FOR TAT met another TIT FOR TAT program, both would cooperate, receiving 3 points each, and then would cooperate on each subsequent turn. If TIT FOR TAT met a particularly mean program that would defect no matter what, TIT FOR TAT would cooperate on the first play, receiving no points while the defector received 5, but on subsequent plays TIT FOR TAT would do what the other player did last, which was to defect. Thus, on subsequent plays, with another TIT FOR TAT, both TIT FOR TATs would receive 3 points each, whereas on subsequent plays with the uncooperative program, they each would receive 1 point.

Axelrod found it interesting that the top-scoring programs in the tournament, including TIT FOR TAT, scored high not by free riding and taking advantage of others but by cooperating and eliciting their cooperation. Axelrod announced the results of his tournament and ran a second tournament with the same rules, this time receiving 63 entries. Even though the entrants knew of TIT FOR TAT's previous strategy for victory, TIT FOR TAT won again; nobody was able to design a strategy that could beat it.

Axelrod then ran an evolutionary tourna-

---

[8]Robert Axelrod, *The Evolution of Cooperation* (New York: Basic Books, 1984).

Figure 6.1 Prisoners' Dilemma Payoff Matrix This matrix shows the payoff in Axelrod's computer tournament. The game is a prisoners' dilemma, in which each player's best short-term strategy is not to cooperate with the other player. But when the game is played many times, both players do better by cooperating with each other. Axelrod found that a TIT FOR TAT strategy, in which the player does this time what the other player did last time, was most effective in providing an incentive for cooperation.

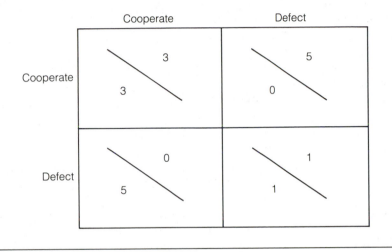

ment in which programs could multiply based on their scores in the previous generation. This meant a high-scoring program in the first generation would have more clones in the next generation than a low-scoring program. In the evolutionary tournament the process continued, with the high-scoring programs increasing their numbers and the low-scoring programs dying out. Eventually, TIT FOR TAT was the dominant (but not the only) strategy left in the tournament.

Implications of Axelrod's Tournament for the Real World

Axelrod's results have some interesting implications for the real world. No rules outside of the payoff matrix were given to people who interacted, so nothing like a government was available to keep people from free riding, yet the dominant strategy, as already noted, was not one that tried to take advantage of other players but rather one that elicited their cooperation. TIT FOR TAT would not cooperate with an uncooperative program, but it was happy to continue cooperating with another program as long as the other was also willing. The implication in the long run was that the way to get ahead (in this game, and perhaps in life) was not to try to take advantage of others but rather to cooperate with them.

TIT FOR TAT employed a very simple strategy, but Axelrod found that it had four important properties that helped it do well in the tournament. First, it was a "nice" strategy, by which Axelrod meant it was never the first to defect. This characteristic was desirable because it gave other players the greatest opportunity to cooperate. Second, by retaliating against defection, it did not allow another strategy to exploit it. TIT FOR TAT was happy to cooperate, but it would retaliate against uncooperative behavior. Third, it was forgiving; if, after defecting, the other strategy tried cooperating again, TIT FOR TAT would cooperate. After retaliating to show that it would not be taken advantage of, TIT FOR TAT would forgive and cooperate again if the other strategy was willing. Finally, it was a very simple strategy, so the other player could easily understand it. If the other player saw that by cooperating both could get 3 points, whereas by not cooperating each would get only 1 point, the other player could figure out that the highest payoff would come from mutual cooperation.

Axelrod's study is interesting because it shows that in at least some circumstances cooperation can emerge as the dominant strategy even when there are no rules forcing players to cooperate. The key to this cooperation is that players can recognize each other and remember their past interactions. People do develop reputations in any type of society, so it might be argued that in the real world the free rider problem might not be as extreme a problem as an abstract discussion implies. For example, on a congested freeway people let other people onto the road even though they do not have to. People stand in line at crowded movies and restaurants rather than push to the front. The fact that we consider exceptions to cooperative behavior to be aberrant behavior shows the extent to which cooperation is accepted as a social norm. Just because there could be a free rider problem in the real world does not necessarily imply that people

will not tend to cooperate for the good of the group.

The Results of Human Action but Not of Human Design

Axelrod's tournaments suggest that cooperation can evolve in a social setting without explicitly designing mechanisms to foster cooperation. Indeed, the market economy represents a good example of the emergence of cooperation as a result of human action but not of human design—nobody planned out the operation of a market economy; it just evolved. Furthermore, when centrally planned economies have tried to design a superior economic system, the results have always fallen short of market economies in similar circumstances. Social institutions can evolve in much the same way as biological species, and efficient characteristics of social systems thrive and grow while inefficient characteristics die out.

This is the theme of a great deal of work done by Nobel Prize-winning economist Friedrich A. Hayek.[9] Hayek emphasizes that in trying to plan efficient institutions, the planners will always lack the specialized knowledge unique to each individual in the economy. Thus, efforts to replace existing institutions with institutions designed to be "bet-

---

[9]See, for example, Hayek's three-volume work *Law, Legislation, and Liberty* (Chicago: University of Chicago Press, 1973, 1976, 1979). The theme that is being considered here is explored in Friedrich A. Hayek, "The Results of Human Action but Not of Human Design," *Studies in Philosophy, Politics, and Economics* (Chicago: University of Chicago Press, 1967), ch. 6. For the reader interested in Hayek's work along these lines, his article "The Use of Knowledge in Society," *American Economic Review* 35, no. 4 (Sept. 1945), pp. 519–530, is highly recommended.

ter" will not take advantage of the vast amount of information held by every individual in the society. Institutions evolve over time as a result of human action but not of human design, and they will contain features that central planners do not understand and that, perhaps, nobody understands. But existing institutions are efficient, because efficient characteristics have evolved over time while inefficient characteristics have been weeded out. Any attempt to design social institutions will not be able to incorporate these results of human action but not of human design, and perhaps more significantly, newly designed institutions may replace old institutions that have unrecognized efficiency characteristics.

The lesson here is that special care must be taken in trying to design social policy to deal with cases in which the market appears to be less than perfectly efficient; the tendency is to seek government intervention to address perceived problems. Consider Axelrod's prisoners' dilemma game. In the real world the government might have been empowered to alleviate the inefficiency inherent in a prisoners' dilemma situation, but as Axelrod's tournament results suggest, cooperation might evolve as a result of human action, but not of human design, if the government does not intervene. Therefore, we should be cautious in trying to design new and better institutions to replace the ones we have.

Demand-Revealing Mechanisms

This caution should not inhibit us from studying the characteristics of alternative institutions; economists have done just that in attempting to design demand-revealing techniques that provide individuals with the incentive to express their true preferences. Recall that the free rider problem, and related problems (such as the holdout problem and other types of strategic behavior), result from individuals having strategic reasons for not revealing their true preferences. Although such behavior may benefit the individual, the fact that everyone shares the same incentives can tend to cause inefficiencies in collective activities. Collective undertakings can be more efficient if demand-revealing mechanisms are employed to get each individual to reveal his or her true preference. Some examples can illustrate how these mechanisms operate.

The Mean Versus the Median

Consider a case in which students vote on the thermostat setting in the classroom. Each student writes down the temperature he or she prefers, and the ballots are collected and tallied. This example will consider two possible methods of tabulating the votes. First, the average temperature could be selected by adding up the temperatures voted for and dividing by the number of ballots. Second, the median temperature could be selected by arraying the ballots from highest to lowest and choosing the temperature in the middle.

If the average temperature is used, each voter has an incentive to strategically misstate his or her preference if the voter feels that the preference will be different from the average. For example, assume that you like a temperature of 68 degrees but believe that most

Table 6.1 Demand Revelation with Two Options and Three Voters

	VALUE OF OPTION IN DOLLARS		
Voter	A	B	Tax
X	50		30
Y		70	0
Z	40	—	20
Total value	90	70	

people honestly prefer, on the average, a temperature of around 74 degrees. In this case you can bring down the average by strategically misstating your preference and casting a ballot for, say, 50 degrees. Indeed, all voters, whether they prefer the room to be relatively cold or relatively hot, could employ such a strategy. Clearly, this method of voting does not give voters an incentive to reveal their true preferences.

Now consider the alternative of taking the median preference. Again, assume that you prefer a temperature of 68 degrees but think that the median voter will prefer 74 degrees. In this case the outcome of the vote is not affected whether you cast a ballot for 68 degrees or 50 degrees or any other temperature below the median. The only effect that your ballot has on the outcome of the election is whether it is above or below the median, so there is no incentive to misstate your preference. In short, selecting the median vote provides a motive for all voters to vote their true preferences, whereas selecting the average vote does not.[10]

The Clarke Tax—A Discrete Case

Selection of the median vote gives voters an incentive to reveal their true preferences, but it does not necessarily produce a Pareto optimal result. There is a method by which an incentive can be provided for voters to reveal their true preferences and for the election system to choose the optimal result.[11] The system is slightly more complicated than simple majority rule.

Table 6.1 illustrates a situation in which three individuals—X, Y, and Z—are asked to vote either for option A or for option B in an election. The options can be thought of as, say, two candidates running for office. In this system voters are asked to do more than simply state which option they prefer; they are also asked to state how much money they would be willing to pay to have their most preferred option selected over the alternative. They will not necessarily have to pay this amount, although, as will be explained, under some circumstances they might have to.

Assume for the moment that voters reveal their true preferences, as expressed in Table 6.1. Voter X prefers option A and is willing to pay as much as $50 to have option A chosen over option B. Voter Y prefers option B by a $70 margin, and voter Z prefers option A by $40. When the votes are added up, option A wins by $90 to $70.

In order to give voters an incentive to reveal their true preferences, they may have to pay a

---

[10]This system of selecting the median vote was actually used for a time in voting for tax rates for schools in Florida school districts. For more discussion on the theory of median voting and a description of the sys-

tem actually used in Florida, see R. G. Holcombe, "The Florida System: A Bowen Equilibrium Referendum Process," *National Tax Journal* 30 (March 1977), pp. 77–84.

[11]This material is based on a demand revelation system developed in Edward H. Clarke, "Multipart Pricing of Public Goods," *Public Choice* 12 (Fall 1971), pp. 17–33. A clearer exposition of Clarke's system can be found in T. Nicolaus Tideman and Gordon Tullock, "A New and Superior Process for Making Social Choices," *Journal of Political Economy* 84 (Dec. 1976), pp. 1145–1160.

Clarke tax (named after the developer of this voting system), which is assessed only on voters whose votes affect the outcome of the election. The tax is calculated as the smallest amount that the voter would have had to have voted in order to change the election's outcome.

If voter X had not voted in the election, option B would have been selected by a $30 margin. Therefore, voter X's vote changed the outcome of the election, and X would have had to have voted $30 to bring option A's vote up to the $70 received by option B. Therefore, voter X is assessed a Clarke tax of $30. By the same logic, voter Z must pay a tax of $20, but because Y's vote did not affect the outcome, Y pays no tax.

The first thing to understand about this tax is that it provides an incentive for all voters to reveal their true preferences. Consider voter X. X would have been willing to pay up to $50 to have option A selected, but X actually had to pay only $30, so X is better off because of the vote. What if X had tried to reduce the potential tax by voting only $40? In this case the final vote would have been $80 to $70, but because of the way that the tax is calculated, the Clarke tax for X still would have been $30. Note that if X had voted $100 or even $1000, the tax would have been the same. If voter X had voted less than $30, then X would not have paid a tax, but option B would have won. Because voter X could state a true preference and have option A win for only $30, X has no incentive to understate that preference.

Likewise, a voter has no incentive to overstate a preference. If a voter's option would have won because of an honest statement of the voter's preference, the tax will be the same no matter how high the vote. But if the voter's option would have lost, the potential Clarke tax will end up being more than the voter would have been willing to pay. For example, voter Y could have misstated a preference of

$100 for option B, and B would have won. However, the Clarke tax would have been $90, or $20 more than the most voter Y actually was willing to pay. With this system voters have an incentive not to overstate or understate their preferences.

The Clarke Tax and Pareto Optimality

This type of election selects the outcome that has the highest dollar value for the voters, and voters will have an incentive to reveal their true preferences. In other words it selects the Pareto optimal outcome, because the Clarke tax has the effect of charging each voter the marginal social cost of his or her action. For example, if only Y and Z are members of the group, option B will have the higher value by $30. Because X is in the group, option A has the higher value, but the inclusion of X's preferences means a net cost of $30 is placed on the remainder of the group. By asking X to pay this cost, X therefore has the incentive to take account of the cost of his or her actions on others in the group.

The Clarke tax functions similarly to a corrective tax on an externality. In being held responsible for the tax, individuals have an incentive to take account of the costs they impose on others. Although in this example voters had discrete options, the same type of voting system can also be used in a continuous case, in which any option along a continuum can be chosen. An example would be voting on the quantity of a publicly provided good to be produced. The continuous case, described in the appendix to this chapter, is more complex, but the principle is the same as in the discrete case. Voters are asked to state their true preferences and then are charged for the marginal social cost that they impose on the rest of the group.

This type of voting system is more complicated than voting systems typically used in the real world, but it is interesting for several reasons. First, it illustrates that, at least in theory, it is possible to design a system that takes away the incentives of strategic behavior and free riding and forces individuals to reveal their true preferences. Second, it provides a mental springboard for considering ways in which a

democratic government might be modified and improved. As previously noted, one should be cautious in altering the results of human action, but political institutions, by contrast, are fundamentally of human design and are constantly subject to modification.

The Normative Basis for Government

In closing this chapter it is worthwhile to note once more that normative issues assume more importance when studying the public sector of the economy than when examining the private sector. Through the collective decision-making institutions of the government, individuals choose what types of activities the government will engage in. Some governments may be run for the benefit of a few individuals, but most governments, including dictatorships and socialist states, claim to be acting in the best interests of the nation's citizens. And in democratic governments citizens as a group have significant input into the actual activities of the government. If a government exists to further the best interests of its citizens, then it is certainly reasonable to ask what those interests are, and how they are to be achieved, even though ultimately the question is a normative one.

In the past few chapters we have dealt with this question in terms of the Pareto criteria. There is a good reason for this, for although the social welfare can be judged in many ways, it is hard to argue that society is not better off if a change improves at least one person's well-being without harming anyone else. And we have extended the Paretian framework to show that a representative democracy is not necessarily inconsistent with the Pareto criteria.

Considering collective activity within the

club model, it is understandable why a group unanimously agrees to some decision rule of less-than-unanimity rule, such as majority rule. Furthermore, it is understandable why a group of more than a few members elects representatives to act in the group's behalf. The decision-making costs involved in having the whole group participate are reduced, and the elected representatives are in a position to specialize in activities related to the group. In short, lower decision-making costs and the benefits of specialization will cause groups to choose representative democracy as a form of government.

Another reason why it is easy to see that individuals could voluntarily choose representative democracy as a form of government is that many groups that are obviously clubs rather than governments also routinely choose this form of organization. Fraternities, tennis clubs, civic groups, and the like all constitute voluntary organizations that are run by representative democracy. The Paretian model can be extended to the coercive activities of government—under some circumstances everyone benefits if all agree to be coerced. This does not mean that the government's activities actually are in the best interests of everybody; it only means that a representative democracy that forces people to abide by its rules is not necessarily outside the bounds of the Paretian model.

Clearly, the government undertakes certain activities that cause some people to incur costs to provide benefits for others; whether the government should take such actions is a normative issue. For example, one might argue that rich but miserly individuals, as members of the society, have an obligation to help those less fortunate than themselves, whether they want to or not. Such an argument requires an interpersonal utility comparison stating that society will be better off, but in the realm of normative economics, people are entitled to make such value judgments. They should recognize, however, that they are making value judgments, and they should articulate what those values are. Furthermore, they should realize that actions based on the more general values of the Pareto criteria are preferable to actions based on applications of interpersonal utility comparisons. At the least, this should be the case if the individual making the judgment places a value on individual freedom; of course, this, too, is a normative question.

Conclusion

Ultimately, what the government should do represents a normative question that must be dealt with in any society that collectively chooses its government's activities. Therefore, it is necessary to examine the types of value judgments that can be made regarding public sector activity to have a complete understanding of public sector economics. Even though most of the material in the previous two chapters has focused on the Pareto criteria, they are in fact relatively weak criteria for deciding when something is in the public interest. Nevertheless, a representative democracy that has the power to force its citizens to obey its rules is not necessarily acting inconsistently with the Pareto criteria. As already noted, individuals might hold values that go well beyond the Pareto criteria. Because there is no way to show that one set of values is better than any other, one cannot object to normative conclusions about economic activities that do not meet the Pareto criteria. Nevertheless, it is important to understand the difference between positive and normative analysis and to recognize what value judgments are being made in such an analysis.

At this point we will set aside these normative issues. The next two chapters provide a strictly positive analysis of the way in which governmental decisions actually are made. Chapter 7 examines issues of public sector demand to see how the individual demands of voters are totaled through elections into an aggregate demand for public sector activity. Chapter 8 evaluates the public sector supply process so that the relationships between public sector supply and demand can be analyzed.

Questions

1. Why does normative analysis play a more significant part in analyzing public sector activities than private sector activities?

2. Explain the problems of free riding and shirking that exist when goods and services are produced collectively. How do these problems lead to inefficiency, and how can government involvement help to overcome them?

3. What is the relationship between the free rider problem, a positive externality, and a collective consumption good? Do the problems caused by them suggest a need for the government involvement rather than market allocation of resources?

4. Explain the social contract theory of the state. How can it be said that individuals in a society are in agreement with the terms of the contract? Is the social contract theory relevant to the real world?

5. What is meant by a procedural theory of justice? Explain the difference between a procedural theory and one that judges outcomes. How could the concept be applied to antitrust law?

6. Explain the strategy of TIT FOR TAT in the prisoners' dilemma game. What characteristics does this strategy have that makes it an effective overall strategy in both the game and the real world?

7. Is it possible that people can agree to being coerced? Explain why or why not, and then consider the implications of such an argument when applied to a government in the real world.

8. Explain how a demand-revealing mechanism works. Do you think that such mechanisms are feasible in a collective group? Under what conditions would you expect them to work best? Under what conditions would you expect them to work least well?

Appendix to Chapter Six
Demand Revelation
with a Continuous Decision

Recall that the demand-revealing mechanism, as described in Chapter 6, provides a method for making a collective decision from discrete options.[1] This appendix applies the same principle to determine the amount of a publicly provided good to produce, which constitutes a continuous choice. As in the discrete case voters have to state their preferences for the various options. In the discrete case voters were assessed a Clarke tax equal to the cost that their choice imposed on all other voters; this also is true for the continuous case. The continuous case is illustrated in Figure 6A.1.

Assume that voters are asked to state their preferences for the good under consideration. The quantity of the good to be produced has yet to be determined, so the voters must state their entire demand curve for the good. For example, individual i has demand curve d_i for the good. Because a single quantity of the good is to be provided to everyone, the total demand for the good is determined by vertically adding everyone's demand, which results in demand curve D. The marginal cost of the good is MC, so the optimal amount of the good to be produced is Q^*, where D intersects MC. Note that the optimal amount of the good can be produced as long as all voters reveal their true demand curves—that is the purpose of the demand-revealing mechanism.

Each voter is assigned some tax price; for example, voter i's assigned tax price is P_i. The system will work no matter what tax price is assigned to any voter because of the use of the Clarke tax, so the tax prices could be assigned arbitrarily. The tax is computed in the continuous case in much the same way as in the discrete case. The outcome is calculated without the voter's vote, and then the voter is charged a tax equal to the marginal social cost imposed on the rest of the group by the individual's vote.

$MC - P_i$ is the marginal cost curve without individual i's share of the cost, and $D - d_i$ is the

[1]Although the example in the text dealt with only two options, any number of options can be considered with the process. See T. Nicolaus Tideman and Gordon Tullock, "A New and Superior Process for Making Social Choices," *Journal of Political Economy* 84 (Dec. 1976), pp. 1145–1160 for a more complete discussion.

Figure 6A.1 Demand Revelation with a Continuous Decision Curve $D-d_i$ is the demand of everyone but individual i, and $MC-P_i$ is the marginal cost of the good minus individual i's tax share. By including individual i's preferences, the outcome is altered from Q' to Q^*, imposing a cost on everyone else equal to the shaded triangle. This shaded triangle is the amount of the Clarke tax, which must be charged to the individual in order to elicit an honest response about the individual's demand for the good.

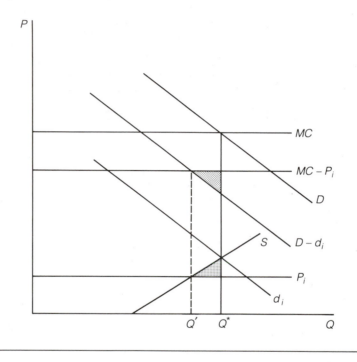

total demand for the good minus individual i's demand. Without individual i in the process, output would have been Q'. Therefore, individual i is charged a Clarke tax equal to the marginal social cost of including his preference, which causes the output to be Q^* rather than Q'.

The tax is calculated by constructing a synthetic supply schedule for the individual, which is the marginal cost curve minus everyone else's demand, or $MC-(D-d_i)$; that curve is labeled S. In other words Curve S

depicts the cost of the good minus its value to everyone else, or the net cost to all other individuals. Because the individual is already paying P_i as a share of the cost, the marginal social cost of individual i's preference will be the difference between the individual's price and the net cost to everyone else, which is the difference between S and P_i. That difference is shown by the lower shaded triangle, so the size of the shaded triangle gives the amount of the Clarke tax.

The upper shaded triangle and the lower

shaded triangle are the same size and represent two different ways of looking at the Clarke tax in the continuous case. Looking at the upper triangle, the individual pays a tax equal to the difference between everyone else's demand for the good and everyone else's cost. Although illustrating the principle is a bit more complicated in the continuous case, the principle is the same: The individual is charged a tax equal to the marginal social cost imposed on everyone else.

Is the individual better off voting and paying the tax? Just as in the discrete case, the answer is yes. The value of voting to change the outcome from Q' to $Q*$ is the area under the individual's demand curve, d_i, but the cost is the area under the synthetic supply curve, S, between Q' and $Q*$. Because up to $Q*$ the demand curve lies above the synthetic supply curve, the individual is better off by an amount equal to the difference in the two areas. Note that just as in the discrete case, though, the individual would not benefit from misstating preferences. The individual has an incentive to reveal his true preferences, and because everybody shares the same incentives, the market demand curve can be calculated and the optimal output produced.

Demand-revealing mechanisms such as this one are interesting theoretical devices because they enable the analyst to see how individuals can be given the incentive to reveal their true preferences for collectively produced goods. However, from a practical standpoint they are not quite so useful. For one thing, individuals must know quite a bit about their preferences to cast a vote. In typical voting systems voters must indicate simply which option they like the best. But with demand-revealing mechanisms they must state how much more they like one option than another, and in the continuous case this means being able to reveal one's entire demand curve. Voters must be able to accurately cast a complex ballot for the system to work as well in practice as it does in theory.

Another problem with the system described here is that it is subject to manipulation by coalitions.[2] Furthermore, when many voters vote, each will have only a small effect on the outcome, meaning that there is little incentive to cast an informed ballot. Though this is a problem with voting systems in general, it applies especially to the demand-revealing process.

Perhaps the major criticism of this type of system, however, is that it runs counter to the generally accepted political norm of one person—one vote. Because individuals cast ballots indicating the value of one option over another, individuals with greater wealth will be willing to express more intense preferences and thus will have an undue influence on the outcomes of such elections. This is no different than in any other market; we are not surprised to see rich people driving expensive cars and living in expensive houses while poor people drive inexpensive cars and live in modest houses. However, we may like it even less if wealthier people have more clout at the ballot box, too.

---

[2]The coalition problem is discussed in Tideman and Tullock, "A New and Superior Process . . . ," referenced earlier.

CHAPTER SEVEN

Public Sector Demand

To this point we have discussed why government activity can be desirable, but we have not examined the way in which a government acts, nor how a government makes its decisions. In previous chapters we noted the inherent efficiency of resource allocation through the market, but we also observed that, for several reasons, the market does not always allocate resources perfectly, and that in those cases it may be desirable to allocate resources through the public sector. Furthermore, we explained why representative democracy is a good mechanism for making collective decisions when large groups are involved. Chapter 7 is the first of several chapters that study the results of the public sector decision-making process. We examine the way in which the preferences of individual voters are translated through majority rule into the demand for public sector output. And, along with Chapter 8, which deals with public sector supply, we examine the supply and demand for public sector output in much the same way that microeconomic theory explains the supply and demand process in the private sector of the economy.

The logical place to start is with an examination of majority rule decision making, because majority rule decisions comprise the foundation of democratic governments. There are several different ways of making majority rule decisions, but they all share an important feature. In each case the preference of the median voter is critical in determining the outcome of a majority rule election. This is called the *median voter model*. As will be seen, several different models exist, but they all arrive at the median voter result.

The Median Voter Model

The median voter model examines decisions made by majority rule and concludes that a majority rule voting system will select the outcome most preferred by the median voter. A majority rule decision can be made in a number of ways, but the median voter model ap-

Figure 7.1 The Median Voter Model The median voter is the voter whose demand is in the middle of all other voters. This figure is used to demonstrate several circumstances under which majority rule decisions choose the outcome most preferred by the median voter.

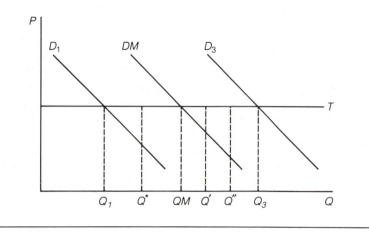

plies to a fairly general set of majority rule election processes. Three common majority rule voting institutions are discussed here.

The Committee Process

First, consider the case in which a majority rule decision is to be made by a committee of three individuals, who are trying to decide how much of a collective consumption good should be produced.[1] The preferences of the three individuals are depicted in Figure 7.1 as demand curves D_1, DM, and D_3, where DM is the demand curve of the median voter, that is, the voter whose preferences are in the middle. Individual D_1 has a lower demand for the good than the median, and individual D_3 has a higher demand than the median. T represents the tax price per unit that must be paid

for the good to be produced. In this example everybody pays the same price per unit—T. Given their demands and the tax price the voters are faced with, individual D_1 most prefers level of output Q_1, individual DM most prefers QM, and individual D_3 most prefers Q_3.

In this committee process any individual may make a motion to produce any level of the good, and any other individual may offer a counter motion. A vote is then taken between the motions. The motion that gets a majority of the votes is the standing motion, and anyone else is free to propose another counter motion, at which time another vote is taken. This process can continue as long as there are motions to be considered, with individuals voting for the motion closest to their own most preferred outcome.

For example, individual D_3 might propose that Q_3 be produced, that being D_3's most preferred level of output, and individual DM might then propose a counter motion that QM be produced. Individual D_3 will vote for

[1]This example follows along the lines of a model developed in Duncan Black, *The Theory of Committees and Elections* (Cambridge: Cambridge University Press, 1958).

Q_3, while individual DM will vote for QM. Because QM is closer to D_1's most preferred level of output than Q_3, D_1 will vote for QM as well, and QM will defeat Q_3 by a vote of two to one. Now, with QM on the floor, individual D_1 can propose Q_1, but only D_1 will vote for Q_1, because, according to the reasoning given above, DM and D_3 will vote for QM. Thus, QM will win again.

In fact, there is no possible motion that can beat QM. Individual DM will always vote for QM, and if the counter motion is above QM, individual D_1 will prefer QM to the counter motion, whereas if the motion is below QM, individual D_3 will vote for QM rather than for the counter motion. Thus, QM will always defeat any counter motion on either side of QM. The significance of QM is that it represents the preference of the median voter. The motion that wins the vote of the median voter will also win all votes to one side of the median and therefore have the majority needed to win the election. This example is constructed with only one voter on either side of the median, but the reader should have little trouble demonstrating that the same result will hold no matter how many voters there are on either side of the median. As long as there is an equal number of voters on either side of the DM, then the committee process will choose QM by majority rule.

A Referendum Model

Not all elections are voted on by committees, however. For some issues, such as school financing in many states, referenda are held where voters determine the amount they want to spend on a collective consumption good, which indicates the quantity to be produced. Consider once again the median voter model in Figure 7.1. This time, a referendum is being held proposing to produce a certain amount of a given good. If the referendum is defeated, then another referendum will be

held, this time proposing a marginally smaller amount of the good, and so on until some level of output is approved by a majority. Assume that in the first referendum, Q_3 is proposed. Individual D_3 will vote for Q_3, but DM and D_1 will vote against Q_3, preferring to wait and vote for a smaller amount. In the next referendum Q' is proposed. Once again, D_3 will favor Q', but the other two voters will vote against Q', waiting for a smaller amount to be proposed. The same result will occur when Q'' is proposed, for the same reason. But when QM is proposed, D_3 will again vote in favor, and this time DM will also vote in favor, so output QM will be approved by majority rule. Thus, in this referendum setting the outcome most preferred by the median voter is the one chosen by majority rule.

The referendum quantity can also be determined by gradually increasing the amount to be voted on. Assume that initially a small amount of the good is produced and referenda held to approve marginal increases in the amount of the good to be produced. The reader can see that a majority will approve of Q_1. The majority will also vote for an increase from Q_1 to Q^*, and an increase from Q^* to QM, but only D_3 will vote for a further increase to Q''. Thus, once again, QM, the outcome most preferred by the median voter, will be chosen by majority rule.[2]

The Median Voter in a Representative Democracy

In a representative democracy voters typically do not have the opportunity to vote directly on the level of output to be produced in the

---

[2]This referendum setting of the median voter model was developed in Howard R. Bowen, "The Interpretation of Voting in the Allocation of Economic Resources," *Quarterly Journal of Economics* 58 (Nov. 1943), pp. 27–48. The median voter equilibrium is sometimes referred to as a Bowen equilibrium.

public sector. Rather, they elect representatives by majority rule, and the elected representatives make those decisions. Thus, voters choose the representative who most closely reflects their views. Consider again the three voters in Figure 7.1, but this time instead of directly voting on the level of output to produce, they are voting for one of two representatives who argue for different levels of output of the public sector good to be produced.

Assume that initially the two candidates take extreme positions. One candidate prefers a small level of government spending and so proposes to produce Q_1, whereas the other candidate prefers a larger government and so proposes Q_3. The first candidate will win the vote of D_1 and the second candidate will win the vote of D_3, so the outcome of the election will depend on which way the median voter votes. The candidate proposing Q_3 will try to win the median voter's vote by moving closer to the median voter's most preferred outcome. By proposing Q' the candidate will be closer to the median than the candidate pro-

posing Q_1 and will gain the vote of DM and D_3. This strategy invites a counter strategy, though. The candidate proposing Q_1 can modify the platform to propose Q^*, which will still be preferred by D_1 but will be closer to the median than Q'; thus, this candidate will gain the median voter's vote. But this invites yet another counter strategy by the candidate proposing Q', who will now propose Q'' to move closer to the median.

The strategy will continue until the two candidates propose platforms converging on QM, because the candidate who wins the median vote will also win all votes to one side of the median and so will win the election.[3] Once again, in representative democracy the outcome most preferred by the median voter will be the outcome selected by majority rule. The three different types of majority rule elections examined here illustrate that the median voter model is really several different models, in all of which the outcome most preferred by the median voter will be the outcome selected by majority rule.

Representative Democracy

The outcome of the median voter model can be generalized to an election setting with any number of voters as long as the issues can be ranked on a single continuum and as long as voters always prefer outcomes closer to their most preferred outcome to outcomes farther away. Note that political candidates are frequently viewed on a continuum from political left to political right.

The Decisive Median Voter

This is illustrated in Figure 7.2, where the curve represents a density function of voters—the higher the curve, the more voters

prefer the outcome at that point. The median voter outcome in this setting will be identical to the results in the previous section. If a right-wing candidate selects platform R_1, then the left-wing candidate can select platform L_1, closer to the median, and gain the median vote and all votes to the left of the median. As a counter strategy the right-wing candidate

---

[3]This type of median voter model was originally discussed in Harold Hotelling, "Stability in Competition," *Economic Journal* 39 (March 1929), pp. 41–57. The model was further developed in Anthony Downs's major work, *An Economic Theory of Democracy* (New York: Harper & Row, 1957).

Figure 7.2 A Model of Representative Democracy If political issues can be expressed in a continuum from political left to political right, the candidate who wins the median vote will win all votes to one side of the election and will win the election. This explains why all candidates tend to look alike. It also explains why extreme candidates cannot win elections. If a new party arose to one side of the median, it would split the votes with the other party on that side, so the party would not be viable; thus, the median voter model also explains why two will be the equilibrium number of political parties in a winner-take-all representative democracy.

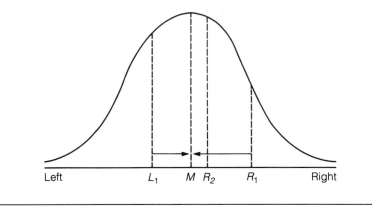

Left L_1 M R_2 R_1 Right

can adjust the platform from R_1 to R_2, closer to the median, but this will provoke a counter move from the left-wing candidate toward the median, until both candidates end up proposing M. Again, majority rule ends up selecting the outcome most preferred by the median voter.

Although the median voter model is presented in fairly abstract terms here, the concept is well understood by politicians, who frequently find themselves, in the interest of political survival, modifying their stands on issues to move toward the median. For example, former President Nixon, in response to vocal protests about some of his actions, claimed to be aiming his policies at the "silent majority" rather than the vocal minority. Nixon's silent majority is the equivalent of our median voter; Nixon's overwhelming reelection victory in 1972 provides some casual evi-

dence for his claim, and for the median voter model in general.

Candidates Tend to Adopt Similar Platforms

Application of the median voter model lends some insight into many aspects of the political process. Frequently, voters lament that they really do not have a choice, because the candidates all seem alike. This sentiment was expressed regarding Nixon and Humphrey in the 1968 presidential election, and regarding Ford and Carter in the 1976 election. Both elections were close, suggesting that in each case the candidates were successful in their appeals to the median voter. The median voter model readily explains this situation, because to win an election candidates must aim their platforms at the median voter. If both candidates are successful, voters should have trouble differentiating the platforms of the candidates.

Extreme Candidates

The median voter model also suggests that extreme candidates cannot win elections. For example, if one candidate chooses platform M in Figure 7.2 while the other chooses an extreme platform at R_1, then the candidate aiming at the median should win the election by a wide margin. Goldwater in 1964 and McGovern in 1972 were both viewed as extreme candidates, and as the median voter model suggests will happen, both lost by a landslide. Likewise, whereas Carter and Ford appeared similar to voters in 1976 and had a close race, Reagan was clearly differentiated from both Carter in 1980 and Mondale in 1984, and Reagan won both elections by comfortable margins. In terms of the median voter model Reagan appears to have selected a platform close to the median, whereas his opponents were some distance from the median.

One might raise legitimate questions about the application of the median voter model to elections; after all, political platforms are but one factor in the public's perception of candidates. For example, the decisive victories of Reagan in 1980 and 1984 perhaps were based on his charismatic image and his ability as a speaker rather than on his political platform per se. However, it is interesting to note that when voters perceive no substantial differences between the candidates, as with Nixon and Humphrey in 1968 and with Carter and Ford in 1976, the elections tend to be close. The landslide victories noted above have occurred when the candidates in the election have clearly differentiated themselves.

Mondale's strongest challenger for the Democratic nomination in 1984 was Gary Hart, who recognized Mondale's popularity with the Democrats. Hart argued that he should be nominated because, despite that popularity, Mondale would not do as well against Reagan as he would. Certainly we cannot test the veracity of Hart's claim. But his argument that although Mondale was closer to the median of the Democratic voters, he was closer to the median of the total population of voters, is worth considering in light of Mondale's crushing defeat.

The median voter model, like economic models in general, represents a very simple depiction of a complex world, and certainly there are factors other than the platforms of candidates that determine the outcomes of elections. Yet the median voter model seems to have a great deal of descriptive power, in addition to its theoretical applications. If nothing else, arguments like Hart's, and like Nixon's claim of catering to the silent majority, show that politicians themselves view the election process from within the median voter framework.

The Equilibrium Number of Political Parties

An interesting phenomenon can be observed in democracies where a single candidate is chosen in each election by majority rule. The political systems in these democracies tend to be two-party systems, even though there are no restrictions on the number of parties that can exist. In this type of democracy, two parties naturally emerge as the equilibrium number of political parties. This can be explained by referring again to Figure 7.2.

Consider a two-party system in which both parties follow the optimal strategy and have platforms near M. Now introduce a third party, which must be on one side of M or the other; assume that the third party takes platform R_1. In this case the party to the right of M will have to split the votes to the right of M with the new party, meaning that the party to the left of M will get far more votes than either of the other parties. Neither of the parties to the right of M can hope to get enough votes to win an election, so they will cease to be viable political parties. Because political parties function to get their candidates elected, this situation cannot persist. Either one of the parties to the right of M will have to go out of business or the two parties will have to merge so that one of them can elect candidates. Thus, in a winner-take-all democracy the equilibrium number of political parties is two. In American politics, even though no laws prevent new parties from emerging, the two dominant parties will tend either to absorb small third parties or put them out of business.

To summarize, the median voter model is quite descriptive of majority rule elections. The model can be demonstrated in a committee setting, or when a referendum is held, or even for a representative democracy. And it illuminates why, in democratic politics, all candidates tend to look alike, and why, when they differ, the candidate perceived as extreme cannot win an election. Furthermore, it explains why two constitutes the equilibrium number of political parties in a representative democracy. However, there are sometimes impediments to the operation of a majority rule election as described by the median voter model. The first such situation that warrants discussion is the cyclical majority.

The Cyclical Majority

Two of the basic assumptions of the median voter model are that the alternatives to be voted on can be ranked on a single-dimensional continuum and that every individual prefers outcomes closer to his or her most preferred outcome to outcomes farther away. Although these assumptions are not necessary to produce the median voter outcome, when they are violated the possibility exists that the median voter's most preferred outcome will not be chosen by majority rule. The most widely discussed problem in this regard is that of the *cyclical majority*, in which no one outcome will dominate all others.[4]

For example, consider a situation in which the amount of money to be spent on the public school system is to be voted on. As in Figure 7.1, there are three voters, who prefer a high,

middle, and low amount of expenditures, respectively. As long as voters prefer outcomes closer to their first preference to outcomes farther away, the median voter model explains the outcome of the election.

To illustrate the cyclical majority, assume that the first voter prefers low expenditures to a middle level, and a middle level to high expenditures. This is shown in Table 7.1, where voter 1's preferences are listed in their rank order, with L (low) above M (middle) and M above H (high). Voter 2 prefers a middle level of expenditures but would rather have high expenditures than low expenditures. Both voter 1 and voter 2 have preferences that are consistent with the median voter model outcome. Voter 3 prefers a high level of expenditures, but if a high level is not approved, she will send her children to private schools and so will prefer a low level of expenditures to reduce her tax bill. This voter's least preferred outcome is the middle level, because she will be paying more taxes than at

---

[4]The cyclical majority problem is sometimes called the Arrow problem because it was discussed in Kenneth J. Arrow's famous book, *Social Choice and Individual Values* (New Haven: Yale University Press, 1951), ch. 1.

Table 7.1 The Cyclical Majority		
VOTER		
1	2	3
L	M	H
M	H	L
H	L	M

Table 7.2 A Cyclical Majority		
VOTER		
1	2	3
Ford	Reagan	Carter
Reagan	Carter	Ford
Carter	Ford	Reagan

the low level but will still choose to send her children to private school. Voter 3's preferences are therefore ordered H, L, M.

What if the school budget is determined by majority rule in a committee-type procedure? If L is considered against M, then L will be favored by voters 1 and 3 and will win the election. If L is considered against H, H will be favored by voters 2 and 3 and will win. But if H is considered against M, M will be favored by voters 1 and 2 and will win. Thus, according to majority rule L beats M, H beats L, and M beats H. In this case no single outcome can defeat all the others, so there is no median voter outcome as in the previous section.

Single-Peaked Preferences

The reason why the cyclical majority outcome arises is because voter 3's preferences do not satisfy the assumption that outcomes farther away from the voter's first preference are preferred less than closer outcomes. Although voter 1 most prefers a high level of spending, that voter also prefers a low level to a middle level. When a voter prefers alternatives less as they move farther away from the voter's first preference, this is called *single-peaked preferences*. In this example, because voter 3 does not have single-peaked preferences, the cyclical majority problem arises. Note, however, that although the absence of single-peaked preferences may produce a cyclical majority, it does not necessarily have to do so. For ex-

ample, leaving voter 3's preferences as they are in Table 7.1, look at the outcome if voter 1's preferences were H, M, L. In this case outcome H would defeat all other alternatives even though one voter does not have single-peaked preferences. Thus, multiple-peaked preferences may generate a cyclical majority, but they will not necessarily do so.

Cycles and the Primary System

Consider another example of the cyclical majority. When campaigning in 1976, Reagan urged Republicans to nominate him as their presidential candidate because, he said, he could defeat President Carter, whereas Ford would not be able to. However, Ford defeated Reagan in the primaries to become the Republican nominee, and as Reagan predicted, Ford lost to Carter in the general election. Ford did not run in 1980, and Reagan was nominated and went on to defeat Carter in the presidential election. Thus, Ford can beat Reagan, Carter can beat Ford, and Reagan can beat Carter.

This is illustrated in Table 7.2, where again the preferences of three voters are listed in ranking order. As the table indicates, if any two candidates enter a runoff, or primary, and the winner of the runoff then runs against the third candidate, the third candidate will win the election. Thus, with the winner of Reagan-Ford running against Carter, Carter would win.

Of course, many things happened in the intervening years from 1976 to 1980, and Reagan might not have beaten Carter if they had competed in 1976. Likewise, Ford might have beaten Carter in a 1980 rematch, or Ford might not even have been nominated. This historical example may or may not hold true because of the changes that occurred from 1976 to 1980, but the real purpose of the example is to show the effect that the primary system could have on an election outcome if preferences did exhibit cycles.

Given the potential for the cyclical majority problem, it is apparent that when the problem arises, the winner of the election will be determined by the order in which the choices are presented to the voters.[5] The preferences listed in Table 7.2 would produce the cyclical majority just described for Ford, Reagan, and Carter. A runoff between Ford and Reagan for the Republican nomination would enable Carter to win the general election, but if Reagan and Carter had a runoff, Ford would defeat the winner, and if Carter and Ford had a runoff, Reagan would win. Quite clearly, the primary system is a system for deciding the order in which candidates will compete with each other. If preferences are cyclical, then the winner of the general election may be chosen as a result of the order in which the candidates compete rather than because voters prefer that candidate to any other candidate.

Information and Incentives

The cyclical majority represents but one of the factors that sometimes interfere with the median voter model's smooth operation. Perhaps a more serious problem concerns the incentives to become informed and politically active in a representative government. Although some people are motivated to become informed about some political issues, most people are not. The result is that those who are better informed about particular issues tend to be more influential on those issues.

Voters lack an incentive to become informed about political issues because the individual voter's vote is unlikely to affect the outcome of an election. Nor is an individual voter's opinion on any issue likely to have any effect on the issue's outcome. In this sense voters are rationally ignorant of most political issues. By contrast, special interests do have an incentive to become informed about political issues that affect them directly, with the result that special interests have an undue influence on political decisions. Some discussion about the rational ignorance of most voters and the influence of special interests will clarify these points.

Rational Ignorance of Voters

When the incentive structure of the public sector decision-making process is examined, it is apparent that the general public has little incentive to become informed about political issues. Voters may collect some political information just because they are interested in keeping abreast of current events, but any information they collect will have virtually no bearing on the outcome of any political issue.

Consider casting a vote in an election. Every voter knows that an election will never be de-

---

[5]Gordon Tullock, "Why So Much Stability?" *Public Choice* 37, no. 2 (1982), pp. 189–202, discusses the cycle problem as it has been portrayed by economists and political scientists since Arrow's presentation of the problem.

termined by one vote. At the national level even the closest elections will be won by thousands of votes, so each individual voter knows that he or she will never cast the decisive vote. Even though the result of an election is decided by all of the votes taken together, no one individual vote will affect the outcome. For example, for a voter to cast the deciding vote in a presidential election, the following improbable scenario would have to take place. The electoral vote would have to be nearly tied, not taking into account the electoral votes from the voter's state, and the state vote would have to be within one vote. The likelihood of that happening is minuscule.

This implies that no individual voter has much of an incentive to become well informed about the candidates. Although most voters will be aware of the general characteristics of a candidate's platform, they will tend to be ignorant about the details of a candidate's proposals for foreign policy, social security, military spending, and so on. Each voter knows that his or her individual preferences are not likely to have any effect on, say, the level of support for NATO, cuts in social security benefits, or military hardware procurements. Therefore, there is not much point in collecting such information.

The typical counter argument to this is that there are thousands (or more) of other people who share the same views as any particular voter, and if they all vote, they can determine the outcome of the election, affect foreign policy, and so forth. But the point is that it takes thousands of people, not just one, and each individual has an incentive to free ride and allow others to be informed voters. The result is that voters collect political information only for their own personal interests, preferring to be rationally ignorant.[6]

---

[6]This problem of rational ignorance in political matters is noted in Downs, *An Economic Theory of Democracy* (New York: Harper & Row, 1957).

Indeed, some people do follow politics in much the same way other people follow sports, collecting a great deal of information from television, newspapers, magazines, and so on, while aware that ultimately they will have little impact on the outcome. People also vote because they feel a civic responsibility or because they enjoy participating in the political process. But again, knowing that their individual votes will have no effect on the election, they have little incentive to become informed about the issues in any detail.

Special Interests

By contrast, special interests have an incentive to become informed about the specific political programs that can potentially provide them with concentrated benefits. For example, most voters may not know how their representatives voted on the most recent legislation aimed at tobacco farmers, but the Tobacco Institute knows. The reason is that a program to provide millions of dollars in support to tobacco farmers will cost each individual voter only a few tax dollars. Even if the individual voter spent the time and effort to become informed about the issue, the voter's opinion would not be likely to sway a representative, nor would the representative be likely to sway the rest of Congress to change the legislation. And even if the voter were successful, that voter would save only a few tax dollars as a result. It is just not worth the effort.

However, the Tobacco Institute certainly will be well aware of such legislation because a few tax dollars from each taxpayer can mean millions of dollars to the tobacco farmers, which gives them a large incentive to become informed about these government programs. Indeed, special interest groups go to great lengths to make sure that their representatives know their views and that they have campaign dollars and the votes of constituents who share their views. These special interests will be rationally ignorant about most political programs, but they will be very well informed about political issues that relate to their special interests. In general, special interests profit by having the government spend money on them or pass favorable regulations. Many voters will spend a few dollars for the special interest, but most of the voters will be rationally ignorant of the fact. Meanwhile, special interests will receive the concentrated benefits that result from the contributions of the large number of taxpayers.

Special Interests Versus the Public Interest

The result is a government in which most voters are rationally ignorant on most issues whereas special interests are well informed. Special interests promise to deliver votes and contributions to elected officials who support their positions, which gives representatives strong incentives to yield to the desires of the special interests. This is true whether the representative is a self-serving and greedy political manipulator or the most public-spirited citizen imaginable. The civic-minded representative can serve the public only if reelected, and to get reelected, the representative must gather more political support than the competition. With special interests carefully evaluating each representative's voting record in their specific areas, and with most voters being rationally ignorant, the incentive structure is set up such that the representative is motivated to favor special interest legislation over legislation benefiting the general public.

Because information is costly to obtain, many people for whom the information has low value will not obtain as much of it as they would if it were costless. The situation is analogous to some of the property rights problems examined in Chapter 4. Recall that with a relatively small group, externalities can be inter-

nalized by voluntary group agreements. With large groups, however, the information and bargaining necessary to internalize the externality generate such high transaction costs that voluntary agreements become infeasible. People simply do not have the incentive to become informed. The result is a government that tends to favor special interests.[7]

To the extent that the information problems of rational ignorance, coupled with special interests, affect political outcomes, the median voter model is not as descriptive of the actual results of democratic decision making as previously suggested. The politician still directs policies at the median voter, but the median voter's demand for public sector output is affected by the voter's rational ignorance. If the individual actually were able to choose public policy as an individual, the voter would have an incentive to be more fully informed, and the median voter's demands would represent an expression of the general public interest rather than the effects of rational ignorance. The implications of the rational ignorance of most voters, coupled with the effects of special interests, will be discussed in more detail in Chapter 8.

The Demand for Immediate Results in Politics

Another problem related to the rational ignorance of the general public is the tendency of the government to follow shortsighted policies rather than policies that provide long-run benefits for the nation. Voters tend to give incumbent politicians credit when the nation is prospering whether the politicians are responsible or not. Likewise, politicians tend to be blamed for negative occurrences whether

---

[7]These issues are discussed at greater length in R. G. Holcombe, *An Economic Analysis of Democracy* (Carbondale: Southern Illinois University Press, 1985).

they are at fault or not. For instance, Hoover's name is often linked with the onset of the Great Depression, even though most people agree that the Depression was brought on by factors beyond his control. Kennedy's victory over Nixon in the 1960 presidential election is often perceived as the result of a recession, for which Nixon, because he was vice president, was held partly responsible. Ronald Reagan's landslide victory over Carter in 1980 stemmed in large part from general dissatisfaction with the performance of the economy, but by 1982 Reagan himself was experiencing political difficulty because of the severe recession. By 1984 the economy was making a strong recovery, and Reagan again won a landslide election.

Are election results really influenced by economic conditions at the time of the election, as the evidence seems to suggest?[8] Even if politicians only think that they may be, certainly they have an incentive to manipulate the economy to make things look good before an election. They can accomplish this in a number of ways. Through monetary and fiscal policy they can try to improve the macroeconomic condition of the economy. Also, prior to an election they can promise government programs and regulations that will benefit special interests. The special interests will recognize the positive effects at the time the

programs are announced, but the true costs of such promises typically will not show up until well after the election.

Such promises to special interests, and the monetary and fiscal policy manipulations that make the economy look good before an election, are examples of the general principle that politicians have an incentive to pursue short-run policies. Often, campaign promises and economic policy measures reflect a greater awareness of the next election than of the long-run best interests of the nation. Because politicians must always be concerned with winning the upcoming election in order to keep their jobs, public policies will necessarily tend to be shortsighted.

This conclusion is simply the result of examining the incentive structure facing politicians and in no way is intended to imply that politicians are any worse (or better) than anyone else. Self-serving politicians, of course, will try to manipulate programs for their own benefit, but even the most well meaning and honorable politicians can keep their jobs only if they are reelected. Therefore, they must be concerned about the effects that their proposals will have on their reelection bids. And pursuing long-run policies that do not have easily recognizable short-run benefits may result in someone else being elected and taking credit for the long-run benefits when they do occur.

Public Sector Demand in Theory and in the Real World

Recall that in terms of externalities and public goods, the market does not allocate resources efficiently because people follow their own

self-interests rather than act in the public interest. Politicians are just as likely to act in their own self-interests as those in the private

---

[8]There is an extensive literature on the political business cycle. For some examples, see William D. Nordhaus, "The Political Business Cycle," *Review of Economic Studies* 42 (April 1975), pp. 169–190, C. Duncan MacRae, "A

Political Model of the Business Cycle," *Journal of Political Economy* 85 (April 1977), pp. 239–263, and Bruno S. Frey, "Politico-Economic Models and Cycles," *Journal of Public Economics* 9 (April 1978), pp. 203–220.

sector; in this sense the problems posed by special interests and shortsighted policies in the public sector are analogous to the problems of externalities, collective consumption goods, and poorly defined property rights in the private sector. In both the public and the private sectors, resources are not allocated as efficiently as they might ideally be. But just because the models are not perfectly descriptive of the real world does not mean that they cannot lend some insight into the political allocation of economic resources.

The Median Voter Model and Political Competition

In economic models of market structure, the model of pure competition presents an extreme view of the way in which a competitive market allocates resources. In the public sector the median voter model plays the same role as the competitive model in the private sector. Both models represent idealized depictions of how resources are allocated, but whereas the competitive model deals with economic competition, the median voter model deals with political competition. The fact that both models make unrealistic and simplified assumptions about the real world does not keep them from describing how resources might be allocated in an ideal setting.

When the market does not conform to the extreme assumptions of the competitive model, some resource misallocation can occur. In the market such factors as externalities, nonexcludability, and monopoly power can cause the market's performance to deviate from the competitive model. Likewise, in the public sector such factors as the rational ignorance of voters, the influence of special interests, and the potential for cyclical majorities are analogous to the private market problems just listed, because they cause political results to deviate from the outcome most preferred by the median voter. Nevertheless,

both the competitive model in the market and the median voter model in the public sector provide valuable insights into the way in which the ideal system works.

A fuller understanding of the operation of the political marketplace will be provided in Chapter 8, which discusses the public sector supply process. At this point, though, it is important to understand the role of the median voter model as a benchmark for democratic decisions. In an ideal setting political outcomes cannot be any better than the median voter model predicts. This naturally leads to the question of the economic efficiency of the median voter model, which will be considered after a brief discussion of some empirical studies on the median voter model.

Empirical Evidence

Most empirical studies on the median voter model find evidence consistent with the median voter model but that might also be consistent with other models of public sector resource allocation.[9] This is because typically it is not possible to identify the median voter specifically, so some other characteristics associated with the median voter must be used as proxies. For example, a study might find an association between median income in a jurisdiction and the level of spending on a particular public sector service, providing indirect evidence that the median voter is the decisive voter.[10]

Sometimes more information is available about voters' preferences. For example, when

---

[9] For example, see James L. Barr and Otto A. Davis, "An Elementary Political and Economic Theory of the Expenditures of State and Local Governments," *Southern Economic Journal* 33 (Oct. 1966), pp. 149–165.

[10] In Robert P. Inman, "Testing Political Economy's 'As If' Assumption: Is the Median Income Voter Really Decisive?" *Public Choice* 33, no. 4 (1978), pp. 45–65, Inman concludes that the median voter is indeed the decisive voter.

a referendum passes by, say, 60 percent, this provides an indication that the sixtieth percentile voter was almost indifferent between voting for the measure and voting against it. If more than one referendum is held on an issue, then information about more than one voter in the distribution becomes available. Holcombe[11] and Munley[12] have used this type of information on the distribution of voters and have found that the outcomes of referenda closely reflect the median voter's preferences.

In another interesting test McEachern[13] found no difference between the level of local debt in states that had no referenda on debt and states that required the approval of 50 percent of the voters in a referendum. However, states with referenda that required more than 50 percent approval had lower debt levels than the other two types of states. McEachern observed that local officials tended to pick the level of debt most preferred by the median voter, as in the representative democracy variant of the model, and that if a referendum were held, voters would approve this level. This meant there was no difference between the states that required 50 percent approval in a referendum and the nonreferendum states. However, the states requiring more than 50 percent approval placed an additional constraint on the debt process, resulting in lower overall levels of debt. McEachern concluded from this that the median voter model was indeed descriptive of election outcomes.

Overall, though the median voter model does seem to be descriptive of public sector outcomes, not all economists who have studied the process agree with that assessment.[14] Note also that all of the empirical studies of the median voter model have been conducted for state and local rather than national elections. Furthermore, if the median voter model is viewed as analogous to the competitive model in the market, it is plausible that sometimes the median voter model will be descriptive and sometimes not. The next chapter, on public sector supply, will shed more light on the issue. Meanwhile, it is appropriate to examine whether economic resources are allocated efficiently if the median voter's most preferred outcome is produced by the political process.

Economic Efficiency and the Median Voter

Certainly there are factors that might hinder the median voter equilibrium from being the result of a democratic process, just as there are real world factors that keep any market from acting like an ideally competitive market. Nevertheless, the median voter model does provide some insight into the way that decisions are made by majority rule. What concerns us here is whether the median voter

[11] R. G. Holcombe, "An Empirical Test of the Median Voter Model," *Economic Inquiry* 18, no. 2 (April 1980), pp. 260–274.

[12] Vincent G. Munley, "Has the Median Voter Found a Ballot Box He Can Control?" *Economic Inquiry* 22, no. 3 (July 1984), pp. 323–336.

[13] William A. McEachern, "Collective Decision Rules and Local Debt Choice: A Test of the Median-Voter Hypothesis," *National Tax Journal* 31, no. 2 (June 1978), pp. 129–136.

[14] See, for example, Thomas Romer and Howard Rosenthal, "Median Voters or Budget Maximizers: Evidence from School Expenditure Referenda," *Economic Inquiry* 26, no. 4 (Oct. 1982), pp. 556–578.

Figure 7.3 Efficiency in the Median Voter Model The efficient level of output, Q^*, is determined by the intersection of the sum of the demands for the output and its marginal cost. Majority rule, following the median voter model, will produce the level at which the median voter's demand intersects his marginal tax price, or QM. The two will be equal only if the median voter's demand is the same fraction of the total demand as his tax price is of the marginal cost of the output.

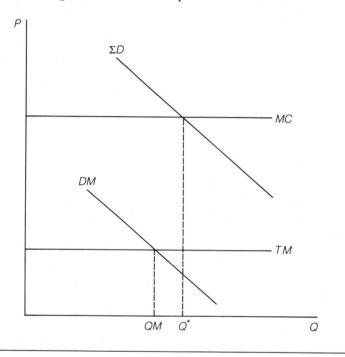

equilibrium provides an economically efficient level of public sector output.

Public Sector Efficiency

Recall from Chapter 3 that the efficient level of output for a good produced in the public sector is that level at which the vertical sum of the individual demand curves for the good is equal to the marginal cost of the good. This is illustrated in Figure 7.3, where Q^* is the level of output that equates ΣD with MC. The median voter equilibrium exists where the me-

dian voter's demand curve equals the median voter's tax price, or where DM equals TM; thus, the median voter equilibrium output is QM. As drawn in the figure, the level of output most preferred by the median voter is less than the optimal level of output.

It is obvious from Figure 7.3 that QM does not have to equal Q^*, so the question is, Under what conditions will the two be equal? In other words, When will the median voter equilibrium produce the efficient level of output? Note that at point QM, because $DM = TM$, $DM/TM = 1$; likewise, at Q^*, $\Sigma D/MC = 1$. By combining the two equations, we see that $Q^* = QM$ when $DM/\Sigma D = TM/MC$. On the left side of the equation, $DM/\Sigma D$ is the fraction of the total demand that is made up of the median voter's demand. On the right side of the equation, TM/MC is the fraction of the total marginal cost of the good that is paid by the median voter. Thus, the median voter equilibrium is efficient when the median voter's share of the total demand equals the median voter's share of the total cost.[15]

Efficiency in the Real World

Although median voter equilibrium is unlikely to be achieved often in the public sector, taxing schemes are frequently implemented in such a way that voters who have a higher demand for a good pay a larger share of the taxes that finance the good. Using the gasoline tax to finance highways is an obvious case, but other taxes may fit the principle as well. For example, if wealthier people tend to live in more expensive houses, and if they tend to demand more educational expenditures, then using the property tax to finance public schools is a way of charging a higher price to those who demand more. If each voter pays taxes in proportion to his or her demand, then the median voter will be paying taxes in proportion to the amount of the good demanded; or, $DM/\Sigma D = TM/MC$. In other words majority rule will produce the efficient level of output.

The Lindahl equilibrium represents a special case of the median voter equilibrium. Recall from Chapter 3 that the Lindahl equilibrium is the condition in which each individual's marginal valuation of the good equals the individual's marginal tax price. If the marginal tax price equals the marginal benefit for all individuals, then this condition must hold true for the median voter as well. Therefore, the median voter's most preferred outcome will be efficient with a Lindahl equilibrium. Note, however, that while the preferences of voters other than the median voter do not affect the median voter outcome, the Lindahl equilibrium specifies the tax and demand conditions of all individuals, which implies that efficiency with a Lindahl equilibrium is more difficult to achieve.

Conclusion

The goal of this chapter has been to explain how the votes of individuals can be translated into the demand for public sector output in a democracy. Though it has many complications, the basic procedure can be described in the median voter model. The median voter model illustrates that under many different circumstances where majority rule is used, majority rule decisions produce the outcome most preferred by the median voter.

In a committee-type setting, when various motions are proposed and evaluated against one another by majority rule, the motion most preferred by the median voter is the only motion that can defeat all others. In a referendum setting, when marginal changes to the status quo are proposed, the median voter's most preferred outcome again will be selected by majority rule. The median voter model is

---

[15]This condition is explained in R. G. Holcombe, *Public Finance and the Political Process* (Carbondale: Southern Illinois University Press, 1983), ch. 2.

most significant when applied to representative democracy, because here voters rarely have the opportunity to vote on issues directly. Rather, they elect representatives who determine the characteristics of public sector output and who, when competing to be elected, will adjust their platforms to try to represent the median voter.

However, the median voter model may not be completely descriptive of majority rule institutions. For one thing, when the cyclical majority problem occurs, no median voter equilibrium outcome can be achieved, in which case the specific characteristics of the election process end up determining the election outcome. For another, voters tend to be rationally ignorant about the activities of government because they have little incentive to collect such information, thus allowing special interests to gain a disproportionate influence over the political process. Furthermore, elected representatives, to obtain reelection, have an incentive to pursue shortsighted policies rather than policies that benefit the nation in the long run. Despite these problems the median voter model provides valuable insights into the way that majority rule decisions are made, particularly by describing the demand side of the market for public sector output, which will be the same as the median voter's demand.

The median voter's demand for public sector output is not necessarily the optimal level of output, but under reasonable taxing institutions, in which people pay taxes roughly equal to their demand for public sector output, it will come close. For the median voter's most preferred output to be the efficient level of output, the median voter's share of the total marginal benefits must equal the median voter's share of the total marginal cost. This type of taxing system can be approximated when people are taxed in proportion to the benefits they receive for public sector output.

In summary, the median voter model in the public sector is analogous to the competitive model of the private sector. It is roughly descriptive of the way that voting allocates resources, in the same way that the competitive model is roughly descriptive of the way that the market allocates resources. Despite some possible complications the voters in a representative democracy can be viewed as demanding the type of government most preferred by the median voter. Thus, the median voter's demand curve for government goods and services is, in essence, the demand curve for government in a representative democracy. There may be complications such as the cyclical majority, special interests, and so forth, but there are also problems with market structure, externalities, and information in private sector resource allocation. These complications must be taken into account, of course, but they should not obscure the workings of either the invisible hand in the market or the median voter model in the public sector. With this basic model of public sector demand in mind, the next chapter examines the other side of the market—public sector supply.

Questions

1. What is the conclusion of the median voter model? Explain three different models that arrive at this median voter conclusion.

2. Why is there a tendency for competing candidates in an election to have similar platforms? Why are extreme candidates unable to win an election?

3. Why are there only two major political parties in the United States, despite the fact that there are no legal restrictions on the number of parties and despite the fact that throughout the history of the nation many small parties have tried to become major parties?

4. Using the median voter model, explain what President Nixon meant by the term *silent majority*. Within the same model explain why Nixon defeated McGovern by a landslide in the 1972 presidential election.

5. In 1984 Reagan defeated Mondale in the presidential election. Hart, Mondale's biggest challenger in the primaries, claimed that the Democrats should nominate him because he could beat Reagan, whereas Mondale would surely lose. Could Hart's claim have been true?

6. Explain why it is natural for voters to be rationally ignorant about most political issues.

7. Explain how special interest groups affect resource allocation through the public sector. Why can special interests have a large impact on public policies in a representative democracy?

8. How does the incentive structure in politics provide incentives for even the most public-spirited representatives to pursue shortsighted public policies?

9. What condition must be satisfied so that the median voter's most preferred level of output will be economically efficient? Explain why this condition makes sense. Is there any reason to believe that real world institutions might come close to satisfying this condition?

10. Who are the U.S. senators in your state? What are their positions on tax reform? What nuclear arms agreements are currently in effect? What are the provisions of these agreements? Can the individual who does not know the answers to these questions be considered rationally ignorant of important political issues?

CHAPTER EIGHT

Public Sector Supply

*I*n Chapter 7 we concluded that the demand for public sector output approximates the demand of the median voter. In Chapter 8 we examine the other side of the market to see how public sector suppliers can be expected to respond to the demand for public sector output. In terms of supply conditions in the private sector of the economy, firms are assumed to be profit maximizers. Of course, the individuals who run firms have other goals as well, but the assumption of profit maximization in the private sector has produced simple models that have significant explanatory power. Public sector suppliers differ in important ways from private sector suppliers, one of the most significant differences being that suppliers in the public sector do not have the incentive to maximize profits. In fact, most public sector output—public schools, highways, national defense—is not sold directly on the market but is allocated to the user at little or no charge when compared to the costs of production. If public sector suppliers do not

maximize profits, then how do they decide how much output to produce?

The profit maximization assumption for private firms can be explained in terms of the incentives faced by suppliers. The individuals in the firm benefit most when they maximize the profits of the firm, and in many situations the only way that a firm can remain in business is to act like a profit maximizer. Likewise, the behavior of the public sector suppliers can be explained in terms of the incentives faced by those suppliers, who are motivated to maximize their budgets in the same way that private sector suppliers are motivated to maximize profits. In examining the institutions within which the public sector suppliers work, we can see exactly what it means to be a budget maximizer in the public sector. Combined with the discussion of public sector demand in Chapter 7, a general framework for understanding demand and supply conditions in the public sector will thus be provided.

Incentives in Bureaucracy

The public sector counterpart of firms that produce output in the private sector of the economy is the government bureaucracy; the

Department of Defense oversees the production of defense, the Department of Energy runs a number of energy programs, and so on. In the private sector of the economy, the market evaluates the worth of a firm's output, and a firm's profits represent the difference between the value of the resources the firm uses in production and the value of the firm's final output. By contrast, public sector output is not usually sold in the market, so market tests cannot be used to determine whether the value of the government's output is greater than its resource cost. Nor can the success of a government bureau be measured by its profits, unlike the success of a firm in the private sector.

Utility and Budget Maximization in the Public Sector

The goal of profit maximization in the private sector is based on the concept of utility maximization. The managers of firms have an incentive to maximize profits because this provides them with the most income. The people who work for the government are not necessarily any better or worse than those who work in the private sector of the economy, and they are probably motivated by the same types of things. Certainly they want to further the public interest, just as citizens in the private sector want to do, but they also are interested in pursuing their own self-interests. To fully understand their behavior, we must understand the incentives they face and the actions they must take to achieve those goals.

In the private sector managers are rewarded based on the profits that they bring to the firm, which obviously gives them an incentive to maximize profits. But in the public sector managers do not seek, and cannot be rewarded for, the profits they generate; rather, they are typically rewarded for the budgets that they oversee. Because bureaucrats who oversee larger budgets receive higher incomes, bureaucrats have an incentive to be budget maximizers.[1]

Undoubtedly, bureaucrats have other mo-

tivations besides increasing their incomes, but these other incentives tend to be positively related to the size of the budgets that they oversee as well. For example, a bureaucrat may be interested in the power and prestige associated with the job, in which case the larger the bureau that the bureaucrat oversees, the more power and prestige the bureaucrat will have. One way to achieve this is by enlarging the budget of the bureau. The bureaucrat might also be interested in a congenial working environment, which is more likely to occur in a growing bureau than in one that is stagnant or shrinking. In a growing bureau there will be room to promote current employees to make room for new workers underneath, which will contribute to a more positive working environment. Thus, the bureaucrat again has an incentive to maximize the budget of the bureau.

The Public Interest and Budget Maximization

The bureaucrat may also be concerned about the public interest, but those working in government bureaus probably believe more strongly in the value of the bureau's service than the median voter does. It is likely, for instance, that those working in the Department of Education believe in the value of federal education programs, that those working in the Department of Energy regard the government's energy programs as beneficial, and that those working for the Environmental Protection Agency think that the government has an important role to play in protecting the environment. In general, people are more likely to apply for jobs in agencies that they feel provide valuable services, and once

---

[1]The budget-maximizing hypothesis with respect to bureaucracy was popularized in William A. Niskanen, *Bureaucracy and Representative Government* (Chicago and New York: Aldine-Atherton, 1971).

hired, it is in their self-interest to continue believing so.

This public interest argument should not be considered too seriously, however. The individual in the EPA may think it is in the public interest to reduce pollution, but the individual still has an incentive to pursue his or her own self-interest. After all, if individuals can be counted on to pursue the public interest when it conflicts with their narrow self-interests, then managers of polluting firms can be expected to reduce pollution of their own accord, without the government requiring it. In reality, we should expect the people at the EPA who regulate pollution to behave in their own self-interests, just as we expect the people in the private sector to do so. In the private sector we expect to see firms act in order to maximize their profits. By the same reasoning, in the public sector we expect to see bureaus act in order to maximize their budgets.

The Bureaucrat's Maximand

The hypothesis that bureaucrats are budget maximizers is persuasive, but it is only one hypothesis among many put forward by students of bureaucracy. While Niskanen formulated the budget maximization hypothesis, he also considered a more complex formulation of his model, in which bureaucrats try to maximize the amount of discretionary funds in their budgets rather than the budget per se.[2] Following this line of reasoning, funds used to produce the bureau's output are not as valuable to the bureaucrat as discretionary funds that can be used for such benefits as vacations disguised as fact-finding trips and funds for conferences to which bureaucrats can invite all of their out-of-town friends for "conference" luncheons at expensive restaurants.

There is undoubtedly much truth to this view, but the hypothesis of maximization of discretionary funds doesn't consider the benefits, such as power and prestige, inherent in overseeing a large budget. In reality, the bureaucrat probably wants both a large total budget and a large amount of discretionary funds within the budget.

There is a subdiscipline related to economics called organization theory that has tried to determine how individuals in organizations actually do make their decisions. Like profit maximization in the private sector, the budget maximization hypothesis represents a simplification of reality. Herbert Simon has suggested that in a complex world individuals do not actually maximize, but "satisfice," to use Simon's language.[3] They choose a level of achievement that would be acceptable and aim for that level. Within the context of a bureaucracy, this means attempting to perform to some acceptable measure, whatever measuring rod is applied. Once the bureaucrat has accomplished this, the rest of the bureau's budget can be used at the bureaucrat's discretion.[4]

Again, just as profit maximization is an oversimplification of the activities of individuals running firms, so is budget maximization an oversimplification of the behavior of bureaucrats. But recognizing the complex, and sometimes conflicting, incentives facing bureaucrats, the budget maximization hypothesis is a good first approximation. Many useful implications can be drawn from that hypothesis even while recognizing its limitations.

---

[3] Herbert Simon, *Models of Man* (New York: Harper & Row, 1957).

[4] A good overview of this literature as it relates to economics can be found in P. M. Jackson, *The Political Economy of Bureaucracy* (Totowa, N.J.: Barnes and Noble, 1983). Along these same lines, see also Ronald A. Heiner, "The Origins of Predictable Behavior," *American Economic Review* 83, no. 4 (Sept. 1983), pp. 560–595.

---

[2] See William A. Niskanen, "Bureaucrats and Politicians," *Journal of Law & Economics* 18 (Dec. 1975), pp. 617–643.

The Public Sector Bargaining Process

Having established that bureaus are budget maximizers in the same way that firms are profit maximizers, this still does not provide enough information about the public sector supply process to understand how much output will be produced by public sector suppliers. For example, although all firms in the private sector have an incentive to maximize profits, a monopolized industry will produce less output and sell at a higher price than a competitive industry under similar circumstances. This section will examine the public sector bargaining process to see what type of bargain is likely to emerge between the bureau and the bureau's sponsor.

The Bureau's Interaction with Its Sponsor

The bureau's sponsor is the organization that determines the bureau's budget. For example, the U.S. Congress is the sponsor of the EPA, the Department of Defense, and so on. Likewise, state and local governments sponsor other bureaus. The term *sponsor* is used by Niskanen to refer to the budget-approving group and will be used here as well, because the model of bureaucracy described here largely follows Niskanen's.[5]

An important difference between the bargaining process that determines a bureau's output and the process that determines the output of a firm in the private sector is that the private sector firm sells output at a certain price per unit and customers decide how much to buy at that price. By contrast, a bureau's total output is determined at the same time as its budget. Thus, the sponsor decides to purchase a certain amount of output from the bureau at a certain price, simultaneously negotiating both the price and the quantity of output. This puts the bureau in the position of being able to make an all-or-nothing sale to the sponsor, extracting all of the sponsor's consumer surplus from the bureau's output.

This is illustrated in Figure 8.1, where the sponsor's demand curve for the bureau's output is labeled *D* and the associated marginal revenue curve is labeled *MR*. The bureaucracy is assumed to have supply conditions like a constant-cost industry, so the marginal cost curve of the bureau, *MC*, would also be the supply curve if the bureau's output were to be produced by a competitive industry.

A competitive industry would produce output level *QC*, and a monopolist, setting marginal cost equal to marginal revenue, would restrict output to produce *QM*. If a government bureau were to produce *QC*, the amount produced by a competitive industry, the bureau would produce consumer surplus for the sponsor equal to the area of the shaded triangle above the *MC* curve. In an effort to maximize its budget, the bureau will propose to its sponsor a level of output larger than *QC*, and if the sponsor sees no better alternative, the sponsor will be willing to accept the bureau's proposal as long as there is some consumer surplus produced by the bureau.

The Bureaucratic Bargaining Process

The challenge to the budget-maximizing bureau, then, is to propose the budget that the sponsor will accept. The bureau will try to propose output level *QB* at price per unit *P** in order to maximize its budget. At *QB* the consumer surplus gained from the production of the units below *QC* (the shaded

---

[5] In addition to his book cited earlier, Niskanen also wrote two frequently cited, related articles, "The Peculiar Economics of Bureaucracy," *American Economic Review* 58 (May 1968), pp. 293–305, and "Bureaucrats and Politicians," cited previously.

Figure 8.1 Output in Monopolistic, Competitive, and Bureaucratic Markets
Compared with the competitive level of output *QC*, a monopolist will produce less, equating marginal revenue with marginal cost and producing *QM*. A bureaucracy will produce *QB*, more than a competitive industry, by producing at the point where the all-or-nothing demand curve intersects marginal cost.

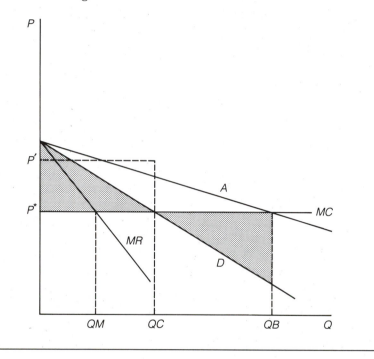

triangle above *MC*) is slightly more than the consumer surplus lost on units above *QC* (the shaded triangle below *MC*). The shaded triangle above *MC* is slightly larger than the triangle below *MC*, meaning that the sponsor will get very little consumer surplus from approving the bureau's budget to produce *QB* at price *P**.

The sponsor might try a counter offer, stating that it prefers less output at that price, but because the bureau bargains for a total level of output in exchange for a total budget, it is likely to tell the sponsor that if the level of output is reduced, the price per unit will rise dramatically. For example, if *QC* is desired by

the sponsor, the bureaucrats will claim that the lowest possible price per unit for that quantity is *P'*. As a result, the sponsor believes that its best alternative is to accept output level *QB*, which is the budget-maximizing level of output for the bureau.

Curve *A* represents the sponsor's all-or-nothing demand curve. An all-or-nothing demand curve shows the price-quantity combinations where the purchaser receives no consumer surplus from the purchase. For example, at quantity *QB* and price *P** the sponsor is indifferent between that amount at that price and no output at all if the shaded triangle of consumer surplus gained for output below QC is equal to the shaded triangle for consumer surplus lost at QB. The budget of the bureau will be maximized when the bureau offers the sponsor QB, where the sponsor's all-or-nothing demand curve intersects the bureau's marginal cost curve. By contrast, a competitive industry will produce the optimal amount of output, QC, and a monopolist will produce QM.

The Bureau's Bargaining Advantage

In essence, the bureau and its sponsor are engaged in a bilateral bargaining situation, and the bureau will have the superior bargaining position necessary to capture the gains from trade for a number of reasons. First, the bureau has only the single sponsor to deal with in the bargaining process and so can specialize in trying to work out a favorable bargaining agreement. Most sponsors, however, oversee many bureaus. For example, the Department of Defense must deal with only one sponsor, whereas the U.S. Congress must deal with DOD, EPA, DOE, and an alphabet soup of other agencies. Thus, the bureau is able to devote more time and effort to the bargaining process than the sponsor.

Second, the sponsor typically gets all of its information about the bureau's characteristics from the bureau itself, so the bureau can reveal to the sponsor only the information that is in the bureau's interest. This means information on the true cost of various program options must be obtained by the sponsor from the bureau. The bureau is, in effect, the sponsor's source of expert information. The sponsor, on the other hand, will typically reveal its demand curve by votes on issues, speeches, and so on. In short, while the bureau will have good information about the sponsor's demand conditions, the sponsor will have only the information about the bureau's supply conditions that the bureau chooses to reveal to the sponsor.

Third, much work is done in committees before the sponsor's full body votes on an issue. Members on the defense committee, for example, will tend to be high demanders of the particular services, thus making it easier for the bureau to present to the sponsor a proposal for a larger-than-optimal budget. All of these factors suggest that a bureau will tend to have a budget that is larger than optimal.

Special Interests and Government Programs

As the focus of federal government spending in the 1960s and 1970s shifted from national defense to transfer programs, special interests increased their efforts to receive a share of the transfers. It makes sense that if the government has more money to transfer, then special interests have a larger incentive to lobby for a share of that spending. Recall from Chapter 7 that special interests have a disproportionately large influence over federal spending

decisions because of the incentives faced by the general public, the elected representatives, and the special interests themselves.

Public Sector Demand and Special Interests

In the previous chapter we argued that the general public is rationally ignorant of most of the government's activities, whereas special interests have an incentive to become informed about specific political programs that potentially will provide them with concentrated benefits. A special interest program provides such benefits to the relatively small number of people in the special interest group by spreading the cost out over everyone in the nation. For example, the costs of the dairy price support program are shared by all taxpayers and all purchasers of dairy products, so that each individual pays only a few dollars a year. The taxpayer and consumer have little incentive to become informed because the time and effort required to do so would save the individual only a few dollars a year.

However, a few dollars paid by each individual becomes thousands of dollars in benefits to the special interest group members. Because they receive concentrated benefits, the special interest group has an incentive to become informed about issues facing the legislature that might directly affect them and to propose measures that will benefit them. This explains why the demands of special interests are more visible to the legislature than the demands of the general public, and also why the legislature has more of an incentive to respond to special interests than to act in the general public interest.

This orientation of representative democracy toward special interests is accentuated by the geographical nature of representation in a democracy such as the United States has. Senators and representatives are elected specifically to represent subsets of the population rather than the nation as a whole, leading voters to reasonably expect that each representative will promote the interests of his or her particular constituents. Although voters in a given area might like to have a representative who is a national leader, they can benefit more directly by having a representative who is able to provide special interest government programs. Therefore, considering this system of representation, one should not be surprised at the influence of special interests.

Special Interests Versus the General Public Interest

The logical conclusion is that the incentive structure built into a representative democracy favors the passage of legislation beneficial to special interests rather than to the general public. Special interests are well informed about the particular issues that affect them, whereas the general public is rationally ignorant about most of what the government does. Because representatives must be reelected to keep their jobs, they need political support, which they can get from special interests in exchange for passing legislation that benefits the special interest. By contrast, the general public is poorly organized and poorly informed and can offer no comparable benefits to the legislator for favoring the public interest rather than the special interest. For any particular representative, aiding special interests amounts to a matter of political survival; for the government in general, favoring special interests over the general public interest is merely a logical extension.

An important question remains, however. Note that although a special interest can influence its representative to support a program in its benefit, this is only one representative among many in the legislature. How is it possible for one legislator to gather enough support for a special interest program that it can gain a majority of the legislature's votes?

Logrolling and Political Exchange

Logrolling is the exchange of political support on one issue for political support on another issue. For voters at large logrolling is not feasible because of the large number of voters and the difficulty posed by the secret ballot in verifying that any given voter has kept the bargain. For representatives logrolling is feasible because of the small number of legislators and because their votes are a matter of public record. In this type of situation representatives can engage in political exchanges to gain support on particular issues they favor by trading their votes on issues they do not care as much about.[6]

Logrolling and Special Interests

The rational ignorance of the general public combined with the informed political pressure of special interests on issues suggests that logrolling is more likely to produce special interest legislation than legislation in the general public interest. If everyone was perfectly informed about all issues, the Coase theorem would apply, and resources would be allocated efficiently in the public sector. But in reality, the special interests promise political support and campaign contributions in exchange for legislative support. Furthermore, the general public tends to be ignorant of programs in their interest even if those programs are passed. The result is that each representative has an incentive to favor special interests over the general public interest.

Legislators obtain votes on special interest programs basically by trading votes with other legislators, though the logrolling process may be more complex at times. A legislator may receive needed votes on a particular program in exchange for an IOU to vote for an unspecified future program for the other legislator. In a relatively small group such as a legislature, a legislator has an incentive to repay IOUs to retain a reputation for cooperation. Otherwise, the legislator will soon find that others are not willing to trade, and that legislator will not be able to get programs passed. Logrolling thus facilitates the legislative process in general and special interest programs in particular.

Gainers and Losers

This special interest theory of legislation provides a somewhat different view of gainers and losers in the political process from the traditional perception of majority rule politics as a process in which the majority wins at the expense of the minority. Considering the incentives for special interest legislation and the need to trade votes for special interest programs to pass, a more realistic view is that individuals and groups can benefit from the political process in direct proportion to the effort and expense they are willing to put into it.

Some people have little incentive to do so. For example, individual milk drinkers have little to gain from lobbying Congress to eliminate dairy price supports. Even though the gains in the aggregate could be large if the individual succeeded in getting the price supports removed, each individual's gains would be small. Nobody has a large incentive to produce what amounts to a collective consumption good for others without compensation.

---

[6]James M. Buchanan and Gordon Tullock, *The Calculus of Consent* (Ann Arbor: University of Michigan Press, 1962), is a classic discussion of the economic implications of logrolling.

Table 8.1 Political Exchange with Cyclical Preferences, in Dollars

Options	VOTERS		
	1	2	3
A	1000	1	2
B	2	3	1
C	1	2	3

Special interests do have an incentive to lobby for these types of benefits, but the benefits they receive will depend on the amount of political support they can offer in return. It is an oversimplification to suggest that if lobbyists can muster a majority of the legislature's votes, they will be winners, and if they cannot, they will be losers. In fact, legislatures can grant some benefits to all interest groups, and groups can be bigger winners by getting more benefits. Interest groups that can promise publicity, campaign contributions, and, most importantly, votes will have more political power and will be able to receive more special interest benefits from the legislature. Those with less power will receive fewer benefits.[7]

Rather than looking at majority rule as a system that produces winners (the majority) and losers (the minority), taking account of logrolling and competition among special interests indicates that the legislature can exchange some benefits for political support with all interest groups. The legislature, in trying to determine the benefits going to each group, weighs the marginal political benefits against the marginal political costs and supports each group such that the net benefits are the same at the margin.[8]

Logrolling and Economic Efficiency

To this point logrolling has been presented as a mechanism whereby special interests can get their programs approved by the legislature. This can occur because nobody has an incentive to represent the general public interest in the logrolling process. However, when all individuals are represented in the logrolling process, resources will be efficiently allocated, because when votes can be traded, individuals are willing to pay more for issues that are worth more to them. An example can illustrate this principle.

Table 8.1 lists the hypothetical preferences of three voters numbered 1, 2, and 3 for three projects labeled A, B, and C. Assume that the three voters must select one of the options by majority rule. The dollar figures reflect the value each voter places on each option. Thus, for example, voter 1 places a value of $1000 on option A, $2 on option B, and $1 on option C. Which option will be chosen by majority rule?

The preferences listed in the table will produce a cyclical majority if each voter can express a preference by casting only one vote. Under simple majority rule A can defeat B, C can defeat A, and B can defeat C. There is no clear majority winner, so the winning option will be chosen based on the way in which the alternatives are considered. For example, if A and B are considered and then the winner of that vote faces C to determine the overall winner, C will be selected. Thus far, this example

---

[7]This idea is developed in Gary S. Becker, "A Theory of Competition among Pressure Groups for Political Influence," *Quarterly Journal of Economics* 98, no. 3 (August 1983), pp. 371–400.

[8]See Sam Peltzman, "Toward a More General Theory of Regulation," *Journal of Law & Economics* 19, no. 2 (August 1976), pp. 221–240, for a development of this line of reasoning.

is identical to the cyclical majority examples in Chapter 7.

If logrolling is possible, however, project A is almost certain to win. Option A is clearly worth more to voter 1, so with logrolling voter 1 can offer to trade for the votes of 2 or 3. Because their votes are worth more to voter 1 than to themselves, a mutually advantageous trade can certainly be made. The total value to the voters of option A is $1003, whereas the value of B and C is $6 in each case. In the absence of logrolling a cyclical majority, occurs, but with logrolling the highest valued project is selected.

This simple example implies that logrolling can lead to economic efficiency when all parties are able to trade. This is an application of the Coase theorem, which states that when transactions costs are low, resources will be allocated to their most highly valued uses. When logrolling is possible, individuals can trade votes so that the alternatives chosen by the democratic process will be those that are most valuable to those trading the votes.

Special interest legislation tends to be inefficient, because the special interests are engaging in political exchange to try to produce their most highly valued outcome, but the general public finds it too costly to participate in the process. Because the general public is not participating, political programs tend to favor special interests. However, among the special interests who engage in political exchange, there will be a tendency for the programs that are most highly valued by the special interests to be produced through the political process.[9]

Agenda Control

In the previous chapter on public sector demand, the suppliers of legislation were depicted as engaging in what might be viewed as competitive political behavior. In other words they attempt to produce legislation that is as close to satisfying the demands of voters as possible. Because the collective demand in a majority rule process is equivalent to the demand of the median voter, this means that suppliers are attempting to satisfy the demands of the median voter. Thus, the purpose of elections in this type of model is to reveal the median voter's demand in the political market.

This competitive political behavior makes a great deal of sense when voters are equally informed about political issues and when candidates must satisfy the demands of the median voter in order to maximize their chances of reelection. In cases where some voters are not well informed or where there is little direct competition for reelection, legislators may behave monopolistically; this monopolistic behavior can be exhibited through the control of the agenda. This is likely to happen, for example, when bills are presented by committees, because committees can shape the terms of legislation before it reaches the floor of the legislature. In a competitive setting one might expect for the terms of legislation to meet with the median representative's preferences. However, representatives are not

---

[9]Extensive discussion on efficiency and inefficiency of political exchange can be found in Buchanan and Tullock, *The Calculus of Consent*. Additional discussion on the possibility of efficiency in political exchange can be found in Becker, "A Theory of Competition."

elected by the legislature but by voters who are rationally ignorant about much of what the legislature does. This gives committees, and committee chairmen especially, more power over their bills than if the setting were more competitive.

The political agenda is simply the collection of issues that are to be decided. In all settings other than a pure direct democracy, some individuals will have more control over the agenda than others. As previously noted, in a competitive setting the agenda setter has an incentive to provide the agenda most preferred by the median voter, but sometimes the agenda setter will be exempt from a high degree of political competition and will be able to manipulate the agenda to produce an outcome closer to the setter's preference than the outcome most preferred by the median voter.

Consider, for example, a referendum setting like the one presented in Chapter 7, but in which only one referendum takes place. In the previous chapter small adjustments were made to produce the outcome most preferred by the median voter, but now assume that the agenda setter is a budget-maximizing bureaucrat who wants as large a budget as possible for a particular program. This situation is depicted in Figure 8.2. If the referendum to approve spending for the program does not pass, the level of spending will be QR, the reversion level.[10] The median voter's demand curve is DM, so the level that the median voter most prefers is QM. Because the median voter's vote will determine the outcome of the referendum, the agenda setter must propose the largest amount possible that will be approved by the median voter.

If QM is proposed by the agenda setter as the alternative to QR, then the median voter will vote in favor and receive the consumer surplus represented by triangle abc. The agenda setter can propose to produce still more and the median voter will vote in favor (against the alternative of QR) as long as the consumer surplus gained from the amount from QR to QM exceeds the consumer surplus lost from the amount greater than QM. The agenda setter can therefore propose QA, such that the area in triangle cde (the consumer surplus lost) is marginally less than the area in triangle abc. The agenda setter proposes QA, the median voter votes in favor, and QA, larger than the median voter's most preferred level, is produced in the referendum. In short, by controlling the agenda it is possible to have some power over the outcome of a political decision.[11]

Agenda Control in the Real World

The referendum case clearly illustrates the principle of agenda control, although, because few decisions are made by direct referendum, it has relatively limited applications to the real world. However, the agenda can be controlled in other types of political settings, too; the power of committees and committee chairmen in the U.S. Congress is a good example. As previously noted, committees are responsible for delivering bills in their particular areas to the floor of Congress, which gives them an undue influence over the terms of those bills. Special interests can concentrate their lobbying efforts on the committee members who determine the provisions of bills,

---

[10] This terminology is that used in Thomas Romer and Howard Rosenthal, "Political Resource Allocation, Controlled Agendas, and the Status Quo," *Public Choice* 33, no. 4 (1978), pp. 27–43.

[11] A referendum case like this one was examined for millage referenda in Michigan in R. G. Holcombe, "An Empirical Test of the Median Voter Model," *Economic Inquiry* 18, no. 2 (April 1980), pp. 260–274.

Figure 8.2 Agenda Control in a Referendum The reversion point, QR, represents the level of output that will be produced if the referendum fails. A budget-maximizing government could present the median voter with an all-or-nothing offer in a referendum and pass a budget as large as QA, which is substantially more than the median voter's most preferred outcome of QM.

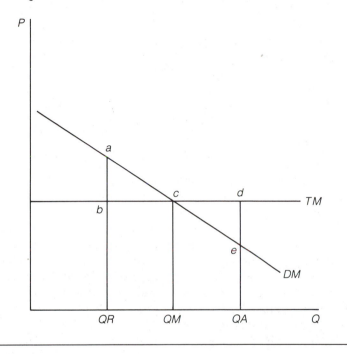

and though the resulting bill may not be exactly what the median member of Congress would prefer, the member may vote in favor anyway, preferring that bill to no bill at all. And logrolling can accentuate this process. Indeed, when looking at the supply side of the public sector, decision makers can manipulate the supply process in a number of ways, so that the outcome is not always what the median voter most prefers.

The agenda can also be controlled when committees nominate candidates for office in an organization. For example, in the Soviet Union the citizens do get to vote for their president in periodic elections, but the nominating committee puts only one candidate on the ballot. Clearly, the nominating committee controls the agenda such that they force the election to turn out the way they want it. The same thing occurs in many other organizations. The Southern Economic Association holds an annual election to select a president, but again only one candidate's name appears on the ballot. Needless to say, the nominating committee's choice is always selected. Even in smaller organizations such as clubs and fraternities, a group of officers often determines the agenda of a meeting ahead of time, which enables them to achieve the results they want.

In this sense control over the agenda of a group enables the agenda controller to manipulate the outcome of the group's collective decisions, even if the entire group votes on the final outcome.

Fiscal Federalism

One way to limit the influence of special interests in government is to produce government goods and services at the lowest possible level of government. *Fiscal federalism* is a system in which government programs are undertaken by different governmental levels, such as local, state, and national governments. Because Chapter 19 focuses on federalism, here we simply introduce the topic. The federal government is made up of many levels—under the national government are state governments, and under state governments are many local governments. Special interests operate at each level of government, but the problems posed by special interests can be reduced by producing government output at lower levels, for three main reasons.

Federalism and Special Interests

First, the influence of special interests can be limited if the government producing a program does not extend beyond the special interests that will benefit from the program. Consider, for example, waterway shippers in Alabama, who benefit from the federal government's maintenance of navigable waterways in the state. A study of the costs and benefits of these waterways estimated that the total cost of maintaining them was greater than the total benefits produced by them.

However, Alabama was a net beneficiary of the program because most of the benefits accrued to shippers in that state while most of the costs were paid by taxpayers in other states. It makes sense that people in Alabama would favor maintenance of the waterways by the national government because the cost to those people was less than the benefits, even though the cost to the nation was greater than the benefits.

Because the benefits of the program accrue to people in Alabama, it would make more sense for Alabama to finance the waterway program through taxes levied on people in Alabama. In this case the people of Alabama would be much less likely to favor the special interest expenditures because they would bear the total cost. The same would be true of other federal government programs. If the people of North Carolina paid for their own tobacco price support programs and the people of Wisconsin paid for their own dairy price support programs, special interests would have a lot more trouble getting these programs passed. At the federal level the total cost to each taxpayer is very diluted, but if such programs were financed at the state level, the costs would be, on average, fifty times higher, giving taxpayers more incentive to actively oppose them, or at least to become more aware of the relative benefits and costs.

Federalism and Consumer Choice

Second, producing government programs at the lowest possible level will offer voters more of a choice of what types of programs they want. For example, if public education were produced by the federal government, citizens who wanted public education would be restricted to the education provided by the government. However, when public education is produced by local governments, people can choose to live in areas that provide the kind of education they want at a price they are willing to pay. By moving to jurisdictions that are more in line with their preferences, voters can, in a sense, "vote with their feet." They can move to local governments that will provide them with the types of government services they want.[12]

Comparisons with Other Governments

The third, and perhaps most important, reason for producing government goods and services at the lowest possible level is that it enables voters to compare what they are getting for their tax dollars with what other people are getting for their tax dollars. If voters are not satisfied with how their local government compares with other, nearby governments, they can either move or they can vote their local officials out of office. This provides local government leaders with an incentive to look good in comparison to other, nearby governments. This type of intergovernmental competition need not require that people continually move from one jurisdiction to another; it only requires that voters replace their existing elected officials if their government does not compare favorably with others.

Production at Lower Levels of Government

All of these issues will be discussed more thoroughly in the chapter on federalism. At this point we need only reiterate that producing government programs at the lowest level of government will limit special interest activity for three reasons. First, by having fewer taxpayers in a smaller jurisdiction pay for the special interest programs, taxpayers will bear a bigger cost, which gives them an incentive to oppose special interest programs not in the general public interest. Second, with many jurisdictions, voters can move to the one that best satisfies their demands for government goods and services. Third, voters will have other, similar governments to compare against theirs to see if their government is providing good service for their tax dollar.

This does not mean that the federal government should do nothing. Some government programs are truly national in scope. National defense is a good example—everyone should contribute their tax dollars in exchange for a program that protects everyone in the nation. Interstate highways are another good example. Local traffic will use the highways, of course, but people who are passing through a state on a limited access highway also benefit. Thus, for programs that are national in scope and that provide benefits to people in all areas of the country, the national government is the appropriate level of government to produce the good. But when the benefits of government programs are geographically concentrated, it makes more sense to produce the program at a lower level of government, thereby limiting the ability of special interests to foster programs that are not cost effective.

---

[12]The classic article on this subject is Charles M. Tiebout, "A Pure Theory of Local Expenditures," *Journal of Political Economy* 64 (Oct. 1956), pp. 416–424.

The Government as an Interest Group

The role of special interests in government has been discussed at some length. One significant factor in the perpetuation of government programs once they are instituted is that government agencies themselves can act as interest groups. Before a particular program is started, there will be a demand for the program from some constituency, but the program may also have opponents. Once the program is passed, a government bureaucracy will be created (or an existing one expanded) to administer the program, and the people in the bureaucracy will become another interest group favoring the program.[13]

This means that in addition to the interest groups that wanted the program passed in the first place, the government employees who run the program will form yet another interest group. Government employees exert significant influence because they are the government's source of expertise on the program. For example, in determining whether a program should be continued, the government can check with its experts—the individuals in the administering agency—whose jobs depend on the continuation of the program. Furthermore, individuals who work for agencies will tend to believe that they produce valuable output, so the agencies' employees will defend the programs they work for.

The result is that once government programs are instituted they are very difficult to eliminate. The interest groups that originally wanted the programs will still want them, and a new and powerful interest group created by the program will help ensure its survival. This explains why a government program, once created, will tend to perpetuate itself.

Public Versus Private Provision

Some goods that are produced in the public sector are also produced in the private sector of the economy, which allows comparisons to be made between the efficiency of public and private provision. In general, public sector provision tends to be less efficient than private sector provision, for several reasons. First, as previously discussed, the general public is poorly informed about public sector production, which permits legislators and bureaucrats to favor special interests over the general public interest. Second, the model of bureaucracy presented at the beginning of the chapter suggests that the incentives for budget maximization in bureaucracy allow the level of output from a bureaucracy to be larger than would be the case in the private sector. Third, as Chapter 4 explained, without private ownership resources tend to be used inefficiently. Some examples can help to illustrate these principles.

David Davies describes a very interesting

---

[13] Milton Friedman, "Economists and Economic Policy," *Economic Inquiry* 24, no. 1 (Jan. 1986), pp. 1–10, offers some insightful comments on the role of economists in policy matters, considering the interests of policymakers as well as the public interest.

case in Australia.[14] Australia has two airlines, one government-owned and the other privately owned, that have no appreciable difference in aircraft, load, route, schedule, or wage rates paid their employees. Davies examined the productivity of the two firms as measured by tons of freight carried per employee, passengers carried per employee, and revenue generated per employee. In an eleven-year span he found that the privately owned airline was more productive than the government-owned airline, by some measures more than twice as productive.

Another study, by Cotton Lindsay, compared Veterans Administration hospitals to private hospitals.[15] Lindsay noted that the productivity of VA hospitals was measured in patient-days rather than profits, which gave VA hospitals the incentive to generate patient-days rather than produce efficient medical care with their budget. Lindsay looked at the average length of stay in a hospital for various surgical procedures and found the stays for the same procedure to be consistently longer, sometimes two to three times longer, in VA hospitals than in private hospitals. For example, an individual hospitalized for kidney stones had an average stay of 18.6 days in a VA hospital, but only 8.2 days in a private hospital.

Lindsay's study is interesting not only because it shows the relative inefficiency of government versus private hospitals, but also because it illustrates how people respond to incentives. When businesses are rewarded for generating profits, they tend to generate profits; but when the VA hospital output is measured in patient-days, the hospital tends to produce patient-days. Undoubtedly, these figures would be different if hospital productivity were measured in the number of procedures performed rather than in patient-days, but this might give the hospital an incentive to discharge patients too soon and to perform unnecessary procedures.

Two other studies illustrate the general principle that government suppliers tend to be less efficient than private suppliers. Crain and Zardkoohi examined government- versus privately operated water utilities in the United States and found that operating costs were significantly higher for the government-operated utilities.[16] Blair, Ginsburg, and Vogel found that Blue Cross–Blue Shield as a nonprofit health insurer had inefficiently large administrative costs that could be captured as profit if a profit-making private sector firm handled their insurance.[17]

In short, whether for airlines or hospitals, water utilities or health insurance, the lesson is the same. Private sector profit-making firms tend to produce more efficiently than government-operated firms. This does not necessarily mean that the government should never produce output. For goods such as national defense, no private sector alternative exists; for other goods, such as interstate highways, the government may be better able to overcome problems that might be encountered

---

[14]David G. Davies, "The Efficiency of Public versus Private Firms: The Case of Australia's Two Airlines," *Journal of Law & Economics* 14, no. 1 (April 1971), pp. 149–165.

[15]Cotton M. Lindsay, "A Theory of Government Enterprise," *Journal of Political Economy* 84 (Oct. 1976), pp. 1061–1077.

[16]W. Mark Crain and Asghar Zardkoohi, "A Test of the Property-Rights Theory of the Firm: Water Utilities in the United States," *Journal of Law & Economics* 21, no. 2 (Oct. 1978), pp. 395–408.

[17]Roger D. Blair, Paul B. Ginsburg, and Ronald J. Vogel, "Blue Cross–Blue Shield Administration Costs: A Study of Non-Profit Health Insurers," *Economic Inquiry* 13, no. 2 (June 1975), pp. 237–251.

with market provision. However, when a good private sector alternative exists, there is ample evidence that private sector production will be more efficient, as Chapter 20 will discuss in detail.

Conclusion

In the earlier chapters of the text, we argued that the market may not always allocate resources in the most efficient manner possible due to problems of externalities, public goods, and incomplete assignments of property rights. However, this does not necessarily mean that the government can do any better—the government can also encounter problems in allocating resources efficiently.

Some of these problems were touched on in the previous chapter. For example, individual preferences may be such that majority rule produces a cyclical majority, and even if there is a median voter outcome, it may not be completely efficient. However, the government is no more likely to produce the output most preferred by the median voter, as the problems with the incentive structure of the public sector suggest.[18]

First, government output is typically produced by government bureaucrats, who have an incentive to maximize the budgets of their bureaus in the same way that managers of private sector firms have an incentive to maximize the profits of their firms. This tendency toward budget maximization means the government produces greater-than-optimal output. Second, most voters are rationally ignorant of most activities of the government,

whereas special interests have an incentive to become informed about the particular issues that affect the interest group. Therefore, elected representatives, who need political support to keep their jobs, are more inclined to favor special interests than the general public interest. These tendencies can be offset somewhat by producing government output at the lowest level of government possible.

In small settings such as representative bodies, logrolling and vote trading can lead to the passage of special interest programs that would not be passed individually. Also, the fact that some individuals can control the agenda of a representative body for their own benefit contributes to a level of production of public sector output not completely reflective of the demands of the median voter.

Placed in proper perspective, though, this picture is not as grim as it looks. Just as the discussion on externalities, public goods, and so on implied that market allocation of resources was inefficient, so much of the discussion in this chapter has made the government's allocation of resources seem inefficient. However, in the real world things rarely work perfectly, and by understanding the limitations of governmental activity we can better utilize the government. Frequently, resources are allocated most effectively through the public sector. Few people would want to rely on anything but the federal government for national defense, nor is it likely that any other organization, including state

---

[18]On this subject see James M. Buchanan, "Public Finance and Public Choice," *National Tax Journal* 28 (Dec. 1975), pp. 383–394.

governments, could have developed and produced the interstate highway system. But while the government most effectively allocates resources for some purposes, it is clearly not the answer to all—or even most—resource allocation problems.

Where externalities and public goods exist, or where property rights are not well defined, there is good reason to regard the government as a possible solution to the resource allocation problem. However, the successes of the government in some areas should not obscure the fact that in many other areas the incentive structure of the government is inappropriate for efficient resource allocation. Moreover, understanding the strengths and limitations of government resource allocation is of more than just academic interest, because ultimately a democratic society chooses the activities that it wants its government to perform. That most people will be ignorant of most of what the government does is good reason for choosing carefully when the opportunity arises. It is ironic that in these matters that collectively are so important, individuals have a minimal incentive to become informed.

Questions

1. Why is budget maximization the goal of a government bureau in the same way that profit maximization is the goal of a private sector firm?

2. Explain the bargaining arrangements that lead to the level of output that will be produced by a government bureaucracy. Compare the level of output produced by a bureaucracy with the levels that would be produced by a competitive market and by a monopolist, respectively.

3. Explain why the typical college student knows more about the differences between various brands of pizza than about nuclear arms agreements, even though nuclear arms agreements are more important than pizza.

4. If voters tend to be rationally ignorant, why are special interests well informed about issues? Are special interests well informed about all issues or just some issues?

5. How can control over a group's agenda give an individual control over the decisions that the entire group will vote on? Illustrate in a graph how the agenda can be controlled using an example of a referendum.

6. What is meant by the term *logrolling*? What are the effects of logrolling on legislative outcomes? When will logrolling be efficient or inefficient?

7. What is fiscal federalism? Why is it desirable? List and explain several reasons why programs produced at lower levels of government tend

to be more efficient when it is feasible to produce the programs at lower levels.

8. Explain how the government acts as an interest group. What are the implications of government agencies acting like special interests?

9. How does the use of a secret ballot in elections aid in preventing the outright buying and selling of votes?

PART FOUR

Taxation

CHAPTER NINE

Positive Principles of Taxation

*I*n the first eight chapters of the text we were interested primarily in what the government does, and why. In the next several chapters we focus on how the government raises revenues to finance its activities. Recall that the government can raise revenue in three ways—taxation, borrowing, and money creation. The next few chapters are devoted specifically to taxation, with a separate chapter on borrowing and money creation.

The principles of taxation can be divided into two general categories. The first category is the positive principles of taxation, which concern the effects of taxation, such as who will bear the burden of a particular tax and what other economic effects can be expected to result. The most important positive principles of taxation are tax shifting and the excess burden, or welfare cost, of taxation. In Chapter 9 we discuss in detail the positive principles of taxation.

The second category of taxation deals with tax policy. Included in this category are such issues as who should bear the burden of taxation and what each person's fair share of taxation is. Ultimately, these normative questions revolve around how tax policy can be used to design as desirable a tax system as possible. Of course, what constitutes a fair, desirable system depends on the positive effects of particular types of taxes, so before the normative issues can even be discussed, the positive issues of taxation must be examined.

Once the positive and normative issues of tax policy are understood, the political incentives involved in developing tax policy must be explained to provide a fuller understanding about how tax policy is designed. The positive principles of taxation discussed in this chapter can be used as a foundation for Chapter 10, which focuses on the issues involved in designing tax policy.

Tax Shifting

The principles of tax shifting apply to all types of taxes, but for purposes of simplicity they will be examined within the framework of a *unit tax*, which is a tax charged per unit of a good exchanged. For example, cigarette taxes are typically applied as a certain amount per

Figure 9.1 Tax Incidence with a Tax Placed on the Supplier When a unit tax is placed on suppliers in a competitive market, the tax shifts the supply curve up by the amount of the tax, and part of the tax is shifted to demanders.

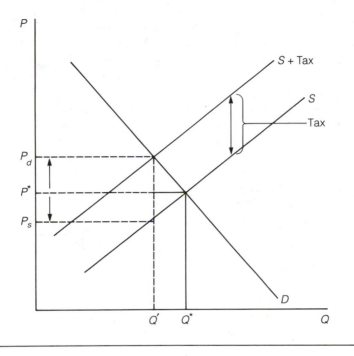

pack of cigarettes, taxes on beer as a fixed price per can, and taxes on gasoline as a certain amount per gallon; in each case the amount of tax due is based on the number of units sold. By contrast, these goods could be subject to an *ad valorem tax*, which is based on the dollar value of the goods sold. For example, an *ad valorem* tax might be 12 percent of the value of beer sold, whereas a unit tax would be 10 cents per can sold. A retail sales tax, which is calculated as a percentage of retail sales, is always a type of *ad valorem* tax, but excise taxes, which are taxes placed on particular selected goods, can be either unit or *ad valorem* taxes.

A Unit Tax Placed on Suppliers

What will happen if a unit tax is placed on the suppliers of a good produced in a competitive market? This situation is illustrated in Figure 9.1, which depicts supply curve S, demand curve D, equilibrium price P^*, and quantity without tax Q^*. Because suppliers have to pay a unit tax on every unit of the good that they sell, each unit is more costly by the amount of the tax, which shifts the supply curve up the same amount. The new supply curve is labeled S + Tax, with the arrow between S and S + Tax indicating that the curves differ by the amount of the tax. Given the tax and the resulting new supply curve, the price rises to price P_D and the quantity produced declines to Q', determined by the intersection of the new supply and demand curves. Just as one might expect, when a tax is placed on the supplier in the market, the price goes up and demanders end up bearing some of the burden of the tax.

Note, however, that the price does not go up by the full amount of the tax. The tax is the distance between S and S + Tax, but the distance from P^* to P_D is less than the tax. Tracing down from the intersection of S + Tax and D to the old supply curve S gives the total amount of the tax, which means that the revenue per unit left for the supplier after the supplier pays the tax is P_S. That is, P_S is the price per unit that goes to the supplier after the tax is paid. This means that although the tax is initially placed on the supplier, part of the tax burden is shifted to the demanders in the form of a higher price and the rest of the tax ends up being paid by the suppliers. This phenomenon is known as *tax shifting*, because although the tax is initially placed on the suppliers, some of the tax is shifted to demanders. The arrow drawn up from P^* shows the proportion of the tax borne by demanders, while the arrow pointing down from P^* shows the proportion borne by suppliers. These proportions will vary depending on the elasticities of supply and demand, which will be discussed in more detail later in this chapter.

An Excise Tax Placed on Demanders

Now consider the effect if an excise tax of the same amount per unit is placed on the demanders in the market rather than the suppliers, as in Figure 9.2. Here the supply and demand curves are the same as in Figure 9.1, but the excise tax causes the demand curve to shift downward to D − Tax. When purchas-

ing a good, demanders are concerned with the total price they have to pay, so if a tax is placed on a good, their demand will fall by the amount of the tax. Thus, the difference between D and D − Tax is the amount of the tax.

With the new demand curve the new equilibrium price is P_S and the new equilibrium quantity is Q', determined by the intersection of the supply and demand curves. The market price falls from P^* to P_S, which shifts some of the tax originally placed on the demanders to the suppliers. But while demanders pay P_S to suppliers, they must also pay the tax, which is the difference between D − Tax and D. Tracing up from the intersection of S and D − Tax to D shows the amount of the tax, and demanders end up paying P_D for the good, including both the amount they pay suppliers and the amount they pay in tax. As in Figure 9.1, the arrow in Figure 9.2 drawn up from P^* indicates the proportion paid by the demanders and the arrow drawn down from P^* indicates the proportion paid by suppliers.

A Tax on the Supplier Versus a Tax on the Demander

As Figures 9.1 and 9.2 illustrate, a tax placed on the suppliers in a market can be partially shifted to demanders and a tax placed on demanders can be partially shifted to suppliers, so that in either case suppliers and demanders end up sharing the burden of the tax. What difference does it make, then, if the tax is placed on the suppliers or on the demanders in the market? This question is addressed in Figure 9.3, which uses the S and D curves from Figures 9.1 and 9.2, the S + Tax curve from Figure 9.1, and the D − Tax curve from Figure 9.2. In effect, Figure 9.3 is a composite of Figures 9.1 and 9.2.

The distance between S and S + Tax is the same as the distance between D and D −

Figure 9.2 Tax Incidence with the Tax Placed on the Demander When a unit tax is placed on demanders in a competitive market, the tax shifts the demand curve down by the amount of the tax, and part of the tax is shifted to suppliers.

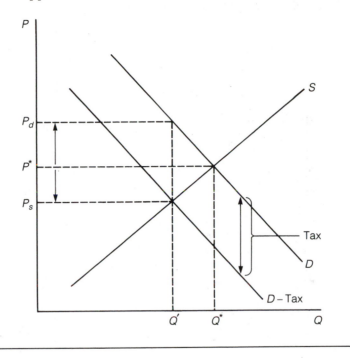

Tax—both are equal to the amount of the tax—so the heavy arrow in Figure 9.3 shows the amount of the tax in both cases. Note that the supply curve shifts up in the first case by the same amount that the demand curve shifts down in the second case. This means that P_D in Figure 9.1 is the same as P_D in Figure 9.2, and that P_S in Figure 9.1 is the same as P_S in Figure 9.2. In both cases the amount paid by the demander, including the tax, is the same regardless of who the tax is initially placed on; likewise, the amount paid by the supplier is the same regardless of who the tax is initially placed on.

Thus, it makes no difference whether the tax is placed on the suppliers or the deman-

ders in a particular market—each ends up paying the same amount no matter who is taxed initially. However, the tax paid by the suppliers usually will not equal the tax paid by the demanders, because the proportion of the tax paid by each group will depend on the relative elasticities of supply and demand.

An important lesson here is that the actual burden of a tax may be different from the legal assignment of the tax. For example, consumers may be charged sales tax, but as this analysis shows, some of the burden of the sales tax can be shifted to suppliers. Likewise, the social security payroll tax nominally is shared between employers and employees, with each paying half. But because the employees are

Figure 9.3 Comparison of a Tax on the Supplier with a Tax on the Demander This figure combines the information presented in Figures 9.1 and 9.2. It shows that suppliers and demanders will pay the same amount of tax regardless of whether a tax is initially placed on suppliers or demanders in a market.

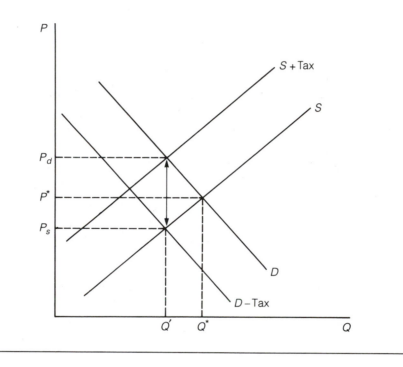

the suppliers of labor and the employers are the demanders, the actual burden of the tax would be the same whether the entire tax was paid by the employees or the employers or whether is was split between them as it is now. Regardless of what the government says, the laws of supply and demand determine who ultimately bears the burden of a tax.

Elasticities and Tax Incidence

The effects of elasticities on tax incidence can be summarized as follows. In general, the more elastic a schedule, all other things held equal, the more the burden of the tax will fall on the other side of the market. For example, the more elastic the demand curve, the smaller the proportion of the tax paid by the demanders and the larger the proportion paid by the suppliers; conversely, the more elastic the supply curve, the greater the pro-

Figure 9.4 The Effects of Demand Elasticity on Tax Incidence This figure compares tax incidence with two different demand curves—elastic demand curve *DE* and inelastic demand curve *DI*. The more elastic the demand, the greater the burden of the tax is on suppliers and the lower the burden of the tax is on demanders. Also note that the more elastic the demand, the more the quantity exchanged will fall as a result of the tax.

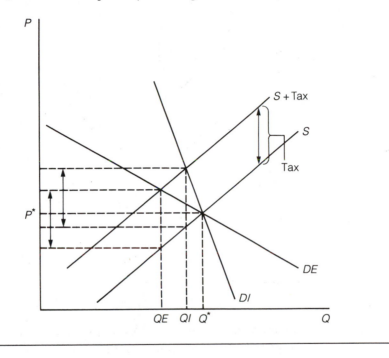

portion of the tax shifted to demanders. In the extreme case of a perfectly inelastic supply curve, the entire tax will be borne by suppliers; conversely, for a perfectly elastic supply curve the entire tax will be shifted to demanders. These ideas can be illustrated graphically.

Figure 9.4 resembles Figure 9.1 in that it shows a tax placed on the suppliers in a market. In Figure 9.4 *DE* is a relatively elastic demand curve, and *DI* is a relatively inelastic demand curve. For *DE* the burden of taxation can be found, as in the previous section, by adding the amount of the tax to the supply curve. Recall that the final effects of the tax

will be the same whether the tax is placed on the suppliers or the demanders. With demand curve *DE* the quantity exchanged is reduced to *QE*, and the tax is represented by the arrow closest to the *P* axis. By contrast, for inelastic demand curve *DI* the quantity exchanged is reduced to *QI*, and the tax is represented by the arrow further away from the *P* axis.

A comparison of these taxes suggests two things. First, the more inelastic the demand curve, the less the quantity exchanged is reduced; the implications of this will be discussed shortly. Second, the more elastic the demand curve, the greater the share of the tax paid by the suppliers. This illustrates

Figure 9.5 Perfectly Inelastic Supply With a perfectly inelastic supply curve the entire burden of the tax falls on suppliers.

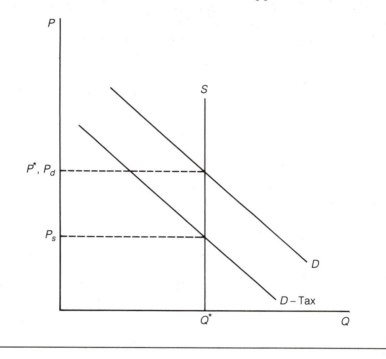

the general principle that the more elastic the schedule, the greater the percentage of the tax that is borne by the other side of the market. The same thing will be true on the supply side of the market. The reader is invited to draw a graph like Figure 9.4 but with a more elastic and a less elastic supply curve to verify that the more elastic the supply curve is, the greater the proportion of the tax paid by demanders will be.

Perfectly Elastic or Perfectly Inelastic Supply

Figures 9.5 and 9.6 show two extreme cases. In Figure 9.5 the supply curve is perfectly inelastic, representing some good for which there will always be a fixed supply on the market. With a perfectly inelastic supply curve a tax can be put on the demanders, but the entire tax will be borne by the suppliers. In other words the price paid by demanders does not shift, and $P^* = P_D$. Note also that when the supply curve is perfectly inelastic, the quantity exchanged is not affected by the tax. The same principle holds for the other side of the market—if the demand curve is perfectly inelastic, the entire tax will be borne by demanders, and the quantity exchanged will not be affected.

Figure 9.6 illustrates the other extreme—a perfectly elastic supply curve. In this case the entire tax is borne by demanders, because when a supply curve is perfectly elastic, the entire tax is shifted to the demand side of the market; thus $P^* = P_S$. The reader can verify

Figure 9.6 Perfectly Elastic Supply With a perfectly elastic supply curve the entire burden of the tax falls on demanders.

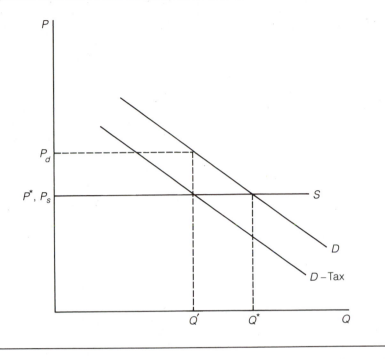

that the same would hold true for the demand curve. Likewise, a perfectly elastic demand will leave the suppliers bearing the entire burden of the tax. The case of perfectly elastic supply is relevant to competitive industries characterized by constant costs, where the long-run industry supply curve will be perfectly elastic. In this case the demanders in the market will end up bearing the entire burden of the tax in the long run.

These conclusions make intuitive sense if one thinks about them. An inelastic supply or demand schedule means that the suppliers or demanders are unwilling to substitute out of the good in question. If this is so, then the group can do little to avoid a tax on the good in question. Conversely, an elastic supply or demand schedule means that the group is willing to forego supplying or demanding the good in question if the price changes adversely. In this case, in order to keep the elastic suppliers or demanders trading in the market, the other side of the market has to bear most of the burden of the tax. Simply stated, the more willing the group in question is to substitute out of the taxed good, the more able it is to force the other side of the market to bear the burden of the tax.

Shifts in the Tax Burden

The general principles just depicted graphically can also be illustrated algebraically. In Figure 9.1 (or any of the other figures) the burden of the tax borne by demanders will be $P_D - P^*$, while the burden placed on suppliers will be $P^* - P_S$. Thus, the ratio of the demanders' share of the tax to the suppliers' share will be $(P_D - P^*)/(P^* - P_S)$, which is the ratio of the change in the demanders' price paid to the change in the suppliers' price received after the tax is paid. Both the numerator and the denominator of this expression can be divided by $(Q^* - Q')$, which is the change in the quantity exchanged, without changing the ratio, to yield

$$\frac{(P_D - P^*)/(Q^* - Q')}{(P^* - P_S)/(Q^* - Q')}$$

This expression states the ratio of the slope of the demand curve to the slope of the supply curve, which means that the ratio of the burden of the tax borne by demanders to the burden borne by suppliers will be equal to the ratio of the slopes of the demand curve and the supply curve.

Although no general relationship exists between the slope of a curve and its elasticity, when two curves pass through the same point (as, for example, the demand curves in Figure 9.4), the flatter curve is the more elastic. Thus, the more elastic the curve is, the greater the share of the burden borne by the other side of the market will be. Furthermore, at the point of intersection the ratio of the slopes of the curves will be equal to the ratio of the elasticities, so that for small changes the ratio of the burden borne by suppliers to the burden borne by demanders will be the ratio of the elasticity of supply to the elasticity of demand. Economists prefer to think in terms of elasticities rather than slopes, but we should note that the precise relationship is between the ratio of the slopes of the curves and the share of the tax ultimately paid by each side of the market.[1]

To summarize, taxes placed on one group in an economy can be shifted through the market to other groups, so that the individuals on whom a tax is initially placed will not necessarily be the ones who ultimately bear the burden of the tax. More specifically, the more elastic a supply or demand schedule is, the greater the proportion of the tax that can be shifted to the other side of the market will be. Also, the proportion of the tax borne by demanders will be the same regardless of whether the tax is placed on the suppliers or the demanders in a particular market. The same will be true of suppliers. Finally, the ratio of the demanders' tax burden to the suppliers' tax burden will be the same as the ratio of the slopes of the demand and supply curves.

The Welfare Cost of Taxation

The welfare cost of taxation is sometimes referred to as the excess burden of taxation or the deadweight loss of taxation; the three terms can be used interchangeably. The *welfare cost of taxation* arises because the taxpayer incurs not only the actual cost of the tax but also the cost of having to alter his or her behavior from the behavior that would have been most preferred without the tax. The taxpayer's behavior is altered because of actions that the taxpayer takes to try to avoid the tax, but in so doing the taxpayer is worse off than

---

[1] In Richard A. Musgrave's classic treatise, *The Theory of Public Finance* (New York: McGraw-Hill, 1959), p. 292, he argues that the ratios of the elasticities are equal to the ratios of the burdens of the tax shares of demanders to suppliers. This is not quite true for the arc elasticity, which would be appropriate for a discrete change of this type.

Figure 9.7 The Excess Burden of Taxation The excess burden of the tax results from the change in behavior caused by the tax. The tax causes people to consume Q' rather than Q^*, resulting in a cost equal in value to the shaded triangle. This cost is in addition to the amount of tax revenue collected, which is represented by the shaded rectangle.

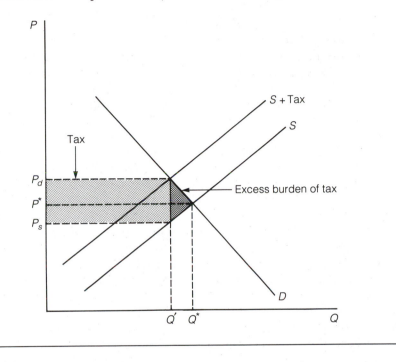

if he or she could have simply paid the same amount of money to the government and not behaved differently.

For example, suppose that the government decides to raise more revenue by placing a tax on gasoline. The taxpayers will be worse off for two reasons. First, the taxpayers must pay the tax every time they purchase gasoline. Second, the tax on gasoline will cause the price of gasoline to rise, which means less gas will be consumed. In other words the tax causes taxpayers to alter their consumption patterns by purchasing less gasoline. The welfare cost to the taxpayers of consuming less gasoline is an excess burden to the taxpayer over and above the amount of the tax paid.

The effects of the excess burden were mentioned briefly in the previous section. Recall that when a tax is levied in a market, the quantity exchanged declines, and this decline in the quantity exchanged is responsible for the welfare cost of taxation.

This concept is illustrated graphically in Figure 9.7, which closely resembles the other figures in the chapter. The tax per unit is $P_D - P_S$, as in the earlier examples. The quantity exchanged is Q' after the tax is imposed, so the tax is $(P_D - P_S) \times Q'$, the area of the shaded rectangle. For example, if there is a 10 cent tax on a gallon of gasoline (this would be $P_D - P_S$) and 1000 gallons of gasoline are sold (this would be Q') then the total tax collected will be the tax per unit times the quantity sold, or $100, and the quantity exchanged will drop to Q'. Therefore, the exchanges from Q' to $Q*$ that could have taken place and provided net benefits to buyers and sellers will not take place.

The welfare cost of the reduction in output from $Q*$ to Q' can be calculated by taking the gain to buyers that would result from consuming the additional units and subtracting the opportunity cost to sellers from producing the additional units. Using the demand curve as a measure of the marginal gain to consumers from the good and the supply curve as a measure of the opportunity cost of producing the good, the net gain that could have been produced from the units between Q' and $Q*$ is the area in the shaded triangle between the demand and supply curves. This triangle represents the dollar value of the burden of taxation resulting from the altered behavior due to the tax; in other words, it is the excess burden of taxation. Recall that the terms *excess burden, welfare loss,* and *deadweight loss of taxation* all mean the same thing, and also that excess burden exists because the tax alters people's behavior in addition to collecting revenue from them.

Within this framework consider the costs of taxation to the taxpayers. The shaded area marked Tax in Figure 9.7 represents the amount of taxes paid by the taxpayers in this market. This is a cost to the taxpayers, but the revenues from this tax are then used to pay for public sector goods and services. The more darkly shaded area marked Excess Burden of Taxation represents the cost to the taxpayers in terms of foregone output in this market. Output level $Q*$ would have been produced without the tax, but the tax causes output Q' to be produced. This is a cost to the taxpayers just the same as the cost of taxes paid, but whereas the revenues from the tax can be used to pay for public sector output, the cost of the excess burden is simply lost.

Thus, the government produces output, presumably of some value, in exchange for the cost of the tax revenues it collects, but the cost of the excess burden is a net social cost.

The Excess Burden as a Cost of Taxation

Because the excess burden represents one of the costs of taxation, it should be taken into account when calculating the total cost of taxation to finance activities in the public sector. A tax that collects a given amount of revenue while altering the behavior of people the least is most desirable, all other things being equal. In other words the tax with the minimum excess burden is preferable because it engenders the least total cost.

A look back at Figure 9.4 can illuminate this issue. Note that when a tax is placed on a good with a more elastic demand, the quantity exchanged falls more than when the tax is placed on the good with the less elastic demand. Thus, placing a given tax on a good with a more inelastic demand tends to minimize the excess burden of the tax. This becomes even more obvious in the extreme case depicted in Figure 9.5. In that case, where the supply curve is perfectly inelastic, the quantity exchanged is not affected by the tax, so the tax causes no excess burden.

In general, the excess burden of a tax can be minimized by placing larger taxes on goods with very inelastic demand or supply schedules. When supply or demand is inelastic, the group with the inelastic schedule will not alter their behavior appreciably, no matter what happens to the price of the good. With an inelastic supply curve suppliers will not reduce production, even though prices are lower; with an inelastic demand curve demanders will not reduce purchases, even though prices are higher. The inelastic schedule implies that the tax will not affect peoples' behavior, meaning there will not be much of an excess burden.

Lump Sum Taxes

A tax that completely eliminates the excess burden of a tax is called a *lump sum tax*, a tax placed on an individual that does not vary no matter what the individual does. The simplest type of lump sum tax is a tax levy of a certain amount that has to be paid by every individual at the time the tax is announced. For example, the government could announce that as of today everybody owes the government a tax of $1000, with no exceptions permitted. Because there would be no way to avoid paying the tax, the tax would have no effect on the behavior of people (except that they would have to raise the money to pay the tax), which means it would have no excess burden. In this sense the lump sum tax is ideal from an efficiency standpoint, because it minimizes the burden of taxation.

However, it is difficult to conceive of how lump sum taxes could be applied in the real world. For example, if the hypothetical $1000 tax were extended so that from now on everybody had to pay a tax of $1000 every year in the future, it would in effect be a tax on having children. Obviously, a young child could not raise the tax money, which would place the burden on the parents and give people an incentive to have fewer children. Likewise, an income tax gives people an incentive to earn less income and take more leisure, so it is not lump sum tax either. Indeed, there are few taxes that will not cause people to alter their behavior in some way.

A tax in a market with a completely inelastic supply or demand curve could act like a lump sum tax if it signified that people would never alter the quantity supplied or demanded of the good—in other words if the good really were of fixed supply or if demanders would always demand a constant amount under any circumstances. A tax on such a good might qualify as a lump sum tax, but no such fixed supply or demand for a good actually exists. And for many goods that have relatively inelastic demands, there is frequently a reluctance to tax them for reasons of equity. For example, medical care is often cited as a good with a relatively inelastic demand, yet medical services, drugs, and so on tend not be taxed so as not to place an additional burden on those who need the care in the first place. Food comprises another category of goods that has a relatively inelastic demand, yet in many states there is no sales tax on food, again for equity reasons.

In general, goods we think of as necessities have relatively inelastic demands, yet it is argued that necessities should not be taxed for reasons of fairness. Conversely, luxury goods have relatively elastic demands, yet they are typically taxed at higher rates, again for reasons of fairness. Thus, in the attempt to minimize the excess burden of a tax, equity issues tend to conflict with efficiency issues. From an efficiency standpoint the best tax is the one with the minimum excess burden, because that tax imposes the lowest total cost on an economy for a given amount of revenue raised.

Excess Burden and Individual Choice

The principle of the welfare cost of taxation can also be illustrated with indifference curves to show how the excess burden of taxation makes individuals worse off than if a lump sum tax is used. Consider the individual whose utility function is depicted in Figure

Figure 9.8 Excess Burden and Individual Choice A tax on good Y rotates the budget constraint inward around point X_1, causing the individual to be at point B rather than point A. However, if the tax took the same amount of income away from the individual without altering the relative prices of X and Y, the individual could be at point C, on a higher indifference curve. The difference between the individual's welfare at point B and point C is the excess burden of the tax.

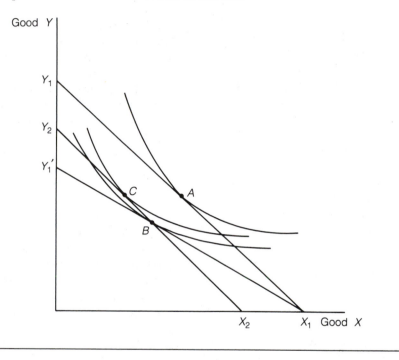

9.8. The individual is faced with the budget constraint X_1Y_1 without a tax and chooses to consume the combination of X and Y given by point A. But when a tax is placed on good Y, the budget constraint rotates inward to budget constraint X_1Y_1'. At this new budget constraint the individual can consume the same amount of X as before the tax on Y if the individual consumes only good X. However, the amount of Y that the individual can consume if the individual consumes only Y will fall as a result of the tax. By considering the tax in this way, it is relatively easy to see how

the budget constraint should be rotated to illustrate a tax on one of the goods. With the tax placed on good Y, the slope of the budget constraint has changed, and because the slope of the budget constraint depicts relative prices, the new slope illustrates that with the tax on good Y, the price of Y relative to X has risen.

With this tax placed on good Y, the individual will now consume the combination of X and Y given by point B, where the individual's indifference curve is tangent to budget constraint X_1Y_1'. By being on a lower indifference curve, the individual is worse off at point B than at point A, for two reasons. First, the individual is worse off because of the amount of the tax paid, and second, because the tax causes the individual's behavior to change to try to avoid the tax. To avoid paying the tax associated with the purchase of good Y, the individual consumes less of Y. From the consumer's standpoint the excess burden arises because the relative price of the taxed good, Y, rises.

But if, instead of levying a tax on good Y, a lump sum tax is applied, the same amount of tax can be collected without the excess burden. The amount of tax collected can be measured either in terms of good X or good Y, but in either case it is the distance from point B to the original budget constraint. A new budget constraint, labeled X_2Y_2, can be drawn in running through point B but parallel to the original budget constraint. Along this new budget constraint the same amount of tax can be collected as at point B, but relative prices remain the same as along the original budget constraint.

The new budget constraint depicts the effect of a lump sum tax on the individual that raises the same amount of revenue as the tax on good Y. The utility-maximizing point for the individual is point C; because point C is on a higher indifference curve than point B, the individual is better off with the lump sum tax than with the tax on good Y. The difference in the individual's well-being is the difference in utility between the indifference curve at point B and the higher indifference curve at point C.

To summarize, recall that the excess burden, in addition to taking tax revenue away from the taxpayer, discourages the consumption of the taxed good. The taxpayer is better off if the tax simply extracts revenue from the taxpayer without altering the relative prices facing the individual. Compare the individu-

al's situation at point B and at point C. The tax revenue collected is the same in both cases, but the relative price of Y is higher on the budget constraint X_1Y_1'. Therefore, the individual is worse off, because the tax gives the individual the incentive to consume less of good Y and creates the excess burden. At point C the lump sum tax allows the individual to purchase X and Y at their original relative prices, so the individual consumes more of good Y. The individual is better off because the consumption choices are not distorted by the lump-sum tax.

Inelastic Labor Supply and the Welfare Cost of an Income Tax

In considering the excess burden of a tax, we argued that if either the supply or demand curve for a good is completely inelastic, there will be no excess burden from a tax in that market. This is true because individuals in the market will not alter their supply or demand quantity under any circumstances. Here we consider another possibility, however. A perfectly inelastic schedule can result from offsetting income and substitution effects, with the substitution effect causing an excess burden of taxation.

This can be illustrated by viewing the effect of an income tax on labor supply. Consider the reaction of an individual to an increase in an income tax. The higher tax makes it more costly to supply labor relative to taking leisure time, so the individual will want to substitute out of work and into leisure. But the higher tax will also mean that the individual has less income and may therefore want to work harder to make up for the income that has been taxed away. In this case, while the substitution effect makes it relatively more attractive not to work, the income effect causes the individual to want to work more. The two effects work in opposite directions.

Figure 9.9 The Excess Burden of an Income Tax The excess burden of taxation is a result of people substituting out of the taxed activity due to the tax. In this example an income tax does not cause the person to alter the amount worked because the income effect and the substitution effect offset each other. There is still an excess burden because of the substitution effect, however. This shows that the excess burden of taxation is the result of the substitution effect alone, and the income effect plays no part in determining the excess burden.

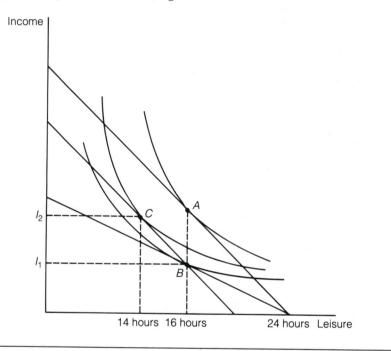

It is possible that the individual might work the same amount with or without the income tax, so the individual's labor supply curve will be perfectly inelastic. However, because there is still a substitution effect, the individual will be better off with a lump sum tax rather than a tax on income. This can be illustrated in Figure 9.9, which is very similar to Figure 9.8. Here the individual worker has twenty-four hours a day to allocate to either work, which earns income, or leisure. The amount of leisure time is recorded on the horizontal axis, and the slope of the budget constraint shows the rate at which leisure time can be transformed into income through working. With no income tax the individual locates at point A, just as in the previous figure.

An income tax raises the relative price of income because the individual must now work more hours in order to take home the same amount of income, so the budget constraint rotates inward and the individual chooses to locate at point B. Note that at both points A and B the individual chooses sixteen hours of leisure per day, and so works for eight hours a day. Because the individual works the same amount regardless of the income received for working, the individual's labor supply curve is completely inelastic.

However, in this case the inelastic labor supply curve is due to offsetting income and substitution effects. If the individual pays a lump sum tax designed to raise the same amount of revenue as the income tax, the budget constraint for the lump sum tax will pass through point B but it will be parallel to the original budget constraint, and the individual will choose to be at point C. At point C the individual works more (takes less leisure), and the after-tax income rises from I_1 to I_2. As in Figure 9.8, the excess burden of the income tax is the difference in welfare of the individual at point B as compared to point C. Because the individual is on a higher indifference curve at point C, the individual is better off with the lump sum tax than with the income tax.

A perfectly inelastic supply or demand curve implies that there will be no excess burden from a tax in that market if individuals in the market do not alter their behavior and supply or demand a different quantity under any circumstances. However, a perfectly inelastic schedule can result from offsetting income and substitution effects and give rise to an excess burden resulting from the substitution effect. A tax on a good causes the individual to substitute out of the taxed good. Thus, as long as there is some substitution effect in response to a change in the relative price of a good, there will be an excess burden of a tax in that market.

Minimizing the Excess Burden of Taxation

In this chapter we have dealt mainly with the theory of taxation rather than specific applications of the tax principles; in subsequent chapters we apply these principles to the real world. Nevertheless, the reader should have a sense of the general magnitude of the welfare cost of taxation. Clearly, the tax system does influence the behavior of individuals, whether by discouraging the consumption of some goods relative to others, influencing an individual's choice of occupation, or altering a corporation's production decisions.

One study has estimated that the welfare cost of the tax system in the United States is between 13 and 24 cents per dollar of revenue raised.[2] This is hardly an insignificant figure compared to the amount of revenue raised. Because government spending accounts for over one-third of *GNP*, the results of this study suggest that the welfare cost of the tax system is at least 5 percent of *GNP*. Given the magnitude of the excess burden of taxation, there is good reason to want to try to minimize it.

The Ramsey Rule

The Ramsey rule, named after its originator, is a theoretical proposition explaining how the excess burden of taxation can be minimized for a given amount of tax revenue to be raised.[3] The *Ramsey rule* states that in order to minimize the excess burden of taxation, the

---

[2]Charles L. Ballard, John B. Shoven, and John Whalley, "The Total Welfare Cost of the United States Tax System: A General Equilibrium Approach," *National Tax Journal* 38, no. 2 (June 1985), pp. 125–140.

[3]Frank P. Ramsey, "A Contribution to the Theory of Taxation," *Economic Journal* 37 (1927), pp. 47–61.

Figure 9.10 The Marginal Excess Burden of a Tax Increase As a tax on a good is increased in equal increments from T to $2T$, the excess burden of taxation increases more than proportionally, as the increase in the size of the welfare loss triangle shows. This illustrates the Ramsey rule, which states that to minimize the excess burden of taxation, taxes should be placed on goods in inverse proportion to their elasticities of demand.

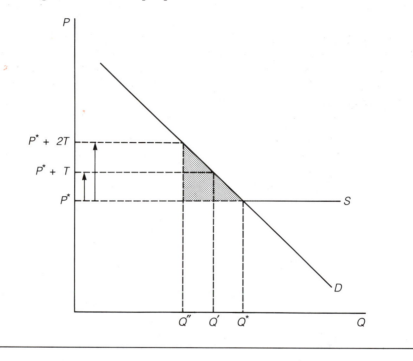

taxes should be placed on goods in inverse proportion to the elasticity of demand for the goods. In other words if the tax on a good is represented by T and its elasticity of demand by E, then the condition defining the optimal tax on goods 1 and 2 to minimize their combined excess burden can be stated as

$$T_1/T_2 = E_2/E_1$$

Proving this proposition in a formal manner is a complex undertaking, but the logic behind it is relatively straightforward.

We have already seen that the more elastic the demand for a good is, the greater the excess burden from a tax on that good will be. This implies that taxes should be placed on all goods with inelastic demands, given that the supply elasticities are the same. Indeed, the Ramsey rule summarized in the equation just given specifies that the large tax is placed on the more inelastic good. But the larger the tax, the greater the excess burden from any additional tax on the good will be; this is illustrated in Figure 9.10.

Figure 9.10 shows the marginal increase in

the excess burden of taxation as a result of a tax increase. For the sake of simplicity, we will consider a market in which the supply curve is assumed to be perfectly elastic. With equilibrium price P^* and quantity Q^* without the tax, a tax equal to T is placed on the good. The price rises to $P^* + T$ and the quantity falls to Q'. The amount of tax collected is the rectangle with vertical side from P^* to T, shown by the short arrow, and horizontal side from the origin to Q'. The excess burden of the tax is represented by the small shaded triangle between Q' and Q^*.

Now assume that the tax rate is doubled from T per unit to $2T$ per unit, as shown by the longer arrow. However, because the higher tax will lead to a lower quantity being exchanged, tax revenue will not be doubled. Note that the darkly shaded box, which was part of the tax revenue collected with the smaller tax, is no longer collected because the quantity exchanged in the market has fallen from Q' to Q''. But while the tax revenue has not doubled, the excess burden of the tax has more than doubled, now encompassing the entire shaded area.

As Figure 9.10 suggests, when a tax becomes larger, the excess burden from increasing that tax grows faster than the corresponding tax revenue. Therefore, even though it makes sense to place larger taxes on goods with more inelastic demands, there is a trade-off between placing ever-larger taxes on the inelastic goods and placing some smaller taxes on goods with more elastic demands. How should these taxes be placed in order to minimize the excess burden? Here is where the Ramsey rule comes in. The excess burden of taxation is minimized when taxes are levied in inverse proportion to the elasticities of demands for the goods.

This does represent a bit of an oversimplification for several reasons. First, we have neglected to consider the elasticities of supply for the goods, but it should be evident that the same type of relationship will hold. Also, we have assumed the goods to be unrelated in consumption (neither complements nor substitutes), so that a tax on one good will not affect the demand for another good. But these simplifying assumptions should not detract from an understanding of the underlying principle of the Ramsey rule, that to minimize the excess burden of taxation, goods with relatively inelastic demands should be taxed more heavily than goods with relatively elastic demands.

Additional Costs of the Tax System

It should be apparent by now that there are costs to taxation over and above the dollar amount of taxes paid. The excess burden is one example, but there are other costs imposed by taxation as well, including compliance costs, administrative costs, and political costs.

Compliance Costs

Anyone who has filled out an income tax form will be familiar with compliance costs, which are the costs imposed on taxpayers to comply with the tax laws. Collecting and keeping records is a big part of compliance costs, as are filling out tax forms and filing taxes. If a taxpayer is audited, additional compliance costs are incurred in demonstrating to the government that the taxpayer indeed is in compliance.

Many individuals, and almost all businesses, find the tax laws so complex that they hire accountants and tax lawyers to help them comply with the tax laws and find ways of minimizing their tax burdens. The largest compliance costs are borne in conjunction with the income tax, because it is the most complicated tax to compute, but even relatively simple taxes, such as the sales tax, have compliance costs.

Although compliance costs are difficult to measure, one study has estimated that compliance costs for the individual income tax in the United States are between 5 and 7 percent of the revenue raised from the tax.[4] The study found that compliance costs in 1982 were between $17 billion and $27 billion, including $3 billion paid for professional tax assistance and about 2 billion hours of taxpayers' time. In view of the fact that this study looked only at the personal income tax, it is clear that compliance costs are a significant part of taxation as a whole.

Administrative Costs

Whereas compliance costs are the costs borne by taxpayers, administrative costs are the costs borne by the government to collect taxes. For example, the Internal Revenue Service (IRS) must print and mail tax forms to taxpayers, process the completed tax returns, and mail refund checks to those who are due refunds. All of this costs the government money. The IRS also has auditors to check on taxpayer compliance, and the auditing procedure itself costs money. Records must be kept for any type of tax, so administrative costs include tax collection and record keeping. Although administrative costs are significant, most economists believe that in the United States compliance costs exceed administrative costs by a considerable margin. That is, it costs taxpayers more to pay their taxes than it costs the government to collect them.

Political Costs

Another cost associated with the tax system is the political cost borne by taxpayers and the government as a result of taxpayers trying to influence the tax laws. The tax laws are always subject to modification, and taxpayers continually attempt to change the tax laws in their favor. For example, realtors have incurred considerable costs hiring lobbyists to try to retain—and, indeed, improve—the home mortgage interest deduction, one of the largest deductions on federal income tax returns. The lobbying effort of realtors represents a real cost of using the tax system, and their efforts have paid off, because the major tax reform bill passed in 1986 retained the home mortgage deduction while many other deductions were eliminated.

Realtors are not alone, of course, in lobbying for favorable tax treatment. As another example, businesses lobby to improve the tax write-offs available for depreciation, research and development, and so on. It is difficult to estimate the political costs to both taxpayers and the government that political activities aimed at influencing tax legislation generate, but in an economic framework a taxpayer has an incentive to spend up to the expected value of the change in the tax law in order to get the law passed. Political costs are discussed in more detail in Chapter 18 in the section on rent seeking.

---

[4] Joel Slemrod and Nikki Sorum, "The Compliance Cost of the U.S. Individual Income Tax System," *National Tax Journal* 37, no. 4 (Dec. 1984), pp. 461–474.

Earmarked Taxes

Earmarked taxes are taxes whose revenues are designated to a particular spending activity. For example, tolls collected at a toll bridge may be earmarked toward paying for the bridge, the federal gasoline tax to the building of highways, and a federal tax on commercial airline ticket purchases for airport improvements. The largest earmarked tax is the social security payroll tax, which goes toward paying social security benefits to recipients. All of these taxes are earmarked because the tax revenues from the particular source go toward a particular spending area.

General Fund Financing Versus Earmarking

General fund financing is the alternative to earmarking. With *general fund financing* the tax revenues are placed in a general fund, from which government programs are financed. For example, in the case of national defense, federal taxes from many sources are collected and placed in the Treasury, and then Congress spends the amount it deems appropriate for national defense without regard to where the revenue was raised. As an alternative, national defense could be financed by earmarking the corporate income tax for national defense. However, this option would require either cutting the defense budget, increasing corporate income tax collections, supplementing the corporate income tax with another tax source, or perhaps combining several of these options.

As with the taxes on gasoline and airline tickets, earmarked taxes are often used in cases where the taxed activity is closely related to the ultimate use of the funds. In these cases earmarked taxes are similar to user charges. However, as the hypothetical defense department example suggests, the earmarked tax

source need not be closely related to the ultimate expenditure.[5] Earmarked taxes only must be collected for a specific purpose.

Earmarked taxes are most often used at the local level of government. For example, schools are often funded by a specific portion of the local property tax, though school funding can vary greatly from state to state. Some states earmark property taxes for schools; others finance their elementary and secondary education out of the general fund of a larger budget, such as a city or county. In some areas a portion of the sales tax could be earmarked for a specific purpose. For example, 1 percent of the sales tax might be earmarked toward financing a new courthouse or county jail.

The Advantages and Disadvantages of Earmarking

Funding government programs entirely by earmarked taxes lacks the flexibility of general fund financing because a particular tax base may be too small or too unstable to provide the revenue generation for a given program that citizens desire. If citizens are allowed to vote on the level of expenditures of various programs for which taxes are earmarked, they have a much better opportunity

---

[5] Earl A. Thompson, "Taxation and National Defense," *Journal of Political Economy* 82, no. 4 (July/August 1974), pp. 755–783, presents a rather novel argument that the income tax can be viewed as a corrective tax on an externality. The earning of income results in a wealthier society, which makes the country a more attractive target for military aggression. But a tax on income discourages income-earning activity; within this framework it can be considered as a type of user charge paying for national defense. Regardless of the validity of this argument, the income tax is not an earmarked tax, because income tax revenues go into a general fund.

to receive the amount of public sector output they find most satisfactory. For example, if citizens can vote on the amount of property tax revenue that will go toward financing public schools, they are more likely to get the level of education they want than if public schools are financed out of a general fund.

Sometimes policymakers can manipulate the budget mix in order to increase spending on particular programs under general fund financing. For example, a city council might desire additional spending to improve the offices in city hall, while taxpayers are more interested in police and fire protection. Under general fund financing it would be possible for the city council to allocate a larger-than-optimal share of the budget to city hall improvement and a smaller-than-optimal share to the police and fire departments. Voters would then vote for a larger government budget to get the increased police and fire services, for which they have relatively inelastic demands, and the city council would get an improved city hall, for which demand is more elastic. The general principle here is the more the budget mix is skewed toward public sector output with more elastic demands, the larger the budget voters will favor.[6]

Earmarked revenue sources provide the benefit of making it clear to taxpayers how much they pay for particular activities of government. For example, most taxpayers have a better idea about how much the social security system costs them than how much the Defense Department costs them. However, earmarked taxes are also less flexible than general fund financing. Still, earmarking has much to recommend it, because the government is required to allocate revenues to particular expenditures before the fact, making the cost of government clearer to taxpayers. The government can always choose to allocate revenues to match the current expenditure patterns, but an explicit match between revenue sources and expenditures can help to control the cost of government.[7]

Conclusion

The principles of taxation can be divided into two general groups—positive and normative. Positive principles of taxation, which examine the effects of taxes on individuals in the economy, can be further analyzed in terms of tax shifting and the welfare loss of taxation. Tax shifting refers to who ultimately bears the burden of a tax. Taxes initially placed on one group can be shifted through the market so that they end up being borne by another group. When a tax is placed on a particular market, the ratio of the tax ultimately borne by the demander to the tax ultimately borne by the supplier is equal to the ratio of the slope of the demand curve to the slope of the supply curve.

The welfare loss of taxation, also called the excess burden or deadweight loss of taxation, is the cost the tax places on the economy over and above the tax revenues collected. In addition to collecting revenue, a tax alters the economic behavior of individuals by causing

[6]See James M. Buchanan, "The Economics of Earmarked Taxes," *Journal of Political Economy* 71 (Oct. 1963), pp. 457–469, for a discussion and diagrammatic demonstration.

[7]This idea can be traced back at least to Knut Wicksell, "A New Principle of Just Taxation," in Richard A. Musgrave and Alan T. Peacock, eds., *Classics in the Theory of Public Finance* (New York: St. Martin's Press, 1967), pp. 92–118.

them to substitute out of the taxed activities. The less people are willing or able to substitute out of the taxed good, the smaller the excess burden will be. Therefore, taxes on goods with very inelastic supplies or demands will minimize the excess burden of taxation.

Other positive principles of taxation, such as earmarking of tax revenues, ease of collection, and ease of monitoring taxpayer compliance, will be discussed in conjunction with the principles of tax shifting and excess burden when specific taxes are examined in the next few chapters. As the studies cited in this chapter suggest, the costs of the tax system are significant, both in absolute dollar terms and as a percentage of tax revenue raised. One of the goals of a tax system, therefore, should be to minimize the excess burden of taxation.

In addition to these positive principles, normative principles of taxation must be considered. Tax systems are designed with tax equity in mind, but the fairness of a particular tax policy can only be evaluated after the actual effects of the tax are understood. The material in this chapter forms a foundation for understanding the positive effects of taxation; in the next chapter we examine equity issues as they relate to the design of a desirable tax structure.

Questions

1. What are the three methods by which the government can finance its expenditures?

2. Explain the difference between a unit tax and an *ad valorem* tax.

3. What is meant by tax shifting? Who bears the burden of an excise tax placed on the suppliers of a good? Who bears the burden of an excise tax of the same amount placed on the demanders of a good? Using a graph, compare the effects of a tax placed on the suppliers of a good with a tax placed on the demanders.

4. In a market where an excise tax is levied, how can one compute the ratio of the tax paid by the suppliers to the tax paid by the demanders?

5. What is meant by the excess burden of taxation? How is the excess burden measured, and why does it arise? What can be done to minimize the excess burden of revenue raised by taxation?

6. What makes a tax efficient? Discuss some of the issues involved in trading off equity and efficiency in the design of tax systems.

7. If the excess burden of a tax is generated because of the actions people take in order to avoid taxes, then a tax that is difficult to avoid will have a minimal excess burden. An oft-cited advantage of a well-defined tax code is that certainty in the tax structure enables firms and individuals to adjust to the tax code; by the same token this adjustment causes the excess burden. In this sense the excess burden of taxation could be minimized by making frequent unannounced changes to the

tax structure, making it difficult to plan ahead to avoid taxes. Comment on the idea that the more uncertain the tax structure is, the lower the excess burden will be, other things held equal. Consider the merits (and demerits) of uncertainty in the tax structure from both an equity and an efficiency standpoint.

8. Can a tax have an excess burden if the supply curve in the market is completely inelastic? Explain, using labor supply as an example. Use your explanation to illustrate exactly what gives rise to the excess burden of taxation.

9. What is the Ramsey rule? Explain the logic behind the Ramsey rule.

10. What is an earmarked tax? Discuss the advantages and disadvantages of earmarking. Would it be feasible to earmark all taxes?

CHAPTER TEN

Principles of Tax Policy

*I*n Chapter 9 we discussed some positive principles of taxation. By understanding these principles, it becomes possible to understand how specific types of taxes affect both individuals in the economy and the economy as a whole. But positive principles supply only a foundation for designing a desirable tax system, because while positive principles might identify the effects of certain types of taxes, they do not provide a means for determining whether the effects of these taxes are desirable.

Some positive principles have straightforward implications for tax policy. For one thing, it is generally preferable to minimize the excess burden of taxation, though even this is not universally true. For example, the stated goal of taxes on certain goods, such as alcohol and tobacco, is to reduce the consumption of those goods. These types of taxes are called sumptuary taxes, and they will be discussed later in this chapter. But sumptuary taxes notwithstanding, the more efficient a tax system is, the lower the excess burden of taxation will be.

Although an efficient tax system is desirable, it is not the single criterion by which tax systems are judged. Indeed, equity in the tax system is viewed by many people as more important than efficiency. When equity goals are similar to efficiency goals, no problems arise in the formation of tax policy, but when the goals of equity and efficiency conflict, as they often do, normative judgments must be made. In this chapter we will examine some generally accepted principles of equity in taxation.

In the development of tax policy, the fundamental goal is to balance the demands of equity and efficiency. However, to fully understand the process by which tax policies are actually developed, we must also consider the political environment in which tax systems are designed. Therefore, after considering some principles of equity in taxation, we close this chapter with a discussion of the politics of taxation, which become especially relevant when considering the major issues of tax reform that have surfaced during the 1980s.

Recall that the principles of taxation can be divided into equity and efficiency issues. An efficient tax is one that minimizes the excess burden of taxation. Other efficiency issues are sometimes raised in conjunction with a specific tax. For example, how easy it will be to monitor the taxpayer for compliance and how easy it will be to collect the tax. By contrast, equity issues, because they deal with fairness, are inherently normative in nature. This implies that there are no scientifically foolproof principles of tax equity; nevertheless, there are a number of generally accepted principles of tax equity. Because in the real world a society collectively chooses its tax institutions, and because in general people want their tax system to be fair, equity issues are at least as important as efficiency issues in the determination of tax systems.

Two of the most important principles of tax equity are the benefit principle and the ability-to-pay principle. Briefly, according to the *benefit principle* people should pay taxes in proportion to the benefits they receive for government output; according to the *ability-to-pay principle* people should pay taxes in proportion to their ability to pay. Although these two principles seem relatively straightforward, a number of problems can arise in trying to implement them.

The Benefit Principle

The benefit principle states that the people who benefit from the government's expenditures should be the people who pay for them. This principle has obvious appeal from an equity standpoint. It seems only fair that people should pay for the benefits they receive and, conversely, that people should not be forced to pay for benefits that go to others. The benefit principle, in effect, views a tax as the price that is paid for a governmentally supplied good. Just as it is fair for people to pay for the goods they receive in the private sector, so it is also fair for people to pay for the benefits they receive from public sector production.[1]

Efficiency and the Benefit Principle

Apart from its appeal on equity grounds, the benefit principle also has some appeal on efficiency grounds, because it can be applied in such a way as to minimize the excess burden of taxation. If a unit tax is placed on consump-

tion of public sector output, then the tax serves essentially the same function as a price in the private market. In this sense a tax can be seen as a user charge. Note that the excess burden will be minimized when actual user charges can be levied. For example, many parks have admission charges that (at least partially) cover the costs of maintenance and operation. Likewise, toll bridges and toll roads frequently charge the tolls to cover the cost of the good. Such charges may be inefficient when the facilities are not congested, but they do serve as a measure of the demand for a particular good or service.[2] And when the facility is congested, the charges act as a rationing device, just like prices in the private sector.

Using a gasoline tax to finance highways has the features of a tax based on the benefit principle. Those who use highways must also use gasoline, which suggests that the costs of building and maintaining highways will be

---

[1] See James M. Buchanan, "Taxation in Fiscal Exchange," *Journal of Public Economics* 6 (July/August 1976), pp. 17–29, for an elaboration of this argument.

[2] For an elaboration of this argument, see Jora R. Minasian, "Television Pricing and the Theory of Public Goods," *The Journal of Law & Economics* 7 (Oct. 1964), pp. 71–80.

borne by those who benefit from the highways. Although such a tax does discourage the use of highways, to the extent that the highways are congested the tax acts as a rationing device. Thus, basing a tax on the benefit principle will tend to be efficient as well as equitable.

In the next chapter we discuss the application of user charges in more detail, raising a number of issues regarding their efficiency. At this point it is sufficient to note that user charges represent a direct method of implementing the benefit principle and offer potential efficiency reasons for applying user charges as well.

Actual Taxes and the Benefit Principle

Certain other taxes may be seen as sharing at least some of the characteristics of the benefit principle. For example, people with more children may tend to have larger (and more expensive) houses; thus, using a property tax to finance public schools will satisfy some of the criteria of the benefit principle. Such a tax only approximates the benefit principle, though. The correspondence would be closer if tuition simply were charged for each child, but a tuition charge might be viewed as inequitable to poorer households. Therefore, the property tax represents a compromise between the benefit principle and the ability-to-pay principle.[3]

---

[3]Earl A. Thompson, "Taxation and National Defense," *Journal of Political Economy* 82 (July/August 1974), pp. 755–783, argues rather creatively that individuals who earn more income make a nation more vulnerable to foreign aggression, because aggressors are more interested in taking over a wealthier country. Therefore, an income tax is a corrective tax on an externality (because one person's wealth makes everyone else in the nation more vulnerable to attack), in addition to being a user charge based on the proportion of defense effort used to protect the particular individual's wealth holdings.

The payroll tax used to finance social security programs might also fit easily into the mold of the benefit principle. The payroll tax was designed to resemble insurance payments in some respects, with beneficiaries paying a payroll tax now in exchange for future benefits. Although the correspondence between insurance payments and the social security payroll tax is not complete, it is apparent that the social security tax is modeled at least in part according to the benefit principle. Social security is discussed more fully in Chapter 15.

User charges, such as tolls for bridges, admissions fees to parks, and rent paid for use of a local civic center, are the most obvious examples of the application of the benefit principle of taxation. But the gasoline tax for highway improvement and the payroll tax for social security also contain certain features of the benefit principle. Indeed, the overall design of the tax system is strongly oriented toward the benefit principle. Note that local taxes tend to pay for public sector output produced for individuals in the locality, while state taxes produce goods to benefit a wider constituency, and federal taxes finance public sector output that produces even more broadly based benefits. The production of civic centers by local governments and national defense by the federal government illustrates how the overall tax system is constructed with the benefit principle in mind.

Despite the inherent appeal of the benefit principle, it cannot be used as the sole principle of taxation. For one thing, it is often difficult to identify the actual beneficiaries of governmental activities perceived to be in the public good. More importantly, some of the government's activities involve providing benefits to less fortunate individuals as a way of improving their welfare. Welfare programs obviously do not satisfy the criteria of the benefit principle; the very idea of welfare programs is that those who are better off in a society will be helping those who are less well off. In Chapter 14 we focus on redistributive issues, but for now it is sufficient to observe that the goals of a redistributive program would not be furthered if those receiving the benefits paid for those benefits themselves.

The Ability-to-Pay Principle

The ability-to-pay principle is the second main principle of tax equity. The ability-to-pay principle, as its name suggests, states that individuals should pay taxes in proportion to their ability to pay. In practice, implementation of the ability-to-pay principle involves a number of difficult issues, but before dealing with these issues, the basic appeal of the general principle needs to be discussed.

Ability to Pay and the Public Interest

Many government activities are carried on for the general public good. Examples include national defense, the court system, the prison system, and the legislature that develops laws and government programs. Adam Smith, in *The Wealth of Nations*, argued that in these cases a close link exists between the benefit principle and the ability-to-pay principle.

> The subjects of every state ought to contribute towards the support of the government, as nearly as possible, in proportion to their respective abilities; that is, in proportion to the revenue which they respectively enjoy under the protection of the state. The expence of government to the individuals of a great nation, is like the expence of management to the joint tenants of a great estate, who are all obligated to contribute in proportion to their respective interests in the estate.[4]

In other words Smith viewed the benefit principle and the ability-to-pay principle as implying similar things about the tax structure. Smith stated that one's benefits from government are in proportion to the income that one receives under the protection of the state, but that one's income is also a good measure of ability to pay. In this sense no real conflict exists between the benefit principle and the ability-to-pay principle.

Although Smith's argument links these two principles theoretically, it also obscures some important practical problems in trying to implement the principles. One immediate problem is that modern governments are heavily involved in redistributive activities, and if the strict benefit principle were used to assign taxes for redistributive purposes, the recipients of, say, food stamps or housing subsidies would be assigned the taxes to pay for these programs. Obviously, food stamps could not be used to help the needy if the needy were asked to pay the taxes to finance the food stamp program.

But while redistributive programs are intended to benefit the recipients of the redistribution, the programs themselves presumably were enacted because society seeks to help out its less fortunate members. If this is a general social goal, then the benefit and ability-to-pay principles may be closer than they first appear on redistributive issues. Redistributive activities are a major part of government expenditures, but it may be difficult to assign benefit shares to individual citizens.

---

[4]Adam Smith, *The Wealth of Nations* (New York: Modern Library, 1937), p. 777.

Everyone benefits to some degree, but in what proportion is less clear.

Because one of the government's goals is to help out those less fortunate, and because in a sense those who are better off benefit more from the protection of the government (they have more to protect), it stands to reason that taxes to finance the general benefits of government should be paid in proportion to the citizens' abilities to pay. It is only fair that those who are more able to pay should pay more, thus lessening the burden on those less able to pay. Although this argument is normative, and so not demonstrably "true" in the same way as a positive principle of taxation, it is a value generally observed in attempting to devise a fair tax system.

Implementing Ability to Pay

As a general principle, ability to pay has much appeal, but two main problems arise. First, is it fair for someone to pay more simply due to a greater ability to pay? The answer to this question involves a value judgment, albeit a necessary one in implementing tax policy. Second, in deciding when individuals have an equal ability to pay and when they do not, how much more should be paid by the individual with the greater ability to pay? For example, if one individual has twice as much income as another, how much more should the high-income person pay in taxes than the low-income person? What if the person with twice the income has a wife and two children to support, whereas the low-income person is single? These types of questions can be analyzed more precisely within a framework that makes a distinction between horizontal equity and vertical equity.

The concepts of horizontal equity and vertical equity are subsets of the ability-to-pay principle of taxation. The principle of *horizontal equity* is satisfied when people with an equal ability to pay end up paying the same amount of tax. The principle of *vertical equity* is satisfied when people with a greater ability to pay end up paying the appropriate amount more in taxes than people with a lesser ability to pay.

How the appropriate amount is calculated will be explained in turn, but first, consider horizontal equity, which specifies that people with an equal ability to pay in fact pay the same amount in taxes.

Horizontal Equity

Some of the problems involved in evaluating horizontal equity have already been mentioned. The idea that individuals with equal abilities to pay should pay the same amount in taxes might imply that two individuals earning the same income should pay the same amount in income taxes. However, as the previous example suggested, if one individual is single while the other is trying to support a family on the same income, then it might be argued that the individual supporting the family does not have the same ability to pay. Therefore, it would be inequitable to tax the individual with family as much as the single individual, because even though they have the same income, they do not have the same ability to pay.

The current U.S. income tax code takes this type of situation into account, levying a lower tax rate on married individuals than on single people and allowing deductions for children as well. In this sense the concept of horizontal equity has been applied—the decision to have a large family lowers the individual's ability to pay and therefore lowers the tax burden. Similarly, current tax law allows the deduction of medical expenses over a certain amount, implying that an individual with high medical payments has a lower ability to pay than one without these expenses. Because such a judgment is normative, it cannot be proved the way a positive statement can be. Nevertheless, there does seem to be a certain element of fairness in regarding someone with high medical expenses as having a lower ability to pay.

Note the possibility that the concept of equity as used here may be at odds with the benefit principle of taxation. Consider again the individual with several children, who, it was argued, has a lower ability to pay than a single person with the same income and should therefore pay a smaller amount of tax. But assume that the family sends its children to public schools, whereas the single person has no children in school. The benefit principle states that the family should pay a higher amount of tax for the greater educational benefits received. But the ability-to-pay principle states that the person should pay a lower tax because of the lower ability to pay.

Certainly equity should be considered when designing a tax system. Problems arise in trying to decide how to implement concepts of equity, though. As the previous example illustrates, two different tax policies can logically be applied to one situation; perhaps the benefit principle can argue against a narrow interpretation of horizontal equity. Because these issues are fundamentally normative, disagreements cannot be easily resolved. This is not meant to minimize the importance of normative issues, however; ultimately, a society must decide through the political process what type of tax system to have. And as diffi-cult as the concept of horizontal equity may be to apply to taxation, it is relatively straightforward when compared to the notion of vertical equity.

Vertical Equity

The concept of vertical equity states that people with greater abilities to pay should pay more in taxes than those with lower abilities to pay. Assuming that one can actually decide who has the greater ability to pay, the concept of vertical equity does little to actually specify how much more one should pay if one has a greater ability to pay. For example, if one individual has twice the income of another, all other things being equal, should the high-income person pay twice the tax of the low-income person? More than twice the tax? Only slightly more?

The concept of vertical equity provides no answers to these questions. The income tax code in the United States is designed so that an individual with twice the income of another will pay more than twice the income tax, but this only tells part of the story. Because the tax code is so complex, higher-income individuals can often take advantage of methods to avoid paying taxes, in ways that lower-income individuals cannot (although much of the tax reform enacted in 1986 was designed to reduce these loopholes). In addition, other taxes besides the income tax must be considered to get a complete picture of the equity of the overall tax system.

How might this notion of vertical equity be implemented? An argument could be made that taxes should be paid in direct proportion to a person's income if one believes that the rewards provided by the market system are fair. If the market compensates people fairly for their contributions to society, then a tax proportional to income would preserve the differential provided by the market and thus would be a fair tax. However, if one believes that the market does not reward people in proportion to their contributions, then a tax that takes an increasingly larger fraction of people's incomes as income rises might be more fair. If higher-income people earn some of their income through luck, whereas lower-income people are the victims of misfortune, then a progressive tax that takes some steps to equalize the differences in income would seem to better satisfy the concept of vertical equity.

The notion of vertical equity is important to the design of a fair tax code. There is widespread agreement that high-income individuals should pay their fair share of taxes and that low-income people should not be burdened with excessive taxation. However, there is less agreement on exactly what a high-income individual's fair share of taxes is, and to what degree low-income individuals should be able to avoid taxation. Our purpose here is simply to introduce the notion of vertical equity and to suggest some of the difficulties involved in incorporating vertical equity into the tax system. We will continue to discuss the concept in subsequent chapters, particularly in conjunction with the income tax. For now, we turn our attention to the concept of progressivity in taxes, which is a key factor in determining the vertical equity of a particular type of tax.

Progressive, Proportional, and Regressive Taxes

Tax systems, and individual taxes, can be classified according to the proportion of income that an individual taxpayer pays in taxes. A tax that is the same percentage of a taxpayer's income no matter what the level of income is called a *proportional tax*. A tax that is a larger percentage of the taxpayer's income as income rises is a *progressive tax*. A tax that is a smaller percentage of the taxpayer's income as income rises is a *regressive tax*. These taxes are depicted graphically in Figure 10.1. Note that we refer to the percentage, not amount, of income paid as tax. For example, if a person with $10,000 in income pays $1000 in taxes and a person with $100,000 in income pays $5000, then the tax is regressive. The person with the lower income pays 10 percent in taxes, and the person with the higher income pays 5 percent.

These concepts are positive—whether a tax is progressive, proportional, or regressive is a matter of fact. However, they have normative overtones, because the percentage of a person's income paid in taxes should be fair relative to the percentage paid by other taxpayers. For example, many people think that regressive taxes are unfair because the lower a person's income, the larger the percentage of that person's income taken in taxes. Furthermore, questions of degree must be considered—two people might favor a progressive income tax and yet disagree on how progressive the tax should be.

For example, from 1965 to 1981 the income tax brackets for the personal income tax in the United States varied from 14 percent of income to 70 percent of income. In 1982 tax rates were lowered so that the brackets varied from 12 percent to 50 percent of income. In both cases progressive tax schedules were in

Figure 10.1 Progressive, Proportional, and Regressive Taxes A progressive tax takes a larger percentage of a person's income the larger the income is. A regressive tax takes a smaller percentage of income the larger the income. A proportional tax takes the same percentage of income regardless of the level of income. Note that the percentage of income paid, and not the dollar amount, determines whether a tax is progressive, proportional, or regressive.

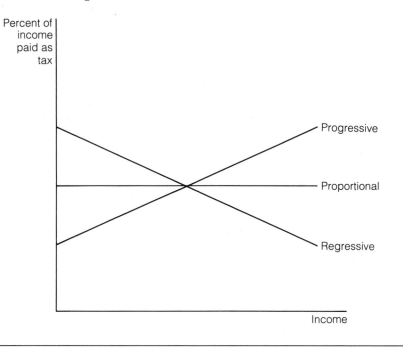

effect, but there are obvious differences in the degree of progressivity. The tax reform measure passed in 1986 provides for even less progressivity in the tax schedule, although progressivity remains a feature of the tax system. Whether one of these rate schedules or some other degree of progressivity represents the fair distribution of the tax burden is a normative question, but an important one.

Here we merely touched on the concept of progressivity, having considered income taxes but not sales taxes, property taxes, or any other taxes, for that matter. These are difficult issues, based partly on the positive concepts of taxing outlined in the previous chapter. For example, if a tax nominally paid by one individual can be shifted to someone else, how is the degree of progressivity in the tax affected? We will discuss the concept of progressivity in subsequent chapters as it applies to specific types of taxes.

Sumptuary Taxes

Taxes designed to discourage the consumption of a good are called *sumptuary taxes*.[5] Recall that the welfare cost of taxation derives from the fact that the tax on a good discourages people from consuming that good. Indeed, this is sometimes the goal of a tax, as in the case of tobacco and alcohol, where legislatures seek to control or to discourage the purchase of the good in question.

Sumptuary Taxes and the Excess Burden

Note that the excess burden of taxation still exists when sumptuary taxes are applied— both demanders and suppliers would consider themselves better off if the tax did not discourage consumption of the taxed good.[6] What then is the rationale for sumptuary taxes? It must be that the consumption of the good by some people makes other people feel that they are worse off, in effect creating an externality. If this is the case, then the sumptuary tax can be viewed as a corrective tax on the externality; some people are taxed for smoking because other people suffer an external cost.

Another possible explanation for sumptuary taxes is that the tax is actually applied be-

cause some people use the government to try to alter the behavior of others, in effect legislating morality through the tax system. Yet another possibility is that the government simply uses the taxes to raise revenue, finding it easier to justify a tax on a good that some people regard as undesirable to consume anyway.

The Rationale Behind Sumptuary Taxes

During the energy crisis of the 1970s, President Carter advocated a 50 cent per gallon tax on gasoline, supposedly, according to Carter, to reduce the consumption of gasoline. This tax, if enacted, would have fallen in the same category as the sumptuary taxes already discussed. President Carter's rationale was that people were harming the nation by consuming—and therefore importing—so much gasoline. The tax would indeed have discouraged the consumption of gasoline, but a closer examination of the situation suggests that the tax Carter proposed was not the right one, given his premises.

Presumably, President Carter did not mind that people were consuming gasoline, but only that the nation had to import so much oil to meet its consumption needs. A tax on gasoline consumption, however, would have not only reduced consumption but also discouraged domestic production. Thus, the effect on the level of imports would have been mixed, as Figure 10.2 suggests. Here a tax is placed on the consumption of gasoline, such that the price suppliers receive for the same output is reduced from P^* to P_S. A lower retail price of gasoline means it is less profitable to produce gasoline, which causes domestic production as well as less consumption to decline. The best tax to discourage the level of

---

[5]Richard Musgrave, in *The Theory of Public Finance* (New York: McGraw-Hill, 1959), refers to this type of a good as a de-merit good, which should be taxed to discourage its consumption. A merit good, by contrast, is a good that should be subsidized in order to encourage its consumption.

[6]One might argue that individuals desire a tax to be imposed on their behavior to get them to reduce some activity when the individuals have insufficient willpower without an additional incentive. This line of reasoning is explored in M. Crain, T. Deaton, R. G. Holcombe, and R. Tollison, "Rational Choice and the Taxation of Sin," *Journal of Public Economics* 8 (1977), pp. 239–245.

Figure 10.2 A Tax on Gasoline Consumption A tax on gasoline consumption to reduce imports may not further that goal because, although consumption falls from Q^* to Q', the price received by suppliers falls from P^* to P_S, and the lower price discourages domestic production. Thus, domestic production could fall by more than domestic consumption. To discourage imports, a tax should be placed directly on the imports rather than on consumption.

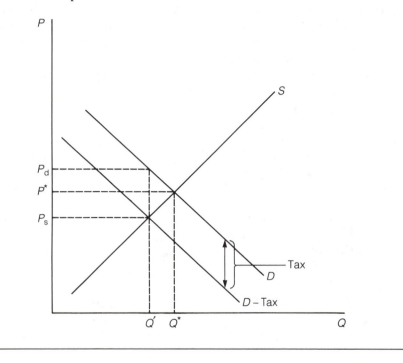

imports would be a direct tax on imports, which would provide an incentive for increased domestic production. In short, an import tax would benefit the goal of energy independence much better than a sumptuary tax on gasoline consumption.

This example illustrates the advantage of understanding the principles underlying tax policy and clearly stating the goal of the tax (increased energy independence). It may well be that by importing a large amount of oil the nation becomes more vulnerable to the whims of potentially erratic foreign suppliers. In this case the consumption of gasoline creates an externality because the user, even while paying for the gasoline consumed, imposes a cost on everyone else in the nation by making the nation more vulnerable to threatened and even actual import interruptions. It is the importing of oil for consumption rather than the consumption itself that creates the externality, though, so the corrective tax should be placed on imported oil rather than on gasoline consumption in general.

In summary, there are several possible rationales for sumptuary taxes. One is that the consumption of some goods creates an externality, in which case the tax is essentially corrective in nature. Another is that a good may be taxed because some people are able to convince the legislature to control morality through tax policy. Yet another is that a legislature trying to raise tax revenue might find it easier to tax goods whose consumption meets with the disapproval of a segment of the population. The rationales are close enough to each other that they can become confused. For example, an individual may be offended simply knowing that some people are smoking cigarettes. Because their smoking imposes a cost whether that person can see it or not, the smoking is viewed as an externality, so a tax is warranted. However, the individual may be using the externality argument simply to justify legislating personal views into law, or as a mechanism for raising more revenue for the government. One might question the fairness of using the government to control a person's private behavior, but here we get to some of the normative, and difficult-to-resolve, issues of taxation. Nevertheless, these issues must be taken into account in a governmental system that decides its tax policy by majority rule.

Politics and Tax Policy

To this point tax policy has been discussed mainly within the framework making the tax system as efficient and equitable as possible. Efficiency and equity are certainly important goals, but to fully appreciate how tax policy is developed, the political motivations of the individuals who are instrumental in shaping tax policy must also be taken into account. After all, the tax system is not designed by a wise and benevolent overseer who considers only the equity and efficiency aspects of taxation, but rather through the political process analyzed earlier in the text. In order to fully understand how the tax system has evolved to its present form, one must consider the incentives facing the individuals who are instrumental in designing it.

Special Interests and Taxation

The tax structure is a product of legislation, and the same political process that determines government programs also determines how those programs will be paid for. Clearly, there are similarities between federal tax policy and the tax policies of state and local governments; these will be detailed shortly. But first, some significant differences should be noted.

First, the federal government depends primarily on income taxes for funding, whereas states and localities rely more heavily on other sources for tax revenue. Individual and corporate income taxes comprise well over half of the taxes collected by the federal government, and when the social security payroll tax is included, over 90 percent of federal revenues is accounted for. Note that income and payroll taxes have been much more readily manipulated to benefit some groups at the expense of others than have other tax bases.

Federal tax policy is decided by Congress, with the Senate Finance Committee and the House Ways and Means Committee having particular influence over the process. As discussed in Chapter 5, congressional committees are responsible for drawing up the proposals for changes in the tax structure that eventually are voted on by the entire Congress. These committees do not form their ideas in a vacuum, but rather operate in a political environment in which lobbyists apply constant pressure for tax reforms that will benefit a particular special interest.

Recall that while special interests have an incentive to lobby for tax reforms that benefit their particular group, nobody has an incentive to lobby for the general public interest. The result is that the legislators who design tax policy are more inclined to design tax policies favorable to special interests rather than the general public. Therefore, when a bill passes that provides some special tax benefits to, say, the oil industry, those in the oil industry show their gratitude by giving the legislators campaign contributions and votes in the next election. Meanwhile, the general public, which has little incentive to pay attention to tax reform, is probably unaware of the tax provision, which means the legislator's general support is unaffected. Just as with government spending, there is a built-in bias in tax reform to favor special interests rather than the general public interest; the result is a complex tax code filled with special interest provisions.

This scenario of tax reform suggests that changes in the tax code will tend to be additions to the code that provide special interest benefits to some subset of the population rather than simplifications of tax law, and in fact this describes the evolution of the tax code. In Chapter 12 this evolutionary process of the tax code to its current, complex form is examined.

Federal Versus State and Local Taxation

The influence of special interests over the tax code seems to be more pronounced in federal rather than state and local taxation. One reason could be the higher stakes involved. Because the federal government collects so much more in taxes than any other level of government, there may be economies of scale in pooling resources and lobbying at the fed-

eral level. Another reason could be the tax bases involved.

The structure of the income tax lends itself to special interest provisions. The numerous instances where deductions, exemptions, and the like allow taxpayers to avoid paying income tax offer a ready precedent for special interests to lobby for additional exemptions in their benefit. Also, the progressivity of the income tax is often changed, which lends legitimacy to the idea that the legislature has the right to alter the relative amounts of tax due from each taxpayer. By contrast, this is not usually the case with state and local tax bases.

States do tax income, but at lower rates than the federal government. Furthermore, states tend to base their income taxes, at least to some degree, on the federal tax code. Thus, an alteration in the federal tax code may affect state taxes in a similar way, but the reverse will not be true. Also, it is difficult, though not impossible, to charge differing rates to different individuals for such taxes as sales taxes or property taxes. A progressive property tax might be a possibility, but ownership can be easily hidden or altered, which means it would be more difficult to enforce than a progressive income tax. Still, these types of taxes are not completely exempt from provisions that seem to benefit special interests. For example, in some areas, agricultural land is assessed at a lower property tax rate than residential land is. Special interests can, and do, work at all levels of government, but with regard to tax policy, they seem to make a greater effort, and exert a greater influence, at the federal level.

Tax Reform

We have painted a somewhat pessimistic picture of the prospects for tax reform in the public interest, but the federal income tax reform that was instituted in 1986 indicates that reform widely viewed as in the public interest can be produced through the political process. Specific changes to the federal income tax will be discussed in Chapter 12; here we can apply our knowledge about the way that the political process works to understand how tax reform in the public interest is most likely to be produced.

First, note that alterations in the tax code made one small change at a time are unlikely to be in the public interest. Rather, each individual change will be for the benefit of some special interest. The reason for this should be clear. Nobody has an incentive to promote changes in the general public interest, whereas special interests have significant incentives to promote alterations in the tax code that will be to their benefit. With special interests being especially interested in designing changes to the tax code and the general public rationally ignorant of tax reform efforts, political forces will naturally favor the special interests.

The best possibility for tax reform in the public interest, then, is not by incremental changes in the tax code to move it in the direction of efficiency. Rather, tax reform truly in the public interest can best be achieved by overhauling the tax code to eliminate all of the special interest provisions. Obviously, special interests will always oppose the elimination of their special interest provisions in the tax code, but if all special interest provisions are eliminated at once, a strong foundation for political support of the reform can be laid. This is exactly the strategy that was used in producing the major tax overhaul enacted in 1986.

This type of major tax overhaul can withstand the negative influences of special interests for two main reasons. First, special interests may actually be better off if their special interest provisions are eliminated along with everyone else's. In this sense members of Congress do not risk losing the political support of special interests, as they would if they tried to eliminate special interest provisions one at

a time. Second, because a major reform of this type will probably simplify the tax code and make it appear more fair, the general public, who ordinarily are not interested in the details of tax reform, will support it.

Political proposals that are opposed by special interests will never have an easy time being passed by the legislature. But in light of the realities of the politics of tax reform, it is apparent that beneficial tax reform is much more likely if it is undertaken as a major overhaul of the tax system rather than one small step at a time, where each step is so vulnerable to the manipulation of special interest politics. This strategy was what enabled the major tax reform in 1986 to be enacted.

Even the 1986 tax reform did not eliminate all of the special interest provisions in the tax code, which implies several things about the prospects for the tax system. The obvious observation is that if the major overhaul actually did produce a much better tax structure, there is much less potential after the tax reform for another major overhaul to produce a tax structure even more in the public interest. But because the process by which tax changes are enacted has not changed, the possibility of minor changes in the tax code remains.

Thus, future changes in the tax code are likely to be small ones that benefit special interests rather than the general public interest. Cynics might even assert that by 1986 Congress had created just about all of the special interest loopholes that it could fit into the tax code, and that to create any more would have required taking someone else's. Therefore, Congress moved to eliminate all special interest loopholes so that it could start giving them out again, one at a time, in exchange for renewed political support of favored special interests.

An optimist can hope that once a better tax system has been enacted, Congress and the general public will resist tampering and might even try to improve upon it. But the realities of the tax reform process suggest that Congress will overhaul and "fine tune" the tax system a little at a time and that such changes are likely to benefit special interests at the expense of the general public.

Tax Policy in the Real World

This overview of the politics of tax policy is not meant to imply that politics are the sole determinant of tax policy. In fact, the equity and efficiency arguments that have been discussed in this chapter as well as previous ones play an important role in determining the ultimate design of tax policy. But because tax policies are designed through the political process, our understanding of how tax policy is made cannot be complete without integrating the politics of the process into the economic ideas that provide the foundations.

Equity and Efficiency

Certainly equity considerations are a significant part of the formation of tax policy. One reason that federal income tax reform has been successful in the 1980s is that the income tax is often viewed as the least fair tax in the United States.[7] In this context a prime consideration in tax reform is the creation of an equitable tax structure, though problems arise in determining what exactly constitutes fairness. Because fairness is a normative concept, legitimate disagreements about equity in taxation can take place, but a major tax reform cannot receive popular support unless it is generally viewed as being fair.

Efficiency aspects of taxation, which also play an important role in tax reform, are a bit easier to pin down because they are positive rather than normative concepts. A major thrust of what is known as supply side economics is that the current tax system hinders productivity in the economy and that any tax reform undertaken should have as a major goal the preservation of incentives for economic production. An inefficient tax code, which generates a large excess burden, hinders the productivity of the economy. This means that there is less output to go around and everyone is potentially worse off. Indeed, both equity and efficiency goals contribute to the development of tax policy. Therefore, a complete understanding of tax policy requires a knowledge of the principles of equity and efficiency in taxation, as well as an awareness of the political environment in which tax policy is formulated.

Individual Taxes Versus the Tax System

In the next several chapters the principles of tax policy introduced here will be applied to an analysis of the various types of taxes in the tax system. Taxes will be considered individually, with some discussion devoted to the sales tax, the personal income tax, the corporate income tax, wealth taxes, and so on. To facilitate comprehension of the tax system, taxes almost have to be considered in this manner—one at a time—but to fully appreciate the overall effect of the tax system, taxes must also be viewed collectively. Therefore, we should keep in mind, even as different

[7]See Richard Vedder, "Federal Tax Reform: Lessons from the States," *Cato Journal* 5, no. 2 (Fall 1985), pp. 571–590. Vedder gives some evidence on pages 584–586 from surveys conducted in the 1970s and 1980s that the federal income tax is viewed as the least fair tax.

types of taxes are analyzed individually, that the ultimate impact of a tax depends on how other taxes are used in the economy.

To clarify this point, consider the effects of taxing an individual's income from interest and corporate dividends, which will depend on how dividend payments are treated in the corporate income tax system. For example, corporations now must pay dividends out of after-tax income, but they can deduct interest payments from taxable income and pay interest out of before-tax income. This provides corporations with an incentive to use bonds rather than stock for financing. We will examine this case in more detail in upcoming chapters; for now, note that the effects of taxing interest and dividends as personal income will depend in part on how those items are treated by the corporate income tax.

As another example, we might be interested in the effects of a tax on wealth. Wealth is a stock concept, and from a stock of wealth comes a flow of income. Thus, if an individual owns an asset worth $100,000 that produces a flow of income of $10,000 per year, this in-come can be taxed with a wealth tax. But note that a 1 percent tax on the stock of wealth will be the same as a 10 percent tax on the flow of income produced by the wealth. In both cases the same $1000 tax is due; these are just different ways of taxing the same stock of wealth, which has value because it can produce a flow of income. Therefore, the effects of a wealth tax cannot be completely understood without taking into account how the income tax taxes the flow of income that comes from the stock of wealth.

These specific examples are meant to illustrate a general point. Even though for the sake of comprehension taxes will be analyzed one at a time in upcoming chapters, a complete analysis of a tax must take into account other taxes and evaluate how a particular tax fits into the total tax system. In looking at general tax principles in this chapter and the preceding one, we have tried to develop a framework within which all types of taxes can be analyzed. In this way we can view the tax system as a whole rather than as a collection of individual taxes.

Conclusion

The development of tax policy in the real world is a complex process encompassing a number of issues. A primary goal of tax policy is to raise revenues in as efficient a manner as possible; another goal is to take full account of equity issues as well in designing a tax structure.

The benefit principle states that each individual should pay taxes in proportion to the benefits received from the government. Recall that the government produces many goods because the private sector of the economy cannot do so efficiently. One way to implement the benefit principle is to finance government output with user charges, but often such charges are not feasible. There may be other ways to levy taxes, however, that approximate the benefit principle of taxation.

The ability-to-pay principle states that individuals should pay taxes in proportion to their ability to pay. This principle may generally be regarded as a tenet of fairness in taxation, but the benefit principle and the ability-to-pay principle may sometimes conflict. For example, an individual with several children in public schools may have a lower ability to pay taxes for public education than an individual with no children, but the individual with children is receiving a larger benefit from public education. According to the benefit principle the person with the children should pay more in taxes, but according to the ability-to-pay principle that person should pay less.

There are two distinct concepts of equity that follow from the ability-to-pay principle of taxation—horizontal equity and vertical equity. Horizontal equity implies that individuals with an equal ability to pay should pay equal amounts of taxes. Although this principle seems relatively straightforward, questions arise as to whether individuals in different circumstances have equal abilities to pay. Does the person who chooses to have a large family have a lesser ability to pay than the person who chooses not to have a family? Does a person who has high medical expenses have a lesser ability to pay than an individual who has equally high home repair expenses? In this regard the concept of horizontal equity becomes more difficult to apply in practice than in theory. The concept of vertical equity is even more difficult to apply, for although it suggests that people with a greater ability to pay should pay more in taxes, it does not specify how much more. Both proportional and progressive taxes satisfy the criteria of vertical equity of taxation, and some regressive taxes qualify as well.

Sumptuary taxes are taxes deliberately designed to reduce the amount of a good consumed. Taxes on tobacco, alcohol, and gambling can fall into this category. To be sure, one motivation for taxing these goods is to raise revenue, but the underlying rationale is that the consumption of these types of goods is undesirable and that a heavy tax can help to discourage their use. In this sense the application of a sumptuary tax is distinctly normative.

Despite the occasional difficulty in specifying concepts of equity in taxation, the importance of equity principles should not be minimized. Fairness in taxation is a generally agreed-upon goal, and so a society must consider equity arguments in choosing its tax system.

A full appreciation of the tax system requires that the political environment in which taxes are determined be understood along with the positive and normative principles that go into shaping tax policy. After all, tax policy is ultimately determined through the political process; it would be naive to assume that tax issues are determined on equity and efficiency grounds without considering the incentives facing individuals who shape the tax laws.

In this chapter and the previous one we have introduced some basic principles of taxation and laid a foundation for examining in detail actual taxes in the tax system in the next several chapters. All of these specific taxes can be evaluated in the context of the general principles of taxation presented here. Because individual taxes are all part of a comprehensive tax system, we must relate the various types of taxes to each other so that we understand not only what the effects of individual taxes are but also how each of them relates to the others.

Questions

1. Discuss the trade-offs that take place between equity and efficiency aspects of tax policy. How might conflicts be resolved?
2. Explain the benefit principle of taxation. How can the benefit principle

of taxation be implemented? Are some methods of implementation better than others?

3. Evaluate the benefit principle as a normative criterion for desirable tax policy. What are its strengths and weaknesses?

4. Explain the ability-to-pay principle of taxation. What are its strengths and weaknesses? Evaluate the appropriateness of using the ability-to-pay principle as the foundation for designing tax policy.

5. Explain the notions of horizontal and vertical equity. Are they legitimate principles on which to build a tax system? What problems might arise in the real world in attempting to implement these principles?

6. What is meant by progressive, proportional, and regressive taxes, respectively? Which type of tax fits most closely with the concept of fairness in taxation? Why?

7. What is a sumptuary tax? How can a sumptuary tax be justified? Do you find these justifications convincing? Why or why not?

8. Do the benefit and ability-to-pay principles of taxation ever conflict with one another? How should a conflict be resolved?

9. How are politics likely to affect the design of tax policy? Discuss some ways in which political influences over tax policy can be minimized.

CHAPTER ELEVEN

Taxes on Economic Transactions

*I*n the next several chapters the principles of taxation presented in Chapters 9 and 10 will be applied to different types of taxes. This chapter begins by reviewing *ad valorem* taxes, unit taxes, and excise taxes. Then user charges and some applications of the benefit principle are discussed. We also consider international transactions in terms of import taxes, duties, and quotas. Finally, general sales taxes and the value added tax are analyzed. Note that the common element in the various taxes is that they are all levied on economic transactions as the transactions occur.

In subsequent chapters we will consider other types of taxes, beginning with the income tax and continuing on to wealth and property taxes. There is no need to remember the names of particular taxes and their effects. For now it is enough simply to recognize that they all have different economic effects. The various types of taxation can all be understood within the framework of the basic principles of taxation discussed in the previous chapters, and the analysis here builds on that foundation.

Excise Taxes, Unit Taxes, and Ad Valorem Taxes

Recall that an excise tax is a tax placed on the sale of some specific good or service, as opposed to a general sales tax, which is placed on all sales. The taxes that most states levy on cigarettes and beer are excise taxes, as are the federal taxes levied on the sale of airline tickets, gasoline, and long distance telephone calls. The effects of an excise tax will be compared to the effects of a general sales tax later in the chapter, but first, the effects of an excise tax should be examined in isolation.

Unit Taxes Versus Ad Valorem Taxes

In Chapter 9 the concepts of tax shifting and excess burden were explained within the context of an excise tax on a specific good; but the general principles outlined there carry over to other types of taxes as well. In all of the examples in Chapter 9, a per unit tax was placed on either the suppliers or the demanders of one specific good.

When a per unit tax is placed on a good, the tax is called, appropriately, a unit tax. All of the excise taxes mentioned previously could be implemented as unit taxes, in the form of a fixed charge per pack of cigarettes, per can of beer, per airline ticket, per gallon of gas, per phone call, and so on. Another type of excise tax is the *ad valorem* tax, which is a tax based on a fixed percentage of the price of a good. Thus, a tax of 10 cents per can of beer is a unit tax, whereas a tax of 10 percent of the retail price of the beer is an *ad valorem* tax. It might seem that if beer sold for $1 a can, a tax of 10 cents per can would have the same effect as a 10 percent tax on the retail sales of beer, but as we will see, even in this simple case the two taxes have different effects.

The same general tax analysis applied in Chapter 9 to unit taxes also applies to *ad valorem* taxes. In both cases taxes can be shifted from one side of the market to the other. Furthermore, the amount of the tax shifted depends on the elasticities of supply and demand, and the principle of excess burden applies in the same way to both taxes. The difference between the two is that whereas the unit tax causes the supply or demand curve to shift by a constant amount (because of the constant tax per unit), an *ad valorem* tax causes the supply or demand curve to shift by a constant percentage. This is illustrated in Figures 11.1 and 11.2. Figure 11.1 depicts the effect of an *ad valorem* tax placed on the suppliers in a particular market; compare this to the effects of a unit tax illustrated in Figure 9.1. The quantity of output in the market is still reduced to Q', and the prices P_S and P_D to suppliers and demanders are the same as in the unit tax case. The difference is that the tax per unit becomes larger as the price rises, be-

cause the *ad valorem* tax is a constant percentage of the good's price rather than a constant amount per unit. Thus, the S + Tax curve in Figure 11.1 is always a constant percentage, rather than a constant amount, higher than the supply curve.

Figure 11.2 depicts the effect of an *ad valorem* tax on demanders in the same market. Again, when compared with Figure 9.2, the effects of the tax are the same, but as in the case with a tax on the suppliers, the tax gets larger as the price of the good rises. In short, most of the analysis of unit taxes can be applied to *ad valorem* taxes as well.

There are some differences between the two types of taxes that deserve mention, however. The most obvious difference is that the unit tax will not change in response to changes in the price of the good, whereas the *ad valorem* tax will. This implies that the real value of a unit tax can be affected by inflation, whereas the real value of an *ad valorem* tax cannot be. For example, if over a period of time prices double, the real value of a unit tax will fall by half while the real value of the *ad valorem* tax will be unchanged.

Advantages and Disadvantages of Each Tax

Which is the more appropriate type of tax depends largely on how legislators want the tax to respond to price changes. In general, it is preferable to design a tax that is unaffected in real terms by inflation; that is, the nominal magnitude would change in proportion to the amount of inflation. In this case *ad valorem* taxes will be superior to unit taxes. Prices might change for reasons other than inflation, however. For example, in the 1970s the retail price of gasoline increased by approximately four times. About half of that price increase was due to inflation, but the other half was due to the higher real price of gasoline.

Figure 11.1 An **Ad Valorem** *Tax on Suppliers* This figure can be compared with Figure 9.1 to show that an *ad valorem* tax on suppliers will have effects similar to a unit tax. The taxes differ because an *ad valorem* tax is a constant percentage of the price of the good whereas a unit tax is a constant amount per unit.

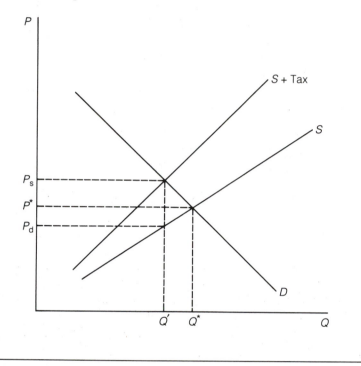

During that time excise taxes on gasoline were in the form of unit taxes, which meant the gasoline tax did not increase automatically—as an *ad valorem* tax would have—despite the increase in gas prices.

One might expect that when the gasoline tax was approved, legislators would have wanted the tax to have a constant real value; in this light an *ad valorem* tax that adjusted with inflation would have been more appropriate. However, the authors of the tax bill probably did not intend for the tax to vary with the price of gasoline, which is why they preferred the unit tax. Indeed, which type of

tax is preferable will vary depending on the circumstances.

Unit taxes are also more appropriate when the value of a good cannot be easily determined. For example, if a tax is being placed on a good at the wholesale level or on an imported good, it may be difficult to calculate a price on which the tax should be levied. Some wholesalers may sell to retailers, while others may retail the goods themselves. At this level it may be easier to count the units of a good than to assign a value, in which case a unit tax is easier to use.

Producers of goods may respond differ-

Figure 11.2 An **Ad Valorem** *Tax on Demanders* Comparing this figure with Figure 9.2 illustrates the similarity between an *ad valorem* tax on demanders and a unit tax on demanders. Tax shifting occurs in the same way, and the excess burden is produced in both cases. But the *ad valorem* tax is a constant percentage of the price of the good, whereas the unit tax is a constant amount per unit.

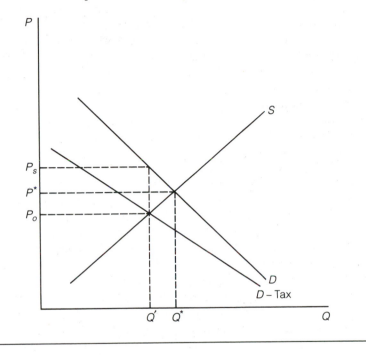

ently to unit taxes and *ad valorem* taxes. Because a unit tax taxes the number of units regardless of value, producers have an incentive to increase the value of the units that they sell in order to minimize the tax to consumers. For example, a unit tax on a pack of cigarettes will give producers an incentive to increase the size of the cigarettes. If the tax on a pack of king-size cigarettes is the same as on a regular pack, the king-size pack will minimize the tax per puff. The same principle holds for other types of goods. A unit tax on wine, when compared to an *ad valorem* tax, will favor expensive wines over cheap ones, because the

tax will comprise a smaller percentage of the purchase price of the expensive wine.

One disadvantage of unit taxes is that they favor expensive units over inexpensive units, thereby distorting the packaging and quality decisions of sellers. To minimize the tax burden as a percentage of the sales price, sellers have an incentive to produce both larger and higher-quality units. Another disadvantage of unit taxes is that inflation can have an adverse effect on the real tax. The advantage of a unit tax is that the amount of the tax is not affected by the price of a good. This means that relative price changes have no effect on the tax per unit and, perhaps more importantly, that when the price of the taxed unit cannot be pinpointed, it is still easy to identify the amount of tax due. This is the case, for example, when a firm imports the taxed good to use as an input into the production of another good.

Excise taxes levied on specific goods do not comprise a very large source of government revenue. At the state level excise taxes tend to follow the framework of sumptuary taxation, levied on things such as alcohol, tobacco, and gambling (in states where gambling is legal). Revenues do, of course, vary from state to state, but because the tax base is relatively small, the revenues are necessarily limited as well. By contrast, a general sales tax, levied on most retail transactions, has a larger tax base and generates more revenue. For example, in 1982 state governments raised $50 billion from general sales taxes, as compared to $28 billion from excise taxes of all types.[1] For states the largest source of revenue from ex-cise taxes was from taxation of motor fuels, which raised $10 billion, or about 20 percent of the total raised from general sales taxes. Taxes on utilities raised about $5 billion, to-bacco $4 billion, and alcohol $3 billion. Thus, although excise taxes do not raise large amounts of revenue, they are responsible for slightly more than 15 percent of state government revenues—enough revenue to be no-ticeable in state government budgets.

At the federal level excise taxes tend to be more closely related to user charges. A federal tax on long distance phone calls is not directly linked to some item of federal output, but a federal excise tax on gasoline is earmarked for highway expenditures, and a federal ex-cise tax on airline tickets is used for airport development. Overall, excise taxes represent a small portion of the federal government's revenues. In the 1985 fiscal year federal excise taxes comprised slightly less than 5 percent of total federal revenues.[2]

User Charges

One type of taxation that can be used to min-imize the excess burden of the tax is a user charge; toll roads and toll bridges are good examples of the application of user charges. In these cases the goods and services are pro-duced in the public sector, but at least some of the revenues used to maintain the services are paid directly by the users. The user charge minimizes the excess burden of the tax by act-ing as a price to be paid for the good, thus rationing the good in the same way that a mar-ket price does. If the user charge is set equal to the marginal cost of providing the public sector output, then there will be no excess burden at all, just as there is no excess burden associated with a simple market price. How-ever, even when the cost of the public sector output, once produced, is essentially zero, as with an uncongested highway, the applica-tion of a user charge still has much to recom-mend it.

---

[1] These figures are from the Department of Commerce, *State Government Finances in 1982*, pp. 23–24.

[2] *Economic Report of the President*, February 1986, p. 341.

User Charges and Economic Efficiency

Strictly in terms of efficiency a toll road or other public sector output financed by user charges does not require financing with taxes collected in other sectors of the economy. One might argue that the marginal cost of allowing another driver on the road is zero, so it would be efficient to have no user charge, but this argument neglects to consider where the money comes from to build the road in the first place. If the road is financed from user charges, then other taxes, and the resulting excess burden, are not necessary. The point is that taxes must somehow be raised to pay for the public sector output.

Even if a user charge has some excess burden, it is preferable to apply the excess burden on the good being financed by the tax rather than on some other good (or income in general). The user charge will still act as a mechanism to ration the good, although if the charge is higher than marginal cost, output of the good will be less than optimal. However, lowering the user charge will create an excess burden somewhere else in the economy.

There are other reasons why a user charge might be desirable even when the marginal cost of the good essentially is zero. For one thing, often the capacity of a good is variable. For example, a highway can be two lanes wide, four lanes wide, or more. Wider highways can always be built to accommodate more people, who naturally will demand the road at a zero price, but by applying a user charge, some demand for the good can be reduced, thus reducing the amount of the good needed to satisfy the demand. In this light, an uncongested good without a user fee may have been overproduced in the first place.

User Charges and Demand Revelation

Pricing a good also gives the good's producers some yardstick by which demand for the good can be measured.[3] If the good is not priced, people will consume it as long as it has any value over zero, but with a user charge on the good, producers can gauge consumer demand and provide the amount in line with that demand. Minasian makes this argument with regard to pay television. According to the standard public goods view, television broadcasts should be priced at zero because there is no marginal cost involved in adding viewers once the show is produced. However, when the programs are free, viewers have no way of sending a market signal about how much the programming is worth to them, and they will watch as long as the value is anything greater than zero. With pay television, viewers' demands can be measured by the amount that they pay to watch certain programs or channels.

In Britain television is paid for by a tax on television ownership, and the government produces programs. Despite some very good programming, on the whole, British viewers seem to prefer American shows. American television is paid for by advertisers, who have an incentive to sponsor shows that their potential customers will watch, making American television much more market-oriented. However, even here the government has much to say by dictating advertising and editorial policies, restricting the types of programming, and limiting the ownership of stations and the ability to purchase and sell the rights to broadcast on a certain frequency.

The British system simply requires owners of televisions to pay a tax, which is a user charge of sorts, but it would be more of a user charge if users paid only for the programs that they wanted to watch. This happens to a degree when advertisers pay, and it happens

---

[3]See Jora A. Minasian, "Television Pricing and the Theory of Public Goods, *Journal of Law & Economics* 7 (Oct. 1964), pp. 71–80.

even more with services like Home Box Office, Showtime, and Cinemax, which allow people to subscribe to a channel if they like the programming. With the advent of video-cassette recorders, this will happen even more, because viewers can purchase (or rent) exactly the programming they want. Note that the production of the show still fits the definition of a collective consumption good, but it may be distributed in a way that charges users for their use in order to provide a market signal regarding how production dollars should be spent.

Another interesting case along these lines is microcomputer software. As microcomputer users know, software can be copied endlessly, which means an additional consumer can consume the good without reducing the consumption of any existing consumer. This is exactly the definition of a collective consumption good. However, the market seems to be doing a good job of producing it, in essence charging a user fee to software users.

User Charges and Equity

To this point user charges have been recommended solely for efficiency reasons, but there are strong equity reasons for applying user charges as well. Taxes are really the price that we pay for consuming public sector output, and according to the benefit principle people who benefit from output should pay for it. User charges represent the most accurate way of applying the benefit principle. Those who use the good pay for it in proportion to their use; those who do not use the good do not have to pay.

Sometimes, user charges will not be appropriate, as in the case of redistributional programs such as food stamps, where some people fund the consumption of others. Obviously, the program would not be redistributing anything if the people receiving the distribution also paid for it. At times it is not clear

who benefits, or by how much, from the goods in question, making it difficult to apply user charges. For example, how would national defense, courts, and legislatures fit into the user charge framework? At other times it is very costly to charge a direct fee to users because of the difficulty in excluding users who do not pay or in measuring the use of a publicly provided good directly.

Approximating User Charges in the Real World

Occasionally, user charges can be approximated, as with the use of the gasoline tax to fund highway construction and maintenance. Certainly it would be impractical to collect tolls on all roads. But people use roads more or less in proportion to the gasoline they use, so a gasoline tax to finance roads approximates a user charge. Note that it is not a perfect substitute, though, because, as in the television example, no information is available on which roads are more heavily demanded.

Other taxes have a passing resemblance to user charges. For example, a person benefits from the protection of national defense in proportion to the amount of property that is being protected, so an income tax can approximate a user charge—if there is a close relationship between income and wealth.[4] This was the general thrust of the statement by Adam Smith, quoted in Chapter 10, relating the benefit principle with the ability-to-pay principle. Along the same lines, larger families are likely to live in larger homes and demand more public education, so a property tax to finance public education may approximate a user charge. Still, these examples more

---

[4]See, for example, Earl Thompson's creative argument in "Taxation and National Defense," *Journal of Political Economy* 82, no. 4 (July/August 1974), pp. 755–783.

closely resemble Lindahl prices than user charges. Furthermore, tax payments for education and defense, as for gasoline, don't indicate the actual demand for those services or goods, unlike a true user charge.

User Charges as Taxes

User charges are similar to market prices in that the user pays a fee in exchange for a good or service, but they differ from market prices in significant ways as well. First, user fees often do not cover the entire cost of the good or service provided. For example, landing fees at airports do not cover the costs of building and maintaining airports, so additional revenues must be raised. In some cases, such as parks, the potential rental value of the land cannot be calculated because the land is not for sale, but again the user fees charged are clearly not sufficient to cover the park maintenance costs, nor do they come close to matching rental value of the land were it in private hands.

In addition, the government often does not price its goods and services in a manner consistent with profit maximization. For example, the cost of mailing a letter at a post office to a post office box in the same building is the same as sending a letter to a rural locale on the other side of the continent. The user, by paying per unit of service, does pay in a manner similar to a market price, but local users of postal services also subsidize longer-distance users, which would not occur if the market were allowed to determine the price. Nevertheless, user charges, when feasible to apply, are among the most effective and fair methods of taxation.

User Charges and Public Enterprise

Sometimes, user charges appear to be almost exactly the same as market prices, such as when the government produces output that private sector producers also provide. For example, in 1982 state and local governments raised $9 billion from the sale of water, $16 billion from the sale of electricity, and $3 billion each from selling liquor, gas, and transit services.[5] Private sector companies are involved in varying degrees in selling each of these items.

In these cases the sale of government output can be considered as a fourth method by which the government can raise revenues. But note that often the government is simply a reseller, as is the case with gas and liquor, and also that some element of taxation is involved in the prices of all of these goods. It is difficult to separate out the tax component from the price of the good. For example, in some states the government owns no liquor stores and simply taxes liquor, whereas in other states the government sells liquor from state-owned stores. For the United States as a whole, the amount of revenue raised by taxing private sales of alcohol is about equal to the revenue raised through government sales of liquor. Likewise, governments generate more revenue from selling public utility output than from taxing private utilities. Some of the government's revenue from such sales goes toward covering the cost of the business, and some represents taxation included in the purchase price. It is not clear how much of the price belongs in each category, especially because most of these government enterprises are legal monopolies, and the monopoly profit should also be counted as a tax.

For purposes of comparison, consider government waste disposal versus government water provision. Waste disposal (both sewage and garbage) tends to be paid for by a tax, whereas water tends to be financed through

---

[5] Figures are from the *Statistical Abstract, 1985 Edition,* p. 269.

metering and user fees.[6] The differences in financing methods are probably due in large part to the fact that it is easier to monitor water usage than waste production.[7] However, in both cases the government is charging individuals for services provided, which is the essence of the benefit principle of taxation. When user fees can be employed as the method of taxation, though, output can be more efficiently allocated.

Import and Export Taxes and Quotas

Another type of tax that falls in the same general category as excise taxes is the *import duty,* which is levied on many types of goods. There is no need to analyze the positive effects of an import or export tax, though, because the effects will be the same as those of any other excise tax, as discussed in Chapter 9. Import taxes are levied for two main reasons—to generate revenue and to discourage imports— both of which will be discussed in this section.

Import and Export Taxes and Revenue Generation

When the United States was founded, import duties were the major source of tax revenue, but in 1985 customs duties amounted to about $1.2 billion, or 1.7 percent of the total tax revenue raised by the federal government in that year.[8] However, import and export taxes remain the major source of tax revenue in many lesser-developed countries today.[9] An important reason for this is that imports and exports are relatively easy transactions to monitor, especially when much of an economy operates with a barter system or when people produce most of the goods they consume themselves. One of the challenges of any tax system is to monitor the economy so that taxes are collected when they are due and collection costs are kept to a minimum. An income tax in a developed country fulfills these criteria very well—as mentioned earlier, the income tax is the main source of tax revenue in the United States. Most people earn their income as wages and salaries, and the companies that pay them not only monitor their income but withhold a portion of it and send it to the government.

By contrast, in lesser-developed countries people are more likely to be self-employed, in which case it is very difficult for the government to monitor transactions to know when a tax is owed. Furthermore, much income tends to be in the form of bartered goods rather than cash, making it difficult to place a monetary value on the transactions. As a result,

---

[6]This is not universally true, though. For example, in New York City water is not metered and people pay a flat fee (tax) for water.

[7]Another factor might be that the government wants to minimize the incentive for individuals to dispose of waste in destructive ways, such as dumping it in public parks in the middle of the night, that might occur more frequently if individuals were charged for the amount of waste they disposed of.

[8]*Economic Report of the President,* February 1986, p. 341.

[9]See chapters by David Greenaway, G. K. Shaw, and Leif Muten, in Alan Peacock and Francesco Forte, eds., *The Political Economy of Taxation* (New York: St. Martin's Press, 1981), for discussions along these lines.

lesser-developed countries cannot rely on an income tax to the extent that more advanced economies can.

At the same time, in lesser-developed countries imports and exports are more easily monitored, because they must pass through the country's borders, meaning that only the borders need to be watched. Also, imports and exports usually have relatively well-defined values, which makes it easier to collect the taxes. In many cases a unit tax is used, for example, a certain tax per barrel of oil, but it is still relatively easy to collect. In short, lesser-developed countries rely on import and export taxes because imports and exports provide the tax base that can be most easily monitored and taxed.

Import Taxes and Trade Restrictions

Even though in developed countries import and export duties make up a small fraction of total tax revenues, they are still used. But such taxes typically are levied not to generate revenue but to discourage the importing of the good in question. Domestic steel manufacturers claim they are suffering from unfair competition from overseas producers, as do garment and textile workers, shoe manufacturers, and others. Whether the claims are true or not, it is not clear that the government should do anything about it. For example, assume that foreign governments are subsidizing the manufacture of steel in their countries, so that foreign steel is cheaper in the United States than domestic steel. If foreign governments want to spend their money to make goods cheaper in the United States, it would seem that we should be grateful rather than try to stop it. Cheaper goods in the United States benefit most of the nation's residents.

If this is so, why would foreign governments subsidize U.S. consumption, and why would the U.S. government try to do something about it? In answering this question, note first that the industry being subsidized in the foreign country benefits from its government's subsidy, in effect acting as a special interest group to obtain favorable government programs. Although U.S. consumers also benefit, the real intention of the foreign government is to provide a special interest benefit to the subsidized industry. Furthermore, while most people in the country benefit from the lower prices of imports, some people—namely, those working in the competing domestic industry—are made worse off because their competitors are selling at lower prices. Thus, those in the domestic industry act as a special interest to lobby Congress to stop what they see as unfair competition. The general public, which benefits from the lower prices on imports, is nevertheless rationally ignorant of most of the issues, making it easier for the special interests to get the Congress to pass an import tariff on the good in question. The tariff causes the good's price in the United States to rise, thus reducing the foreign competition faced by the domestic firm.

The effects of the tariff can be easily understood. As is the case with any other excise tax, the price increase of the imported good resulting from the tariff causes the quantity exchanged to fall. Because imports now cost more, fewer of them enter the country, which means the demand curve for the domestic firm's product shifts outward. The domestic firm can sell more output, and at a greater price.

Without the tariff the domestic firms in the industry would produce less, supporting the claim that the imports were costing Americans their jobs. But this claim is only partially true, because it fails to take account of all the effects of the tariff. If more imports come into the country, then foreigners have more dollars with which to buy American goods. The

Figure 11.3 The Effects of Quotas and Tariffs Either a quota or a tariff could be used to reduce the amount of the good exchanged from $Q*$ to Q' and raise the price to P_S. However, a tariff will collect the difference between $P*$ and P_S as tax revenue, whereas a quota allows importers to retain that amount as additional profit. Therefore, for the same amount of import restriction, a tariff provides more benefit to the general public, while the quota provides a benefit to importers.

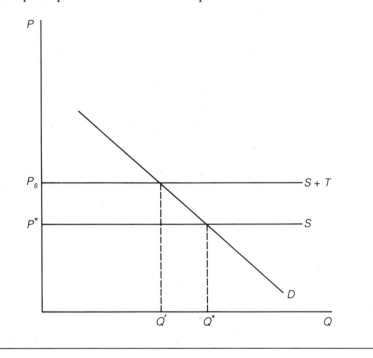

increased foreign demand for American goods will create additional jobs to produce the exports. In fact, because industries protected by tariffs tend to pay higher wages than exporting industries, the number of jobs gained by eliminating the tariff will actually exceed the number lost in most cases, though they will be lower-paying jobs. Problems arise in trying to guess ahead of time what goods will be exported. We do not know exactly what industries will benefit, and by how much,

from the reduction of a trade barrier. It is easier to identify the losers than the gainers, but in general, the gain from eliminating a trade barrier will outweigh the loss.

Quotas Versus Tariffs

Another type of frequently employed trade barrier is the *quota*, which simply restricts the quantity that can be imported. A quota is even less beneficial to the general public than a tariff, but even more beneficial to special interest groups, so the enactment of a quota signals more of a special interest victory than a tariff. Figure 11.3 compares the two types of import restrictions to show why.

In this figure, the market supply curve S, by being horizontal, is perfectly elastic, as it would be in the long run with constant returns to scale in a perfectly competitive world market. $S + T$ is the supply curve that results from the imposition of tariff T, with an accompanying rise in the price of the import to P_s and decrease in the quantity imported to Q'. This is no different from any other tax. A quota could have the same effect on the quantity of imports by restricting the amount of the good that can legally be imported into the country to quantity Q'. The reduced quantity imported will cause a movement along the demand curve and an increase in the price of the imported good to P_s. Thus, domestic producers benefit just as much from the quota as from the tariff.

There is an additional benefit, however. Because no tax is collected, the importer can buy the good at price P^* in the world market and sell it at the domestic market price P_s in the protected country, making an extra profit of $P_s - P^*$ on each unit sold. In this light the importer obviously prefers the quota to the tariff because of the additional profits it generates. However, because no tax is collected, either tax revenues decrease or some other item has to be taxed to compensate for the lost revenue. Thus, a quota is even less in the public interest than a tariff because, in addition to the increased cost of goods and the misallocation of resources, no tax revenues are generated.

General Sales Taxes

A general sales tax is an *ad valorem* tax placed on all retail sales, though sometimes, specific items will be exempt from general sales taxes. For example, some states do not tax groceries, and some do not tax prescription drugs; this varies from state to state. Except for specifically exempted goods, all retail sales are taxed. Sales taxes are a relatively important source of revenue for state governments. In 1984 states raised $54 billion from general sales taxes, which was about 32 percent of total state revenues.[10] Note that transactions at the wholesale level are not taxed under the sales tax. A tax on all sales, whether at the retail level or not, is called a *turnover tax*.

A General Sales Tax as a Consumption Tax

A general sales tax has effects similar to an excise tax placed on all goods for sale in that it restricts the level of output and raises prices, but it has an additional effect as well. A general sales tax can be viewed as an *ad valorem* tax on clothes, plus an *ad valorem* tax on record albums, plus an *ad valorem* tax on books—in short, an *ad valorem* tax on every good sold. Because the sales tax is placed on all goods, it represents a tax on the taxpayer's level of consumption. The tax is not paid on

[10]These figures are from the *Statistical Abstract of the United States*, 1985 edition, p. 279.

the portion of the person's income that is not consumed (for example, saving), so a general sales tax serves to discourage consumption in general.

To illuminate this idea, consider again the notion of the excess burden of taxation discussed in Chapter 9. The excess burden of a tax arises because when a tax is placed on a good, the tax makes that good relatively more expensive than other goods, and when the relative price of a good rises, people substitute out of the relatively more expensive good into other goods not affected by the tax. In the case of a general sales tax, the prices of all goods rise by the same percentage, so the general sales tax does not make any good relatively more costly to purchase than any other. However, because the general sales tax is levied only on consumption goods, it makes consumption relatively more expensive than untaxed activities as saving and leisure. This gives people an incentive to substitute out of consumption into untaxed activities.

Is the Sales Tax Regressive?

Most sales taxes are state taxes, and some localities have sales taxes as well. Because sales taxes represent a constant percentage of the retail sales price of a good, some people argue that sales taxes tend to be regressive with respect to income. If everybody spent a constant percentage of their incomes on consumption, then the sales tax would be proportional with respect to income. For example, if everybody spent all of their income on consumption and the sales tax was 5 percent, then the sales tax would tax 5 percent of everybody's income. However, poor people tend to spend a larger percentage of their incomes on consumption and save a smaller percentage. Thus, if a poor family spends all of their income on consumption goods while a rich family spends only 80 percent, then with the 5 percent sales tax the poor family ends up spending 5 percent of

their income on the sales tax, whereas the rich family spends only 4 percent (80 percent of 5 percent).

Other people argue that viewing the sales tax as regressive is an overly simplistic conclusion when all factors are taken into account. First, they state that income at a given point in time is a static concept. When an individual's lifetime income is considered, there will be far greater income equality than when looking at the income distribution at one point in time. For example, many college students have low incomes and consume most of their income; with the assistance of loans, they may even consume more than their income. Thus, college students, as low-income individuals, are paying a large percentage of their incomes as sales tax. When college students graduate, however, their incomes rise, and sales tax as a percentage of income decreases. Several decades later, after retirement, incomes generally decline, so people again pay a relatively large percentage of income as sales tax. Thus, in the larger context of an individual's lifetime income, the sales tax is not necessarily regressive. The same individual might be both a high-income person and a low-income person at different points throughout the individual's lifetime.

This brings up a second argument, related to the first. Over a person's lifetime income will equal consumption plus what the person bequeaths to others at death. Ignoring bequests, which become the income of the recipient, a person's lifetime income equals the person's lifetime consumption. Although people save more during some points in their lives and consume more at others, the sales tax, viewed over a person's lifetime, thus represents a proportional tax. Because sales taxes do exempt certain consumption items from taxation, this will not be strictly true. Furthermore, because tax laws vary from state to state, it will be more true in some places than others. However, a completely comprehensive sales tax could be equated to a proportional income tax over an individual's lifetime.

Another factor to consider is that a sales tax taxes consumption but not saving. This provides an incentive to save and thus increases capital accumulation in the economy. More capital means an increase in the capital/labor ratio and a resulting increase in wages. By relying on the sales tax to raise tax revenue, an increase in wages might make the overall impact of the sales tax progressive, because lower-income people tend to earn a greater percentage of their income as wage income, whereas higher-income people tend to earn a greater percentage of their income as capital income.

Income and Substitution Effects

Earlier, we suggested that a general sales tax might cause an individual to work less. In evaluating the validity of that statement, we must first consider the two distinct effects a tax can have on a person's behavior—the substitution effect and the income effect. According to the substitution effect the higher relative price of the taxed good compared to other goods causes the consumer to substitute out of consuming the taxed good into consuming other goods. According to the income effect the tax, by taking some income away from the taxpayer, leaves the taxpayer with a lower disposable income. Most excise taxes do not take a large enough fraction of a person's income to have any measurable income effect, but a general sales tax can significantly affect a person's total income in one of two ways. The person might work less because the tax creates a disincentive to earning income, or the person might want to work harder to earn additional income to replace some of the potential consumption that is taxed away. Thus, the reduction in the quantity of output of all goods might not be as great under a general sales tax as under an excise tax on one good.

This can be illustrated in Figure 11.4, which depicts the case of an individual who has the alternative to either work to purchase consumption goods or to take leisure. The framework here is similar to that of the income tax described in Chapter 9. Without a sales tax the individual is on the budget constraint furthest from the origin and consumes at point A. The sales tax raises the relative cost of consumption, so the budget constraint rotates in. The individual now consumes at point B, assuming that the individual's indifference curve is the solid curve tangent to the new budget constraint. In this case the individual increases the amount of leisure time taken from L_1 to L_2. It makes sense for the individual to substitute out of consumption and into leisure due to the higher relative price of consumption.

But the possibility also exists that the individual will now work harder and take less leisure because of the lower income. In this case the individual will locate at point B', and the indifference curve will be the dashed curve. Note that in both cases the individual's consumption level has fallen below what it would be without the tax, but it is possible to draw the diagram in such a way as to depict increased consumption as well.

As a general rule in economic analysis, when only a substitution effect is depicted, there is a clear-cut substitution out of the more costly alternative into the less costly alternative. However, with income effects the individual might substitute either way. This conclusion can be applied specifically to public finance: The more a tax affects an individual's total income, the less predictable in theory the overall effects of the tax will be.

Income and substitution effects will obviously enter into our discussion of the income tax in Chapter 12. For now simply note the following key points. First, all taxes have a substitution effect that discourages the taxed activity—an excise tax on gasoline discourages gasoline consumption, and a general

Figure 11.4 Possible Effects of a Consumption Tax This figure illustrates that a consumption tax, which raises the price of consumption relative to leisure, might cause a person to work more or less, depending on the person's utility function. Whether the individual actually works more or less depends on the income effect.

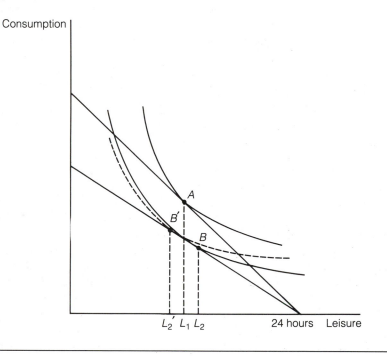

sales tax discourages consumption in general. Second, taxes that have a large effect on a person's income can have a significant income effect, though that effect can work in one of two directions. The reduction in income can discourage the person from working as hard, adding to the substitution effect, but it can also cause a person to work harder to make up the income lost to the tax, which in some cases could more than offset the substitution effect.

Turnover Taxes

Recall that a turnover tax is like a sales tax, except that a turnover tax taxes all transactions, not just retail sales. For example, if a leather tanner sells leather to a shoe manufacturer, who then sells the finished shoes to a shoe store for retail sale, a retail sales tax will place a tax only on the retail transaction. But a turnover tax will first tax the value of the

Table 11.1 Value Added, in Dollars

GOOD	PRICE	VALUE ADDED	10 PERCENT VALUE ADDED TAX
Logger's wood	4	4	.40
Sawmill's lumber	7	3	.30
Bat-maker's bat	15	8	.80
Sport store's bat	25	10	1.00
Totals		25	2.50

leather sold to the shoe manufacturer, then tax the value of the shoes sold by the manufacturer to the shoe store, and finally tax the value of the shoes sold at retail by the shoe store.

The turnover tax is inefficient because it places a tax on the value of each transaction, thus discouraging transactions. The turnover tax taxes each good multiple times. In the shoe example the value of the leather is taxed once when it is sold to the shoe manufacturer, again when the shoes are sold to the retailer, and yet again when the shoes are sold at retail to the final purchaser. Firms can avoid the multiple tax by merging and producing their inputs themselves rather than buying them in the market. For example, the shoe manufacturer can buy the shoe store, so that after buying the leather, the manufacturer both makes and sells the shoes at the retail level. A turnover tax encourages vertical integration of firms, that is, it encourages firms that buy and sell to each other to merge, thus eliminating some of the transactions that are subject to the turnover tax.

The turnover tax, while not common today, was used in Europe before the establishment of the Common Market. The replacement of turnover taxes by other types of taxes is a good example of how economic theory can be applied to improve the efficiency of the economy. The turnover tax is an inefficient method for raising revenue because it discourages potentially profitable exchanges and encourages potentially inefficient mergers. Turnover taxes—and other types of taxes—have been replaced in Europe by the value added tax.

The Value Added Tax

The value added tax is used in the common market countries of Europe, and though not currently used in the United States, it has been considered frequently, especially at the federal level. A *value added tax* is, as its name suggests, a tax on the value added by each producer in the economy.

This concept can be explained with the aid of Table 11.1, which lists some hypothetical data on the cost of producing a wooden baseball bat. In the first step in the process, a logger cuts a tree down and sells enough wood to make one baseball bat to a sawmill for $4. The sawmill cuts the logger's tree into lumber, selling enough lumber to make one bat to the bat manufacturer for $7. The bat-maker then makes the bat and sells it for $15 to a sporting goods store, which sells it to a customer for $25.

If a 10 percent value added tax is in effect, each producer is required to pay a tax on 10 percent of the value added to the final product. In this case the logger who cuts the tree pays a value added tax of 40 cents on the wood used to make one baseball bat because the logger's wood contributes $4 to the value of the product. The sawmill buys the wood for $4, but after cutting the wood up it sells the lumber to make the bat for $7, meaning that it adds $3 in value to the product. Therefore, the sawmill owes 30 cents in value added tax. The bat-maker takes the $7 piece of lumber and makes it into a $15 bat, adding $8 in value to the bat in the process and paying 80 cents in value added tax. The retailer who sells the bat for $25 adds $10 in value to the bat by making it conveniently available to the final consumer and so owes $1 in value added tax. The total tax paid is $2.50, or 10 percent of the retail price of the good.

The total tax figure should not come as a surprise. After all, the total price of the good is going to equal the sum of the values added by each intermediate producer, and if each producer pays 10 percent of the value added, the total tax has to equal 10 percent of the final value of the good. Note also that the total value added tax collected is the same as a retail sales tax of the same percentage. In this light it is worthwhile to compare the effects of the two types of taxes in more depth.

The Value Added Tax Versus the Sales Tax

First, with a value added tax the people who physically pay the tax revenue to the government will be different from the people who pay with a sales tax. With a value added tax, the tax is paid by every producer in the economy. By contrast, a retail sales tax either is

paid by the retail purchaser or, as is usually the case, is collected from the purchaser by the retailer, who then pays the tax on the customer's behalf. In short, the value added tax is levied on the suppliers in a market; the sales tax is levied on the demanders.

Keeping in mind the principles of tax shifting discussed in Chapter 9, who ultimately bears the burden of each tax? Recall that regardless of whether a tax is levied on suppliers or demanders in a particular market, the suppliers end up bearing the same tax burden in either case and the demanders end up bearing the same tax burden in either case. Consider the chain of suppliers in the baseball bat example. It makes no difference if the logger pays the value added tax or if the logger is exempted from the tax and the sawmill pays the logger's share. Likewise, it makes no difference if the bat-maker pays the shares of the logger and the sawmill, and so on down the chain of production. Thus, the ultimate burden of a value added tax is the same as the burden of a sales tax. Even though the taxes initially are levied on different people, because of tax shifting, the same people ultimately end up paying a value added tax as would end up paying a sales tax of the same amount.

However, the sales tax is preferable to the value added tax in most areas. For one thing, a retail sales tax is definitely easier to collect than a value added tax. Only retail sellers need be bothered with a retail sales tax, whereas every seller in the production chain must pay a value added tax, meaning many more individuals have to contend with the record keeping and payment schedules.

Second, the sales tax is much easier to calculate. A retail establishment need only add up its total revenues and take a fixed percentage of that to pay as a sales tax. But with a value added tax the same retail seller would have to add up its total revenues and then subtract its purchases on which the tax had already been paid to compute the amount of tax owed. Thus, fewer people need be bothered with the sales tax, and even those who must collect the sales tax will find the record keeping much easier with a sales tax than with a value added tax. The costs of compliance with the sales tax will be much lower than with the value added tax.

Third, it is far easier to enforce the provisions of the sales tax law. Because fewer taxpayers are involved, fewer taxpayers need to be monitored, and compliance costs to the government will be lower. Also the relative simplicity of calculating the sales tax makes it easier for each taxpayer to accurately determine the tax due. The difficulty in understanding the value added tax may open the door to abuse; the complexity of administering the value added tax in Europe certainly makes it more difficult to monitor. Thus, on enforcement grounds the sales tax comes out on top again.[11]

Exempting Goods from Taxation

In light of the relative advantage of a sales tax over a value added tax, it might reasonably be asked why a value added tax is ever used. One argument often cited is that with a value added tax it is easier to exempt certain goods and services from taxation. However, complications arise almost immediately with this argument. For example, if food and medical supplies are to be exempted from value added taxation, as is now done with the sales tax in many states, the tax becomes almost unworkable. How is one to know, when cotton is harvested, whether it is to be used in manufacturing shirts, in which case the tax should be paid, or whether it will be used to make bandages, in which case it is tax exempt. Of course, it would be possible to exempt the final retail seller from the tax (e.g., grocery stores and drug stores), but by then most of the value added tax on the good would have already been paid by earlier producers in the chain. Thus, it is virtually impossible with the value added tax to exempt final products from taxation, except by giving a credit to the retailer for the tax previously paid on the good. There are obvious inefficiencies, however, in administering tax policy by first collecting taxes and then rebating taxes previously paid.

Although it is difficult to exempt certain retail products from taxation under the value added tax, the value added tax can be used to exempt certain types of producers from taxation. Again using the cotton example, it would be difficult to exempt cotton farmers from the sales tax because most products combine cotton and other inputs, such as weaving, dyes, and perhaps other fabrics. Cotton farmers could easily be exempted from the value added tax, though. In this sense the value added tax represents a much better vehicle by which special interest groups can exempt themselves from taxation. Rather than the socially desirable effects often produced by exempting necessities such as groceries and medical supplies from taxation, certain competitive benefits can be obtained by using the value added tax to exempt selected industries from taxation. Indeed, the value added tax can be applied in much the same way as tariffs and import quotas, for the benefits of special interests.[12]

---

[11]See Valerie Strachen, "The VAT in the U.K.," in Alan Peacock and Francesco Forte, eds., *The Political Economy of Taxation* (New York: St. Martin's Press, 1981), pp. 177–191, for a discussion of the administrative difficulties of the value added tax. See also C. T. Sandford, M. R. Godwin, P.J.W. Hardwick, and M. I. Butterworth, *Costs and Benefits of VAT* (London: Heineman Educational Books, 1981).

[12]Richard W. Lindholm, *The Value-Added Tax and Other Tax Reforms* (Chicago: Nelson-Hall, 1976), discusses this and related issues.

Levying the Tax Where the Good Is Produced

Another argument in support of the value added tax is that often much of a good is produced in one area, then shipped out of the area and sold elsewhere. If the sales tax is in effect, taxes are paid in the area where the good is sold rather than where it was produced. But according to this argument a value added tax that is levied where a good is initially produced rather than where it is sold is fairer. This argument seems especially relevant in Europe, where a good may cross many borders before being completed and sold. Why should all of the tax be collected by the selling country rather than by the producing countries in proportion to the value added by each one?

Although this argument sounds plausible, it does not hold up under closer scrutiny. When international (or interstate) trade takes place, the value of the goods flowing out of an area will approximately equal the value of the goods flowing in. After all, places that export goods use the resulting income to buy goods of equal value. Therefore, it makes little difference to the total amount of tax revenue collected whether the tax is placed on the goods produced at home before they are exported or on the goods sold at home after they are imported. The total tax collected by any area will be approximately equal under either a value added tax or a sales tax.[13]

The reason why the value added tax and not a sales tax or some other type of tax is used in Europe is more a matter of historical accident than any sound economic choice. In trying to agree on a compatible tax structure, the European common market countries, who had very different tax structures, selected the value added tax as being least disruptive to the Common Market as a whole. The decision was a political rather than an economic one, and it has produced unforeseen complexities in taxation in Europe.[14]

Revenue Generation

Another argument frequently made for a value added tax is its ability to generate revenue. The large budget deficits of the 1980s might warrant a tax that can generate large amounts of revenue, such as a value added tax. Although a value added tax can certainly generate large amounts of revenue, its revenue-generating capabilities are nevertheless exactly the same as a sales tax. Therefore, there is no reason to favor a value added tax on the grounds that it can generate needed revenue; the same is true of a sales tax.

The Visibility of the Tax

In terms of visibility politicians tend to favor the value added tax to the sales tax. The sales tax is paid at the time of the retail purchase and typically is added on to the price of the good at the time of sale, which means the purchaser can easily determine how much of the total cost of the good represents tax. With a value added tax, on the other hand, the tax is included with all of the other costs of the good, so that the proportion of the price that is actually tax is not readily apparent to the retail customer. This is especially true if spe-

---

[13]Note that in Europe the value added tax is rebated for exported goods and charged on imports. See Allan A. Tait, *Value Added Tax* (London: McGraw-Hill, 1972), ch. 1, for details on the operation of the value added tax in Europe.

[14]J. A. Kay and M. A. King, *The British Tax System*, 3d ed. (Oxford: Oxford University Press, 1983), p. 125, note that the value added tax costs roughly twice as much to administer as the purchase tax that it replaced in the United Kingdom.

cial interests manage to exempt some producers from the payment of the tax. Thus, the value added tax is more hidden than the sales tax.

One consequence of the value added tax being more hidden is that taxpayers may be less resistant to paying the tax. For example, in a state with a 5 percent sales tax a person who buys a $10,000 automobile will be well aware of the $500 in sales tax that is paid on the transaction. But with a value added tax the individual who purchases a $10,500 car will not have as clear a notion of the amount of taxes paid. Likewise, in the United States today a purchaser can never be sure how much of the price of a good is due to the corporate income tax.

There are two views on the relative lack of visibility of the value added tax. According to one view, because the tax is hidden, the government may be able to get away with taxing more and providing less to taxpayers in return for the taxes paid. If the tax is not hidden, taxpayers can better evaluate their elected representatives and communicate to them what they want the government to do. According to the other view the government needs revenues to operate, and the best tax is the one that collects this revenue from taxpayers in as painless a manner as possible. In this sense the value added tax is preferable because the taxpayers are unaware of the extent of taxation.

In addition, because the value added tax is initially levied on producers while the sales tax is levied on retail purchasers, many voters and taxpayers may misunderstand the effects of the two taxes. A taxpayer might favor a value added tax over a sales tax, not realizing that ultimately the two types of taxes end up being paid by the same people. Thus, consumers might vote for a value added tax and be opposed to a sales tax, reasoning that the value added tax will be paid by producers whereas the sales tax will be paid by consumers. Likewise, politicians who want to increase taxes can argue for a value added tax (and perhaps receive popular support), even though the effects are the same as with a sales tax. Thus, the value added tax may be favored by politicians because its effects are more likely to be misunderstood and taxpayers are more likely to think that someone else will end up paying the tax. Yet, on these grounds a voter should favor a value added tax only if the voter also favors a sales tax of an equal magnitude, and even then, due to the lower costs of collection, administration, and compliance, the sales tax is preferable.

Conclusion

In this chapter we analyzed several types of taxes, building on the foundation laid in Chapter 9. Excise taxes can be either unit taxes or *ad valorem* taxes, and the two types of tax can have similar, but not identical, effects. Likewise, the general sales tax has effects similar to an excise tax on all goods sold at the retail level. Although the substitution effect of a general sales tax discourages people from buying consumption goods, thus discouraging the earning of income as well, the income effect can mitigate the substitution effect. We will discuss the income effect in more detail in Chapter 12. The value added tax, commonly used in Europe, has the same economic effects as the sales tax, though the value added tax is less visible to taxpayers, is harder to calculate, requires the compliance of more taxpayers, and is more difficult to monitor.

We also examined import tariffs and quotas. Lesser-developed countries tend to rely more heavily on import and export duties as a source of tax revenue because they have relatively little income to tax and because economic transactions tend to be difficult to monitor. By contrast, it is relatively easy to collect taxes on imports and exports as they cross the country's borders.

In developed economies import duties are a relatively insignificant source of revenue, though they are often used to discourage imports of certain goods and protect domestic industries from foreign competition. In this sense import duties represent a type of special interest legislation. Quotas are an even more effective form of special interest legislation, because even though no tax is paid, the importer can purchase the good in the world market at a competitive price and sell it at a higher price in the domestic market. Restraint of trade by either quotas or tariffs is generally not beneficial to the overall economy, but from the general public's standpoint tariffs at least have the advantage of providing tax revenues. With quotas importers profit from selling the restricted quantity of imports, taking the revenue that could have been collected in taxes from a tariff and instead giving it to the importer as excess profit.

Early in the chapter we pointed out that user charges are an excellent source of revenue for public sector expenditures. User charges, when feasible, act in a manner similar to market prices—they minimize the excess burden of taxation, they ration the public sector output in the same way a market price rations a market good, and they provide a good signal of the demand for the output. User charges also satisfy the criteria of the benefit principle, because the people who pay for the good are the beneficiaries of the output. Indeed, user charges have much to recommend them for both efficiency and equity reasons.

This chapter has analyzed the economic effects of a number of different types of taxes. The next chapter picks up where this one leaves off by analyzing the personal income tax, which is the most important type of tax revenue in developed economies. In Chapter 12 we evaluate the personal income tax along the same lines that taxes on economic transactions were evaluated in this chapter. In subsequent chapters we examine the corporate income tax, the property tax—a major source of tax revenue at the local level—and other types of taxes.

Questions

1. Explain the differences between *ad valorem* and unit taxes. Assuming cigarettes sell for $1 per pack, what would be the difference between a 10 percent tax on cigarettes and a 10 cent per pack tax on cigarettes?

2. Under what circumstances is a unit tax appropriate? Under what circumstances is an *ad valorem* tax appropriate?

3. What is the relationship between user charges and market prices? Discuss both the pros and cons of user charges when the marginal cost of using a good is zero. Explain how user charges help to monitor the demand for a good and how this provides an efficiency benefit even when an additional user could use the good at no marginal cost.

4. Explain the differences in the economic effects of a true user charge, such as a highway paid for by the users' tolls, and an earmarked tax approximating a user charge, such as a gasoline tax used to finance highways.

5. How do Lindahl prices and user charges differ? Is one a subset of the other? What are the efficiency characteristics of each?

6. Why do developed economies tend to rely heavily on income taxes to finance government operations, whereas developing economies rely more heavily on import and export duties and taxes?

7. Explain who gains and who loses from import restrictions such as quotas and tariffs. If there are both gainers and losers, how are those in favor of the restrictions able to get them passed?

8. Why is a country better off with a tariff than with a quota that produces the same import restriction? Why do importers prefer quotas to tariffs?

9. Is the sales tax regressive? Explain both sides of the argument.

10. Compare and contrast the sales tax and the value added tax. What are the economic effects of each tax? What are the advantages and disadvantages of each tax?

11. Considering your answer to question 10, explain why politicians are likely to argue for a value added tax rather than a retail sales tax of the same magnitude.

12. What is the difference between a retail sales tax and a turnover tax? What are the economic effects of each? Will one of these types of tax generally be more desirable than the other? Why?

CHAPTER TWELVE

The Personal Income Tax

*T*he most significant source of tax revenue in developed economies is the income tax. The general principles of taxation presented in Chapters 9 and 10 apply to income taxation just as they apply to other types of tax. Income taxes discourage people from earning income, causing a substitution from income to leisure activities not subject to the tax. However, an offsetting effect can occur if people work harder to make up for the income lost through taxation. One of the important topics covered in this chapter is the income and substitution effects of the income tax.

Our discussion of the income tax encompasses a number of other significant issues. One is whether the tax discourages saving and capital formation. Certainly, a tax on consumption rather than on income will encourage more saving, but some people oppose a consumption tax for equity reasons. Another topic is tax reform, a major issue in the 1980s. Therefore, we examine the tax reform process in some detail, describing how the tax system has been modified by the Tax Reform Act of 1986. The issues prompting the tax reform are important not only in terms of understanding why the tax system has been reformed but also for indicating how future reforms could affect the income tax system.

To provide some background for the discussion, the chapter also sketches a brief history of the income tax in the United States and an overview of some of the current provisions in the U.S. income tax system. But first, in the interest of continuity with the ideas discussed in the previous chapter, we compare income taxation to sales taxation and the taxation of consumption.

Sales, Consumption, and Income Taxes

In the previous chapter we equated the sales tax with an excise tax placed on every good sold at the retail level. The tax has the effect of reducing consumption of the taxed goods and encouraging substitution into untaxed activities, so the substitution effect from the sales tax works exactly as described for an excise tax on all retail goods. Although income effects will probably have little influence in the case of a narrowly based excise tax, the income effects of a broadly based tax such as a sales tax are significant. In this chapter we extend our comparison of excise taxes and general sales taxes to include consumption and income taxes.

The object of taxation is referred to simply as the *tax base*. Thus, for a gasoline tax, the tax base is sales of gasoline; for a general sales tax, retail sales; for an income tax, income. A person's gross income is allocated to three basic spending categories: consumption, saving, and taxes. Assuming for the moment that there is no saving in the economy, this means all income not paid in taxes is used for consumption, so the retail sales tax is levied on all income. Within this framework the tax base is the same for all three types of taxes—with no saving a sales tax amounts to a tax on income.

However, an important difference exists between the way that sales taxes and income taxes are collected. Because a sales tax is collected at the time of the sale, there is no practical way to charge different tax rates to people with different income levels. Some goods might be exempt from the sales tax (or taxed at a different rate), but for those goods that are taxed, all individuals have to pay the same tax rate. By collecting the tax on income, however, progressive tax rates can be built into the system, so that individuals who earn more income pay a higher proportion in taxes.

Sales and Consumption Taxes

A sales tax is one type of *consumption tax*, which is usually levied on consumption as the consumer buys the consumer good. Consumption can be taxed in other ways, though. One way of instituting a consumption tax might be to apply a tax on value added. As the previous chapter made clear, the tax base is the same for a value added tax and a retail sales tax, and both types of tax on consumption levy the tax as an economic transaction takes place. One way to overcome the difficulty in charging different rates to different individuals for such transaction-based taxes would be to add up consumption spending over the period of a year and then, as with the income tax, have the taxpayer remit the entire tax due on consumption over the year at one time. Consumption could also be calculated by subtracting saving from income (because income equals consumption plus saving plus taxes). A consumption tax paid in this manner would resemble the income tax in collection method, even though it would retain a conceptual link to the sales tax by sharing the same tax base.

Consumption and Income Taxes

Recall that if there is no saving in an economy, a tax on consumption will constitute a tax on income. Without saving to consider, a consumption tax, computed annually, would only require that an individual pay tax on the year's income. But if saving is considered, the consumption tax is computed by totaling the individual's income, subtracting saving, and paying a tax on what remains. The tax base is the same as under the transactions-oriented sales tax; only the method of computation and collection is different. Computing the consumption tax in this way has the advantage of allowing different tax rates to be charged to different individuals. This might be desirable on equity grounds, because a tax that collects a constant percentage of consumption spending is likely to be viewed as regressive with respect to income.

Indeed, a sales tax collects a constant proportion of consumption expenditures, but people who earn lower incomes tend to save a lower percentage of their income. For example, a person with $10,000 in income might spend all of it on consumption, whereas someone with $100,000 in income may spend $70,000 on consumption and save $30,000. Now consider the effect of a 5 percent sales tax on all consumption goods. Both people pay 5 percent of their consumption as tax, but the low-income person spends 5 percent of total income on the tax while the high-income individual spends 5 percent of $70,000, or $3500, which is 3.5 percent of the person's total income of $100,000. Because higher-income people generally save a larger percentage of their income than lower-income people, the sales tax is regressive with respect to income. Thus, for equity reasons income taxes tend to be favored over sales taxes as a source of revenue.

There were, however, persuasive counter-arguments to this view made in Chapter 11. Essentially, a person's lifetime income and lifetime consumption amount to the same thing. But in Chapter 10 we noted arguments in favor of progressive taxes in general on equity grounds, so even if a proportional tax on consumption is not regressive, progressive tax rates on consumption might still be viewed as desirable. If this is so, then a consumption tax calculated periodically by subtracting saving from income would be preferable to a transactions-based consumption tax.

Taxes on Saving

The difference between a consumption tax of this type and an income tax is that the latter taxes income going toward saving in addition to taxing consumption. Because of this, the income tax is often viewed as providing an incentive against saving. We will discuss this issue in more detail later in the chapter. As previously noted, the United States could substitute a consumption-type tax for the income tax. Currently, the U.S. tax code contains provisions that, to a limited extent, adhere to the consumption tax framework by permitting certain methods of saving income without paying taxes on the income. Most common is some type of deferred pension plan, such as the Individual Retirement Account (IRA) that some taxpayers are eligible for. With a deferred pension plan the taxpayer can save a certain amount of money in a special account and deduct that amount from taxable income. When the money is drawn out of the account at retirement, tax is paid on the income at that time.

The only step necessary to move from the current U.S. income tax system to a consumption tax system would be to allow unlimited amounts of money to be placed in deferred pension plans and permit withdrawals at any time without paying a penalty (income tax would be paid at withdrawal, though). Taxpayers in the United States would thus have the alternative of paying tax in a consumption tax system rather than in an income tax system. In fact, as will be discussed more fully, the Tax Reform Act of 1986 moved the tax system further from a consumption tax system by eliminating some of the major opportunities for sheltering saving from the income tax.

Definitions of Income

The discussion of income and consumption taxation has been greatly simplified because it assumed that there is no difficulty involved in determining what constitutes income for the purpose of taxation. On the surface the definition of income seems relatively straightforward, but some ambiguities arise, especially concerning income in kind and the treatment of changes in the value of a person's wealth, when one is trying to measure income for tax purposes. Furthermore, it is not always clear-cut what income should be exempt from taxation. All of these issues add to the complexity of designing an effective and fair tax system.

In-Kind Benefits

When a person is paid in goods or services rather than in dollars, that person has received *income in kind*. For example, a company might provide an employee with a company car or pay for a health insurance plan for employees as one of the benefits of employment. The company could pay the employee a larger salary and allow the employee to buy his or her own car and insurance, but the payment in kind might be preferred by both parties for a number of reasons. First, the company may find it cheaper to buy automobiles and insurance in quantity and pass some of the savings on to the employee as a benefit than to pay the employee the additional salary needed to purchase such items. Second, the payment in kind may not be taxed as regular income to the employee, so the payment in kind comes to the employee as tax-free rather than taxed income. Traditionally, many types of payments in kind have not been treated as taxable income to the recipients, although the Tax Reform Act of 1986 reduced the ability of employers to give untaxed benefits in kind to their employees.

There does not seem to be a good reason to treat payment in kind differently from monetary income, and while some types of payment in kind are excluded from taxation, others are supposed to be reported to the Internal Revenue Service (IRS) as taxable income. Often, it is easy to determine the value of a payment in kind—the cost of a company's employee insurance program will be well doc-

umented—but other times it is not so easy. How much in-kind income does a traveling sales person receive by driving the company car home from work every day and using it on weekends? How much in-kind income should be reported to the IRS if a person borrows the company ladder to do some work around the house?

Some fringe benefits, such as the company car and the company insurance policy, are items that the employee would likely buy personally if the company did not provide them. Other fringe benefits, such as a large carpeted office and a reserved space in the company's indoor parking garage, might cost the company extra even though the employee would not pay for them personally. The company provides these fringe benefits as a deductible expense of doing business—by offering a more pleasant environment they can hire employees more cheaply. Indeed, neither the company nor the employee pays taxes on the fringe benefits.

In principle, these payments in kind and fringe benefits should be treated no differently from ordinary income for tax purposes, but in practice it is often difficult to draw the line between payments in kind and expenses of doing business. Even when some payment in kind clearly has been made, as when the traveling sales person uses the company's car for personal business, it is still not clear what portion of the expense of the car should be considered a business expense and what portion is personal income.

Changes in Wealth

Another problem in defining income for tax purposes is in deciding how changes in a person's wealth resulting from unrealized capital gains should be figured into taxable income. The Haig-Simons definition of income, named after Robert M. Haig and Henry C. Simons, regards income as the dollar value of the maximum amount that one can consume over a given time period without reducing the value of one's wealth.[1] The salary a wage earner brings home is included in income, as is any increase in the real value of any property owned. For example, if the value of a person's home rises from $50,000 to $60,000 in a year with no inflation, the $10,000 increase in the value of the home counts as income. Likewise, if a person owns stocks or bonds whose values go up, the increase in value is treated as income.

Using the Haig-Simons definition of income for tax purposes, one can imagine a case in which a person buys a business for $100,000 that generates $10,000 a year in net income. The discount rate, which determines the value of the business, here appears to be 10 percent. But if the person makes some changes in the business such that it now generates $50,000 in income annually, at the same 10 percent discount rate the business is now worth $500,000. In this case the increase in income from $10,000 to $50,000 increases the worth of the business by $400,000; under the Haig-Simons definition of income, income tax would have to be paid on this amount.

Although the Haig-Simons definition has a certain theoretical appeal, some problems can arise in implementing it. First, with assets such as homes, businesses, or artwork, it is not always clear what the value of the asset is until it is sold. Second, it is conceivable that a person who experiences a capital gain on an asset would have to sell the asset to raise enough money to pay the taxes on the gain. From an equity standpoint some would consider this unfair.

Irving Fisher defined income differently, as the sustainable flow of purchasing power available to an individual.[2] Under Fisher's definition a capital gain would not count as income because it would not represent a sustainable flow; only the increased income from the increased value of wealth would be taxed. In the flat tax section of this chapter, we examine the proposal of economists Robert Hall and Alvin Rabushka, following along the lines of Fisher's definition, for an income tax system that does not tax capital gains. Such a system makes sense because if the income from the capital is taxed, then taxing the capital as well amounts to taxing the same source twice. Indeed, under current tax law saving is subject to a double tax, as we will discuss. For now, simply note the ambiguities involved in defining income for tax purposes.

Imputed Rental Income

Some increases in wealth can produce more monetary income subject to tax; other increases may not. For example, consider two identical homes, side by side, one of them occupied by the owner and the other by renters. If the capital value of each house increases, the owner of the rental house will have more rental income, which will be subject to tax. The owner who lives in the house, however, receives the value of the rental as an in-kind benefit of home ownership while not receiving any taxable income from the increase in the value of the asset. Because unrealized capital gains in owner-occupied housing are not subject to taxation, the homeowner does not pay tax on the increase in the value of the property. One way to tax such an individual would be to place a tax on the value of rental

---

[1]For the original sources of this definition, see Robert M. Haig, *The Federal Income Tax* (New York: Columbia University Press, 1921), and Henry C. Simons, *Personal Income Taxation* (Chicago: University of Chicago Press, 1938).

[2]Irving Fisher, *The Theory of Interest* (New York: Macmillan, 1930).

services that the homeowner receives from the home, or the imputed rental income. The renter pays rent equal to the value of using the residence and also pays tax on the income that is earned to pay the rent. On equity grounds the homeowner, who receives the same flow of services from a home as the renter, should perhaps pay taxes on the rental value of the owner-occupied home.

Note that the value of the home is a stock, and the rental service received from the home is a flow. If the stock were taxed (by taxing the increase in the value of the house), then an additional tax on the imputed rental value would constitute a double tax. Although the current tax system often does tax certain types of income twice, we should at least realize when this occurs. But note that in the case of owner-occupied housing, neither changes in the stock (unrealized capital gains) nor the flow (imputed rent) are taxed under most circumstances in the current tax code.

In fact, in the current tax code none of these ideas regarding the definition of income are followed consistently. Capital gains are subject to taxation, but only when the asset is sold and the gains are realized—as long as the asset is not sold, no tax is due. Some in-kind benefits must be reported as taxable income to the IRS, but others do not have to be. Also, the current tax code exempts some income from taxation. In addition to the standard deduction allowed for all taxpayers, many items of expenditure, such as interest payments on home mortgages, state and local income taxes (but not sales taxes), and charitable contributions, can be deducted from income for tax purposes.

In summary, many difficulties are involved simply in trying to define income for purposes of taxation, even though income seems like a fairly straightforward concept. In the next section we discuss how income tax rates have changed in the United States since the tax was established, and then we examine in more detail how the current tax system deals with computing taxable income.

A Brief History of the U.S. Income Tax System

A brief history of the tax system can help put the current tax code into perspective. Britain installed an income tax on a permanent basis in 1842. An income tax law was first passed in the United States in 1861 to help finance the Civil War, and it remained on the books until 1871. With a few exceptions the rate was 3 percent on all income over $800, which was substantially greater than the median income at the time. When Congress tried to reinstate an income tax in 1894, the Supreme Court declared it to be unconstitutional on the grounds that it was a direct tax not distributed among the states according to population as the Constitution required. This led to the passage in 1913 of the Sixteenth Amendment to the Constitution, which allowed an income tax. The first income tax law allowed a personal exemption of $3000 and taxed the remainder of income at graduated rates from 1 percent (for incomes up to $20,000) to 7 percent (for incomes over $500,000).

The personal exemption in 1913 was high enough relative to the average income that initially less than 1 percent of the population was subject to the tax, but over time more of the population came to be covered. The rates have been raised as well, reaching a peak of

Table 12.1 Federal Income Tax Rates for Selected Years

YEAR(S)	PERSONAL EXEMPTION ($)	FIRST BRACKET		TOP BRACKET	
		Percent Rate	Income ($)	Percent Rate	Income Over ($)
1913–15	3,000	1	20,000	7	500,000
1918	1,000	6	4,000	77	1,000,000
1921	1,000	4	4,000	73	1,000,000
1925–28	1,500	1.125	4,000	25	100,000
1936–39	1,000	4	4,000	79	5,000,000
1944–45	500	23	2,000	94	200,000
1954–63	600	20	2,000	91	200,000
1965–67	600	14	500	70	100,000
1970	625	14	500	71.75	100,000
1977–78	1,000	14	2,700	70	102,200
1979–81	1,000	14	3,400	70	108,300
1982	1,000	12	3,400	50	41,500
1983	1,000	11	3,400	50	55,300
1984	1,000	11	3,400	50	81,800
1985	1,040	11	3,540	50	85,130
1986	1,080	11	3,670	50	88,270
1987*	1,900	11	1,800	38.5	54,000
1988*	1,950	15	17,850	28	89,560
1989*	2,000	15	17,850	28	89,560

*Years marked * are from the Tax Reform Act of 1986. For 1988 and 1989, single taxpayers with incomes between $17,850 and $43,150 are in the 28 percent bracket. Taxpayers with incomes between $43,150 and $89,560 have a marginal tax rate of 33 percent.

Sources: *Historical Statistics of the United States*, p. 1095, and IRS personal income tax forms.

92 percent during the 1950s before being cut to 70 percent by the 1965 tax year. Prior to the Economic Recovery Tax Act of 1981, income tax rates varied from 14 percent to 70 percent, but the act reduced the top rate to 50 percent, lowered rates for all taxpayers, and provided for the indexing of tax rates to inflation. The Tax Reform Act of 1986 lowered rates even further, producing a maximum effective rate of 33 percent and making significant changes in other parts of the tax code as well.

Table 12.1 lists federal income tax rates for selected years since 1913, including the level of income exempt from taxation for a single individual and the tax rate in the lowest tax bracket. Income is taxed at this rate up to the level of income in the next column, labeled Income. The next two columns list the highest marginal tax bracket and the level of income that must be earned to be taxed at the highest marginal tax rate. Note that the initial highest bracket of 7 percent in 1913 was increased in a few years to 77 percent because of World War I, but that large tax cuts were enacted in the 1920s. Rates rose again in the 1930s, and though the table does not show it, the highest marginal tax bracket rose from 25 percent to 63 percent in 1932, went up to 79 percent in 1936, and did not sink back below 70 percent until the 1980s. Still, the highest bracket in the 1930s applied to incomes in excess of $1 million, and the price level has increased by more than six times since that time. As the table indicates, tax rates have risen over time. More significantly, the reduction in the amount of income that must be earned to owe tax and to be taxed at the highest bracket has fallen even more dramatically.

The entries after 1986 reflect the changes brought about by the Tax Reform Act of 1986. Note the dramatic drop in the maximum tax rate from 50 percent in 1986 to 38.5 percent in 1987 to 28 percent in 1988. This drop is even more dramatic when the decline in the maximum rate over the decade of the 1980s is considered—a drop in the marginal tax rate for the highest income taxpayers from 70 percent in 1981 to 28 percent in 1988 is a major change. A taxpayer's marginal tax rate is significant and will be discussed in detail later in the chapter.

Calculating Taxable Income

Some of the conceptual difficulties in calculating taxable income have been discussed, and the purpose of this section is to provide an overview of the current U.S. income tax system to see how the current tax code deals with those difficulties. Discussion of issues related to the tax treatment of savings and capital gains will be deferred until after the calculation of taxable income is examined, because some of those issues can be illuminated by first seeing how they are treated according to current law.

Tax law must be concerned with more than just defining income, though. Designing a tax code that is fair is a primary concern, as is a tax collection system that is as efficient as possible. This means not only trying to minimize the excess burden of taxation but also keeping compliance costs, monitoring costs, and other costs to a minimum. In short, there is not a single goal to strive for in designing a tax code. With this in mind, we can trace the process of determining an individual's U.S. income tax liability, using the Tax Reform Act of 1986 tax code as a model.

Computation of Income

The first step in the process is to calculate total income. This involves adding together all of one's income, including interest and dividends from investments, capital gains, alimony, pension income, business income, rents, royalties, unemployment compensation, and other types of income; indeed, the IRS income tax form even has a line on it for "other income." (They want to make sure you do not leave anything out.)

Before 1987 long-term capital gains (capital gains from selling assets owned more than a year) were taxed at only 40 percent of the rate for ordinary income. With a maximum income tax rate of 50 percent in 1986, this meant that the maximum tax rate on long-term capital gains was 20 percent. Short-term capital gains (capital gains from selling assets owned less than a year) are taxed at the same rate as ordinary income both currently and before the 1986 tax reform. Thus, prior to 1987 capital gains were taxed at a rate significantly lower than the rate for other income.

Furthermore, the previous maximum rate for capital gains was even lower than the present maximum income tax rate.

Whether long-term capital gains should be treated differently from other income will be discussed in Chapter 13. At this point we simply need to note the change in the law. Another issue worthy of consideration is that income from saving, such as dividends and interest, is taxed at the same rate as ordinary income. This gives rise to a double tax on saving, which arises because income from saving—capital gains, dividends, and interest—is treated as ordinary income for tax purposes. Note that the current tax law is much more consistent in this regard than the tax law prior to 1987, when it was easier to shelter income earned on savings from taxation. We will discuss the double tax on saving in more detail later in the chapter.

The definition of income in the U.S. tax code does not follow precisely any of the definitions of income discussed here. It does not tax capital gains at the time they occur, as in the Haig-Simons definition, but when they are realized. In this sense the capital gains tax taxes more than the sustainable flow of income, like in the Fisher definition. Because tax policy has many goals, it will not be possible to point to a single principle and say that the tax laws satisfy that one. But with some exceptions, income for tax purposes is computed as the dollar amount received from all sources by the taxpayer during the tax year.

Exemptions

The tax laws allow individuals to exclude certain items in calculating taxable income, for example, personal exemptions for the taxpayers and their dependents, and fellowships and scholarships up to the amount used for tuition, books, and supplies. Because such items are exempt from taxation, they are called *exemptions*. In addition to this nontaxable income, other items, called *adjustments*, are excluded from taxation by being subtracted from taxable income. These adjustments to income fall into five general categories.

One category is employee business expenses. The rationale behind employee business expense adjustments is that individuals should not have to pay taxes on what they must spend to earn the income. Just as businesses can subtract their expenses from their gross receipts and pay tax only on their net income, so individuals are exempt from paying taxes on the expenses of earning an income. For example, travel expenses might be included if the income earner must travel as a part of the job, though the IRS does not allow expenses incurred going to and from work as a deduction. In addition, the cost of any special tools that the employee must supply or special uniforms that the employee must wear are also exempt, though a coat and tie is not considered a uniform, and the cost is not exempt from income taxation. Moving expenses can also be deducted from taxable income if a person changes jobs and the new job is more than thirty-five miles further away from the individual's home than the old job. The rationale here is similar to the employee business expense—presumably, the move constitutes an expense of earning income.

Although some expenses, such as business travel, can be deducted completely from taxable income, the Tax Reform Act of 1986 specifies that only 80 percent of the expense of meals and entertainment for business purposes is deductible. Thus, if a businessperson spends $100 taking a group of clients out to lunch, where formerly the entire $100 could be subtracted from taxable income as a business expense, the current law allows only $80 to be deducted.

Alimony paid to an ex-spouse is another item that can be deducted from income. Because alimony received is a part of the recipient's income, this deduction keeps the alimony from being taxed twice. The taxpayer can also deduct penalties assessed due to early withdrawal of savings. Some savings instruments assess a penalty if the money is withdrawn before the instrument matures. Because tax is paid on the interest earned before the withdrawal, the penalty for early withdrawal is subtracted against the interest earned (which, remember, was already added into taxable income).

Finally, money contributed to approved retirement plans is exempt from taxation. Many employers have some type of retirement plan for their employees, set up so that the employee pays no tax on the money going into the retirement plan, but pays income tax on the money when it is paid to the employee after retirement. If a person's employer does not have such a plan, the individual can place up to $2000 per year into an IRA account, as long as the taxpayer earns that much in income and is not covered by another plan. These IRA accounts, intended to provide for the retirement years of the contributor, might be kept at banks, stock brokerage firms, or other financial firms approved by the IRS. If the money in the IRA is drawn out before the individual reaches age 62, then a 10 percent penalty must be paid. But as long as the income is saved, no tax is due. After retirement, when the money is withdrawn from the account and used for consumption, tax is paid at ordinary income tax rates. From 1981 to 1986 individuals were allowed to contribute to IRAs regardless of whether they were covered by another plan, so many individuals who are not now eligible to contribute to IRAs have an IRA account established prior to 1987.

Later in the chapter we will discuss IRA accounts in more detail; at this point we are merely outlining how the income tax is calculated. So far we have seen that total income is added up and then certain items not subject to tax are subtracted from that total income; these items are called exemptions. The result of this process is what the IRS calls *adjusted gross income*.

Deductions

After these exemptions are figured, the taxpayer can either take a standard deduction or itemize deductions. A *deduction* is an amount that is subtracted from adjusted gross income before calculating the tax due. The standard deduction for a single person in 1987 was $2540, which the taxpayer can simply subtract from adjusted gross income. Alternatively, the taxpayer can add up a host of other items to be deducted from adjusted gross income, including medical expenses in excess of 7.5 percent of adjusted gross income, taxes other than sales taxes paid to state and local governments, interest paid on home mortgages, and miscellaneous other deductions.

For many taxpayers the largest deduction will be interest paid on a home mortgage. Prior to the Tax Reform Act of 1986, all interest paid by individuals could be deducted from adjusted gross income. A major goal of the act was to broaden the tax base by taxing many items that previously could be deducted from taxable income. In its original form the act did not allow any interest expenses to be deducted, but the real estate lobbyists placed enough pressure on legislators that the home mortgage deduction was preserved, even while all other interest deductions were eliminated. There is no sound economic reason why homeowners should be allowed to take this deduction while interest paid for other purposes is not deductible. Indeed, the inclusion of the deduction in the Tax Reform Act of 1986 is a tribute to the influence of one special interest group. This single item of home mortgage interest makes it worthwhile for most homeowners to itemize deductions rather than take the standard deduction.

The taxpayer can also deduct charitable contributions as well as $1900 (in 1987) for each dependent, that is, each child or parent living at home, for whose care one is responsible. The deduction for dependents is scheduled to increase to $1950 in 1988 and $2000 in 1989 and to be indexed for inflation after that. In addition, miscellaneous deductions—uninsured casualty losses, administrative expenses for investments, business expenses such as subscriptions to journals and professional dues—can be claimed, though only to the extent that they exceed 2 percent of adjusted gross income. For example, if someone has an adjusted gross income of $100,000 and miscellaneous deductions totaling $2500, only $500 can be deducted from taxable income.

Subtracting all of these deductions from adjusted gross income gives taxable income. Note the difference between exemptions and deductions. An item that is an exemption can be subtracted from taxable income regardless of whether or not the taxpayer takes the standard deduction. Therefore, for some taxpayers exemptions will be more beneficial than deductions.

Tax Computation

The taxpayer then figures the tax due on this taxable income. Beginning in 1988 there will be three marginal tax rates at which taxpayers can be taxed, but these will be divided into four brackets. For a single individual the first $17,850 of taxable income is taxed at a rate of 15 percent, and income from $17,851 to $43,150 is taxed at 28 percent. For income between $43,151 and $89,560, an additional 5 percent is added to the individual's marginal tax rate, making the effective marginal tax rate for people in this bracket 33 percent. Above $89,560 in income, the additional 5 percent tax is eliminated, so the marginal tax

Table 12.2 Marginal Tax Rates in 1988 for a Single Individual

TAXABLE INCOME ($)	MARGINAL TAX RATE (PERCENT)
Up to 17,850	15
17,851 to 43,150	28
43,151 to 89,560	33
Above 89,560	28

rate for people earning more than $89,560 returns to 28 percent. These effective marginal tax brackets for single individuals are listed in Table 12.2.

The reason why the additional 5 percent tax is applied to taxpayers in the 33 percent bracket is to phase out the 15 percent rate on income below $17,850. By adding the 5 percent to tax rates in this 33 percent phaseout range, the average rate rises until, at an income of $89,560 for single individuals, the average tax rate is 28 percent. Thus, the highest-income taxpayers pay 28 percent on all of their taxable income, and their average tax rate equals their marginal rate of 28 percent.

Although marginal tax rates rise and then fall as income rises, the average tax rate continually rises with increases in income. And even for individuals in the 33 percent bracket, marginal tax rates for most taxpayers will be lower under the existing tax law than before the Tax Reform Act of 1986.[3] But this is the first time since the income tax was established that the taxpayers with the highest in-

---

[3] For some types of income, tax rates are considerably higher, though. Previously, capital gains were taxed at a maximum rate of 20 percent; under current law the capital gains tax rate could be as high as 33 percent, a 65 percent increase. Compared to the previous law, then, there is much less of an incentive to earn capital gains.

comes are not subject to the highest marginal tax rate.

After computing the tax due, taxpayers are allowed to subtract certain items, called *credits*, from the tax due. Some items for which credits may be taken are expenses to care for children or other dependents who could not care for themselves and taxes paid to foreign governments. There is also an earned income credit for low income individuals that varies depending on the number of dependents the income earner has. The Tax Reform Act of 1986 eliminated several items for which tax credits could previously be claimed, in accordance with the general philosophy of broadening the tax base in order to lower tax rates.

Note that credits are significantly more beneficial to taxpayers than deductions. Deductions are subtracted from adjusted gross income, which means they are worth the amount of the deduction times the taxpayer's tax bracket to the taxpayer. For example, if the taxpayer is in the 33 percent tax bracket and can take a $100 deduction, then the deduction reduces the taxpayer's taxable income by $100 and so reduces the tax due by $33. However, a credit of $100 directly reduces the taxpayer's taxes by $100, making it far more valuable to a taxpayer than a deduction of an equal amount.

The 1986 tax act also makes a provision for an alternative minimum tax for individuals who have many deductions. The alternative minimum tax rate is 21 percent, but it covers a broader tax base that includes some infre-

quently used deductions such as depreciation of personal property and tax-exempt interest on certain bonds, as well as common deductions such as state and local taxes. Because the alternative minimum tax rate is close to the 28 percent regular rate for the highest-income taxpayers, the alternative minimum tax may apply to a large number of taxpayers, especially in states that have high state income taxes.

To review, a taxpayer adds up his or her total income, excluding from the total any income not subject to taxation. Then the taxpayer subtracts certain adjustments to give adjusted gross income. Deductions are subtracted from adjusted gross income to give taxable income, from which the income tax is computed. Finally, tax credits are subtracted from this computed tax to yield the tax due. If all this seems complex, it is. The Tax Reform Act of 1986 was intended, among other things, to simplify the tax code. The final act was issued in two volumes. The first volume contained 925 pages stating the law, and the second volume contained 886 pages of explanation and interpretation. Whether the act actually did simplify tax law is debatable, but at the least it had the effect of lowering tax rates and broadening the tax base. With this background some theoretical issues surrounding income taxation can be viewed within the context of the existing system. The first issue to be considered is the theory behind broadening the tax base in order to lower rates.

Broadening the Tax Base

As just noted, one of the principal objectives of the Tax Reform Act of 1986 was to broaden the tax base in order to lower marginal tax rates. The general philosophy behind this type of reform is to close up some of the numerous loopholes that allowed much income to go untaxed, so that the same amount of tax revenue can be raised, but at lower rates. The

Figure 12.1 A Comparison of Broadly Based and Narrowly Based Taxes
Budget constraint *NT* represents no tax, and a narrowly based tax rotates
the budget constraint to *NN*, placing the individual at point *X*. A broadly
based tax collecting the same amount of revenue produces budget
constraint *BB*, with the individual locating at *Y*. The individual is on a
higher indifference curve and therefore is better off under the more
broadly based tax.

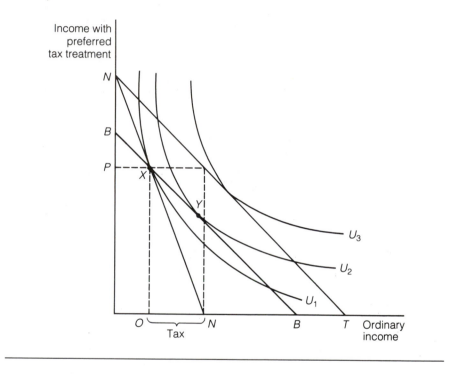

benefits of lower marginal tax rates will be
discussed later in the chapter; here we want to
show how taxpayers can benefit from a
broader tax base when overall tax revenues
remain the same.

It is worth pointing out that a second goal
of the Tax Reform Act was to remain revenue
neutral, that is, to collect the same amount in
tax revenues as the old tax system would have.
Taxpayers as a whole can benefit from a tax
on a broader tax base that collects the same
amount of revenue, as Figure 12.1 illustrates.

The figure depicts an indifference curve in
which an individual faces a trade-off between
earning two different types of income. One
type, measured on the horizontal axis, is ordinary income that will be taxed under any
tax system. The other type, measured on the
vertical axis, is income that receives preferred
treatment, and therefore will not be taxed,
under a narrowly based tax system. With no
taxes the individual's budget constraint becomes *NT*.

But a narrowly based tax, which taxes ordinary income but not income that receives preferred tax treatment, causes the individual's budget constraint to shift to *NN*. The individual locates at point *X* in the diagram, earning amount *O* of ordinary income and amount *P* of income with preferred tax treatment. The amount of the tax, measured in ordinary income, is the amount by which the budget constraint rotates inward from *NT* to *NN* at point *X*, which is shown by the bracketed amount labeled Tax. What is significant about the narrowly based tax is that it changes the relative price of earning the different types of income.

Now consider a broadly based income tax that taxes both types of income at the same rate and raises the same amount of revenue as the narrowly based tax. The budget constraint for the broadly based tax passes through point *X* because it raises the same amount of revenue, shown by the bracketed amount labeled Tax, but it is parallel to the original budget constraint *NT*, indicating that the same trade-off takes place between earning

the two types of income as if there were no tax. Thus, the budget constraint under the broadly based tax is constraint BB. Note that under the broadly based tax the individual moves to a higher indifference curve and so is better off. Also note that the individual earns more of the ordinary income and less of the preferred income if the preferred income does not receive any special tax treatment.

Neither of these findings should be surprising. The relative amounts of the two types of income earned reflect the fact that individuals will substitute into the relatively cheaper option when relative prices change. As Chapter 9 explained, taxation produces a welfare loss because it alters relative prices that individuals face. Therefore, the more broadly based tax, which entails less distortion of the trade-offs faced by taxpayers, has a lower welfare loss. Indeed, tax reformers had this, as well as lower marginal taxes, in mind when they designed the Tax Reform Act of 1986.

The Income-Leisure Trade-Off

A person can derive utility not only from income but from nontaxed activities as well; these nontaxed activities are referred to here as *leisure*. This is a broader definition of leisure than is typically used, and deliberately so, because a tax on income makes nontaxed activities in general relatively more attractive. In this sense leisure activities include not only fishing and golf but also painting one's own house rather than hiring a painter. For example, a mechanic may be able to work overtime for $10 per hour and hire a painter for $7 per hour. Assuming that the mechanic can paint as well as the painter, and also that the mechanic is indifferent between working at

one job or another, whether the mechanic should work overtime and hire a painter or do the job herself depends ultimately on the rate at which the mechanic's wages are taxed.

Taxed Versus Nontaxed Activities

If the mechanic pays no tax on her income, then the best alternative is to work for $10 per hour, hire the painter for $7 per hour, and be better off by $3 per hour. However, if the mechanic is in the 33 percent tax bracket, then $3.30 is taxed away for each hour's work, leaving the mechanic only $6.70 per hour after taxes, in which case the mechanic is better off

Figure 12.2 The Income-Leisure Trade-Off An income tax, which rotates the budget constraint inward, causes the individual to substitute from income-earning activities into leisure.

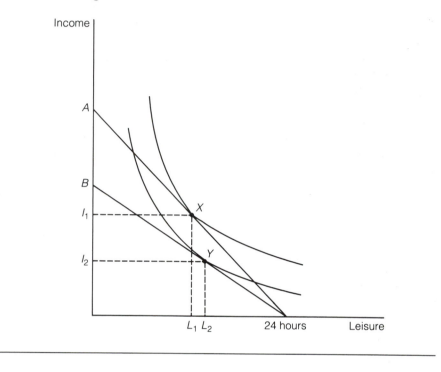

doing her own painting. Note that a profitable exchange could be made were it not for the excess burden of taxes, which discourages the taxed activity. Here the potentially profitable exchange of hiring a painter will not occur if the income tax rate is above 30 percent.

In general terms the income tax gives an incentive to pursue nontaxed activities rather than taxed activities. As the house painting example suggests, this sometimes means doing work for one's self rather than hiring someone to do it, thereby foregoing the gains from trade that could have been produced when the gains are less than the taxes that would have to be paid. It also might mean pursuing activities in the underground economy, where taxes are not collected. For example, one of the incentives for such illegal activities as drug dealing and prostitution is that the income on those activities is kept hidden from the government and therefore not taxed. Income taxes also provide an incentive for such traditional leisure activities as tennis and napping.

Income Versus Leisure

To illustrate the effects of an income tax, all of these untaxed activities are lumped into the category of leisure. The effects of the income-leisure trade-off are depicted in Figure 12.2 through the use of indifference curves. Because the maximum amount of leisure that can be consumed each day is 24 hours, the budget constraint for any individual intersects the leisure axis at the point marked 24 hours.

The amount of income that the person can earn is determined by the person's wage rate. For example, with no tax the person's budget constraint extends from the point marked 24 hours on the leisure axis to point A on the income axis, and by taking no leisure, the person can earn the level of income marked A. Because the individual can take more leisure time only in exchange for less income, the line from 24 hours to A is the budget constraint. The slope of the line represents the wage rate of the individual, or the rate at which leisure time can be transformed into income.

The arcs in the diagram are two of the individual's indifference curves. With no taxes (and the budget constraint intersecting at A) the utility-maximizing point for the person is at X, and the individual takes L_1 amount of leisure and earns income I_1. But by adding in the effects of an income tax, the rate at which leisure can be transformed into income is lowered, so the budget constraint rotates down to intersect the income axis at B. There are still 24 hours of leisure available—leisure is not taxed, so the intersecting point remains unchanged on the leisure axis. But the slope of the budget constraint becomes less steep, reflecting the less desirable trade-off between income and leisure, and B is below A because even if the person takes no leisure time, total income declines as a result of the tax. The person's utility maximizing point is now Y, income has fallen to I_2, and leisure activities have risen to L_2. In short, the income tax causes a substitution from income-earning activities into leisure.

This substitution effect, in which a person substitutes out of the good experiencing a price increase and into a good experiencing a price decrease, will always occur. But recall that when income is significantly affected, the income effect can work against the substitution effect. For example, the tax takes away so much of the person's income that the person's standard of living declines, causing the person to work more to make up for some of the income that has been taxed away. In this case the effect of the income tax is actually to increase the number of hours worked.

This case is illustrated in Figure 12.3, which is drawn the same as Figure 12.2 except for the indifference curves. In Figure 12.3 the individual's preferences are such that the amount of leisure falls from L_1 to L_2 as a result of the income tax. Likewise, after-tax income falls from I_1 to I_2. But what most interests us is that the person could actually work more as a result of an income tax. Another possibility, not depicted here, is that the person could work the same amount with the income tax.

The excess burden of any tax arises because a tax alters the choices that people make. If people make the same choices with the tax as without it, the burden of the tax comprises only the amount of tax collected—there is no excess burden. Note, however, that even if the amount of work remains the same, an excess burden still occurs because people use their time and income differently. For example, the mechanic might paint her own house rather than hire a painter (the substitution effect) even if the amount of income the mechanic earns doesn't change. The excess burden of a tax results solely from the substitution effect and remains the same regardless of the nature of the income effect.

Figure 12.3 An Increase in Work in Response to an Income Tax This figure shows that a person can work more as a result of an income tax, if the income effect works in the opposite direction and is larger than the substitution effect.

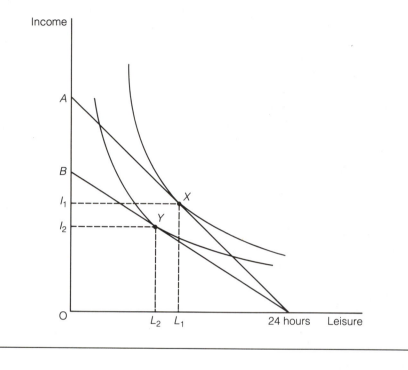

The Backward-Bending Supply Curve of Labor

Because workers work for after-tax rather than before-tax wages, an income tax represents a reduction in the effective wage rate paid to workers. If workers work more to offset an income tax, this implies that workers are willing to work more hours when the wage rate is lower. This suggests that there is a backward-bending supply curve for labor.

A backward-bending labor supply curve is depicted in Figure 12.4. At low wage W_1 workers supply quantity of labor Q_1, but when they are offered higher wages, such as W_2, they work more, so the quantity of labor supplied increases to Q_2. Eventually, however, when

wages increase to W_3, the quantity of labor supplied declines. This happens because at wage W_2 workers have many of the material things in life that give them satisfaction, so they use an increase in income, in effect, to buy more leisure time. The indifference curve diagram in Figure 12.3 illustrates this type of case in which workers who initially are making a wage equal to W_3 in Figure 12.4 react to an increase in the tax rate that lowers their effective wages by working more.

Note that the backward-bending supply curve of labor applies only to the economy as a whole, not to an individual employer. An

Figure 12.4 The Backward-Bending Supply Curve for Labor A backward-bending supply curve of labor can exist because at high wage rates workers want to work less as wages increase. In effect, they are buying more leisure time with their higher wages.

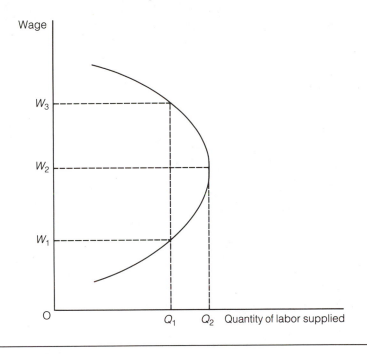

individual employer will always have to pay a higher wage to hire additional workers (unless the labor market is very competitive, in which case additional workers can be hired at the same wage). The individual employer must compete with other employers to hire more labor, so the employer must make that employment possibility more attractive than its alternatives.

This does not answer the question of whether the backward-bending supply curve of labor actually exists, though. In theory, it could exist, but this does not mean that the economy-wide labor supply curve actually is backward-bending. From a positive standpoint this is an interesting question, but from a normative standpoint it has less relevance to

public sector economics. The reason is that the model depicting the relationship between income tax and labor, as shown in Figures 12.2 and 12.3, is built on the assumption that the income tax lowers a person's income. Although the income tax does indeed lower a person's disposable income (income that can be spent in the private sector), presumably the taxes being collected are paying for utility-providing public sector goods such as parks, roads, and national defense. Because these are goods that taxpayers desire, the reduction in private sector income should be offset from the income in kind received from the public sector output.

In this light Figures 12.2 and 12.3 tell only part of the story; Figure 12.5 fills in the missing

Figure 12.5 The Income-Leisure Trade-Off with Taxes and Government Spending Examining an income tax in isolation for its effect on labor supply tells only half of the story. The income tax rotates the budget constraint inward, but the public sector output bought with tax revenues has an income effect that shifts the budget constraint out, leaving only the substitution effect. The substitution effect unambiguously reduces the amount of labor supplied, because leisure increases from L_1 to L_2.

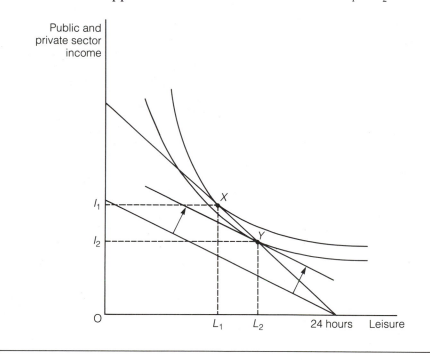

details. First, the budget constraint rotates inward as in the earlier figures, but then the budget constraint shifts outward, parallel to the rotated budget constraint, reflecting the income in kind from the public sector output paid for by the tax revenues. If the resulting output were equal in value to the taxes paid, this would place the individual on the original budget constraint, but the new relative price line reflects the relatively higher price of income in terms of leisure foregone. In this case there is no net income effect, because the negative income effect of the taxes is offset by the positive income effect of the public sector output. All that remains is the substitution effect, which unambiguously causes the individual to substitute away from the more costly activity (income) and toward the less costly activity (leisure).[4]

In conclusion, there may be a backward-bending supply curve for labor, but if it has

---

[4]See James Gwartney and Richard Stroup, "Labor Supply and Tax Rates: A Correction of the Record," *American Economic Review* 73, no. 3 (June 1983), pp. 446–451, for a discussion of this idea.

any relevance to public sector economics it is because taxpayers are not receiving public sector output equal in value to the taxes that they pay. If the income in kind from public sector output compensates taxpayers for their taxes, then the backward-bending supply curve for labor will have no influence on the effects of income taxation.

The Laffer Curve

The *Laffer curve* explains the trade-off between tax rates and tax revenues. There are two factors at work in this trade-off. First, as tax rates rise, a higher percentage of income will be paid as taxes. Second, as tax rates rise, less income will be earned because of the higher tax rates. The Laffer curve, named for its originator, economist Arthur Laffer, is depicted in Figure 12.6, and it can be understood in the following terms. At the origin in the diagram, if tax rates are zero, tax revenues obviously will also be zero, because no tax will be collected on any income. As tax rates rise, tax revenues will also go up because now some taxes are being collected. Beyond some point, however, income will fall in response to the higher tax rates, and when the percentage fall in income is greater than the percentage rise in taxes, tax rates will fall as well.

In the extreme case tax rates could be high enough to tax away 100 percent of all income earned, which would remove any incentive to earn income. With no income earned, no taxes would be paid despite the high tax rates. Thus, in Figure 12.6, when tax rates are either zero or 100 percent, tax revenues will be zero. Because low tax rates will collect some tax revenues, the curve must slope up as long as rates remain below the revenue-maximizing tax rate *RM* and then slope back toward the Tax rates axis when the maximum amount of collectable tax revenue *TM* is passed.

When President Reagan campaigned for his first term in office in 1980, he argued that a reduction in taxes could increase the tax revenue collected. The basis for his argument was his belief that tax rates in the United States were above *RM*. Note that with many different tax rates, this could be true for some taxes (and tax brackets) but not for others. For example, before the tax cut in 1981 the highest marginal tax rate was 70 percent, but it was reduced to 50 percent in 1981 and further reduced to 28 percent for individuals earning the highest incomes in 1988. This means that prior to 1981 the highest-income earners were paying 70 percent of any additional income earned as taxes, but by 1988 the rate will have dropped to 28 percent. For an individual in the highest tax bracket, working to earn an additional $1 in income left the individual with only 30 cents after federal taxes (not including state and local taxes), whereas with the tax cuts the individual will be able to keep 72 cents from every dollar of additional income. This amounts to more than twice the after-tax income for the marginal tax dollar. Thus, it is possible that individuals in higher tax brackets could have been taxed at rates higher than *RM* while individuals in lower brackets were taxed at lower rates.

How could a nation choose tax rates that placed them on the downward-sloping portion of the Laffer curve? Perhaps individuals were not able to adjust immediately to increases in tax rates, causing the amount of revenue raised through taxation to rise initially. But over time, as taxpayers adjusted

Figure 12.6 The Laffer Curve As tax rates rise, the amount of taxable income earned is reduced. Eventually, the reduction in the tax base more than offsets the increase in tax rates, so above *RM*, tax revenues fall in response to an increase in tax rates.

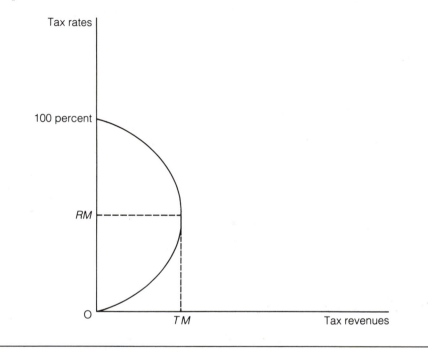

their affairs to account for the new provisions of the tax law, additional tax avoidance and evasion could have caused revenues to fall.

Thus, a tax increase that could be revenue-enhancing in the short run might reduce tax revenues in the long run.[5]

Average and Marginal Tax Rates

In considering income tax systems, it is important to understand the difference between average and marginal tax rates, a distinction that has only been alluded to previously. A person's *average tax rate* is the amount of tax paid divided by the person's income; a per-

son's *marginal tax rate* is the percentage of any additional income paid in tax. For example,

---

[5]This argument is explained in James M. Buchanan and Dwight R. Lee, "Politics, Time, and the Laffer Curve,"

assume that a tax schedule requires a taxpayer to pay 10 percent of the first $10,000 and 20 percent of any additional income as tax. A person who has $20,000 in income will pay 10 percent of the first $10,000 in income, or $1000, plus 20 percent of the other $10,000 in income, or $2000, for a total tax bill of $3000. The person's average tax rate is the total tax—$3000—divided by total income—$20,000—or 15 percent. The person's marginal tax rate, as noted, is the percentage of any additional income paid in taxes, or 20 percent.

This is an example of a progressive tax structure, because the percentage of income paid in tax rises as income rises. Note that with progressive taxation, the marginal tax rate exceeds the average rate. The reason for using a progressive tax structure is its redistributional characteristics—a progressive tax structure applies the ability-to-pay principle by having people with larger incomes pay a higher percentage of their incomes in taxes. Chapter 14 is devoted to redistribution; for now keep in mind simply that a progressive tax structure has the effect of increasing the excess burden of the tax compared to a proportional (or regressive) tax.

Marginal Tax Rates and Excess Burden

Recall that the excess burden of a tax results from the fact that the tax provides an incentive for taxpayers to change their behavior in order to try to avoid paying the tax. Thus, the greater the tax, the greater the incentive to change one's behavior to avoid the tax. In the previous example the taxpayer was in the 20 percent marginal tax bracket, meaning that for each dollar earned, 20 cents had to be paid as income tax. The taxpayer's average tax rate

was only 15 percent, though, so if, instead of a progressive tax schedule a proportional tax schedule that collected tax at a 15 percent rate were in effect, the taxpayer would end up paying the same $3000 in income taxes, but at a marginal tax rate of only 15 percent. In other words, with the progressive tax the taxpayer loses 20 cents of each additional dollar to taxes, whereas with the proportional tax, which raises the same amount of revenue, the taxpayer loses only 15 cents of each additional dollar. Thus, there is less of an incentive to avoid earning income with the proportional tax than with the progressive tax.

This example is intended to illustrate a general point. The revenue collected by an income tax is a function of the average tax rate, but the excess burden of an income tax is a function of the marginal tax rate. Thus, to minimize the excess burden of a tax, the marginal tax rate should be kept as low as possible. Consider a lump sum in this context. The marginal tax rate of a lump sum tax is always zero, which is why there is no excess burden. Progressive taxes are used for redistributive purposes, but this equity justification for progressive rates has a cost in efficiency. The more progressive the tax system, the higher the marginal tax rates, and therefore the higher the excess burden of the tax, will be. This discussion illustrates the justification for the 33 percent tax bracket in the tax code. By increasing marginal tax rates in this range, the average and marginal rates are both 28 percent for the highest-income taxpayers, which produces a lower excess burden than under a progressive system, where marginal tax rates are higher than average.

Journal of Political Economy 90, no. 4 (August 1982), pp. 816–819.

Indexation, Inflation, and Bracket Creep

Indexation of taxes, mentioned earlier, means adjusting tax rates for inflation, so that real taxes paid are independent of the price level. The Tax Act of 1981 provided for indexation of individual income tax brackets in an attempt to eliminate a problem known as *bracket creep*. Bracket creep occurs when the same level of real income is taxed at a higher rate because an increase in the price level causes a person's nominal income to rise for a given level of real income. Because tax rate schedules are based on nominal income levels, a person's tax bracket is determined by nominal income. Thus, if the person's real income remains the same during a year of, say, 10 percent inflation, then the person's nominal income rises by 10 percent. With a progressive tax structure inflation increases the amount of tax that taxpayers have to pay on a given level of real income. This is the result of bracket creep.

In 1961 the tax law provided for marginal tax rates from 20 to 91 percent, but 88 percent of all tax returns filed paid marginal rates from 20 to 22 percent. Tax rates were cut several times between 1961 and 1979, but by 1979, 45 percent of all taxpayers were paying marginal tax rates in excess of 23 percent.[6] The reason for the increase in marginal tax rates despite the tax cuts during that period was that the price level during the period more than doubled. Rates were cut, but not by enough to offset the rise in nominal incomes caused by inflation.

One problem that exists because of bracket creep is that the government can use inflation as a device to raise tax revenues without actually legislating a tax increase. Tax increases are politically unpopular for obvious reasons, giving Congress a clear incentive to use inflation as a revenue-generating device, or at least blunting any incentive to reduce inflation. In this light indexation serves to reduce not only the government's ability to produce unlegislated tax increases but also its incentives to encourage inflationary policies. The indexation provisions of the 1986 Tax Reform Act cover only the tax brackets of the income tax. Thus, for example, if there is 5 percent inflation, indexation provides for a 5 percent increase in the nominal income required to place the taxpayer in a certain tax bracket.

Inflation can also affect the amount of taxes due by a taxpayer from capital gains. The nominal value of real assets will increase in inflationary times, and capital gains taxes are paid on the gain in nominal terms rather than in real terms. For the tax system to be completely indexed, the capital gain would have to be adjusted for the amount of inflation. Again, we discuss this issue more completely in the following chapter; we mention it here simply to point out that the indexation of tax brackets provided for in the current tax code does not completely eliminate the effects of inflation on tax revenues.

---

[6] These figures are given in Robert E. Hall and Alvin Rabushka, *The Flat Tax* (Stanford: Hoover Press, 1985), p. 14.

The Double Tax on Saving

The income tax system in its current form places a double tax on saving—income is taxed once when earned, and then, if it is saved, the proceeds from the saving are taxed again. To illustrate, consider a person planning to spend $1000 on a new stereo. Assume for the moment that there is no tax on income, and also that the interest rate is 10 percent, which means that the person can save the $1000 and earn $100 a year in interest. Thus, the cost of the stereo ($1000) is the same as the cost of buying an income stream of $100 a year from now on; in other words the new stereo costs the same amount as $100 a year in future income.

However, if there is a 50 percent income tax, the person must earn $2000 in income in order to buy the same stereo, because $1000 will be paid in taxes, leaving $1000 to pay for the stereo. How much income will have to be earned to buy the $100-per-year income stream? In order to receive the $100-per-year income stream, the interest earned must be $200, because with a 50 percent tax rate half of the interest will be paid in taxes. Thus to get the $100 per year, $200 in interest must be earned, which means that $2000 must be saved. But with the 50 percent tax rate $4000 in income must be earned to save $2000. The result is that $2000 in income must be earned to buy the stereo, whereas $4000 in income must be earned to receive the $100 per year income stream. With no taxes the two items cost the same amount, but with the 50 percent income tax the future income stream from saving is taxed twice and it costs twice what the stereo costs. Tax is paid on the income once when it is earned and again on the proceeds from the savings, so the relative price of saving rises with an income tax. This is why the

current income tax system places a double tax on saving.

The problem with the double tax on saving is that a reduced amount of saving reduces the amount of income available for investment. Thus, the income tax system favors present consumption over investment. In this case, though, the excess burden of the double tax on saving is shifted forward into the future—lower investment today means lower future productivity. The double tax on saving reduces present capital formation and reduces future output in exchange for more consumption today. In this light the advantages of a consumption tax over an income tax become evident. As long as income is saved, it is not taxed under the consumption tax, but when the saving is withdrawn and consumed, then the tax is paid.

An argument can be made supporting this double tax based on equity grounds. Because people with higher incomes tend to save more, the double tax on saving falls more heavily on those who can best afford it. Furthermore, some people have higher expenses than others, so the ability to save may indicate that the double tax is placed on income not needed for necessities such as food, shelter, or medical care. Indeed, the same arguments that favor progressive taxation can also be used to support a double tax on saving; at the least one should recognize that the double tax exists and that the burden of the tax is shifted into the future.

Individual Retirement Accounts

As noted earlier, the Individual Retirement Account escapes this double tax on saving by allowing contributions to the IRA to be deducted from taxable income. The regular income tax is paid on money coming out of the account. The reason why the IRA is such an advantage to the taxpayer is not because it defers taxes but because it escapes the double tax on saving.

One possible method of moving the current U.S. income tax system from an income tax to a consumption tax would be to allow all taxpayers unlimited contributions into IRA accounts rather than to impose the $2000 limit, and to eliminate the penalty that now exists for withdrawing the money before age 62.

This would produce a consumption tax for those who utilized the IRA option.

The 1986 Tax Reform Act moved in the opposite direction, however, by limiting participation in tax-deferred IRA accounts only to those not covered by other pension plans provided by their employers. The result is that most taxpayers who were previously contributing to IRA accounts are now ineligible to make further contributions. The 1981 tax reform laid the foundation for a move toward a consumption tax, but the 1986 act clearly was a move in the opposite direction.

The Flat Tax

A large part of the intellectual foundation for tax reform in the 1980s was established by proposals for a flat tax, in which all income eligible for taxation is taxed at one uniform rate. The Tax Reform Act of 1986 sought to implement, or at least approximate, some of the principles of a flat tax by broadening the tax base, lowering rates, and establishing only three marginal tax rates. The characteristics of a truly flat tax can be understood in the context of the flat tax model proposed by economists Robert Hall and Alvin Rabushka.

The Hall-Rabushka Flat Tax

The Hall and Rabushka flat tax plan[7] calls for a personal exemption of $4500 in 1985 dollars for the taxpayer, another $4500 for the spouse (if married), and $1800 for each dependent. Thus, for example, a married couple with two children would have an exemption of $12,600 in 1985 dollars. No tax is paid on this amount, and all income above the exemption is taxed at a flat 19 percent rate. Hall and Rabushka designed their system so that all income is taxed at the 19 percent rate (including the income of businesses), but no income can be taxed twice, as is currently the case with the double tax on saving. They argue that their 19 percent tax rate, coupled with the other provisions in their proposal, would raise the same amount of revenue as the current income tax system, that is, it would be revenue neutral.

Indeed, a true flat tax system has only one rate, at which, after a personal exemption, all income is taxed. The 1986 tax act might be called a "modified flat tax" because it reduces the number of tax brackets, but still it does not place all taxpayers in a single tax bracket. To lower tax rates to the levels proposed by tax systems such as Hall and Rabushka's, the tax

---

[7]See Robert E. Hall and Alvin Rabushka, *The Flat Tax* (Stanford: Hoover Press, 1985).

base must be broadened so that more income is subject to taxation and the total amount of tax revenues does not change. This was another goal of the 1986 Tax Reform Act. Although the 1986 tax reform did not institute a flat tax, by comparing it to the Hall and Rabushka plan, the intellectual heritage of the flat tax elements in the 1986 tax bill becomes evident.

Most designers of flat tax proposals have tried to engineer systems that are revenue neutral. They have also tried to design them so that general income classes—rich, middle, poor, and so on—pay the same amount as under the existing system. This makes sense from a political standpoint because if the tax is a Pareto superior move, then it will receive broad general support from taxpayers. Of course, a flat tax that eliminates loopholes and deductions by which income is shielded from taxation is not likely to earn the support of taxpayers who take advantage of these aspects of the tax law, because they will find themselves worse off under the flat tax.

Social Engineering Through Tax Preferences

With a completely flat tax using a broad base including all income, the tax system would no longer be compatible with the concept of using tax loopholes to provide incentives for desirable behavior. Credits, deductions, and exemptions that have been used in the past were in the tax code for several reasons. One is that special interest groups lobbied to introduce provisions favorable to them. Another is that those loopholes were introduced to provide incentives for desirable behavior and to further certain public policy goals. Because tax reform has eliminated some of these provisions, such public policy goals as investment and energy efficiency may have been harmed. Indeed, the 1986 tax act clearly viewed social engineering through the use of tax loopholes to be, in general, undesirable. These loopholes, also known as *tax expenditures*, warrant a further look.

Tax Expenditures

Tax expenditures are reductions in taxation, either through deductions or credits, that are designed to further some goal of social policy. For example, charitable contributions can be deducted from income for tax purposes, which gives individuals more of an incentive to make charitable donations than they would have without the tax incentive. The result is that more charitable donations are made and social goals are furthered without resorting to direct government expenditures. As another example, federal income tax does not have to be paid on interest earned from most bonds issued by state and local governments. As a result, state and local governments can (and do) pay lower interest to bondholders, making it less expensive for these lower-level governments to raise revenue. The federal government could do away with this provision and compensate state and local governments by providing them with more federal grants, but by collecting less in taxes, the same goal is accomplished.

In a comprehensive study of tax expenditures, Surrey and McDaniel list federal tax expenditures for six years in a table that spans eighteen pages.[8] Obviously, tax expenditures are numerous, ranging from certain exclusions for allowances paid to U.S. military personnel to deductions for certain corporate research and development expenditures to tax credits for rehabilitation of certain historical structures; there is hardly space to list them all here. The stated purpose of all of these credits and deductions is to further some goal of social policy.

It is worthwhile to consider why tax expenditures are so named. Assume that the government decides it wants to further research certain kinds of drugs. One way to spur this research is to provide researchers with government grants, but this requires additional government spending. Another method of accomplishing the same goal is to provide a tax credit to firms that undertake the kind of research the government is interested in. Although this method does not result in new taxation, it does reduce the amount of taxes collected by the amount of the tax credit. Thus, the government can either directly spend the money on the program or it can lower the taxes of the researchers who undertake the program. The tax revenue not collected is called a tax expenditure because, at least in the opinion of those who named the concept, those revenues are spent to further the social goal—tax expenditures are just another form of government spending.

One must be careful about taking this term too literally, however, as one government official did when President Reagan was looking for ways to cut government spending early in the 1980s. Having pledged to reduce government spending but not to increase taxes, Reagan sought to cut some government expenditures. The person who suggested slashing tax expenditures apparently did not see that a cut in tax expenditures in fact would not reduce government spending but would increase taxes.

At least in theory, it is possible to substitute selective tax cuts for government spending to further certain social goals. Although tax cuts in certain areas mean the lost revenue will have to be raised elsewhere unless the government's budget deficit is to be increased, this would also be true if the money were spent directly. But problems arise in implementing such a policy. As noted in Chapter 10, tax policy in the real world is heavily influenced by special interests, and there is certainly no guarantee that any special credits or deductions added to the tax code are in the general public interest rather than favoring some special interests. Because the tremendous increase in tax expenditures over the past few decades eroded the tax base, higher marginal tax rates were needed in order to produce the same average tax rates. The concept of broadening the tax base by eliminating many tax expenditures in the 1986 tax act indicates that government is moving away from the utilization of tax expenditures to further social goals. In short, the notion of a broad tax base with low marginal tax rates is antithetical to the concept of tax expenditures.

---

[8]Stanley S. Surrey and Paul R. McDaniel, *Tax Expenditures* (Cambridge: Harvard University Press, 1985).

Conclusion

The personal income tax is the single most important source of tax revenue in the United States today. For this reason its effects are of more interest to the general public and to public finance economists than other taxes. The current income tax system is a result of a major reform that replaced a more progressive tax system. The old system permitted a large number of credits, deductions, and exemptions that were enacted piecemeal for the nominal purpose of providing incentives for certain types of activities. The concept of a broad tax base with low marginal rates is embodied in the 1986 Tax Reform Act, but there are sound theoretical reasons for believing that any piecemeal changes made to the tax code will again move it in the direction of providing particular benefits to special interests. Indeed, it will be interesting to observe, in the years ahead, the reactions of the economy, of politicians, of special interests, and of voters, to tax reforms of the 1980s.

The income tax has the general effect of causing people to substitute leisure and untaxed productive activity for income-earning activity, though the income effect can offset this substitution effect. But if the taxes paid are exchanged for public sector output that is viewed as income in kind by the taxpayers, then the effect of public sector output will offset this income effect, leaving only the substitution effect, which unambiguously causes a substitution of leisure for work.

The income tax places a double tax on saving because income is taxed once before it can be saved and again as interest income from saving. The result of the double tax is that the income tax system provides an incentive to consume now rather than invest. Furthermore, the burden of this double tax is shifted into the future, because less investment now means lower future productivity.

In Chapter 13 we continue our discussion of income taxation by looking at the corporate income tax. We also examine some topics that are relevant to the personal income tax as well, but that have been deferred, including taxation of capital gains and the effect of income taxes on incentives to bear risk.

Questions

1. Why is there a problem in defining income for tax purposes? List some possible definitions of income for tax purposes, and outline the advantages and disadvantages of each. How do these definitions compare to the definition currently applied by the U.S. income tax system?

2. Use a diagram to illustrate why the typical taxpayer is better off under a more broadly based tax rather than a more narrowly based tax when the two taxes collect the same amount of revenue.

3. Will people work more or less if the income tax is increased? Fully

explain the arguments on both sides of the issue. Which argument do you think is correct, and why?

4. What is the Laffer curve? Explain why it is shaped the way it is. Why might a country choose a tax system that places it on the downward-sloping portion of the curve?

5. Explain the distinction between the average tax rate and the marginal tax rate. Why is this distinction important?

6. What is indexation of taxes? What problems does indexation try to solve? Why would the government have less of an incentive to control inflation without indexation?

7. Explain the difference between a sales tax, a consumption tax, and the current income tax. What are the advantages and disadvantages of each?

8. Explain how the current tax system places a double tax on saving. Can this policy be justified? What are the drawbacks of a double tax on saving?

9. What are the main differences between a completely flat tax and the current tax system? What are the advantages and disadvantages of the flat tax compared with the existing system?

10. What are the main differences between the current tax system and the tax system that existed prior to the Tax Reform Act of 1986? How might future tax reform be affected by the Tax Reform Act of 1986?

11. Why did the tax system have so many more complex provisions for deductions, exemptions, and exclusions before the Tax Reform Act of 1986? Explain the relationship between a tax system and the political system that produces a tax system. Given your explanation, how was tax reform that eliminated many of these special interest provisions possible?

CHAPTER THIRTEEN

Taxes on Business Income and Wealth

*T*he previous two chapters have been devoted to an examination of the effects of various types of taxes. In this chapter we continue our analysis of taxation by looking at some other tax bases, the most important of which is the corporate income tax. Though the corporate income tax differs in some fundamental ways from the personal income tax, individuals ultimately end up paying any tax. Stating that a corporation pays a tax really implies that the burden of the tax is borne by the corporation's stockholders. But the tax might also be shifted to the corporation's customers or suppliers. Who actually bears the burden of the tax is but one of a number of issues of interest with regard to the corporate income tax.

Taxation of wealth is another important source of tax revenue, with the most significant wealth tax being the tax on real property. Property is a stock of wealth, and income is the flow that is generated from the stock of wealth. Thus, there is a close theoretical relationship between an income tax and a property tax—one taxes the flow of wealth as it is earned, the other taxes the stock of wealth after it has been accumulated. Both the similarities and the differences between these two types of taxes are examined.

In addition, we touch on some less important tax bases, such as the inheritance tax. Like its predecessors, this chapter is built on the foundation of tax principles developed in Chapters 9 and 10. As before, the effects of specific types of taxes can be better understood within the context of those general principles.

The Corporate Income Tax

The corporate income tax is an important source of revenue for the federal government, but its significance has been declining in recent years in comparison to personal taxes. The corporate income tax was responsible for 6.2 percent of federal tax revenues in

1983; by contrast, corporate income tax payments constituted 23.2 percent of federal tax revenues in 1960.[1] The Tax Reform Act of 1986 was designed in part to increase the corporate income tax's share of total federal tax revenues.

As noted in Chapter 12, the corporate income tax cannot be fully considered independent of the personal income tax. The tax treatment of dividend and interest payments illustrates why this is so. If corporations pay their dividends from after-tax income, then dividends taxed as personal income will be double-taxed. The answer to the question of whether corporations should be allowed to deduct dividends and interest payments depends on how such payments are treated in the personal income tax. Of course, this is a normative issue. One may want to double tax investment income for equity reasons, even while recognizing the inefficiency of such a policy. In any event the appropriate corporate tax policy is inextricably linked to the personal tax structure in use.

Characteristics of the Corporate Income Tax

The federal corporate income tax rate structure taxes 15 percent of corporate income up to $50,000, 25 percent of income from $50,001 to $75,000, and 34 percent of income over $75,000. In a manner similar to the personal income tax, the two lower brackets are phased out, with an additional 5 percent tax on corporate income from $100,000 to $335,000, meaning that the effective marginal rate for corporations earning incomes in that range is 39 percent. Beyond $335,000, the effective marginal rate returns to 34 per-

cent. At this level of income, both the average and marginal rates are 34 percent.

Prior to the Tax Reform Act of 1986, the maximum corporate income tax rate was 46 percent, so corporate rates, like personal rates, have been cut substantially. Despite the reduction in tax rates, corporate tax revenues under the act are greater than they previously were because, again as with the personal income tax, the tax base was broadened considerably with the elimination of many tax preference items that reduced the amount of corporate income subject to tax. One change worthy of note is that prior to 1987 the maximum corporate tax rate was lower than the maximum personal tax rate, providing a tax incentive for high-income activities to be incorporated. But the 1986 act produced a maximum personal tax rate below the maximum corporate rate, thereby removing an incentive to incorporate.

According to tax law dividends are paid by corporations out of after-tax income, meaning that after the corporation has paid 34 percent of its income in taxes, the recipient of the dividend must pay personal income tax on dividend income. As previously noted, ultimately it is individuals and not corporations who pay taxes. Thus, for an individual in the 33 percent tax bracket, the dividend that already has been subject to a 34 percent tax paid is now subject to the 33 percent income tax. This means that 56 percent of the corporate income dedicated to the dividend ends up being paid as taxes. Payment of the personal tax can, however, be deferred if the firm reinvests its income rather than paying it out in dividends.

Interaction Between Corporate and Personal Income Taxes

The preceding discussion illuminates the interaction between personal and corporate in-

---

[1] These figures from the *Statistical Abstract of the United States*, 1985 edition, Table 488.

come taxes and the importance of considering the provisions built into each in evaluating tax policy as a whole. Provisions built into the personal income tax have an important impact on the trade-off between corporate payment of dividends or reinvestment of funds. Likewise, how interest payments and dividends are treated determines whether there will be a double tax on them.

Should dividends be excluded from the corporate income tax? Should interest payments be an allowable expense? To reiterate, the answer to these questions depends on how they are treated in the personal income tax. Presently, individuals are taxed at the same rate for dividends and interest, whereas corporations are allowed to deduct interest expenses but not dividends. This provides a tax advantage to the issuance of bonds rather than stock as a method of financing capital expenditures, but this advantage may be offset by the deferral of taxes if the firm reinvests rather than pays dividends. Because the tax advantage to the individual taxpayer also depends on the individual's marginal tax rate, the calculation of whether debt or equity is treated more preferentially by the tax system can become a complicated issue indeed.

Fringe Benefits

Another area of interest to the corporate income tax is the treatment of fringe benefits for employees. Currently, some insurance plans, company automobiles, and so on can be offered to the employee as a fringe benefit. And while the corporation can deduct the benefit as a legitimate business expense, the recipient is not required to declare the value of the benefit as income on the individual's tax return. Clearly, this allows companies to pay their employees in nontaxed income in the form of goods or services, even though the employees would likely purchase those goods

and services if the company did not provide them. Other fringe benefits, such as carpeted offices and business travel to resort areas, might not be purchased by the individual, and at any rate it is difficult to determine how much (if any) of the expense actually constitutes a necessary business expense. The Tax Reform Act of 1986 closed some of the loopholes that allowed corporations to pay in kind to employees by making fringe benefits taxable, but as the above examples suggest, it is virtually impossible to close completely the loophole of untaxed fringe benefits.

Depreciation

One area of the tax code that is of considerable interest to corporations is depreciation. As an economic concept, *depreciation* is the decline in the value over time of capital equipment, such as buildings and machinery. Many expenditures made by firms can be deducted from taxable income at the time the money is spent as the expenses of doing business, but the cost of capital equipment cannot be deducted when the expenditure is made. Rather, a fraction of the cost of the equipment is taken each year as a depreciation expense.

Conceptually, the amount of accounting depreciation taken each year for tax purposes equals the amount of economic depreciation, which is the decline in the value of the asset. In practice, however, accounting depreciation and economic depreciation are unlikely to be equal for several reasons. First, federal tax law specifies how much depreciation can be taken each year on an asset. Second, under most circumstances firms find it advantageous to take as much depreciation as possible as soon as possible.

In general, firms will prefer to take all of their capital spending as an expense in the year the money is spent rather than have to spread the expense over a number of years through depreciation because of the time value of money. If firms can pay lower taxes today, even if current tax savings are offset by more taxes in the future, they will have the use of that money, which can earn interest. There are many different methods of depreciation, but two general categories are straight-line and accelerated depreciation. Under straight-line depreciation the life of an asset is determined (say, ten years), and then an equal fraction of the cost of the asset (10 percent) is allowed as a depreciation expense in each year. Under accelerated depreciation a larger amount of depreciation (more than 10 percent) is allowed in early years, offset by a smaller amount (less than 10 percent) in later years.

If firms cannot expense their assets, then they will prefer to use accelerated depreciation instead of straight-line, so they can depreciate their assets over fewer years rather than more. By so doing, they can defer their tax payments as long as possible. Although this is true for any particular item, the method of depreciation will not affect the firm's annual tax payments in the long run if the firm invests about the same amount every year. An example can illustrate.

Assume that a firm buys a delivery van for $10,000. If the firm depreciates it over a ten-year period using straight-line depreciation, the depreciation expense will be $1000 per year for each year (assuming no salvage value). At the other extreme, if the firm is allowed to expense the van immediately, taxable income will be lowered by $10,000 this year, meaning the present value of the $10,000 reduction in taxable income will be greater than the present value of a $1000 per year reduction every year for the next ten years. Therefore, the firm is better off expensing rather than depreciating.

Now assume that the firm has ten delivery vans and that it buys a new one every year as an old one wears out after ten years of use. In this case the firm can either depreciate the vans using straight-line depreciation and claim a total depreciation expense of $10,000 ($1000 times the ten vans) or expense the vans as they are bought and claim a $10,000 expense every year. In this steady state situation it does not matter what type of depreciation schedule the firm uses—the deduction for capital expenditures will be the same. Over the long run, a more accelerated depreciation gives more of an advantage to growing firms, although eventually this tax advantage is offset by higher taxes.

Inflation does have a real effect on depreciation expenditures because records are kept in terms of nominal dollars. For example, if the price level doubles over ten years for the firm with the ten delivery vans, after ten years the depreciation on a van will be worth only half of its original real value. This problem can be solved by indexing capital accounts for tax purposes, but this significantly complicates tax accounting. Another solution is to allow immediate expensing of any capital expenditures, thereby eliminating the effects of inflation without affecting the tax burden of the firm in the long run.[2] In addition to its effects on depreciation, inflation also has a major effect on capital gains, as we will discuss later in the chapter.

---

[2]This solution is offered by Robert Hall and Alvin Rabushka, *The Flat Tax* (Stanford: Hoover Press, 1985).

The Burden of the Corporate Income Tax

Recall that the corporate income tax ultimately is borne by individuals. Saying that the corporation pays the tax amounts to saying that the corporation's stockholders bear the burden of taxation, but the principles of tax shifting suggest that corporations may be able to shift the burden of the tax forward to their customers, or even to their suppliers. In this sense the question of who bears the burden of the corporate income tax can be answered by looking at the relative slopes of the supply and demand curves in the relevant market. Note that at any point in time this slope will tend to differ from market to market.

Competitive Markets

In the short run the effect of a change in the corporate tax structure in a competitive market will vary depending on conditions in the market in question. In the long run, however, firms enter particular markets hoping to realize at least a normal rate of return. If demand in a market is more elastic than average, this shifts more of the tax burden to suppliers, who therefore tend to leave that market and enter markets with relatively inelastic demand, where more of the burden is borne by the demanders. This causes an outward shift in the supply curve of the market with the more inelastic demand and an inward shift in the supply curve in the market with the more elastic demand, until the relative shares of the tax burdens borne by suppliers and demanders is the same in each market.

This occurs because in the long run capital is mobile across markets and will leave markets yielding less than the market rate of return for markets yielding more than the market rate of return. But while in the long run the relative shares of the tax borne by suppliers and demanders will not differ from market to market, the effect of the tax on the quantities produced in the markets will differ. This can be seen in Figure 13.1, which illustrates the basic effects of a corporate income tax in different markets.

Panel A depicts a market with a relatively inelastic demand, Panel B shows a market with a relatively elastic demand. Assuming that the rate of profit is the same in both industries, the corporate income tax is the same percentage of the price of the good in each market, so the equilibrium tax is equivalent to an *ad valorem* tax. In both panels the supply curve without the tax is labeled S and the same supply curve with the tax is labeled S + Tax. As the arrow from the original quantity Q' indicates, the larger adjustment takes place in the market with the more elastic demand, whereas the larger adjustment in the original price P_1 takes place in the market with the more inelastic demand. As a result, resources flow out of the market with the elastic demand and into the market with the inelastic demand, causing the supply curves to shift further to S' + Tax in both panels.

After adjustment an equal burden of the tax is borne by suppliers and demanders in each market, but the long-run adjustment increases output in the market that shows the least decrease in output without the tax and decreases output still further in the market with the elastic demand and the largest initial adjustment. Clearly, the excess burden is larger in the market with the more elastic demand, but if capital is mobile across markets, the long-run return to capital in all markets will be equalized and the short-run elasticity of supply becomes irrelevant.

Figure 13.1 The Effects of a Corporate Income Tax in Different Markets
Panel A depicts a competitive industry with a more inelastic demand than
Panel B, all other things being equal. An equal tax on suppliers in each
market will be shifted more to demanders in Panel A, where demand is
more elastic, making industry A relatively more profitable than industry
B. In the long run resources move from B to A, shifting the supply curve
out for industry A and in for industry B, until the returns in the two
industries are equalized. In the long run the relative burdens of the
tax will be the same on suppliers and demanders in both markets, but
note that the excess burden is larger in the market with the more
elastic demand.

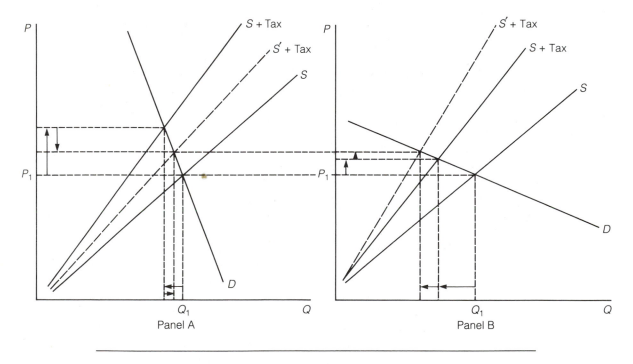

All of this has presumed that the response
of the owners of capital is simply to shift capital from one market to another to equalize the
rates of return to capital in all markets. In fact,
the corporate income tax may also entice potential investors to buy consumption goods
rather than invest, in which case the long-run
supply curve in a market will be even more
elastic. In the most extreme case the long-run

supply curve will be perfectly elastic, in which
case the entire burden of the tax will be borne
by demanders. This extreme case is unlikely,
however, because it implies that investors require a certain rate of return that, if not realized, causes them to withdraw their wealth
from investments until the market pays the
required rate.

Keep in mind, however, that ultimately corporations do not pay taxes, people do. The corporation merely collects the tax, so in stating that a corporation bears the burden of a tax, what we really mean is that the corporation's stockholders end up bearing the burden of the tax. Thus, the increase in the corporate tax burden brought about by the Tax Reform Act of 1986 will initially cost firms in industries with more elastic demands more because less of the tax can be shifted to demanders, but in the long run all firms will be affected equally, with production falling more in industries with elastic demand. Because capital is mobile and in the long run can be diverted to consumption, eventually most of the burden of the corporate income tax will be borne by the firm's customers.

Monopoly

In the short run an income tax on a firm making monopoly profits may have no real effects, unlike a tax on a competitive firm. If the corporate income tax collects a constant fraction of a corporation's profits, as is essentially the case with the U.S. corporate tax, then the monopolist's profit-maximizing level of output will not change. This can be illustrated with the help of Figure 13.2.

The top panel depicts the cost and revenue curves of the monopolist, with Q_M being the profit-maximizing quantity and Q_O being the greatest level of output that will generate positive monopoly profits. In the lower panel the top curve, labeled M, depicts the level of monopoly profits accruing to the monopolist. As in the top panel, profits are maximized at Q_M, Q_O is the largest level of output that will generate monopoly profits, and Q_O' is the smallest level of output that will generate monopoly profits. Looking at the bottom panel, an income tax that taxes a constant proportion of net profits lowers curve M by a constant amount, to look like curve $M - T$. The mo-

nopolist's profits are lower, but because profits are lowered by a constant proportion, the maximum point of $M - T$ is the same as the maximum point of M. The tax on the monopolist does not affect the profit-maximizing level of output, even though it reduces the amount of profit.

This can be seen in a different way in the top panel of the graph. Because profits are rising up to output level Q_M, the tax also rises, adding to marginal cost. However, increased output beyond Q_M lowers profit and therefore the amount of tax due, reducing the cost of increasing output. The income tax adds to marginal cost for output below Q_M but reduces marginal cost beyond Q_M; by adding the tax to MC a new marginal cost curve $MC - Tax$ results. The intersection of both curves with the MR curve is at the same quantity, meaning that the profit-maximizing level of output is unaffected.

Although this is an interesting case, note that it applies only where the firm earns pure monopoly profits and may not be relevant to many situations in the real world.[3] Often, what appears to be a monopoly profit is actually a return on some economic activity, such as the willingness to bear risk. Without the possibility of receiving returns in excess of the market rate of return, the entrepreneur may never invest in the risky venture that ultimately pays off. If this is the case, then the corporate profits tax, even when it taxes seemingly excess profits, results in a reduction in the taxed activity. The effect of taxation on risk bearing will be discussed next.

---

[3]For a discussion of this case, see Anthony B. Atkinson and Joseph E. Stiglitz, *Lectures in Public Economics* (New York: McGraw-Hill, 1980), pp. 206–208.

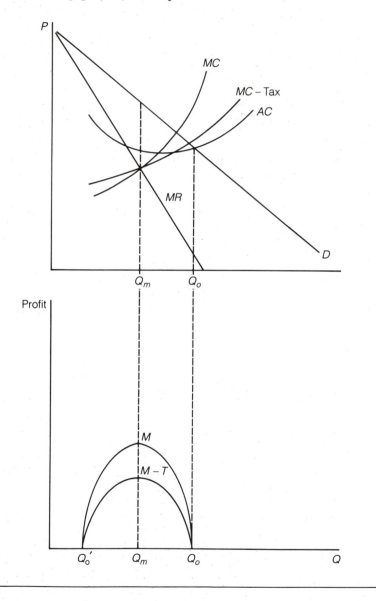

Figure 13.2 Monopoly Response to a Proportional Tax on Net Income A tax on monopoly profits lowers the amount of profit by a constant percent. As such, it reduces the profits of the monopoly without altering the profit-maximizing quantity of output.

The Income Tax and the Return on Bearing Risk

All saving and investing behavior entails bearing some risk. For example, the buyer of a bond takes a risk that the issuing company may default, and even the purchaser of a government bond runs the risk that inflation will lower the real return of the bond. Purchasers of common stocks and entrepreneurs bear even more risk, and it is this bearing of risk that stimulates growth in our economy and facilitates the introduction of new products and technologies to the marketplace. However, the corporate income tax—and the income tax in general—lowers the return on risk bearing because the government shares in the gains that the bearer of risk receives in the market but does not share in the losses.

Any investor in a risky venture hopes that the venture will pay off with above-normal profits. If it does, the income tax will take about a third of those profits from the successful investor. The government will share in any gain resulting from the assumption of risk. On the other hand, if the venture is unsuccessful, the government does not refund money to individuals who take losses, which means the entire burden of the loss is borne by the risk taker. Because the government shares in the profits from risk taking but does not share in the losses, a clear-cut incentive against risk taking is built into the tax system.

There is an exception to this, however. An investor who has income from other sources can write off the loss on a risky venture against the income made from other sources, so that the government does share in some of the risk to the extent of the risk-taker's income from other sources. Although this system creates a bias in favor of people with income from other sources—wealthy individuals, large corporations, and so on—for taking risks as compared to people with no other sources of income, allowing losses from some ventures to offset income in others mitigates, to a degree, the bias in the tax system against risk taking. Furthermore, capital markets exist in which individuals with income from other sources can provide money to risk takers without other income to offset potential losses.

Nevertheless, by potentially lessening the return from risky ventures, the income tax stifles the risk-taking activities necessary for economic growth and technological innovation. Risky ventures, which the risk taker hopes will produce returns in excess of the market rate of return, are taxed at the taxpayer's marginal tax rate rather than the average rate. The marginal rate of 34 percent, for example, applies to most corporate income, even though the average rate may be below that due to the deductions the corporation is allowed to claim. This provides support for the argument in favor of a more comprehensive income tax base with flatter rates, because lower marginal rates will produce a greater return to innovative and risk-taking behavior.

The Taxation of Capital Gains

A capital gain, as previously noted, is an increase in wealth due to the appreciation of the value of an asset that an individual or corporation owns. For example, an individual can become wealthier by owning an asset, such as a house, that appreciates in value, thus making the individual wealthier through a capital gain. Capital gains income is treated in a manner similar to ordinary income in both the corporate and personal income tax system; several issues regarding capital gains taxation merit discussion here.

Unrealized Capital Gains

One issue concerns the treatment of unrealized capital gains. An unrealized capital gain occurs when the value of someone's property increases but the person has not sold it. For example, a person who originally purchased a house for $50,000 that is now worth $75,000 will have an unrealized capital gain of $25,000. Under the Haig-Simons definition of income outlined in the previous chapter, an unrealized capital gain should count as income just as much as a realized capital gain, in which case the person is liable for tax on the unrealized gain of $25,000.

The current tax system in the United States does not, however, levy taxes on unrealized capital gains. Only when the house is sold is the seller liable for taxes on the capital gain. By deferring taxation on unrealized capital gains, the tax system provides an incentive for keeping property rather than selling it. Thus, the owner of the house can keep a house worth $75,000 or sell the house and have $75,000 minus the tax payment due on the sale. Obviously, the house could be worth slightly more to someone other than the current owner, but the current owner might not be willing to sell because of the tax that would be due on sale.

There is a clear efficiency argument in favor of taxing unrealized capital gains, but there are also arguments against it. One argument against taxation of unrealized capital gains in based on equity considerations. A person might buy a house and then find that the value of the house rises so much that the house must be sold in order to get the money to pay the taxes on it. From an equity standpoint this might appear to be little more than government confiscation of someone's property. Another argument against taxation of unrealized capital gains has to do with the possible administrative problems involved in determining the amount of tax due. For many assets, such as houses, paintings, and so on, the actual value of the item may not be precisely known until the item is sold. Therefore, in order to accurately assess the tax due, it might be necessary to wait for the sale of the asset. In this context taxing capital gains only after they are realized represents a way of minimizing disputes between the owner and the government.

Inflation and Taxation of Capital Gains

Another issue regarding capital gains taxation is the effect of inflation on the value of an asset. If taxes are placed on the nominal value of an asset, then one might be liable for a capital gains tax on an item even though the real value of the item has declined. For example, assume that someone purchased an asset for $50,000 in 1970. From 1970 to 1980 the price level approximately doubled, so that the individual sold the asset in 1980 for $90,000. The resulting nominal capital gain is $40,000, and under current tax law the seller is required to pay a capital gains tax on that $40,000. Note, however, that the entire capital gain is due to inflation. If prices had remained the same during the period in question instead of doubling, the asset would have sold for only $45,000, and the individual would have shown a capital loss. Indeed, the individual had a capital loss in real terms but nevertheless was required to pay a capital gains tax because of the increase in the nominal value of the asset. A capital gain in nominal terms that is not a real capital gain is called a *phantom capital gain*, and during inflationary times the taxation of phantom capital gains can place a significant burden on some taxpayers.

Before the Tax Reform Act of 1986, the tax code contained a number of provisions that lowered the tax on capital assets as a partial compensation. Most importantly, capital gains were taxed at a lower rate than ordinary income; by contrast, under the current law capital gains are taxed at the same rate as ordinary income. Furthermore, whereas purchasers of capital equipment formerly were eligible to take an investment tax credit of up to 10 percent of the purchase price of the asset, the repeal in 1986 of the investment tax credit raised the effective price of capital by 10 percent. Thus, although accelerated depreciation for tax purposes, which remains a part of the current tax law, can often provide an incentive for the purchase of capital equipment, the treatment of capital gains as ordinary income and the elimination of the investment tax credit mean capital gains are taxed much more heavily than they previously were.

Even if these repealed provisions remained in the tax code, all taxpayers realizing capital gains would still have higher tax bills if the inflation rate was higher. It makes little sense to offset one distortion in the tax system by introducing another. The simplest way to solve the problem of the taxation of phantom capital gains would be to index capital gains to current price levels and have taxpayers pay taxes on real rather than nominal capital gains. This would fix the problem without resorting to other, complicating additions to the tax code. Another solution would be to allow the immediate expensing of capital expenditures and then count them as income when the item was sold. This way, all transactions would be accounted for in the current year's dollars.

As should be evident by now, inflation introduces considerable complications into accounting for tax purposes. If inflation is not accounted for, distortions arise in the tax structure, and indexation to adjust for inflation, though feasible, adds another layer of complexity to the income tax system. It is unfair to tax individuals or corporations for phantom capital gains. Indeed, homeowners are in a good position to experience the ill effects of the tax on phantom capital gains; homeowners also comprise a large block of voters. As a result, there is a one-time exclusion by which a homeowner can sell a home and not be liable for the tax on the capital gain. Politically, one can understand why the one-time exclusion for homeowners came to be included in the tax code, but it does not make good economic sense to treat this one source of phantom capital gains differently from other phantom gains.

Wealth and Property Taxation

Income as a tax base has been discussed extensively. Another possible tax base is wealth, with the property tax being the most common type of tax on wealth. In theory, there is a close relationship between income taxation and wealth taxation—wealth is the stock of the accumulated flow of past income, and future income is the return on present wealth. Economists refer to an investment in education as the accumulation of human capital, so even pure labor income has its source in the value of the individual's stock of capital.

To illuminate the equivalence in theory between income and wealth taxation, consider an individual who owns a bond that returns $100 per year on an interest rate of 10 percent. The present value of the future stream of income from the bond is $1000, that is, the value of the bond is $1000. But where a wealth tax taxes the stock, an income tax taxes the flow. Thus, the individual could be subject to a 50 percent income tax, which would amount to $50 per year, or a 5 percent wealth tax on the value of the bond that would raise the same amount of revenue by taxing the same source. A tax on the stock of wealth and a tax on the flow of income from that stock of wealth are just two different ways of taxing the same tax base.

Incentives in Income Taxes and Wealth Taxes

Wealth taxes and income taxes do not have identical effects in practice, however, because different methods may be used to avoid taxation under the two types of tax. With the bond it is hard to avoid either the income tax or the wealth tax, but human capital is another case. The flow of income is the return on the individual's stock of human capital, so a tax system can tax either the individual's income-earning potential as wealth or the individual's actual income as a flow. If the flow is taxed, as with the present income tax, people have an incentive to underutilize their human capital, substituting leisure for work. If the stock is taxed (for example, by placing a tax of a fixed dollar amount on the holder of a medical degree regardless of the person's income), then people have an incentive to accumulate less human capital but to work harder to generate income from the human capital they have. Because of the excess burden of the tax, which alters people's behavior as they try to avoid taxation, the two types of taxes have different effects.

In fact, this example is not very realistic, because it is often impossible to determine the value of a person's human capital independent of the person's income. The point is that the incentive structure of an income tax encourages the substitution of nontaxable returns to wealth, such as leisure, whereas a wealth tax discourages the accumulation of wealth. For example, a person subject to an income tax might collect antiques, while that same person, if subject to a wealth tax, might be more likely to use the income to take a vacation.

Unrealized Capital Gains and Wealth Taxation

Earlier we touched on the tax treatment of unrealized capital gains. Recall the example of the homeowner and the renter who live in identical houses next door. If the value of the houses goes up, the renter ends up paying a higher rent while the owner receives the additional benefits of the higher-valued house without paying for them. Under an income tax system the taxation of unrealized capital gains would rectify the inequity, but such a tax might be viewed as unfair, especially if the homeowner had to sell the house to pay the income tax. Under a wealth tax the renter and the homeowner would be treated equally.

Note that both the income tax and the wealth tax, like all taxes, have undesirable secondary effects due to the excess burden of taxation. Indeed, the excess burden is one of the prices we pay to raise revenue to finance government spending. Some sources of wealth, such as human capital, are more easily taxed if the flow of income from the wealth is taxed rather than the stock of wealth itself; other sources of wealth, such as real estate, are more easily taxed directly. That is one reason why both types of taxation are a part of the overall tax structure.

The Property Tax

The property tax is a major source of revenue for local governments. State and local governments combined receive over 30 percent of their tax revenues from the property tax, and local governments receive well over half of their tax revenues from the property tax.[4] Though it is possible to tax all types of property, real estate comprises the major source of property tax revenue, so in this section we focus on the implications of a real estate tax. The taxed components of real estate can be divided into two subcomponents, land and improvements made to the taxed site. The effects of a tax on improvements should be apparent in light of the previous discussions on taxation—the tax provides a disincentive toward improving the value of property.

Locational Decisions and the Property Tax

Because the property tax is the primary source of local government revenue, differences among various locations can influence the locational decisions of businesses. The effect is probably small in determining whether a business will move from its existing location, but when businesses are looking into possible expansion sites, the effects of a property tax can be important. Businesses with expansion plans typically plan to buy property and improve it by building factories, offices, and so on, and the value of these improvements is subject to the property tax. Expanding businesses generally have many sites to choose from, so local officials desiring to foster economic development in their areas need to be aware of the potential competition from other localities and try to keep tax rates reasonable. Indeed, intergovernmental competition is an important aspect of the federal system of government, as will be discussed in Chapter 19.

Locational decisions involve more than just looking at taxes, though. As the fiscal exchange model of taxation suggests, businesses view taxes as the price that they pay for government goods and services and examine the mix of public sector output along with the tax level in an area when making locational decisions.[5] However, this does not alter the fact that a property tax provides a disincentive for improving property.

Site Value Taxation

Although in reality the property tax taxes the value of both the land and the improvements on the land, it is possible to imagine a tax placed only on the value of the site without considering the value of improvements. The simplest type of land tax is a fixed tax per acre of land, which, like a lump sum tax, is virtually impossible to avoid paying (except by abandoning the property). Consider, for example,

---

[4] Note, however, that local governments typically have other significant sources of revenue besides tax revenues. Revenues from the federal and state governments are important to local governments, as are revenues from enterprises such as hospitals, water and sewage facilities, and so forth. The activities of state and local governments are discussed in more detail in Chapter 19.

[5] For discussions of the effects of state taxes on economic development, see Thomas R. Plaut and Joseph E. Pluta, "Business Climate, Taxes and Expenditures, and State Industrial Growth in the United States," *Southern Economic Journal* 50, no. 1 (July 1983), pp. 99–119, and Thomas Romans and Ganti Subrahmanyam, "State and Local Taxes, Transfers, and Regional Economic Growth," *Southern Economic Journal* 46, no. 2 (Oct. 1979), pp. 435–444.

an acre of property that an individual is contemplating purchasing for a certain sum. What happens to the value of the property when, with no changes in public sector services, the per acre tax on property unexpectedly goes up by $100 per year? If we assume a 10 percent interest rate, the present value of the stream of future payments of $100 per year is $1000, so the individual now considers the property to be worth $1000 less. In this sense the property tax is unavoidably linked to the taxed piece of property.

The same analysis applies to the seller of the property who, in keeping the property, has to pay $100 per year more, meaning that the present value of the additional liability is $1000. Ownership of the property is now worth $1000 less to whomever owns it, which implies that the property tax is equivalent to a lump sum tax on the owner of the property at the time that the tax is levied. The tax is not passed on to any future owners because the sales price of the property includes both the value of the benefits of owning the land and the present value of the expected future tax liability attached to the land at the time of sale. In the previous section the conceptual link between taxes on wealth and taxes on income was discussed; here is a good example of an application of that idea. A property tax is a stream of tax payments by the owner of a piece of property, but it has the effect of being a lump sum tax on the wealth of the property owner at the time the tax is levied.

Within the framework of the tax principles discussed in Chapter 9, the reason why the entire site value tax is borne by the owner of the land is that the supply of land is completely inelastic. Note the difference between a tax on land and a tax on capital. Taxing capital provides an incentive to produce less capital, and with capital being more scarce, its price rises. But land is fixed in supply. Although any one individual can reduce his or

her land holdings, it is not possible to reduce the total supply of land, as it is with capital. Therefore, the owner ends up bearing the entire burden of the tax.

Site Value Taxation Versus Property Taxation

There is an important difference between whether the tax is levied only on the land or whether it is levied on improvements as well. In either case the present owner bears the burden of the tax on existing property. However, while a tax on improvements discourages the improvement of the value of a piece of property, a per acre tax on land entails no disincentives because land is in fixed supply. A per acre tax provides a disincentive for creating new acres of land, but with land in fixed supply this is not possible, which means the tax cannot be avoided. Because the tax collects revenue but does not provide other incentives for the taxpayer to alter behavior, the per acre tax is a good example of a lump sum tax. And because most real property is part land and part capital, the property tax does provide a disincentive to making capital improvements on the property, as well as lower the market value of the land by the present value of the tax.

One caveat needs to be added to this conclusion, however. Within the fiscal exchange model of taxation, an increase in taxes is likely to go for some public services that may be of value to the landowner. In this case the increase in tax decreases the value of the land at the same time that the increase in public services increases the value of the land. If the government is successful, the net result ought to be the provision of services in excess of the tax costs, thereby causing the value of the property actually to increase.

Keep in mind that we are equating a per acre tax on land with a lump sum tax. Such a tax, if applied nationally, would not have great revenue-generating capabilities, because the land in, say, downtown Manhattan is very valuable on a per acre basis compared to much land in rural areas. Thus, a per acre tax that raised revenue in urban areas would be prohibitively high in many rural areas, and if the present value of the future tax liability exceeded the present value of the future services of the land, the land would have a negative value and would be abandoned.

By taxing the site value of the land, this can be avoided. The taxable value of the land can be determined by the value of the land in the surrounding area, but independent of how the particular piece of property is being used. In downtown Manhattan, for example, land is valuable because skyscrapers can be built on it. If the site value of the land is taxed, two equal-sized adjoining pieces of land will be worth approximately the same amount and thus will be taxed the same amount regardless of how they are used. The taxation of site value only, by not taxing the value of improvements to the property, removes the disincentive for improving property but retains a tax based on the value of the property. Because the value of a site is almost entirely a function of how adjoining property is being used, the owner has little control over the site value. Furthermore, it is difficult to avoid paying the tax, so little excess burden is generated; in this sense the tax retains the close kinship to a lump sum tax.

In short, the property tax is probably the closest thing to a lump sum tax in our tax system. Land is in fixed supply and cannot be moved from one taxing district to another, which means the basic property tax is difficult to avoid. Because improvements as well as the site value of land are taxed, however, some excess burden results from the fact that the tax discourages improving the value of the property.

Site Value Taxation and the Value of Land

By contrast, the placement of a tax on the site value only, rather than on the value of the site and improvements, provides an incentive to develop the property, because property tax is not paid on the improvements. The answer to the question of how such a tax would affect the value of the site itself depends on whether site value taxation is applied everywhere or only in one locality.[6]

Consider first the case in which site value taxation is used nationwide, and compare this to the nationwide use of a property tax that includes the value of improvements. Assume that tax rates are set such that both tax systems raise the same amount of revenue. In this situation an unimproved piece of property will have a higher tax bill with site value taxation, because the unimproved land's value is a function of what the surrounding land is being used for rather than a function of the value of the improvements to that property itself. The value of the land is the same whether it is improved or not, which implies that site value taxation taxes the value of land more heavily. Therefore, the value of the land will be lower under site value taxation.

This conclusion makes sense. With a higher tax rate applied to unimproved land and a lower tax rate applied to improvements under site value taxation, the value of the unimproved land will fall due to the higher tax burden associated with it. This assumes that site value taxation is a national policy, however; the conclusion will be different if only one locality uses site value taxation.

[6]See Jan K. Brueckner, "A Modern Analysis of the Effects of Site Value Taxation," *National Tax Journal* 39, no. 1 (March 1986), pp. 49–58, for a more detailed discussion of the concepts in this section.

Consider now a single locality within a large metropolitan area. The single locality uses site value taxation while all other parts of the metropolitan area use a property tax that taxes the value of both the land and improvements. In this case a property tax is paid on improvements everywhere except in the locality using the site value tax. This provides an incentive for developers to improve the value of the property in the single locality more than in the surrounding area, increasing the demand for the land in that locality and causing its price to rise. Therefore, if site value taxation is used in a small area and the surrounding area uses a property tax on the site and improvements, the area with site value taxation will have more valuable improvements than the surrounding area, and the increase in the demand for land in the area will cause land values to rise in that locality.

In summary, site value taxation provides an incentive to improve the value of property. If site value taxation is applied to a widespread area, it will decrease land values, because a greater tax will be borne by land (and a lesser tax on the improvements to the land). If, however, a small area uses site value taxation when the surrounding areas use a property tax on land and improvements, this will provide an incentive to develop the value of the property that uses site value taxation, which in turn will cause the value of land to rise.

The Inheritance Tax

The adage that nothing is certain except death and taxes rings especially true for inheritance taxes, where a person is taxed for dying. In the context of the excess burden of taxation, the inheritance tax actually provides an incentive to live longer in order to postpone payment of the tax. There are, however, other ways to avoid the inheritance tax as well, the most obvious being to spend all of your money before you die.

Avoiding the Tax

The inheritance tax is a relatively insignificant source of tax revenue. In 1985 federal estate and gift taxes combined raised about $6 billion in revenue, or less than 1 percent of the total tax revenue of the federal government. Nevertheless, the inheritance tax can siphon away a significant portion of a large estate. The fact that the marginal rate for estates over $5 million is 70 percent provides a large incentive for wealthy people to try to avoid the tax. One method is to set up a trust, through which, under certain circumstances, the estate can be shielded from taxation. Another method is to pass wealth on through gifts while still living. Although at the federal level a gift tax is closely linked to the inheritance tax, it is possible to reduce or even eliminate taxation by spreading gifts over a number of years.

Besides giving one's wealth away or setting up a trust, the other option for avoiding the inheritance tax is to spend one's wealth before death. There is a clear incentive to do so, which has some implications for capital accumulation. One source of saving is money held by older people to pass on to their heirs, but the greater the tax on the bequest, the less the incentive to save, which provides the economy with funds for investment. Older individuals may save for bequests, or they may save to provide a nest egg for their later years. Of course, the same money can serve both functions. Furthermore, the date of a person's death is uncertain, which makes it difficult to plan to exhaust a stock of wealth precisely at the time of death.[7] For whatever reason it appears that older individuals do not draw down their stock of wealth in their later years,[8] even though there would be a greater incentive to save for the purpose of leaving a bequest if the inheritance tax did not exist.

Justifications for the Inheritance Tax

Given the disincentive effects of the inheritance tax and considering that it does not raise much revenue, one might ask why the tax is used. The strongest supporters of the inheritance tax favor it for equity reasons rather than efficiency reasons or its revenue-generating capabilities.[9] For example, they argue that it is not fair for some people to benefit from wealth earned by someone else, or that the inheritance tax fosters the goal of a more equal distribution of income.

These are normative issues, of course, but nevertheless worthy of scrutiny. In terms of

equality the inheritance tax does not raise much revenue, so while heirs of wealthy people will be appreciably less well off because of the inheritance tax, the meager amount collected in tax will not measurably benefit the poorer people in a society. One who endorses the inheritance tax as a means of promoting equality in essence favors making the rich worse off without appreciably improving the well-being of the poor, which is not too far from stating that the heirs of wealthy people should not benefit from wealth they have not earned. Indeed, favoring the inheritance tax on equity grounds comes close to favoring a Pareto inferior move—some people are made worse off, but nobody is made significantly better off.

Arguments in support of the inheritance tax on efficiency grounds can be advanced as well. The most obvious efficiency reason is that, in addition to its revenue-generating capabilities, the inheritance tax closes a loophole in the current income tax structure. Currently, unrealized capital gains are not taxed, giving an incentive to keep property rather than sell it and pay tax on the gain. Under this tax structure it would be possible for unrealized capital gains to pass from one heir to the next without ever being taxed. The inheritance tax puts an end to this chain because the gain must be realized at the death of the current owner.

The most appropriate structure for the inheritance tax will vary depending on the reason for its existence. If one views it as ancillary to the income tax, it should have rates similar to those used for other capital gains. On the other hand, if one views it as a tool to further equity goals, higher (or possibly confiscatory) rates would be justified.

---

[7]It is not impossible, though, even with an uncertain death date. A person can always purchase an annuity that pays a certain amount up to the time of death.

[8]See Thad W. Mirer, "The Wealth-Age Relation among the Aged," *American Economic Review* 69, no. 3 (June 1979), pp. 435–443, and Lawrence J. Kotlikoff and Lawrence H. Summers, "The Role of Intergenerational Transfers in Aggregate Capital Accumulation," *Journal of Political Economy* 89, no. 4 (August 1981), pp. 706–732, for some evidence.

[9]Richard A. Musgrave and Peggy B. Musgrave's comprehensive public finance text, *Public Finance in Theory and Practice* (New York: McGraw-Hill, 1980), pp. 496–497, lists five rationales for inheritance taxes; four of them are equity-oriented reasons for wanting to limit the amount of wealth that one generation can pass on to the next.

Severance Taxes

Severance taxes are taxes charged on the extraction of natural resources. State governments use severance taxes more than governments at other levels, charging for oil and gas, coal, timber, and other natural resources as they are extracted. Severance taxes are applied both as *ad valorem* taxes and as unit taxes. For example, Alabama has a severance tax of 3 cents per ton of coal (a unit tax) and 8 percent of the gross value of oil and gas produced in the state (an *ad valorem* tax). From an individual state's standpoint a severance tax has several advantages, namely, that it is difficult to avoid and it may shift the burden of the tax to individuals in other states.

At the state level there is some degree of intergovernmental competition, which manifests itself, among other areas, in economic development. States must make sure that their tax burdens are in line with the taxes levied by other states, because firms that are making locational decisions will look at the state's tax structure as one key variable. Most industries have a choice of locations, but a firm engaged in natural resource development must locate where the resources are. Of course, firms may choose to do more exten-

sive exploration, mining, and so on in states with low severance taxes, but the fact remains that a firm cannot exploit the natural resource base in a state without paying the state's severance taxes. Firms can move their factories, their warehouses, and their employees, but they cannot move natural resources across state lines without being liable for the severance tax. In this regard a severance tax is similar to a property tax—the owner of a resource owns the value of the resource less the tax liability that must be paid to the state if the resource is extracted.

The supply of the resource is not completely inelastic, because owners of resources can decide to bring them to market now or at a later date. Therefore, owners of the resources have the ability to shift some of the burden of a severance tax to demanders of a resource. Furthermore, because much of a resource is typically exported out of the state, the state can not only generate revenues but also shift the burden of state taxation to other states. Thus, from the state's standpoint a severance tax is an attractive public finance option.

Conclusion

The analysis in this and the preceding chapters has given an overview of the major sources of tax revenue used by governments at all levels, showing how the principles of taxation covered in Chapters 9 and 10 are generally applicable to all tax sources. The government taxes so many activities that some tax sources—fishing licenses, for example—were

not discussed explicitly, but the effects of such taxes adhere to the same principles.

Taxation is necessary for the government to raise revenue, but where the benefit principle cannot be readily applied, taxes have different effects from the market prices that finance private sector goods and services. In evaluating the tax structure, both equity and efficiency criteria must be considered. A tax system should minimize the excess burden it imposes on the population, but at the same time it must treat taxpayers fairly.

The corporate income tax discussed at the beginning of this chapter provides an excellent opportunity to apply the principles of taxation to an analysis of the effects of a tax, because ultimately it is individuals who pay the corporate income tax. All other things being equal, firms in industries with more elastic demands will bear a greater percentage of an increase in the corporate income tax than firms with less elastic demands, but in the long-run adjustments in the market as capital moves from less profitable to more profitable industries will result in the same long-run burden being borne by suppliers in all markets. However, output will be reduced more in markets with more elastic demands.

The corporate income tax as currently structured creates a double tax on dividends, because dividends are paid from after-tax corporate income. The income tax is taxed once through the corporate income tax and then a second time by the dividend recipient. Although equity arguments in favor of double tax can be made—people with investment income may have a greater ability to pay than those with wage income only—the double tax also provides a disincentive to saving and investment. The double tax can be avoided if the investor instead chooses to consume.

The corporation can defer the double tax by reinvesting its profits rather than paying them out as dividends, thereby increasing the worth of the firm by transforming ordinary income into a capital gain. The tax on the capital gain is paid only when it is realized. In the sense that corporations can deduct interest as an expense, the tax system is biased in favor of debt financing over equity; this also provides an incentive not to pay dividends.

Depreciation also plays a significant role in the calculation of the corporate income tax. For any given asset it is to the corporation's advantage to depreciate the asset as quickly as possible, but for a corporation that invests about the same amount every year, the depreciation schedule becomes irrelevant. One year's total investment will be depreciated every year regardless of the type of depreciation used, except when inflation becomes a factor. Inflation erodes some of the real value on the depreciation schedule of the asset to be depreciated, because the depreciation schedule is kept in nominal terms.

The treatment of fringe benefits is another important issue with regard to the corporate income tax. Presently, corporations are allowed many fringe benefits as expenses, but the individual who receives the benefit does not have to pay tax on it, even though the benefit can be equated with personal income. This allows income in kind to effectively escape taxation. Ideally, all income should be treated the same for tax purposes, but it is often hard to draw the line between legitimate business expenses and fringe benefits paid to employees.

Any income tax lessens the return to risk taking because the government shares in the investor's gains if the risky venture pays off but not in the losses if the venture fails. Though losses from one venture can be offset against gains from another, the fact that an individual does not reap the full gains due to the acceptance of risk means that the income tax reduces the risk taking necessary to stimulate innovation and growth in an economy. This is a good argument for keeping marginal tax rates as low as possible, because the returns to risk taking are taxed at the marginal rather than the average rate.

The capital gains tax, and the treatment of unrealized capital gains, have important effects on the behavior of individuals in the economy. Under the Haig-Simons definition of income, unrealized capital gains constitute income because they add to a person's wealth. Nevertheless, unrealized capital gains are not taxed under the current tax laws, thus creating an incentive to hold property rather than sell it. The owner can benefit from the full value of the property by keeping it, whereas by selling it the owner must pay capital gains tax.

Inflation can have a major effect on the taxpayer's liability under a capital gains tax. Because capital gains are measured in nominal terms for tax purposes, an increase in the price level causes a nominal capital gain on which tax must be paid when the gain is realized. Before 1987 capital gains tax rates were lower than rates for ordinary income, but even in that framework, when a nominal capital gain is a loss in real terms, a simple lowering of the tax rate cannot compensate for the effects of inflation. From an economic standpoint the proper way to adjust for inflation is to index the gain, but this adds another layer of complexity to an already complicated tax system.

Wealth is a stock that produces an income flow, and a tax on the stock of wealth can be seen as equivalent to a tax on the flow of income that comes from the wealth. Both types of tax naturally fit into the tax system, not only because it is sometimes hard to measure wealth (as in the case of human capital) but also because the disincentive effects and excess burdens of the two types of taxes differ. Ideally, the tax with the lower excess burden is used. The most common form of wealth tax is the property tax, which has some characteristics of a lump sum tax; a flat per acre tax on land would probably be as close to a lump sum tax as one could probably come. The current property tax, which is a tax on the value of property, produces a disincentive toward improving the value of a site.

The inheritance tax is often justified on eq-uity grounds, but there are efficiency reasons for using an inheritance tax as well. Because the capital gains tax does not tax unrealized capital gains, the inheritance tax can be seen as a tool to tax unrealized capital gains at the end of an individual's lifetime. If this is the motivation for the inheritance tax, its characteristics should be integrated into the structures of the income and capital gains tax system.

Taxes in Isolation and the Tax System

An important lesson of tax policy that cannot be fully appreciated by looking at taxes individually is that the optimal provisions for one type of tax depend on the way in which other taxes are levied. The inheritance tax is a good example of this. Because the current tax structure does not tax unrealized capital gains, an inheritance tax provides a mechanism by which this source of income can be taxed rather than allow it to accumulate tax-free for generations. This being the case, one cannot discuss the provisions of the inheritance tax without considering the way that capital gains are treated in the income tax system.

Similarly, because a wealth tax is a tax on a stock and an income tax is a tax on the flow produced from that stock, the optimal treatment of a tax on the stock depends on how the flow is being taxed. To tax both would constitute double taxation, but often it is either easier or more efficient to tax the stock under some circumstances and the flow under others. Occasionally, double taxation may be the goal of the tax system, but in such cases the double tax aspect should at least be recognized.

The importance of viewing the tax system as an integrated whole is most apparent when taxes on the returns to saving and investment are considered. The answer to the question of what are the effects of allowing firms to deduct their interest expenses but not dividend payments to figure taxable income depends on how dividends and interest payments are treated in the personal income tax. If the goal is to tax them at personal tax rates, then they should be regarded an expense to the corporation and taxed under the personal income tax. Conversely, they could be taxed at the corporate level and then be exempted from tax under the personal income tax. Currently, interest expenses are not taxed under the corporate income tax, but dividends are. Because both are taxed as personal income, they are treated differently under the tax code.

To summarize, although individual taxes can be examined in isolation, different types of taxes can be used to tax the same tax base, so it is important to see not only the effects of individual taxes but also how different taxes interact with each other. Provisions of the tax system may seem reasonable when applied to a single tax source, but when viewed in conjunction with other taxes, a provision may allow certain types of income to escape taxation altogether (fringe benefits) while other types of income (dividends) are taxed twice. Therefore, to evaluate a tax system, all types of taxes need to be viewed as parts of the overall tax structure. The tax system is often viewed as a mechanism for redistributing income as well as a method of revenue generation. This naturally leads to Part Five of the text, which discusses redistribution.

Questions

1. Explain how interest expenses and dividend payments are treated in the corporate income tax. Relate their treatment in the corporate income tax to their treatment as income by the individuals to whom they are paid. What are the economic effects of this type of tax treatment?

2. Explain the effects of inflation on the taxation of corporate income. Be sure to consider both depreciation and capital gains in your explanation.

3. Who bears the burden of the corporate income tax? Explain both the short-run and long-run effects of a change in corporate income tax rates.

4. Assume that a firm is in a steady state situation with regard to capital expenditures, so that it invests about the same amount every year. Explain what difference it would make to the firm's tax bill if it used straight-line depreciation or some form of accelerated depreciation, or if it were allowed to declare all of its capital expenditures as an expense for tax purposes.

5. Outline the effects of an income tax on the willingness of individuals to assume risk. Does the income tax treat all individuals the same in this regard?

6. The present tax system does not tax unrealized capital gains. What arguments can be made both for and against treating unrealized capital gains this way?

7. What is the conceptual link between wealth taxation and income taxation? Given this link, is there any reason to tax one rather than the other? Is there any reason to tax both?

8. Explain the similarities and differences between a property tax and a lump sum tax.

9. How does an inheritance tax fit into the income tax as currently structured?

10. Give several reasons why state governments find severance taxes to be an attractive source of revenue.

11. "If a site value system of taxation rather than the existing property tax system were employed, the Empire State Building would have been built twenty stories taller." Is there any economic justification for this statement?

12. Will site value taxation increase or decrease the value of unimproved land? On what factors does your answer depend?

13. Explain why a complete analysis of the effects of any tax must include an evaluation of how that tax fits into the overall structure of taxation.

14. How will a tax on corporate profits affect a pure monopolist. Discuss some factors that illuminate the way in which this conclusion can be extrapolated to the real world.

PART FIVE

Redistribution

CHAPTER FOURTEEN

Taxation and Redistribution

*I*n the preceding chapters we analyzed specific types of taxes in terms of both efficiency and equity, but we only touched on the concept of the tax system itself as a mechanism for producing a more equitable society. Our implied model of taxation in the previous chapters was the fiscal exchange model of taxation, in which taxes represent the price that is paid for public sector output. In determining how that price should be paid, the two criteria of efficiency and equity come into play. The tax should impose as little excess burden as possible, following the principles of efficiency, and should be shared fairly among taxpayers, following the principles of equity.

This view of taxation is consistent with the model of government as a type of club, in which citizens are bound together by an agreement that enables them to collectively produce goods and services that the market would not otherwise provide. Taxes pay for this public sector output. Frequently, however, the tax system and public sector spending in general move beyond the production of public sector output and pursue actively the social goal of income equality. Although the tax principles of equity underlie such actions, they extend beyond simply seeing that everybody pays their fair share of the tax burden. The government might also undertake social

policies to transfer benefits to those in the society who are less fortunate, with the goal of making them better off. Of course, such social policies are financed by the tax payments of those who are better off. In short, the basic goal of government redistributive programs is to use the resources of some taxpayers to improve the welfare of others.

Note the conceptual division of principles of tax equity here. According to one concept of equity, everyone essentially pays a fair share of the cost of government. According to another concept, those who are less well off have benefits redistributed to them from the tax payments of those who are better off. The benefit principle of taxation clearly applies to the first category of taxation, but the ability-to-pay principle might apply to either category. It can be argued that a person who is more able to should pay a larger share of the tax burden. But it can also be argued that a person who is more able to pay is under some type of social obligation to help those less fortunate and thus should pay more in taxes to redistribute income. This chapter deals with the redistributive issues of public finance.

A number of questions regarding redistributive issues must be addressed, but those questions can be divided into three basic categories. The first concerns the motivation for redistributive government programs. Why is there a demand for them? What are the possible justifications for governmental redistribution? The second category of inquiry deals with the results of redistributive programs. What are their effects? Do they really help those they are intended to help? How should these programs be designed? The third category deals with the incentive structure implied in the redistributive programs. What types of behavior are encouraged by redistribution, and how do the programs affect the way that the government in general is run?

Equality of Opportunity and Equality of Results

Many people view equality as a social goal that the government should try to further through its taxation and spending policies. In a general sense the fact that some people live in luxury while others in the same society (or the same world) live in extreme poverty may be thought of as undesirable for many reasons, each of which has different policy implications. Because a society can, through government, create social policies, an understanding of why inequality might be regarded as undesirable can point the way to the appropriate remedial actions.

In applying the general concept of equality to our discussion, we must first distinguish between equality of opportunity and equality of results. In the United States some government policies are designed to produce equal opportunity, whereas others are designed to produce equal results; often, the distinction is not clearly made.[1] The desire to provide equality of opportunity is not a desire for equality per se but rather a desire to give everyone an equal chance. In this sense it is analogous to the desire for a game with fair rules, but not necessarily a game that ends in a tie. Equal opportunity, as the term implies, simply means that everyone in life starts off with the same opportunity.

Obviously, inequality can result from rules that do not provide equality of opportunity. Apartheid in South Africa, the now-defunct caste system in India, and governmental rules that enforced racial segregation in parts of the United States through the 1960s are all examples of inequality of opportunity. Often, even though the rules do not specifically establish inequality, discrimination can still occur if some individuals are not provided with the same opportunities as others based solely on characteristics such as gender or national origin.

Fair Rules and Fair Outcomes

The inequality that results from discrimination is generated by social conditions that are not considered to be fair; an analogous situation would be a game in which the rules favored some players over others. The obvious solution is to change the rules so that everyone has an equal opportunity. Recall the device of the veil of ignorance used by John Rawls to

[1]For example, Duncan K. Foley, "Resource Allocation and the Public Sector," *Yale Economic Essays* 7 (Spring 1967), pp. 45–98, argues that fairness is essentially defined as equality of opportunity, but William J. Baumol, "Applied Fairness Theory and Rationing Policy," *American Economic Review* 72 (Sept. 1982), pp. 639–651, bases his argument on Foley's definition of fairness and yet ends up with a criterion based on the result of a policy. See R. G. Holcombe, "Applied Fairness Theory: Comment," *American Economic Review* 73 (Dec. 1983), pp. 1153–1156, for a discussion of these two concepts of fairness.

describe what constitutes a fair social structure.[2] Rawls theorizes that all individuals, before knowing anything about their financial status, social position, level of intelligence, athletic ability, race, gender, and so on, must agree on the rules of the society. Rawls argues that rules that could have been agreed on behind this veil of ignorance are fair rules.

Although one can see that there may be some disagreement among those of us not behind the veil as to what might actually be agreed on, the principle seems clear. Everyone should be subject to rules that can be agreed on as fair.

The questions about how the government should implement fair rules are clearly normative. For example, should there be high inheritance taxes, so that some individuals do not start off with an unfair advantage due to inherited wealth, or do inheritance taxes unfairly deprive the wealth holder from the opportunity to pass wealth on to heirs? Would a progressive income tax be agreed to behind the veil of ignorance? If so, at what rates? Although such questions do not have clear-cut answers, what is important here is to recognize that the desire for equality of opportunity is merely a component of the desire for overall equality. Equality of opportunity demands fair rules, but it does not necessarily require that income be transferred from some individuals to others.

The Goal of Equality

However, some individuals think that equality of opportunity is not sufficient, that the less-than-equitable results of equality of opportunity warrant the implementation of income redistribution policies. Specifically, they argue that taxes and government spending should further the goal of creating a more equal society. Again, because the policy implications differ, it is worthwhile to examine the possible reasons why a more equal distribution of income could be viewed as desirable.

Utilitarian Justifications

The first reason stems from the concepts of utilitarianism and the social welfare function that were introduced in Chapter 2. Recall that the utilitarians believed that the utility of one individual could be measured and compared to the utility of another individual. In this context social utility is the sum of all of the individual utilities in a society. If there is diminishing marginal utility of income, then the higher one's income, the less utility is derived from additional income. Therefore, total social utility can be increased by transferring income from high-income individuals (with a low marginal utility of income) to low-income individuals, who will receive more utility from the income. In short, to maximize social utility, the government should transfer income from high-income individuals to low-income individuals.

Economists today do not believe that utility is directly comparable among individuals, but a similar concept is embodied in the notion of a social welfare function. The social welfare

---

[2] John Rawls, *A Theory of Justice* (Cambridge: Harvard University Press, 1971).

function can be thought of as a utility function for a society as a whole, and it admits the possibility that social welfare can be increased by income transfers. This idea has been most explicitly expressed in a body of literature known as optimal taxation, in which a social welfare function compares the utilities of individuals and, in general, determines that a society can maximize its social welfare if income is distributed more equally.[3] Complete equality would not be desirable in this view, because the excess burden of taxation from the redistribution would lower *GNP* so much. However, the goal of tax policy in this view is equality of income, which again can be contrasted to the goal of equality of opportunity.

Utility Maximization of Those Least Well Off

John Rawls argues for a policy that maximizes the well-being of the individual who is least well off in a society.[4] This policy, like the one just discussed, places a high value on equality for its own sake. However, Rawls recognizes that the disincentives toward earning income involved in redistribution programs lower the whole society's income, so he suggests taxing high-income earners and redistributing the income to low-income people until the utility of the person with the lowest well-being is maximized. Note that such a policy will not generate complete income quality. Taxation

on high-income earners would be low enough that the tax revenue raised on their incomes would not fall if rates were raised slightly. The relationship between this idea and the Laffer curve discussed in Chapter 12 should be evident—both concepts recognize that tax rates can be high enough to lower the total amount of tax revenues raised and therefore reduce the total tax revenues available.

Clearly, the idea that more equal income distribution is desirable is normative, and one would expect some people to hold opposing views. Martin Ricketts, for example, has argued against a social policy that justifies the transfer of income from some people to others because it enhances social welfare.[5] Ricketts observes that if income redistribution is justified in this way, then one is essentially condoning government policies that require some people to contribute to the income of other people. The implication of this argument is that to enhance the social welfare, some people can be forced to work for the well-being of others, which, some argue, is no more than a step away from slavery. Therefore, one can object on moral grounds to government policies that redistribute income just because the government thinks that the utility loss to the losers is more than offset by the gain to the gainers.

In summary, some people argue in favor of governmental redistribution programs simply because they find equality of income to be a desirable end toward which government programs should work. This suggests that the tax system should be progressive enough to transfer income from rich people to poor people up to the point at which the cost resulting

[3]See Peter A. Diamond and James A. Mirrlees, "Optimal Taxation and Public Production: I and II," *American Economic Review* 61 (March 1971), pp. 8–27, and (June 1971), pp. 261–278, for a seminal work in the area. More references and a discussion are found in R. G. Holcombe, *An Economic Analysis of Democracy* (Carbondale: Southern Illinois University Press, 1985), ch. 5.

[4]John Rawls, *A Theory of Justice*, (Cambridge: Harvard University Press, 1971).

[5]Martin Ricketts, "Tax Theory and Tax Policy," in Alan Peacock and Francesco Forte, eds., *The Political Economy of Taxation* (New York: St. Martin's Press, 1981), ch. 2.

from the excess burden of the tax just offsets the benefit of a more equal income distribution. In this view taxes represent more than just a means to pay for publicly provided goods and services; they are also social tools by which greater equality in a society can be carved.

There are two significant counterarguments to this viewpoint. One is that when some individuals are forced to give some of their income to others, those forced to give up their income are being unfairly coerced by the government. The other is that inequality often comes about because some people work harder and are more productive than others and therefore deserve the fruits of their labors. In this context it is equality of opportunity—not equality of results—that is desirable. As previously noted, these are normative issues. Nevertheless, such issues can play a significant role in shaping public policy. Ultimately, it is the value judgments of voters and government officials that determine what the goals of government policy will be.

Charity as a Collective Consumption Good

The desire for a more equal distribution of income is only one of many possible justifications for the government to redistribute income. Another reason that deserves consideration is that charity has some of the characteristics of a collective consumption good and so will be underprovided if left to the private sector of the economy.[6]

Charitable Giving as a Pareto Superior Move

People in a society want to see those less fortunate than themselves helped out—this is the motive for charity. Charitable activity, which can increase the standard of living of less fortunate individuals, is a Pareto superior move because both givers and recipients are made better off. Note that to classify voluntary giving as a Pareto superior move is almost tautological. The givers must be made better off or they would not agree to give, and the recipients must be made better off or they would not agree to accept the charity. Furthermore, because potential givers want to see the well-being of the recipients enhanced, they also will receive increased utility from a knowledge of the charitable activities of others.

The Incentive to Free Ride

This implies that charitable activity has some of the characteristics of a collective consumption good. Potential givers, in gaining utility from the knowledge that the recipients are being helped, have an incentive to become free riders. Although they would like for the well-being of less fortunate individuals to be improved, they can free ride off of the charitable activities of others.

The argument here is the same as with any other collective consumption good. Recall

[6]Harold M. Hochman and James D. Rogers, "Pareto Optimal Redistribution," *American Economic Review* 59 (Sept. 1969), pp. 542–557, is an oft-cited article on this idea.

that with national defense, because people share the same incentive to free ride on the protection produced by others, national defense will be underprovided, thus giving the rationale for the government to provide the good collectively. Likewise, with charity people share the same incentive to free ride on the charitable activities of others, which means charity will be underprovided. The role of the government, then, is to overcome the free rider problem by ensuring everyone's participation and providing the optimal amount of redistribution.

In strictly logical terms this argument for public sector production of charity is somewhat shaky. First, redistribution can hardly be considered Pareto superior because someone is sure to be made worse off by the redistribution. Second, the result of the government's redistributive programs can hardly be considered Pareto optimal. Because the demands for redistributive activities cannot be measured, there is no way to know what the optimal amount is in the first place. Therefore, this argument cannot be held as proof that the government should be involved in redistributive activities. On the other hand, the incentive to free ride suggests that public sector production of charitable activity is indeed a collective consumption good, so it is likely to be underprovided if left entirely to the private sector.

Redistribution as Insurance

Another possible reason to redistribute income through the public sector is that it acts as a type of income insurance. People with large incomes who pay taxes that go to redistribution programs are in effect paying a premium, and those with low incomes are receiving the payments. Note that this view of redistributive activities is compatible with the idea of the veil of ignorance discussed earlier. Behind the Rawlsian veil of ignorance—or even early in one's life—a person will not have a good idea about the amount of income one can expect to earn. Before the amount of income is known, a person might well agree to pay a larger-than-proportional amount in taxes if income is higher than average, but also to receive income from high-income people if income is lower than average. In this sense redistribution becomes a form of social insurance that partially protects people from having low incomes.

This will be true not only among different people but even for the same person at various stages in the person's life. In a typical lifetime earning profile a person's income is relatively low when the person first begins work, but income rises as the person moves into middle age and then sinks after retirement to a lower level than existed in middle age. In applying the ability-to-pay principle over the course of this individual's lifetime, the person might choose to pay more in taxes when the taxes could be most easily afforded, thus redistributing income from peak earning years to leaner years. The same might be true of individuals who are self-employed or are paid mostly in commissions. Redistribution through the tax system acts as a sort of insurance plan by which premiums paid in the high-income years are exchanged for payments in the low-income years.

Cash Versus Payment in Kind

Redistributive activities tend to be financed from taxation, but the redistribution itself can be paid either in cash or in kind. Both types of redistributive methods are used in programs in the United States. For example, unemployment compensation and Aid to Families with Dependent Children (AFDC) each distributes cash payments to the recipients. The redistributive programs simply provide income to the recipients, which they may spend in the best way they see fit. Other programs, such as food stamps, housing subsidies, and Medicaid, are designed specifically to provide in-kind payments in the form of food, housing, and medical care. The object of in-kind programs is to help the recipient receive a certain specific benefit rather than general income.

Cash Payments and Utility Maximization

Note that if increasing the utility of the recipient is the only criterion by which the type of benefit to be paid is determined, a cash payment will always be at least as good as, and possibly better than, the in-kind transfer. The reason is that recipients of the benefits can better know their utility function than anyone else. Thus, if food is what will enhance the recipient's utility the most, the recipient can buy it, but if something else will provide more utility, then the recipient will purchase whatever provides the greatest utility for the money.

Some of these issues can be explored in a more analytical framework within the context of Figure 14.1. The vertical axis measures the quantity of the good paid in kind, and the horizontal axis measures all other goods. The solid line through point A is the budget constraint with no government payment, and the utility-maximizing individual is at point A, at which K_1 of the good on the horizontal axis and G_1 of all other goods are consumed. Now consider a government program that provides a payment in kind of K_S of the good on the horizontal axis. If the recipient were to consume the amount paid in kind in addition to the amount of the good that would have been bought even without the subsidy, the individual would consume K_2 of the good, but the individual is more likely to apply some of the income formerly used to purchase K for other goods now that some of good K is being given to the individual as a payment in kind.

Note that Figure 14.1 is drawn under the assumption that the payment in kind provides the individual with more of the subsidized good than the individual would have consumed without the subsidy. The same argument will not hold if the individual is given an in-kind payment of less than the amount that otherwise would have been consumed. Up to a point the payment in kind can substitute for income that would have been used to buy the good, making the payment in kind no different to the individual than a general income transfer.

However, the individual may prefer to consume less of the goods paid in kind and more of other goods. This situation is depicted at point B in the figure. Here, the individual is purchasing none of good K and using all income to buy other goods, but the individual still would prefer to consume less of K at market prices and transfer some consumption of K into consumption of other goods. If a simple income transfer were provided that would allow the individual to buy K_S more of the good, the budget constraint would have

Figure 14.1 Payment in Kind Versus Cash Transfer An individual receiving an in-kind transfer of K_s consumes at point B, but if an equivalent amount of income were given to the individual instead, the individual could locate at point C, on a higher indifference curve, and be better off.

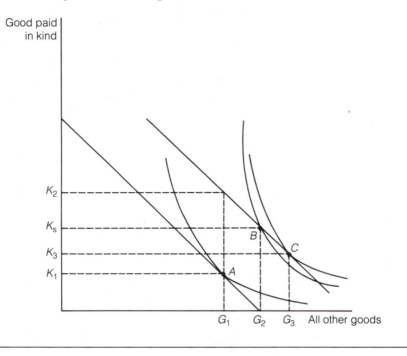

shifted out parallel to the original budget constraint by the amount of the transfer, to become the dashed budget constraint. The utility-maximizing individual would now consume at point C rather than at point B and would be better off as a result. In other words, the income transfer could never make the individual worse off than a payment in kind, and it could make the individual better off.

The Rationale for In-Kind Payments

If income transfers are at least as good as and sometimes better for recipients than in-kind benefits, how can in-kind transfers ever be justified? To answer that question, recall the argument that charity has some of the characteristics of a collective consumption good. In the context of in-kind payments, this means that the goal of the redistributive program is to increase the well-being not only of the recipient but also of the taxpayer, who benefits by knowing that the recipient is better off with the redistributive program.

The taxpayer may only care about the utility of the recipient, in which case the payment of cash will be the best way to redistribute income. However, many taxpayers are willing to contribute to helping less fortunate people buy food, shelter, and medical care, but they do not want to contribute toward their buying cigarettes or playing video games. Therefore, rather than give money that can be spent on activities the donors feel are undesirable, the payment is made in kind. The food stamps can be used to buy food, as the donors have intended, but not record albums. In short, payments in kind can only be justified by considering the utility of the taxpayer as well as the utility of the recipient. If only the recipient's utility is considered, a cash payment will always be at least as good and maybe better than a payment in kind.

This argument does lose some of its force, however, when the fungible nature of money is considered. If, for example, a person normally spends $35 per week on food and is then given food stamps worth $20 per week, the person will not necessarily now buy $55 worth of food in a week. In fact, the person may only spend the $20 in food stamps plus $20 more for a total of $40 on food, using the other $15 to go to the movies. In this case the food stamps really act just like a transfer of income, $5 of which is used on food and the rest of which is spent on something else. The point is that just because a person is given an in-kind payment does not mean that the person uses the payment as intended.

The Negative Income Tax and Other Redistributive Programs

One redistribution program that has been considered from time to time is a negative income tax, which shares some characteristics with other income transfer programs. A negative income tax works in the following way: If a person's income falls below a certain level, then the government pays the person an income supplement. The lower the person's income, the larger the income supplement. Thus, the payment from the government is largest if the person's income is zero.

The negative income tax is illustrated in Figure 14.2, where I^* is the level of income below which the negative income tax is paid and I_0 is the amount the individual receives with no other income. For example, the negative income tax might pay an individual with no income $2500 per year and reduce the payment by 50 cents for each additional dollar of earned income. Thus, for a person earning $2000, the payment is $2500 - .5($2000) = $1500. With this example I^* is equal to $5000—the level at which the negative income tax payments would end—and I_0 is equal to $2500. The budget constraint without the negative income tax—the line starting at 24 hours and extending to I'—will shift to the line $I'AB$ with the negative income tax.

The negative income tax can be analyzed with the same principles used to evaluate the personal income tax. In this case there is an income effect, because the low income individual has a higher income when receiving the payment. With the higher total income the individual can be expected to receive more total income but also to consume more leisure time; that is, when income rises from I_1 to I_2, leisure rises from L_1 to L_2. In essence, some of the extra income is used to buy more leisure time. The income subsidy is shown by the

Figure 14.2 The Negative Income Tax A negative income tax shifts the recipient's budget constraint from $I'24$ hours to $I'AB$. The individual can now reach a higher indifference curve and so is better off.

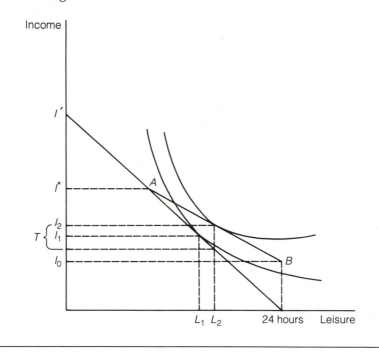

bracketed amount T. Note that the increase in income from I_1 to I_2 is less than the amount of the subsidy due to an increase in leisure.

The Incentive to Substitute into Leisure

A negative income tax also generates a substitution effect, which raises the relative price of earning income. Without the negative income tax each additional dollar earned by the low-income person represents $1 more in total income, but with the negative income tax an additional dollar earned reduces the negative income tax payment by 50 cents, so that the person's total income increases by only 50 cents ($1 − $.50 = $.50). In this sense the

negative income tax imposes the additional cost on the income earner of losing some of the subsidy when income is earned. This gives the low-income person subject to a negative income tax an incentive to substitute leisure for income.

Indeed, it is possible that the substitution of leisure for income might be great enough to actually reduce the total money income of the recipient. This case is illustrated in Figure 14.3, where the recipient substitutes so much leisure for income-earning activity as a result of the negative income tax that total income drops from I_1 to I_2. The recipient is better off because the negative income tax places the recipient on a higher indifference curve, but

Figure 14.3 A Reduction in Income with a Negative Income Tax This figure illustrates the possibility that the individual's money income can fall with a negative income tax (from I_1 to I_2) even though the person's utility rises.

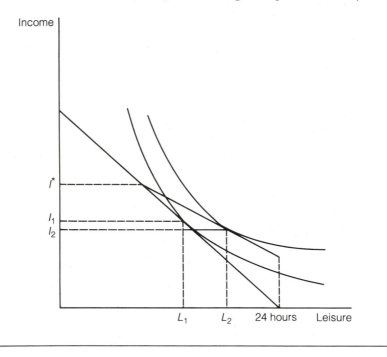

the dollar income of the recipient, including the payment from the government, is lower than before.

Redistribution and the Income of the Poor

This type of analysis illustrates a general principle about redistributive activity. Redistributive programs increase the well-being of the recipients, but they may not appear to do so if only simple dollar figures are examined. The reason is that in order to qualify for the programs, it is necessary to be poor (or perhaps unemployed or in some other way disadvantaged), which provides an incentive for people to substitute out of income-earning activities.

In the case of the negative income tax, Figures 14.2 and 14.3 clearly illustrate this phenomenon. In Figure 14.2 the person receives a payment of T, but the person's total income increases by less than that amount. Thus, for example, if a person were receiving $100 per month from the government, it would be incorrect to say that without the payment the person's income would be $100 less. Although this may be true in some specific cases, in general the elimination of the $100 government payment would reduce the person's income by less than $100, because the person would now have an increased incentive to earn other income. As Figure 14.3 illustrates, the substitution effect can be strong enough that the person's money income will actually fall when the government payment is received. But if the negative income tax were eliminated, that person would have an increased incentive to work and would actually end up with more dollar income than before.

Although our discussion has focused on the negative income tax, the same principles apply to any redistribution program that reduces the benefits paid as the person earns more income. For example, food stamps and AFDC could provide someone with enough income that they would decide to forego work in order to collect income from the government. If the family were working, their total dollar income could be higher, but they would have to work all day and forego the government benefits. In short, the poor person has

an incentive not to earn income and lose the governmental payments.[7]

We can learn several important lessons from Figures 14.2 and 14.3. First, as Figure 14.2 implies, the redistributive program can make the recipient better off—place the recipient on a higher indifference curve—even though the recipient's measured income, including transfers, is lower than if the transfers were not made. Second, when redistributive programs are in effect, it is misleading to look at a recipient's well-being in simple dollar terms, because the income distribution may not change or may even appear worse due to the redistributive programs. Clearly, redistributive programs do not simply add the amount of redistributed income to the person's income without the programs.

Progressive Taxation and Wage Adjustment

The progressive tax system itself can be viewed as a redistributive vehicle, though market adjustments to the wage structure will at least partially offset the redistributive effects of progressive taxation. The reason for this is that workers ultimately work for after-tax income rather than before-tax income. If the tax system is made more progressive in an attempt to redistribute income, workers in higher-paying jobs receive less after-tax income and have an incentive to look for less demanding jobs, albeit at lower pay. Meanwhile, lower-paying jobs become more attractive because those jobs yield higher after-tax income, so the supply of laborers willing to take those jobs increases. The result is that in order for employers to retain their higher-paid employees, they have to pay them more to compensate for the higher taxes the em-

ployees incur, but they can reduce the pretax wages of lower-paid workers because the more progressive taxation reduces the tax bills of those workers.[8]

The net effect is that a more progressive tax structure raises the pretax income of high-income workers and lowers the pretax income of low-income workers to compensate them for the change in the tax structure. In this light progressive taxation has much less of a

---

[7] See Charles Murray, *Losing Ground* (New York: Basic Books, 1984), for an eloquent discussion of how welfare programs have produced poverty and welfare dependency in this way.

[8] See Milton Friedman, *Price Theory* (Chicago: Aldine, 1976), pp. 246–248 for an explanation. See also R. G. Holcombe, *An Economic Analysis of Democracy* (Carbondale: Southern Illinois University Press, 1985), ch. 5, for an elaboration of this idea.

redistributive impact than is commonly believed. Some evidence to this effect is presented by Reynolds and Smolensky, who note that even though the tax system has become much more progressive since World War II, the after-tax distribution of income (including transfer payments) has remained roughly the same and the pretax distribution of income has become more unequal.[9] These findings are consistent with the theory that the pretax distribution of income will adjust to offset the effects of changes in the tax structure.

Distributive Government

In the past several decades an important change in the priorities of government programs in the United States has taken place. In 1960 government spending at all levels of government comprised about 28 percent of *GNP*, more than one-third of which went for national defense. In adding the revenues directed toward traditional areas of government spending, such as education and roads, to this figure, we see a government dedicated to producing goods for collective consumption, with an emphasis on national defense. By 1980 government spending had risen to about one-third of GNP, but less than one-sixth of total government spending was devoted to national defense. Rather, much of the additional spending in those two decades went toward redistributional programs. Indeed, from 1960 to 1980, the focus of government activity shifted from producing goods largely for the public interest to collecting money from some people and transferring it to others.

This transformation has had a number of effects. Earlier in the chapter we saw that individuals could become dependent on government transfers. This welfare dependency could actually cause the distribution of income to become more unequal, thereby thwarting the goal of a more equal distribution of income. In addition, the shift in government spending has had the effect of increasing the amount of money that the government redistributes, thus making it more worthwhile for special interests of all types to lobby the government for some type of special interest benefits. We discussed this in some detail in Chapter 8. Recall that special interests have an incentive to lobby for benefits from the government, whereas the general public is rationally ignorant of most of what the government does. Thus, the government tends to produce special interest benefits rather than serving the general public interest.

The Incentive Structure of Government Programs

Our intention here is not to condemn government activity, but rather, by applying economic theory, to warn that the incentive structure of the government must be monitored carefully to ensure that government programs do what they are supposed to do. Certainly, nobody intended for welfare programs to increase the level of poverty, but as noted,

---

[9]Morgan Reynolds and Eugene Smolensky, *Public Expenditures, Taxes, and the Distribution of Income* (New York: Academic Press, 1977).

Figure 14.4 A Price Floor By holding the price up at P_F, a price floor redistributes income from buyers to sellers of a product. Above-normal profits can be earned temporarily, but eventually the price of inputs in the market will be bid up to reflect the value of the product's higher price, and producers will eventually earn only a normal return.

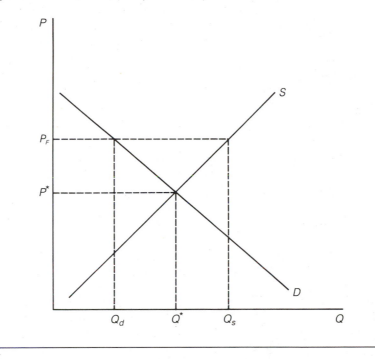

welfare programs often provide incentives for recipients to remain out of work and in poverty.

The incentive structure works for programs other than poverty programs, though. Programs to help farmers have had the effect of making farmers dependent on government subsidies for their survival as well. A good example is dairy price supports, although most any farm subsidy program would serve equally well. Figure 14.4 depicts a price floor that holds the price of dairy products above the market equilibrium price. P^* is the price that would exist in the market without the government program, and Q^* is the amount that would be sold. The government price support, by holding the price at a higher level, P_F, causes the quantity demanded to fall to Q_D and the quantity supplied to rise to Q_S.

In other words consumers consume less while producers produce more, thus creating a surplus. Due to the higher price producers have an incentive to produce more output and even more profits, but this in turn bids up the value of the resources used in producing dairy products. Ultimately, these higher profits will be competed away and farmers make only normal profits when producing quantity

Q_S at the price P_F. The result is that dairy farmers become dependent on the subsidies to stay in business. The establishment of a program creates a transitional, or temporary, gain to the recipients, but after the transitional gain there are only normal returns to be earned, and abolishing the program will result in a transitional loss to those now dependent on the program.[10]

Redistributive Programs and the Poor

On the surface it would seem that if government programs provide income and in-kind benefits to the poor, the well-being of the poor should increase. In considering the issues in more detail, however, we have seen a number of reasons why this may not be the case. The incentives fostered by most transfer programs encourage recipients to earn less income on their own. This can reduce the income of the poor in the short run, and it can make it more difficult in the long run for the poor to escape poverty.

Incentives to Earn Less Income

To reiterate, redistributive programs provide an incentive to earn less income. Programs that redistribute income to low-income individuals in effect make payments in exchange for being poor, and people can be expected to respond accordingly. This is not to suggest that people would rather be on welfare than work for a living, but rather that there will be less urgency to find a job if the government provides support in the interim. Furthermore, a combination of government programs might even reduce an individual's income if the individual takes a job.

For example, a study by Gwartney and McCaleb[11] reported that in 1983 a Pennsylvania mother with two children would actually have more spendable income earning $4000 per year than earning $9000 per year. If the woman's earned income were $4000 per year, she could have $9214 in spendable income, including the transfers she would be entitled to under government programs. But if she earned $9000, her spendable income would be $8798, including transfers and subtracting the taxes due on the income. Considering these incentives, would anyone expect this woman to earn the $5000 in extra income to bring her earnings from $4000 to $9000 if her spendable income would not change?

That same study found that the woman could receive $7568 in spendable income from government programs alone if she earned no income. Thus, if the woman's earned income went from zero to $9000, her spendable income, after taxes and government transfers, would rise from $7568 to $8798—an increase of only $1230. Given these incentives, and given the costs incurred when holding a job, such as child care, work clothes, and purchased rather than home-cooked meals, one can hardly expect this

---

[10]See Gordon Tullock, "The Transitional Gains Trap," *The Bell Journal of Economics* 6 (Autumn 1975), pp. 671–678.

[11]James Gwartney and Thomas S. McCaleb, "Have Antipoverty Programs Increased Poverty?" *Cato Journal* 5, no. 1 (Spring/Summer 1985), pp. 1–16.

woman to accept a job paying $9000 per year rather than remain unemployed.

To further illuminate the disincentives generated by redistributive programs, assume that the woman can work 40 hours a week, 50 weeks a year, for a total of 2000 hours a year, so that a job paying $4.50 per hour will produce $9000 in earned income. Her spendable income with this job paying $4.50 per hour would increase by only $1230. Indeed, the same study found that spendable income would remain roughly unchanged if the individual worked for the minimum wage of $3.35 per hour. Given that the same spendable income can be produced without working, we should be surprised if the woman took a job at minimum wage, only to earn the same spendable income that she could receive without working.

The Hardcore Poor and the Marginal Poor

Gwartney and McCaleb make an important distinction between the hardcore poor and the marginal poor. The *hardcore poor* are individuals who are poor because of injuries, disease, or some other type of disability and who have little control over their incomes. By contrast, the *marginal poor* are poor because of such things as a lack of education, pregnancy, a change in family status, or a general economic downturn. Although these individuals may be the victims of misfortune, they are in a position to improve their economic status and move out of poverty on their own. Workers can find jobs when the economy recovers, mothers of young children can reenter the labor force, and individuals can get additional education or on-the-job training if the incentives for them to do so are strong enough.

A major goal of redistribution programs is to help the hardcore poor, who realistically cannot support themselves. But in the process, redistribution programs provide incentives to the marginal poor to remain in poverty to qualify for government programs. When individuals can earn nearly as much money remaining unemployed as reentering the labor force, there is little incentive for them to work. Eventually, the marginal poor who are unemployed become unemployable and join the ranks of the hardcore unemployed.

Growing Dependency on Government Programs

The term applied to the marginal poor who gradually become hardcore poor is *welfare dependency*, and considering the incentives built into the redistribution system, it is easy to see how this process takes place. For an individual with low skills, one way to develop job skills is from on-the-job training. For example, an individual can take a job in a garage, at minimum wage, and learn automobile maintenance, through training on the job, gradually increasing skill levels until a higher wage can be earned. Of course, on-the-job training can only take place if the person has a job in the first place, and redistribution programs that pay a person as much for being unemployed as for working at a low-skill job provide little incentive to get that first job through which valuable job skills can be obtained. The result is that the person who could have been on an upward-earning track out of poverty remains poor and dependent on government programs for an income.

Another criticism frequently raised regarding redistribution programs is that to qualify, often the recipient must be unable to work. For example, a single mother with children at home has an incentive to continue having children. Furthermore, two-parent families have an incentive to split up so that they can qualify. In short, families have an incentive to split up, individuals have an incentive not to work, and individuals who once had an incentive to escape poverty become dependent on government redistributive programs. According to this line of reasoning, redistribution programs have actually harmed the marginal poor by making it much harder for them to escape the conditions of poverty.[12]

Keep in mind that not everybody agrees with this assessment of the government's redistributive programs.[13] The programs un-

doubtedly help the hardcore poor, and they may provide some transitory assistance to the marginal poor. Nevertheless, we must recognize that redistribution programs contain incentives to remain poor if that is what it takes to qualify. Thus, in designing the most effective redistributive programs, we need to provide incentives to escape poverty rather than to become dependent on the government's redistributive programs.

The Politics of Redistribution

In addition to our normative examination of the foundations of redistribution policy and our positive analysis of the consequences of redistributive programs, we need to consider the political environment in which these programs are formulated and perpetuated. Table 14.1 lists some figures on government spending that suggest that the big increase in spending for redistributive programs came between 1965 and 1975. In 1965 transfer payments comprised 23 percent of total federal government spending, national defense 41 percent. By 1975 transfer payments had increased to 39 percent of federal government spending, but national defense had declined to 26 percent. In 1985 government spending was in roughly the same proportions as in 1975. Before 1972 national defense was a larger proportion of federal spending than transfer payments, but by 1972 each accounted for

about 32 percent of federal spending. After 1972 transfer payments exceeded defense spending.

Recall that as the government spends more money in transfers from some people to others, special interests have an increased incentive to lobby for transfer payments. It also creates a substantial transfer "industry" of individuals—often, but not necessarily, working for the government—who make their livelihood from the redistributive programs of government and thus have an incentive to perpetuate the programs. However, the incentives facing government administrators are not always completely in line with the welfare of those who receive the transfers.

There are two main points to consider here. First, as redistributive programs become a larger portion of the government's budget, special interests have increased incentives to lobby for redistributive benefits. With more money to be redistributed, the potential payoff is greater. Second, the establishment of redistributive programs creates a welfare industry made up of people who administer government programs and people who benefit from the programs (such as owners of low-

---

[12]This is the central theme in Charles Murray, *Losing Ground*, (New York: Basic Books, 1984).

[13]A critique aimed specifically at Murray's book can be found in the University of Wisconsin-Madison Institute for Research on Poverty's *Focus* 8, no. 3 (Fall/Winter 1985), pp. 1–12.

Table 14.1 Government Spending on Transfer Payments and National Defense, 1965, 1975, 1985

YEAR	TOTAL EXPENDITURES	TRANSFER PAYMENTS		NATIONAL DEFENSE	
	Billion $	*Billion $*	*Percent of Total*	*Billion $*	*Percent of Total*
1965	120	28	23	49	41
1975	336	132	39	86	26
1985	963	359	37	256	27

Source: *Economic Report of the President*, February 1986, p. 345.

income housing, who receive much of their rent from government housing subsidies). This welfare industry wields political power that is an important force in perpetuating and expanding its programs. Therefore, to completely understand the government's redistributive programs, we must not only recognize the positive consequences of the programs and the normative equity issues involved but also consider the political environment in which the policies are created and perpetuated.

Incentives of Administrators

The theory of bureaucracy discussed in Chapter 8 suggests that bureaucrats have an incentive to maximize the budgets of their bureaus, and the same principle applies to bureaus engaged in redistribution. But increased spending is not easily correlated with increased well-being of groups targeted for help. Thomas Sowell has studied the effects of government programs designed to help disadvantaged groups and noted, "It would be easier to find an *inverse* correlation between political activity and economic success than a direct correla-

tion."[14] Sowell, a black economist, clearly believes that government programs have, on net, hurt blacks, despite the fact that their stated goals are often to help minorities.

Sowell does not view these net negative effects as the result of well-meaning individuals who have somehow steered government programs in the wrong direction, but rather as the result of the rational self-interests of government administrators and black leaders to maintain the system that provides their livelihood. Sowell argues, "However catastrophic the politicization of race may be in the long run, from the point of view of individual leaders it is a highly successful way to rise from obscurity to prominence and power. . . . In short, despite the unpromising record of politics as a means of raising a group from poverty to affluence, and despite the dangers of politicizing race, there are built-in incentives for political leaders to do just that."[15]

Walter Williams is another black economist who has argued that government policies have, on net, harmed minorities.[16] How should these arguments be evaluated for purposes of public policy? Above all, these arguments indicate that the political process can

---

[14]Thomas Sowell, *Civil Rights: Rhetoric or Reality?* (New York: Morrow, 1984), p. 32.

[15]Sowell, *Civil Rights*, p. 35.

[16]See, for example, Walter E. Williams, *The State Against Blacks* (New York: McGraw-Hill, 1982).

be better understood by looking at the economic incentives of participants in the process. Certainly, some individuals may profit from an expansion of redistributive programs, regardless of whether the poor benefit. This does not imply that we should do away with all such programs, but rather that we need to examine carefully the incentives of both the recipients and the administrators.

The government cannot solve problems simply by indiscriminately spending money on them, and money spent on redistributive programs can be spent wisely or foolishly, just as money spent on any other type of program can be. Wasteful spending at the Pentagon, though perhaps more newsworthy, derives from the same incentives for mismanagement of funds and ineffective programs facing redistributive programs. It is not enough simply to look at the number of dollars being spent to see what the government is doing to assist underprivileged individuals. In redistributive programs, as in all government spending, the political incentives can often cause ineffective programs to be favored over potentially effective ones.

Objects of Redistribution

As Table 14.1 shows, the government collects a lot of money in taxes from some people to redistribute to others. In 1985 there were about 240 million people in the United States, so the amount of redistribution in that year was $359 billion divided by 240 million people, or about $1496 per person. Because many people (for example, children) do not pay much in the way of federal taxes themselves, the amount that an average family of four would have to pay in taxes to support federal redistributive programs is four times $1496, or $5984.

Assume for the moment that all of this money is collected and paid directly to poor

people, and assume that one out of every five individuals in the country is poor. If this method of redistribution were followed, a family of four poor people could collect five times $5984, or $29,920, from the government, enough to place the family well above the poverty line. Obviously, poor people do not get nearly this amount from the government. Therefore, we must ask why redistributive programs do not do a better job of helping the poor when we pay enough into the programs to virtually eliminate poverty.

The main reason is that most transfers are paid not to poor people but to middle-income individuals. Social security payments are a good example of a redistribution program that gives most of its benefits to people who are not poor. Some of the money for redistributive programs also goes to pay federal workers, and some goes to provide buildings for them to work in. Some of the money even goes to needy people.

Table 14.2 lists some figures on money spent through redistributive programs specifically aimed at persons with limited incomes in 1983. For example, $127 billion was targeted for people with limited incomes in 1983; by contrast, social security payments in 1983 were $164 billion, far more than the payments to low-income individuals. Some social security recipients will be poor, of course, but redistribution through social security benefits are targeted to older people rather than poor people. But if the total benefits of $127 billion targeted specifically to low-income people simply were divided up and given to the bottom 20 percent of families by income, this would allow $10,591 for each family of four. This figure is a little more than a third of the amount calculated when all redistributive programs are included, which suggests that most government redistribution is not specifically targeted for low-income individuals.

According to Table 14.2 medical care com-

Table 14.2 Cash and Noncash Benefits for Persons with Limited Income, 1983

CATEGORY	AMOUNT (BILLION $)	PERCENT OF BENEFITS	PERCENT OF FEDERAL SPENDING
Medical care	44	35	5
Cash aid	35	28	4
Food benefits	16	13	2
Housing benefits	13	10	1
Education aid	9	7	1
Total*	127		15

*Total is greater than the sum of listed programs because some small programs are not listed in the table.

Source: *Statistical Abstract of the United States*, 1985 Edition, p. 357.

prises the single largest benefit provided to low-income individuals, accounting for $44 billion, or about 35 percent of the total benefits and about 5 percent of total federal government spending for 1983. Cash aid is the next largest, accounting for about $35 billion. The largest subcategory under cash aid is Aid to Families with Dependent Children, for which $15 billion out of the total $35 billion was spent. Of the $16 billion devoted to food benefits, $12 billion was in the food stamp program. In all, programs targeted to low-income persons amounted to $127 billion in 1983, about 15 percent of total federal government spending for that year.

What lessons can be drawn from these statistics? First, it is obvious that most redistribution is not targeted specifically to needy people. Considered in the political context within which redistributive decisions are made, this should not be surprising. Many people other than poor people have the ability to lobby the government for benefits, and the most visible group in this regard is the aged, who receive social security. Indeed, the next chapter is devoted exclusively to the social security program.

Second, if tax revenue were redistributed directly to poor people, poverty could, at least theoretically, be eliminated. For example, in 1983 a family of four could have received over $10,500 in federal government benefits if the money had been divided up and given to the lowest 20 percent of individuals by income. In fact, even though the U.S. government redistributes enough money so that it could have provided the 20 percent of the most needy families of four with nearly $30,000 in income in 1985, poverty remains. To understand why this happens, we must keep in mind the nature of the political process. Money will tend to be redistributed at least somewhat along the lines of political power. And the welfare industry itself has an incentive to perpetuate the poverty that creates a demand for its services, which suggests that most of the taxes paid for redistributive programs do not reach needy individuals.

This discussion is not meant to argue against redistributive programs, but merely to confront the realities of trying to redistribute income through the political process. Understanding the incentives of everyone involved represents the logical first step toward building a system that can accomplish the goal of effectively redistributing income to those who need it most.

Conclusion

Redistribution is an important area in public sector economics, because it is one of the major activities that governments engage in. Redistribution also encompasses a number of difficult issues. Not only is it based on normative foundations that sometimes are not clearly understood, but also established programs can have consequences very different from those intended.

There are many possible motivations for establishing redistributive programs in government. The most obvious is a simple desire to see more income equality in the nation. Presumably, one could also argue that the social welfare would be increased by transferring income from those who are better off to those who are worse off. This argument requires that some interpersonal utility comparisons be made, because the effects of such transfers will be to make some people better off but others worse off.

Charitable activities share some of the characteristics of a collective consumption good, meaning that there is an incentive for potential givers to free ride off of the contributions of others. Because everyone has the same incentives, charitable activities tend to be underprovided. Thus, the role of the government is to collect taxes in order to finance the optimal amount of redistribution. Redistributive programs also might be viewed as a type of insurance, by which payments are made to lower-income individuals from premiums paid by higher-income individuals. Clearly, some redistributive programs, such as unemployment compensation, are of this type.

In short, many different motivations contribute to the demand for redistributive programs. Another factor that must be considered is the demands of both the recipients of the programs and the government administrators who run the programs. Because both recipients and administrators vote, they rightly view it as in their own interests to have the programs continued.

The results of redistributive programs are often different from what is initially intended. For example, payments to poor people give them an incentive to be poor; likewise, payments to those out of work give them an incentive to remain unemployed. Often, there is no good way around these drawbacks, in which case they must be viewed as one of the costs of producing redistributive programs. However, some economic analysis can often clarify the incentives implied in the programs as well as predict the effects of the programs.

Questions

1. What characteristics might an equitable tax structure have? Differentiate between the concept of equity as applied to a fiscal exchange model of taxation and to redistributive programs.

2. Explain the distinction between equality of opportunity and equality of results. Which is more appropriate as a goal of social policy? Can both be incorporated into the same public policy? Explain the circumstances under which they might be applied.

3. Explain why the private market may provide less than the Pareto optimal level of income redistribution. Is this an argument for using tax revenues as a source of income redistribution? Explain both sides of the argument. Which side do you think is correct?

4. Normative questions, unlike positive ones, do not have single right answers. If this is so, why are normative questions so important to issues such as redistribution? Why can these issues not be resolved solely in terms of positive analysis?

5. Are the goals of redistributive programs better achieved with cash transfers or transfers in kind? Explain both sides of the issue.

6. Describe the operation of a negative income tax. Will a negative income tax necessarily increase a person's money income? Explain why redistributive programs in general do not necessarily increase a person's income as measured in dollar terms.

7. Explain why a progressive tax system has less of a distributive impact than the amount of money taken from some people by the tax system and given to others suggests.

CHAPTER FIFTEEN

Social Security

This chapter is a logical extension of the previous chapter because the social security program constitutes the largest government redistribution program. The social security program was begun in 1935 to provide retirement benefits to those participating in the program and also to provide benefits to surviving dependents of those covered. The program was expanded in 1956 to provide disability insurance to those in the program, and it expanded again in 1965 to give medical benefits to those over age 65 under the Medicare program. The official name of the social security program—Old Age, Survivors, Disability, and Health Insurance—reflects its various functions. Clearly, the program has grown a great deal since it was first established. Indeed, although social security is just one of many government redistribution programs, it has become so large and encompasses so many significant issues that it warrants a separate chapter.

Some of these issues are related to the way that social security is financed. The social security program is unusual in its financing in that an earmarked payroll tax is used to pay for it. From time to time, it has been suggested that social security revenues be augmented by funds from the general treasury, or even that

social security be financed from general funds rather than from the earmarked payroll tax. Though this aspect of the program certainly merits consideration, it is not the most controversial aspect of social security financing. Even more attention is focused on the fact that social security is a pay-as-you-go rather than a funded insurance program, which has significant economic implications. In addition, the social security program generates substantial controversy concerning the benefits paid under the system and the taxes used to finance it.

Social security taxes and benefits have continually risen since the program was originally established. The political factors contributing to this trend are of interest, but anyone covered by the social security system is far more concerned with how those same political factors will affect the future of the program. A key question is whether future taxpayers can be counted on to pay the taxes that finance the program. Keep in mind that a program established through the political system can be curtailed or eliminated the same way. This gives individuals paying social security taxes today legitimate reason to be concerned about such issues.

The Social Security Payroll Tax

The social security program was originally established to function as a government-operated retirement program. It was intended to have many of the characteristics of a private retirement plan in that the individuals participating in the program would make contributions while they were working in exchange for benefits after they retired. The program is different from many other government redistribution programs because there is no requirement of need to collect the government transfer—eligibility for benefits is contingent simply on having contributed to the program in the past.

Contributions

Contributions to the program are made in the form of a payroll tax, which means that only labor income is taxed. Income is taxed at a constant rate up to a specified maximum level. The employer and the employee contribute equal amounts to the program. When the program was initially established, it provided for the employee to contribute 1 percent of his or her salary and for the employer to match this contribution, for a total contribution of 2 percent of the employee's salary up to a maximum wage income of $3000. In other words the tax was 2 percent of the employee's wage for the first $3000 of income, so the maximum contribution would have been $60 per year, counting both the employee's and the employer's share.

The payroll tax works in essentially the same way today, though both the rates and the maximum wage that can be taxed have risen. The tax is still divided evenly between the employee and the employer, but the combined tax for 1987 is 14.3 percent of income up to $46,800.[1] As the program has grown, the taxes used to finance the program have also grown, but they have retained their original form as a flat rate payroll tax up to a maximum amount. This method of financing makes sense if one thinks of the program as a type of social insurance. A person pays a premium into the social insurance plan that bears a relationship to the amount that the person expects to get out at retirement. Benefits are then paid out at retirement based on contributions rather than need.

Table 15.1 lists some pertinent facts about social security and the payroll tax for selected years. As the figures indicate, the program started out as a relatively insignificant part of the total government budget, but it has grown rapidly over the years. In 1950 the program accounted for only 2.5 percent of total federal government spending; today it accounts for over 25 percent of federal spending. In addition, the payroll tax rate is about five times as large today as it was in 1950 and is projected to grow larger. The program's growth history prompts serious questions about whether future taxpayers can be counted on to foot the bill for social security when the current group of contributors reaches retirement age. We will consider this issue later in the chapter.

The Structure of the Tax

Although other federal programs, such as airport improvement and interstate highways, are also financed through earmarked taxes, none of these programs is of the same magnitude as the social security program. Because

---

[1] These figures are taken from Peter J. Ferrara, *Social Security: Averting the Crisis* (Washington, D.C.: Cato Institute, 1982), Tables 1 and 2, pp. 137–140.

Table 15.1 Characteristics of the Social Security Program for Selected Years

YEAR	COMBINED EMPLOYER AND EMPLOYEE TAX RATES	MAXIMUM TAXABLE INCOME ($)	SOCIAL SECURITY AS A PERCENTAGE OF TOTAL FEDERAL EXPENDITURES
1940	2.00	3,000	0.6
1950	3.00	3,000	2.5
1960	6.00	4,800	12.7
1970	8.40	7,800	20.7
1980	12.26	25,900	24.8
1990 (projected)	15.30	56,800	(not estimated)

Source: Peter J. Ferrara, *Social Security: Averting the Crisis* (Washington, D.C.: Cato Institute, 1982), Tables 1, 2, and 4.

the social security payroll tax is over 25 percent of total federal taxes, the tax naturally has received close scrutiny. The tax seems to adhere to the benefit principle in that benefits are paid out as a function of contributions, but the tax has been criticized because of its regressive nature. Note that the tax is applied at a flat rate up to a certain maximum level, which implies that higher-income individuals end up paying a lower percentage of their income in tax. Furthermore, capital income is excluded altogether from taxation.

Whether this tax structure is appropriate depends on how the program is viewed. According to the benefit principle, the tax is equitable, but if social security is viewed as being like other governmental redistribution plans, the tax structure may be viewed as inequitable. When the tax was collected at a combined rate of 2 percent, equity was perhaps not a very significant issue, but as social security tax rates have risen, the structure of the tax has become more important.

The Burden of the Payroll Tax

An interesting feature of the program is that the tax is shared equally between employees and employers. The answer to the question of how this sharing arrangement affects who ultimately bears the burden of the tax depends on a straightforward application of the principles of tax shifting examined in Chapter 9. In the sense that employees are the suppliers of labor and employers are the demanders, we are essentially asking what difference it makes whether the tax is placed on suppliers in a market or on demanders. Recall that according to the principles of tax shifting, it makes no difference.

Tax Shifting and the Payroll Tax

To illustrate, compare a situation in which employers are responsible for the entire amount of the tax to one in which employees have to pay the entire amount. Because the ultimate burden of taxation has no connection with the original placement of the tax, we can conclude that an employee's take-home wage will be the same whether the entire tax is placed on the employer or the employee, provided the tax rate is the same. A slight difference in the tax burden might result if social security contributions were included as taxable income on other taxes, but given the principles of tax shifting, it should make little difference whether the tax is paid by the supplier of labor or the demander.

This makes sense if one reflects on it. An employer is concerned with the total cost of hiring an employee, including any taxes that must be paid on the employee's behalf. Likewise, an employee cares about the after-tax income from a job. Wages are set by the forces of supply and demand, and who ends up paying the tax will be irrelevant to the after-tax income of the employee.

The Visibility of the Payroll Tax

This is not to suggest that it is completely irrelevant whether the tax is levied on the employer or the employee or is shared between them. A tax levied on the employer will be hidden from the employee, at least to some extent. At the end of the year, an employee's W-2 form will list only half of the amount contributed to social security on behalf of the employee. The employer's contribution has identical economic effects and should be

considered as a cost to the employee of the social security program.

A person who thinks that a tax should be as painless to pay as possible will favor placing the entire tax to the employer, in which case the employee's take-home pay will not change, but the tax will be more hidden. On the other hand, a person who believes that the cost of a government program should be readily visible so that taxpayers can easily evaluate whether the program is worth its cost should favor placing the entire tax on the employee. This way, the employee has a clear measure of the cost of social security and is in a good position to evaluate whether the expected benefits from the program are worth the cost.

The use of the earmarked tax to finance social security does give the social security program a characteristic not shared by any other major federal program: It is very easy for the taxpayer to estimate the cost of the program. Due to the program's financing through the payroll tax, the taxpayer need only double the amount shown on the W-2 form (to account for the employer's contribution) to find out the cost to that taxpayer of the program. By contrast, other major programs, such as national defense, are financed out of the personal income tax, the corporate income tax, government borrowing, and other revenue sources, so that an individual taxpayer cannot easily estimate the program's total cost.

Coverage

Approximately 90 percent of workers in paid employment are covered by the social security program, whereas in 1940 less than 60 percent of workers were covered.[2] Excluded from coverage are federal workers, who fall under the civil service retirement system,

members of Congress, and some employees of state and local governments. State and local

---

[2]Some statistics are given in Peter J. Ferrara, *Social Security: The Inherent Contradiction* (Washington, D.C.: Cato Institute, 1980), Table 7.

governments have the option of having their employees covered under the social security system, but they can withdraw from social security and provide their own retirement systems if they choose to. Self-employed individuals are also covered under social security, but the combined employer-employee tax rate for self-employed individuals is lower than for those working for a contributing employer.

Eligibility

To be eligible for benefits, an individual must have worked for forty quarters in a covered job. This means that some individuals may be eligible for social security benefits while also being eligible for another government retirement program, such as civil service retirement or military retirement. The amount of benefits paid is a function of the current legislated formula rather than the amount the retiree paid in. This means that someone who worked nine years and contributed to the system would not be eligible for retirement benefits, whereas other individuals might be receiving several retirement checks if they moved from, say, a civil service or military job to one covered by social security. Although benefits are tied to the individual's contribution level, the benefits paid do not reflect the present value of past contributions, as is the case under a private system.

The Redistributive Nature of the Program

For most workers social security is compulsory; the discussion of the benefit structure suggests why. Because some workers can come out better than others under the system, there would be a tendency for those workers to enthusiastically sign up for the program, whereas those who did not expect to get a good deal would be likely to bypass the system. In insurance terms this is known as the problem of *adverse selection*. It is also true that social security is a pay-as-you-go system rather than a funded insurance plan, which requires new contributors to keep the system solvent. This aspect of the program will be discussed later. At this point note simply that the benefit structure shares elements of both an insurance plan and a redistribution program.

The redistributive nature of the program becomes evident in its treatment of married individuals. A married couple is eligible to receive 150 percent of the social security benefits paid to a single individual. However, if the spouse is also eligible for benefits, both can choose to receive the benefits that they would be entitled to as single individuals. A private pension plan would have to pay the same amount to two individuals with identical earnings independent of marital status, or there would be self-selection, whereby married individuals would be more inclined to join the voluntary pension plan than singles. However, under the compulsory social security system, a married individual could have income and be eligible for benefits and yet do better by choosing the spouse's benefit if the individual's benefits were less than 50 percent of the spouse's benefit. In this case the individual would rather not contribute and receive benefits as a spouse, but the compulsory nature of the system requires contribution. For example, a housewife who raised a family and then decided to reenter the labor force might prefer not to contribute and simply be eligible as a spouse, but the system requires participation.

Federal Employees

From a political standpoint an important omission in social security coverage is Congress and civil service employees. Because federal employees in general do not have to contribute to the system, this politically important group has little direct interest in seeing that the social security system functions efficiently and provides a guarantee of benefits at retirement. Young workers today might reasonably be concerned about whether the social security system will be paying benefits years from now in exchange for the nearly 15 percent per year of one's income that now goes into the system. If Congress and govern-mental employees were tied into that same system, there would be more reason to believe that the system would be viable from a political standpoint. As it is, there could be major changes to the social security system that would not affect the people who run it.

The Pay-as-You-Go System of Financing

As mentioned, the social security system is a pay-as-you-go system, which means that beneficiaries are paid directly from the contributions of people currently working. The alternative would be to have a funded system, which is how private pension plans are structured; indeed, the government requires private pension plans to be funded. A funded pension plan works much like money placed in a bank account. The worker places money into a retirement account at each payday, and the money is invested by the pension plan until the worker retires. Then the retiree receives income from the pension. In essence, the individual contributes a certain amount to the pension plan, and that amount remains in an account until it is paid back at retirement, with interest.

The pay-as-you-go system used by social security looks similar to the participant—money is paid in now in exchange for benefits to be collected later. However, the pay-as-you-go system works differently in that it collects contributions from current workers and redistributes them to current retirees as benefits. Because current contributions are not invested, the link between the contributor's contributions and retirement benefits to be paid later is cut. The plan is simply income redistribution, although it is designed to have the appearance of a pension plan.

As a result, the continuation of benefit payments is dependent on new individuals continually entering the system. Without new participants there will be no source of funds to pay future benefits to those who have already paid into the system; that is, the liabilities of social security are unfunded. The system promises to pay benefits to current contributors, but it can do so only by taking the contributions of future contributors. By contrast, a private pension plan invests the contributions of contributors and pays an individual's retirement benefits out of the individual's contribution. This means the pension plan always has a net worth at least equal to the present value of the future liability of the pensions that must be paid in the future. In other words the private pension plan will have accumulated a fund out of which current liabilities are paid. This suggests another important reason why the social security system is not voluntary—only by forcing people to participate in the future can the system be assured that it will have the ability to pay future benefits.

The Viability of Pay-as-You-Go

This raises the important question about why social security was established as a pay-as-you-go rather than a funded system. The logic behind such a structure is that, in a growing economy with a growing work force, there will be more new contributors entering the system and paying larger contributions (as incomes rise) each generation. Whereas a voluntary system cannot guarantee that future benefits will be paid, a compulsory system, at least theoretically, can. Larger benefits can be paid out immediately without funding, and the growth in benefit payments is virtually guaranteed by the growth in population and per capita income.

However, this ideal model of the pay-as-you-go system has been affected by increased

benefit payments as well as several demographic factors. First, the population is living longer, meaning that each retiree can expect to collect for a greater number of years. Second, the so-called baby boom after World War II will produce a large number of retirees in the first decade of the twenty-first century, and to raise the revenues to pay benefits to these individuals will require either increased taxes, reduced benefits, or both. The future of social security will be examined in a later section.

The Political Determination of Benefits and Costs

From an apolitical standpoint those who participate in the social security system might expect to pay taxes into the system and then receive payments depending on the future taxes paid in when the current contributors retire. In this context the rate of return on contributions is equal to the growth in national income, which in turn is a function of the growth in per capita income and the growth in population. Under this scenario beneficiaries simply divide the current contributions among themselves. This assumes that the tax rate is constant and that the program's characteristics do not change as current contributors retire.

In fact, the program's characteristics are subject to change through the political process.[3] To illustrate, consider first a private pension plan. An individual deciding on con-

tribution rates and benefit levels has an incentive to compare the present value of contributions over the individual's lifetime to the present value of the expected future retirement benefits. With the social security system, on the other hand, the individual's benefits are a function not of taxes paid during the individual's working years but rather of the taxes paid by others during the individual's retirement years. How, then, might the voting-age population react to a proposal to increase social security taxes and benefits?

For simplicity the population can be divided into three groups. One group consists of young workers who are just beginning to participate in the system. The second group consists of middle-aged workers who have participated in the system for years, but who still must make some more contributions before retiring. The third group is retirees, who, by the way, tend to have higher voter participation rates than the rest of the population. Obviously, a proposal to increase taxes to finance current payments will benefit retirees, because any increase in benefits comes at no cost

---

[3]See Edgar K. Browning, "Why the Social Insurance Budget Is Too Large in a Democracy," *Economic Inquiry* 13 (Sept. 1975), pp. 373–388, and Kriss Sjoblom, "Voting for Social Security," *Public Choice* 45, no. 3 (1985), pp. 225–240, for discussions along these lines.

to them. By contrast, young workers might object to the increased burden of the payroll tax to finance what amounts to a transfer to the older generation. But those in the middle group, where the median voter resides, are less likely to object, because they will pay the higher taxes for only part of their working career, and in exchange for the promise of higher retirement benefits.

The point is that the closer one gets to retirement, the more it is in one's narrow self-interest to vote for higher taxes in exchange for higher benefits. The benefits enjoyed by retirees are financed by the taxes of others, unlike the benefits in a private pension plan, which are a function of the amount one pays into the system. One can easily see how the political system introduces a bias in favor of increasing the benefits in the system. Retirees and older workers can vote for increased benefits that will be paid for not by their own contributions but by the contributions of younger people.

Social Security and Capital Accumulation

One effect of the social security system being an unfunded system is that it reduces the incentive for private saving, because money is contributed now in exchange for future benefits. The individual correctly views social security as an alternative to private saving and so rationally reduces the amount saved. The result is that, social security being a pay-as-you-go rather than a funded system, less money is available for investment.

Funded Pensions

To illustrate this, compare a situation in which no public retirement system exists with one in which a funded pension system exists. Without a retirement system individuals would have to save for their own retirements, so the income placed in private pension plans would become available for investment by others. Figure 15.1 depicts the loanable funds market, with demand for funds (for investment) D and supply of funds (saving) S. The equilibrium amount of saving and investing is Q^*, at the intersection of the supply and demand curves, producing interest rate r. But when a funded pension plan is set up, the amount going into the pension plan, R, reduces the amount of private saving by R because individuals can save that much less for their retirement. The pension plan then takes the money contributed at the present time and invests it to earn a return, which is paid to the current contributors when they retire. Note that the amount invested will equal the contributions to the plan, or R. Thus, comparing the funded pension plan to no plan, the amount of individual saving shifts the saving curve back to $S - R$, but the amount R is then invested by the pension plan, shifting the curve back to its original position. Funds from the pension substitute for the private saving they replace, so there is no net effect on aggregate investment.

Unfunded Pensions

Now compare a funded pension plan with an unfunded plan. The contributor still perceives that money contributed today will be

Figure 15.1 The Effect of Social Security on Saving and Investment People perceive social security contributions as substituting for some saving for the future. Therefore, they reduce their saving by an amount *R,* shifting the supply of loanable funds inward to $S - R$, which reduces current investment.

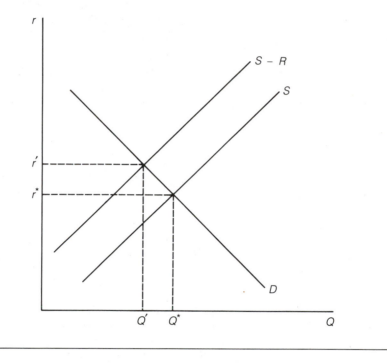

returned in the form of retirement benefits later, so the saving curve still shifts to $S - R$. However, the proceeds, instead of being invested as they would be under a funded system, are simply paid out to current beneficiaries. With no additional funds available for investment, the total amount of funds going to investment falls from Q^* to Q', and the interest rate rises from r^* to r'. Current contributors treat their contributions like saving, but no money is made available for investment. The net effect is a reduction in the amount of investment as a result of an unfunded social

security system.[4] The magnitude of this effect is a matter of current debate among economists. Though we leave the issue here, in Chapter 16 our discussion of the national debt deals with issues regarding capital accumulation that are directly applicable to social security.

---

[4]Martin Feldstein has been a major promoter of this hypothesis. See his "Social Security, Induced Retirement, and Aggregate Capital Accumulation," *Journal of Political Economy* 82, no. 5 (Sept./Oct. 1974), pp. 905–926, for an introduction to these ideas.

The Growth of the Social Security Program

Table 15.2 provides a history of social security financing for the Old Age, Survivors, and Disability Insurance (OASDI) program. Medicare, which was established in 1966, is included in the tax columns but not in the figures on receipts, expenditures, and assets. Table 15.3 lists information on the Medicare program later in the chapter. As previously noted, the original social security payroll tax in 1937 was at a combined rate of 2 percent, of which 1 percent was paid by the employee and 1 percent was paid by the employer. The combined tax remained at this level until 1950, when it was increased to 3 percent. The progression of combined tax rate can be traced through 1984 to give an idea of how much it has grown.

Recall that the social security program was originally established to resemble an insurance program, with contributions required on income up to $3000 per year. Income above that level was not taxed. This meant that the maximum tax up through 1949 would have been $60, counting the employee's and the employer's share. The next column in the table lists how the maximum earnings subject to tax has increased over time. The maximum earnings taxed increased less rapidly than the price level through the early 1970s, but since then increases have exceeded the inflation rate. Note that because these taxes include money going to all branches of the social security program, Medicare is included after 1966.

The remainder of the table deals with receipts, expenditures, and assets only of the OASDI part of the program. The receipts column lists tax revenues collected for the program, while the expenditures column lists money paid out, including administrative expenditures.[5] The total assets column lists the amount of money in the OASDI trust funds, out of which benefits are paid. Recall that social security operates from an earmarked tax and in its present configuration cannot draw on general tax revenues.

The final column, which lists expenditures as a percentage of assets, reveals much about the evolution of the pay-as-you-go nature of the system. Until 1950 the program spent less than 10 percent of its assets every year, but as more people became eligible for social security as a result of having paid into the program, this figure began to rise. At this point Congress could have decided to limit benefits and raise taxes to make the social security system a funded system, but instead it chose to gradually increase benefits without a corresponding increase in taxes. In 1950, for example, benefits were increased by between 50 and 100 percent, followed by increases of 12.5 percent in 1952 and about 13 percent in 1954.[6] Even though taxes were also raised, not enough revenue was generated to maintain a funded system. Indeed, in the early 1950s social security could have been restructured relatively easily into a funded system by raising taxes without increasing benefits, but decisions made then eliminated the possibility of creating a funded system without major restructuring.

Additional increases in benefits granted in the early 1970s further eroded the system's

---

[5] Administrative expenses have recently been slightly more than 1 percent of the total benefits paid, so these expenses are a negligible amount of the social security program.

[6] *Social Security Bulletin*, Annual Statistical Supplement, 1984–1985, p. 5.

Table 15.2 Expenditures, Receipts, and Assets from the OASDI Trust Fund

YEAR	COMBINED TAX RATE	MAXIMUM EARNINGS TAXED ($)	RECEIPTS (MILLION $)	EXPENDITURES (MILLION $)	TOTAL ASSETS (MILLION $)	EXPENDITURES AS A PERCENT OF ASSETS
1937	2.0	3,000	767	1	766	0.1
1938	2.0	3,000	375	10	1,132	0.9
1939	2.0	3,000	607	14	1,724	0.8
1940	2.0	3,000	368	62	2,031	3.1
1941	2.0	3,000	845	114	2,762	4.1
1942	2.0	3,000	1,085	159	3,688	4.3
1943	2.0	3,000	1,328	195	4,820	4.1
1944	2.0	3,000	1,422	238	6,005	4.0
1945	2.0	3,000	1,420	304	7,121	4.3
1946	2.0	3,000	1,447	418	8,150	5.1
1947	2.0	3,000	1,722	512	9,360	5.5
1948	2.0	3,000	1,969	607	10,722	5.7
1949	2.0	3,000	1,816	721	11,816	6.1
1950	3.0	3,000	2,928	1,022	13,721	7.5
1951	3.0	3,600	3,784	1,996	15,540	12.8
1952	3.0	3,600	4,184	2,282	17,442	13.1
1953	3.0	3,600	4,359	3,094	18,707	16.5
1954	4.0	3,600	5,610	3,741	20,576	18.2
1955	4.0	4,200	6,167	5,079	21,663	23.5
1956	4.0	4,200	6,697	5,841	22,519	25.9
1957	4.5	4,200	7,381	7,507	22,393	33.5
1958	4.5	4,200	8,117	8,646	21,864	39.5
1959	5.0	4,800	8,584	10,308	20,141	51.2
1960	6.0	4,800	11,382	11,198	20,324	55.1
1961	6.0	4,800	11,833	12,432	19,725	63.0
1962	6.25	4,800	12,585	13,973	18,337	76.2
1963	7.25	4,800	15,063	14,920	18,480	80.7
1964	7.25	4,800	16,258	15,613	19,125	81.6
1965	7.25	4,800	16,610	17,501	18,235	96.0
1966	8.4	6,600	21,302	18,967	20,570	92.2
1967	8.8	6,600	24,034	20,382	24,222	84.2
1968	8.8	7,800	25,040	23,557	25,704	91.7
1969	9.6	7,800	29,554	25,176	30,082	83.7
1970	9.6	7,800	32,220	29,848	32,454	92.0
1971	10.4	7,800	35,877	34,542	33,789	102.2
1972	10.4	9,000	40,050	38,522	35,318	109.1
1973	11.7	10,800	48,344	47,175	36,487	129.3
1974	11.7	13,200	54,688	53,397	37,777	141.4
1975	11.7	14,100	59,605	60,395	36,987	163.3
1976	11.7	15,300	66,276	67,876	35,388	191.8
1977	11.7	16,500	72,412	75,309	32,491	231.8
1978	12.1	17,700	78,094	83,064	27,520	301.8
1979	12.26	22,900	90,274	93,133	24,660	377.7
1980	12.26	25,900	105,841	107,678	22,823	471.8
1981	13.3	29,700	125,361	126,695	21,490	589.6
1982	13.4	32,400	125,198	142,119	22,088	643.4
1983	13.4	35,700	150,584	152,999	19,672	777.8
1984	14.0	37,800	169,328	161,883	27,117	597.0

Sources: *Social Security Bulletin*, Annual Statistical Supplement, 1984–85, Table D, p. 23, and Table 14, p. 77.

Table 15.3 Medicare, Taxes, Receipts, Expenditures, and Assets

YEAR	COMBINED TAX RATE	RECEIPTS (MILLION $)	EXPENDITURES (MILLION $)	ASSETS (MILLION $)
1966	0.7	1.943	891	944
1967	0.7	3,559	3,353	1,073
1968	0.95	5,287	4,179	2,083
1969	0.95	5,279	4,739	2,505
1970	1.1	5,979	5,124	3,202
1971	1.1	5,732	5,751	3,034
1972	1.1	6,403	6,318	2,935
1973	1.15	10,821	7,057	6,467
1974	1.15	12,024	9,099	9,119
1975	1.15	12,980	11,315	10,517
1976	1.15	13,766	13,340	10,605
1977	1.15	15,856	15,737	10,442
1978	1.55	19,213	17,682	11,477
1979	1.50	22,825	20,623	13,228
1980	1.12	26,095	25,064	13,749
1981	1.3	35,725	30,342	18,748
1982*	1.65	37,998	35,631	8,164
1983*	1.25	44,567	39,337	12,858
1984*	1.0	46,720	43,257	15,691

*Excludes $12,437 million lent to the OASDI Trust Fund.

Source: *Social Security Bulletin*, Annual Statistical Supplement, 1984–85, Table D, p. 23, and Table 134, p. 201.

assets. The table shows the tax increases, partly in the form of higher rates and partly in the form of the increased income, that is covered under the social security system during that period. Assets in the system cannot now be considered a trust fund in any meaningful sense—the system's assets would cover less than two months of benefit payments.

Table 15.3 lists similar information for the Medicare program. Established in 1966, Medicare is funded from a portion of the social security tax. As the table shows, that amount varies from year to year. When initially established, Medicare received 0.7 percent out of the total 8.4 percent tax, or a little more than 8 percent of the system's total revenues. By 1978 that figure had risen to 1.55 percent, but by 1984 it had fallen back to 1 percent, or a bit more than 7 percent of the total. Unlike the other social security programs, Medicare has never had even the potential to become a funded health insurance program. Except in its initial year, Medicare expenses have always exceeded the amount in the Medicare trust fund.

Social Security as an Investment

From a personal standpoint an individual might be interested in whether social security provides a good rate of return on the money paid into the system, especially in light of the fact that in the near future these payments will exceed 15 percent of a person's income when both the employee's and the employer's contributions are considered. The answer to the question of whether social security is a good investment depends on several factors, including the structure of the future system, future tax rates, and the growth of future income in the country. One thing it does not depend on is how good an investment it has been for people in the past. Many early contributors did very well by the system because initially more people were paying into the system than were qualified to collect from it.

The Structure of the System

Many proposals for altering the social security system have been advanced, some of which are discussed in the next section. Keep in mind that social security is a government program established through the political process, which means it could be abolished in the same way; in the extreme case no benefits would be paid out. Other, less radical options for reform could reduce future benefits from the system. At this point we will assume that the basic structure of social security will remain essentially as it is today, but the possibility of a change in the structure of the system cannot be ruled out. One factor that could drastically alter whether the system is a good investment would be a major change in the benefit or tax structure of social security.

Future Tax Rates

The effect of future tax rates is relatively straightforward—higher future tax rates mean larger benefits to future recipients. Even though social security taxes are so high right now that it may be unrealistic to expect them to go much higher, this ultimately will be decided within the political system. It is worth noting that the increases in tax rates in the past have made social security a good investment for past contributors. The combined employee-employer tax rate was 2 percent in 1940, 3 percent in 1950, and 6 percent in 1960. As taxes have increased and the trust fund has been drawn down, current retirees have benefited by realizing a good return on their investment. However, because the trust fund is now depleted and taxes may be as high as is politically feasible, current contributors may find social security to be much worse from an investment standpoint than past retirees.

Growth in Income

The major determinant of whether social security will be a good investment is the growth in real income in the United States. Because retirees receive payments from current taxpayers, the faster income grows, the more money will be available for social security benefits. In a pay-as-you-go system the connection between income growth and future benefits is obvious—more income means more tax collections, which means higher benefit payments. But another important element of income growth must be considered. As the baby boom generation reaches retirement age early in the twenty-first century and more people become eligible for benefits, the more income there is to pay them, the less likely it is that a large-scale restructuring of the social security system will take place. Higher future income means that there will be less of a conflict between future taxpayers and future recipients.

Throughout the history of the system, social security has been a good investment for people who have paid in at low tax rates and received payment from taxpayers paying higher rates. But because tax rates are not likely to increase at the same rate in the future, the future payoff from social security cannot be expected to match its past payoff. Thus, how well current contributors do at retirement depends primarily on how much income rises in future years. One other key determinant concerns future changes in the social security system, to which we now turn our attention.

The Future of Social Security

As long as the basic pay-as-you-go structure of the social security system is retained, the future of social security can be succinctly summarized by stating that the total contributions will roughly equal the total benefits paid during a year. Given current projections, however, the current level of benefits can be paid out only if the payroll tax is substantially increased over and above the current scheduled increases.

A. H. Robertson, formerly chief actuary for the Social Security Administration, projects that a payroll tax of greater than 24 percent will be needed by the year 2035 to finance the current social security program.[7] Under what Robertson calls optimistic assumptions, the required tax could be as low as about 17 percent, but under pessimistic assumptions the tax could be as high as 43 percent. Lest the reader think that 2035 is a long time away, an individual born in 1970 will be 65 in 2035. What Robertson's projections suggest, in addition to the possibility of tax increases to finance the system, is that social security may not be able to survive in a political system where benefits can be voted away by taxpayers.

The Medicare program is responsible for a substantial part of the projected increase. Robertson calculates that a payroll tax of over 8 percent would be required to fund the medical benefits alone. As lifespans increase and as medical technology develops, such a projection certainly seems realistic. If the optimistic scenario holds, then perhaps a payroll tax of 17 percent could be used to continue the program in its present form for the foreseeable future. But under the pessimistic assumptions a payroll tax of 43 percent—in addition to the federal income tax and other taxes—is not realistic, which means the system would have to be changed.

A stopgap measure would be to use some general revenues (from the income tax and other sources) to supplement the payroll tax revenues, though such a solution would not directly address the program's problems. Another possibility would be to cut benefits. This could be done either across the board or perhaps according to a means test. That is, people with higher incomes would no longer be eligible for social security benefits. This would make social security more like other redistribution programs, but it might be viewed as a violation of trust to those who paid in to the program and then were not eligible for the benefits thought to be guaranteed.

---

[7] A. Haeworth Robertson, *The Coming Revolution in Social Security* (Reston, Virginia: Reston Publishing Company, 1981). See especially pp. 82–96.

Proposals for Reform

A number of proposals for reforming the social security system, mainly aimed at overcoming what reformers viewed as the main negative aspects of the program, have been made over the past several decades.[8] One issue that may be relevant to any reform is that the social security program really serves two conceptually distinct functions. It is an insurance plan, but it also is a welfare program. The insurance aspect of social security derives from the fact that contributors pay into the program as workers and receive retirement benefits and health insurance through Medicare when they retire. However, recall that benefits are not paid solely as a function of premiums paid in. For example, married couples with one worker receive a larger benefit than single people with the same contribution history. Furthermore, benefits are not proportional with respect to payments. In this sense the program is part insurance and part welfare.

Insurance and Welfare

The welfare aspect of the social security system can be justified to a certain extent. If a person were not receiving social security ben-efits, then that person would probably require some other type of public assistance. At least the social security program, unlike other redistribution programs, requires some history of earlier contribution to the program in order to receive benefits, and the benefits paid to some extent lessen the burden on other parts of the welfare system. Some reformers have suggested separating these two aspects of the system so that the insurance plan pays benefits strictly as a function of earlier premiums paid into the system while a separate welfare system pays additional benefits based on need. Pechman, Aaron, and Taussig advocate financing the social security system, like other government programs, out of general revenues.[9] Alicia Munnell advocates similar reform but supports retaining the payroll tax to finance the insurance function.[10]

One of the problems with the social security system is that in the past benefits for retirees have been relatively generous given the contributions of the beneficiaries. This is mainly because premiums have risen so much since the beginning of the program. For example, a current retiree can take advantage of relatively generous benefits even though in the early 1940s the combined employee's and employer's contribution was only 2 percent. The system could be a funded system today if benefits were paid as the present value of past contributions; the reason why virtually no fund exists is that past recipients have received benefits in excess of the value of their

---

[8]An overview of many of these programs is found in Peter J. Ferrara, *Social Security: Averting the Crisis* (Washington, D.C.: Cato Institute, 1982), ch. 10. Two government studies in the early 1980s, *Social Security in America's Future*, Final Report of the National Commission on Social Security, March 1981, and *Report of the National Commission on Social Security Reform*, January 1983 (chaired by Alan Greenspan and sometimes referred to as the Greenspan Report), have documented the potential problems with the future social security system and have noted that either benefits must be reduced or taxes increased to keep the system solvent. There seems to be little disagreement on these conclusions.

[9]Joseph Pechman, Henry Aaron, and Michael Taussig, *Social Security: Perspectives for Reform* (Washington, D.C.: Brookings Institution, 1968).

[10]Alicia H. Munnell, *The Future of Social Security* (Washington, D.C.: Brookings Institution, 1977).

contributions. Furthermore, there is little justification for paying generous benefits to those who retire with a relatively high level of wealth. By separating the insurance and welfare functions, all retirees would receive a fair return on their contributions, and especially needy retirees could receive welfare benefits.

Raising the Retirement Age

Another possibility would be to raise the retirement age at which individuals could begin earning benefits or to pay lower benefits to those who retired earlier. Currently, retirement benefits are reduced by 50 cents for every dollar of additional income earned, meaning that there is a substantial inducement to quit work at age 65 and begin collecting benefits. If the social security system itself did not induce retirement, the payments it would have to make to retirees would fall.

Eliminating Pay-as-You-Go

Other reformers want to eliminate the pay-as-you-go nature of the program and also provide for alternatives to the governmentally run retirement system.[11] These proposals involve guaranteeing benefits to those who are currently retired or are close enough to retirement that they can expect a net benefit from the program under its current terms. But younger workers, even if they have already contributed to the system, will end up paying more in in the future than the expected present value of their retirement benefits, which gives them little incentive to continue in the

system. These individuals could simply be required to contribute money that would have gone into social security into a private pension fund, such as an IRA account.

Such a system could require mandatory contributions to be made to the pension plan so as to reduce the number of retirees needing government welfare assistance. The individual's benefits would be guaranteed, because the IRA account would be owned by the individual, rather than just being a political promise that could be rescinded, as with the current social security system. During a phaseout of the pay-as-you-go system, though, revenue would still be needed to satisfy obligations to those who had spent a lifetime contributing to social security. This could be done either from general revenues or through a continuation of the payroll tax at declining rates.

Any realistic reform of social security must somehow deal with the fact that the current system has a tremendous unfunded liability of future claims and that the demographic characteristics of the population indicate that these claims cannot be honored without substantial (and perhaps politically unacceptable) tax increases. If the program must change, options for reform include reducing the welfare aspects of the program, raising the eligibility age for retirement benefits, and even instituting mandatory private pension funds, thereby eliminating the unfunded liability. The future of social security is of major interest, if only because such a substantial portion of wage income goes into the program and because so much of the population will be affected by any program changes.

---

[11] A summary of many proposals along these lines is given in Peter J. Ferrara, *Social Security: The Inherent Contradiction*, (Washington, D.C.: Cato Institute, 1980), ch. 10.

Conclusion

The social security program has grown rapidly since its inception in 1935, now covering about 90 percent of paid employees and consuming approximately 25 percent of the federal government budget. The social security system is unusual among federal government programs in that it is financed by an earmarked payroll tax, which makes it relatively easy for all contributors to see how much they are paying to support the system. Although the tax is shared between employers and employees, a simple tax-shifting analysis shows that it would make little difference to the ultimate burden of the tax whether the tax were borne entirely by employers or entirely by employees.

The social security program is compulsory for most workers, for several reasons. First, if individuals were not required to join, retirees who had not saved for their retirement years would place an additional burden on the welfare system. The requirement to participate helps lessen that burden. In addition, because it is a pay-as-you-go system, the requirement for participation ensures a steady flow of new contributors to finance the benefits of those who are eligible.

The pay-as-you-go system has the additional effect of reducing the amount of capital accumulation in the economy—lower investment today means less economic growth in the future. Capital accumulation is reduced because contributors correctly perceive that money contributed to social security today will be repaid in the future as a retirement benefit. In this sense social security contributions substitute for private saving. But because the contributions are directly paid out to beneficiaries, there is a reduction in saved funds available for investment. This reduction in investment today reduces the future productivity of the economy.

Social security really serves a number of functions. In part, it is a retirement plan, but it also has features of a welfare system built into it. Benefits are not paid strictly according to the present value of past payments, but rather take other criteria into consideration as well. Although the system has some characteristics of an insurance plan, its pay-as-you-go nature means that some people in the economy are financing transfers to others. Ultimately, the benefits that current contributors will receive is determined through the political process rather than based on how much the individual has contributed to the system.

Projections about the future of social security vary widely, but there is almost complete agreement that the present schedule of benefits can continue to be paid out only if the payroll tax is raised, perhaps by a substantial amount. Depending on whether the optimistic or pessimistic projections eventually are realized, the benefits presently promised may be unrealistic, and a major reform of the system may become necessary.

The intention here is not to alarm but to inform. Under optimistic projections current contributors could receive benefits similar to those now provided, but the current contributor cannot count on this. Unlike a private pension plan, in which the contributor owns a share of the plan's assets, future social security benefits for current contributors represent a political promise that future contributors will pay for the benefits. And if current projections concerning future revenues and expenditures for social security prove to be correct, a decision about how to bring revenues and expenditures into balance will have to be made through the political process.

Questions

1. Currently, the social security tax is shared equally between employer and employee. What effect would it have on the burden of the tax if the entire tax were placed on the employee? On the employer? Use graphs to illustrate your answer.

2. How does the unfunded nature of the social security system affect capital accumulation in the economy.

3. Explain why a pay-as-you-go system such as social security can give the initial beneficiaries a good return on their contributions but cannot sustain this return. Considering social security as a government program whose characteristics are therefore politically determined, explain why the political system will produce a pay-as-you-go rather than a funded system.

4. Explain several rationales for making the social security system compulsory rather than voluntary. Do you think that these rationales are adequate justification for a compulsory system.

5. Currently, members of Congress and civil service employees do not participate in the social security system. In view of the political nature of the system, how might social security differ if all government employees had to participate?

6. The social security program is partly an insurance plan and partly a form of welfare. What is the distinction between these two aspects of the program? How could this distinction come into play in any potential reform of the system?

7. In your opinion will the social security system provide a structure of benefits much like the present structure when you retire? If not, how do you think the system will differ? What reforms would you suggest to improve the social security system?

8. Is money paid into the social security system a good investment? Explain what factors you need to consider in formulating an answer.

PART SIX

Economic Activities of Government

CHAPTER SIXTEEN

Borrowing and Money Creation

The government can finance its expenditures in three ways—it can tax, it can borrow, or it can print new money. Where in the preceding chapters we analyzed taxation, in this chapter we discuss borrowing and money creation, examining the process by which financing decisions are made and then evaluating the consequences of borrowing and money creation. Because state and local governments operate under significantly tighter financing constraints than the federal government, the discussion in this chapter focuses on federal government finance. Some issues regarding state and local government finance will be looked at in Chapter 19.

Borrowing and money creation certainly relate to the subject of public finance—they are two of the three ways by which public sector activities are financed—but they are also important to other areas of economics. Macroeconomics examines the effects of debt and money creation on inflation, unemployment, interest rates, and other macroeconomic variables. The subdiscipline of monetary economics deals directly with the way in which money is created by the banking system and the effects of money creation and monetary policy.

In the sense that the mechanics of monetary and fiscal policy are not of as much interest here as their implications for public finance and democratic decision making are, the purpose of this chapter is to present material that will complement the analysis that takes place in these other economic subdisciplines.

We start with an examination of the process by which the government's decisions on public finance are made. How is it determined what combination of taxes, debt, and new money will be used to finance public sector spending? We then focus on the effects of using debt finance. This topic becomes especially relevant to public finance because some economists believe that there is no difference in real terms between the effects of taxation and debt finance.

Another issue of direct relevance is the political consequence of using debt and money creation as a vehicle of public finance. Our premise is that if debt and money creation can affect the economy, the politicians who control the process might use it for their own benefit. The implications of such actions to public sector decision making are significant, and they warrant further consideration. Yet another issue that will be discussed is the possibility of a balanced budget amendment. Why would Congress approve such an amendment, and if they would approve it, why do they not balance the budget without the amendment?

The Government's Financing Decisions

The government's financing decisions begin with the government budget. The government makes decisions on spending independent of decisions on revenue generation. The first step in the process can be viewed as the determination of the level of federal spending. Although the budgeting process involves the president and the Office of Management and Budget, and although the final budget must be approved by both houses of Congress, for now note simply that federal spending programs are approved by Congress with input from the President and that financing decisions must be made to determine how the revenue will be raised to pay for these programs. We will study the budgeting process in more detail in Chapter 17.

In this chapter the level of government spending will be considered as given, determined by the supply and demand process examined in Chapters 7 and 8. Congress must decide how much in tax revenue to raise to pay for the spending that it approves. The U.S. Treasury is then authorized by Congress to make payments for the programs and to collect the taxes that Congress has authorized. The Internal Revenue Service is the branch of the Treasury that oversees the collection of federal tax revenues. Thus, Congress approves a level of government spending and a level of taxes, and the Treasury writes the checks for the spending program and collects the tax revenue authorized by Congress.

Government Borrowing

A government budget deficit occurs when the government spends more than it collects in taxes, a surplus exists when tax revenues are greater than expenditures, and a balanced budget occurs when expenditures equal tax revenues. Since 1960 the government budget has been in deficit in every year except 1969. Therefore, in recent years the government consistently has obligated itself to pay out more in spending than it collects in taxes. The Treasury must finance this deficit by issuing bonds and using the resulting revenue to pay the government's bills. This issuance of government bonds is what is referred to as government borrowing. Because the Treasury must be authorized by Congress to borrow, periodically Congress will vote a higher debt ceiling so that the Treasury can borrow to cover the expenditures that Congress has approved. This is how the level of the national debt is determined.

Table 16.1 provides some idea of the government's borrowing activity and the level of the national debt since 1950. The first column lists the year, followed by the surplus or deficit in billions of dollars. Note that the budget had a surplus for three years in the 1950s and for two years in the 1960s, but from the 1970s on the budget not only has been in deficit in every year but also has been showing larger and larger deficits over time.

Table 16.1 The Federal Debt and Deficit (−) or Surplus (+) as a Percentage
   of Total Federal Spending and GNP*

YEAR	SURPLUS OR DEFICIT (BILLION $)	S OR D AS PERCENTAGE OF BUDGET	S OR D AS PERCENTAGE OF GNP	FEDERAL DEBT (BILLION $)	DEBT AS PERCENTAGE OF GNP
1950	−3.1	7.6	1.2	256.9	96.9
1951	6.1	13.4	2.0	255.3	81.6
1952	−1.5	2.2	0.4	259.1	76.4
1953	−6.5	8.5	1.8	266.0	73.6
1954	−1.2	1.4	0.3	270.8	74.4
1955	−3.0	4.4	0.8	274.4	72.1
1956	3.9	5.5	1.0	272.8	66.3
1957	3.4	4.4	0.8	272.4	62.8
1958	−2.8	3.4	0.6	279.7	63.1
1959	−12.8	13.9	2.7	287.8	60.7
1960	0.3	0.3	0.1	290.9	58.4
1961	−3.3	3.4	0.7	292.9	57.5
1962	−7.1	6.7	1.3	303.3	55.3
1963	−4.8	4.3	0.8	310.8	53.8
1964	−5.9	5.0	1.0	316.8	51.3
1965	−1.4	1.2	0.2	323.2	49.0
1966	−3.7	2.8	0.5	329.5	45.5
1967	−8.6	5.5	1.1	341.3	43.9
1968	−25.2	14.2	3.0	369.8	44.5
1969	3.2	1.7	0.4	367.1	40.3
1970	−2.8	1.4	0.3	382.6	39.5
1971	−23.0	10.9	2.2	409.5	39.7
1972	−23.4	10.1	2.1	437.3	38.7
1973	−14.9	6.1	1.2	468.4	37.4
1974	−6.1	2.3	0.4	486.2	35.3
1975	−53.2	16.0	3.6	544.1	36.8
1976	−73.7	19.8	4.5	631.9	38.5
1977	−53.6	13.1	2.9	709.1	38.1
1978	−59.0	12.9	2.8	780.4	37.3
1979	−40.2	8.0	1.7	833.8	35.4
1980	−73.8	12.5	2.9	914.3	35.5
1981	−78.9	11.6	2.7	1,003.9	34.8
1982	−127.9	17.2	4.2	1,147.0	37.7
1983	−207.8	25.7	6.5	1,381.9	42.9
1984	−185.3	21.8	5.2	1,576.7	44.0
1985	−212.3	22.4	5.4	1,827.5	46.4
1986	−202.8	20.7	4.8	2,112.0	50.4
1987	−143.6	14.5	3.2	2,320.6	51.1

*Percentages calculated by the author.

Source: *Economic Report of the President*, 1986, Table B-73. 1986 and 1987 are estimates.

Due to both inflation and real economic growth, the dollar figures in the table may not provide a completely accurate picture of the size of the deficit relative to the economy. The next two columns in the table list the deficit or surplus as a percentage of the total government budget and as a percentage of *GNP*. No clear trend suggests itself in those numbers until the late 1960s, when the deficit becomes an obviously larger percentage of both the budget and of *GNP*.

The next column lists the total federal debt, which does not show an obvious rapid rise until around 1970. However, inflation began to increase around that time as well, causing nominal *GNP* to increase. Even though the level of debt was increasing during the period, it was decreasing as a percentage of *GNP*, as listed in the final column. The table shows that the national debt was at its low as a percentage of *GNP* in 1981, but that it has increased rapidly as a percentage of *GNP* in the 1980s. These figures merely indicate the trends in the debt and deficit; later in the chapter the implications of deficit financing will be discussed in detail.

Money Creation

The money supply in the United States is controlled by the Federal Reserve Bank, or Fed for short. Although nominally an independent organization owned by member banks, the Fed has the characteristics of a government agency. Its top officers are chosen by the president and confirmed by Congress, it is given the monopoly right to issue money, it regulates the banking industry and both member and nonmember banks alike must abide by the Fed's regulations, and its charter comes from Congress and can be revoked by Congress. One important difference between the Fed and other agencies, though, is that the Fed's budget does not need to be approved by Congress.

Under a gold standard the central bank would issue money backed by gold held on reserve. Like all countries, the United States is not on a gold standard, though. The U.S. money supply is backed primarily by government bonds that are held on reserve by the Fed in much the same way that gold is held under a gold standard. To control the amount of money in the economy, the Fed buys and sells bonds. When the Fed buys bonds, it does so with newly created money, thus increasing the amount of money in circulation. When the Fed sells bonds, it exchanges the bonds for money that is taken out of circulation, thus reducing the money supply. The crucial point here is that the Fed can take the bonds issued by the Treasury and turn them into newly created money. The process is somewhat more complex than just printing up more money to pay the government's bills, but the net effect is the same.

As previously mentioned, Congress decides on the level of taxing and spending, which produces the deficit (or surplus). Then the Fed decides how much of the debt will be monetized, that is, how much to turn into newly created money. In very general terms this is the process by which the government chooses how to finance its expenditures— whether to use taxation, debt, or the creation of new money. With the basic process outlined, we can turn to the effects of these public finance decisions.

The Burden of the National Debt

Perhaps no problem in economics has been analyzed more thoroughly than the question of who bears the burden of the national debt. The history of this question is interesting enough—and closely enough related to the current issues—that it is worth reviewing. French economist Jean François Melon argued in 1735 that the national debt was not really a burden on the nation because the holders of the bonds were fellow countrymen.[1] In other words the debt was not a burden because, in essence, "we owe it to ourselves." Adam Smith noted this argument, and also his disagreement, in 1776 in his famous book *The Wealth of Nations*:

> In payment of the interest of the public debt, it has been said, it is the right hand which pays the left. . . . It supposes that the whole public debt is owing to the inhabitants of the country. . . . But that the whole debt were owing to the inhabitants of the country, it would not on that account be less pernicious.[2]

Smith went on to argue that with government debt borrowers did not need to assess the merits of public spending projects in the same way that they would need to assess private spending projects. A person lending to a private sector borrower would have to assess the merits of the spending project in order to judge the soundness of the loan, because if the money were not wisely invested, the lender would run the risk of having the loan default. In the public sector, however, repayment of the loan is guaranteed by the Treasury, which means the loan can be paid back as long as the government is able to collect taxes. In this light public sector borrowing need not be wisely invested, because taxpayers will have to foot the bill for repayment whether they like it or not. Smith went on to note: "The practice of [deficit finance] has gradually enfeebled every state which has adopted it."[3]

To summarize, Smith's argument was that with government borrowing there is no mechanism to ensure that the borrowed money will be wisely invested, and that, over time, ill-advised investments will eventually "enfeeble" the borrowing nation. Smith therefore found good reason to object to the argument that the debt is no burden because "the people of a nation owe it to themselves."

Ricardo and the Equivalence Theorem

The next major contributor to the debate over who should bear the burden of national debt was David Ricardo, whose views remain relevant even today. Ricardo developed what is known as the *Ricardian equivalence theorem*, which states that there is no real difference between the effects of financing government spending through taxation or through debt. Much of the current economic debate on the

---

[1] Jean François Melon, *Essai Politique sur le Commerce* (Amsterdam: F Changuion, 1735), ch. 23.

[2] Adam Smith, *The Wealth of Nations* (New York: Modern Library, 1937, originally published in 1776), p. 879.

[3] Smith, *The Wealth of Nations*, p. 881.

burden of the debt is built on the foundation that Ricardo laid in the early 1800s.[4]

The Equivalence Theorem

Ricardo reasoned that the burden of deficit finance would be no different from the burden of taxation to finance the same level of government spending because the present value of the future taxes to service the debt would be the same as the taxes if paid now. Keep in mind that the whole argument behind the equivalence theorem assumes that government spending is held constant, and the question is whether there will be any difference in financing the spending through taxation or debt. An example can help to clarify the principle.

With government spending held constant, the government lowers taxes by $1000 and instead borrows $1000, at 10 percent interest. Thus, $1000 in debt replaces $1000 in taxes. In this case taxpayers now have $1000 more than they would have had (due to lower taxes), but the government will owe $100 a year (10 percent of the $1000 borrowed) as long as the debt is not paid off. Future taxes will have to go up by $100 per year to pay the interest on the new debt, so in reducing taxes and substituting debt, the taxpayers get $1000 more today in exchange for $100 more in taxes every year until the debt is paid off.

At a 10 percent interest rate the present value of the $100 in future tax increases every year is $1000, so the present value of the future tax liability due to the debt issue is the same as the present value of the tax cut. The taxpayers receive an asset of $1000 today in exchange for a future liability with the present value of $1000. In essence, the govern-ment has forced the taxpayers to take out a loan by giving them $1000 today in exchange for a $1000 liability. Prudent taxpayers will not allow the government to alter their consumption patterns by exchanging debt finance for taxation, but will save the $1000 tax cut. At 10 percent interest the additional $1000 in savings will pay $100 per year, which can then be applied to the service of the debt. If taxes are ever collected to pay off the debt, then the $1000 can be withdrawn from savings and used to offset the higher taxes.

Ricardo's point is that by holding government spending constant and substituting debt for taxation, the present value of the future taxes to service the debt will just offset the value of the tax cut. The present value of taxpayers' wealth does not change, so the wise taxpayer saves the tax cut to offset the government's financing decision and pay the anticipated higher future taxes. Thus, according to the equivalence theorem, taxation and debt are equivalent in their real effects—it makes no difference whether the government uses taxation or debt to finance its expenditures.

Arguments Against the Equivalence Theorem

Ricardo saw another side to this argument, however.[5] Although an individual given a $1000 tax cut today in exchange for a $100 a year tax increase every year in the future will see no change in the present value of wealth, the individual receiving the money today will probably not save all of it. Rather, having to pay $1000 less in taxes this year, most individuals will probably spend at least some, and

[4]David Ricardo, *The Principles of Political Economy* (London: John Murray, 1817).

[5]See Gerald P. O'Driscoll, Jr., "The Ricardian Nonequivalence Theorem," *Journal of Political Economy* 85, no. 1 (Feb. 1977), pp. 207–210, for a discussion of Ricardo's views on the subject.

perhaps most, of the $1000 on consumption goods instead of saving it all. If the entire tax cut is not saved, then consumption will increase and the amount of resources available for investment will decrease. Recall that national income equals consumption plus investment plus government spending, so with government spending remaining constant and consumption increasing, investment must fall. The reason is that some money that would have been saved for private investment is now used to buy the additional government bonds.

Ricardo argued that if the government substituted debt for taxation, in effect it was forcing people to take out a loan that they would not otherwise have wanted. The rational thing to do, then, would be to save the entire reduction in taxes to offset the effects of the debt, so that the substitution of debt for taxation could have no real effects—this is the equivalence theorem. Ricardo recognized that most people would not save to offset the effects of lower taxes, however, and so argued that the theorem named after him was not in fact true.

The Current Issues

Two factors made the discussion of the burden of the national debt especially relevant after World War II. The first was the fact that the national debt increased by over five times from 1940 to 1945, from $48.5 billion to $259.1 billion. The second was the increasing acceptance among economists of Keynesian economics and the notions of using budget deficits as a tool to expand the economy during recessions or depressions. According to the Keynesian theory, the government might want to run deficits several years in a row to fight a recession, so naturally questions would arise about the burden of the debt, especially in light of the large accumulated debt after the war.

The answer generally accepted at the time was articulated by Abba Lerner in 1948.[6] Lerner argued that the debt was not a burden because for the most part it was owned by

Americans—that they owed it to themselves. This, of course, was the same argument made more than two centuries before by Jean François Melon. Given the history of the debate, it is surprising that Lerner's argument remained generally unchallenged throughout most of the 1950s.

The first serious questioning of Lerner's theory was done by James M. Buchanan in 1958.[7] Buchanan argued that the present sellers and purchasers of the public debt voluntarily agree to the transaction and so are not bearing the burden of the debt. However, future taxpayers who are forced to pay higher taxes as a result of the debt are being made worse off. The government, because of its ability to force future taxpayers to pay higher taxes, pushes the burden of the debt into the future. Once again, note the similarity between Buchanan's argument and the argument made by Adam Smith that deficit fi-

---

[6]Abba Lerner, "The Burden of the National Debt," in *Income, Employment, and Public Policy* (New York: Norton, 1948).

[7]James M. Buchanan, *Public Principles of Public Debt* (Homewood, Ill.: Irwin, 1958).

nance would gradually enfeeble a nation by burdening future taxpayers for repayment or debt service.

This appears to be a case of intellectual history repeating itself, but the story is not complete yet. In 1974 Robert Barro argued that the debt would not be a burden because if debt were used in place of taxation, saving would increase to offset the effects of the debt.[8] Barro, of course, was merely restating the Ricardian equivalence theorem. In the decade after Barro's article was published, a lively debate sprang up among economists, largely revolving around the issues that Ricardo identified over a century and a half ago.

The Equivalence Theorem and the Burden of the National Debt

This intellectual history is interesting in its own right, but the same topics raised in the past are also crucial to an understanding of the current issues about the burden of the debt. The two crucial issues are whether (and by how much) government borrowing affects interest rates, and whether the burden of the debt is passed on into the future.

One argument that has been made about the burden of the debt is that it cannot be passed into the future because only present resources can be used in the present. Thus, any opportunity cost of the debt must be incurred by using present resources rather than future resources—what will exist in the future cannot be used up now. The fallacy of this argument is easily explained. If the equivalence theorem does not hold, then there will be more present consumption and less present investment. Lower investment today means lower production possibilities in the future, so the burden of the debt will be passed on into the future due to lower capital accumulation.

Figure 16.1 illustrates this point. The Q axis measures the quantity of saving and investment and the r axis measures the interest rate. The demand curve D is the demand for funds by private sector investors, who borrow more at lower interest rates to give the demand curve its downward slope. The supply curve measures the supply of saving available for investment and is upward-sloping to indicate that higher interest rates entice savers to save more. Now add government borrowing G to the private sector demand for borrowing to give the combined demand for borrowed funds $D + G$. Total saving will rise from Q_0 to Q_1, but because government borrowing is the distance between D and $D + G$, the amount of private investing falls from Q_0 to $Q_1 - G$. In other words, private sector borrowing is lower due to government borrowing. To use a term frequently employed by economists, government borrowing has *crowded out* private borrowing, and this crowding-out effect is responsible for the lower level of private investment.

This explains how the burden of the national debt can be passed on to the future. Lower investment today lowers the future

[8]Robert J. Barro, "Are Government Bonds Net Wealth?" *Journal of Political Economy* 82 (Nov./Dec. 1974), pp. 1095–1117.

Figure 16.1 The Effect of Government Borrowing on Private Investment
When government borrowing is added to other demands for loanable funds, the demand curve shifts out (to $D + G$), which increases the interest rate and reduces the amount of private investment to $Q_1 - G$.

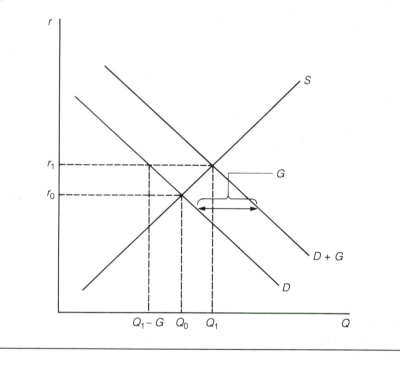

productive capacity of the nation, and it is this lower future productivity that constitutes a shifting of the burden of the debt from the present to the future. Figure 16.1 also answers the question about the effects of government borrowing on interest rates. Note that the interest rate rises from r_0 to r_1 as a result of the government debt, so government borrowing will have the effect of increasing interest rates as well.

The discussion in this section has thus far ignored the equivalence theorem. If the equivalence theorem is true, then private saving should increase to offset the government's borrowing. Figure 16.2 depicts the effect of the equivalence theorem. As in Figure 16.1, government borrowing causes the demand for borrowing to shift out to $D + G$, but according to the equivalence theorem saving will increase by an equal amount, to S', to offset the government borrowing. In this case the interest rate remains the same, as does the amount of private borrowing and investment. Apparently, what the effect of the debt is, who bears its burden, and how it affects interest rates are all dependent on whether the equivalence theorem is true. If it is true, the effects will be like those depicted in Figure 16.2, but if it is not, the effects are similar to those depicted in Figure 16.1.

Figure 16.2 Government Borrowing and the Equivalence Theorem
According to the equivalence theorem, the supply of saving will increase to match any increase in government borrowing, which leaves the interest rate unchanged and does not affect the amount of private investment, Q_0.

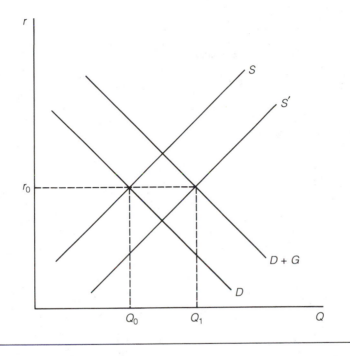

As with many issues, economists do not agree as to whether the equivalence theorem holds, but one way to test the theorem is to see if additional government deficits do lead to additional saving to offset the effects of the deficits. By one estimate an additional dollar of government debt causes an increase in saving of only 20 cents.[9] This suggests that the equivalence theorem does not hold, but rather that government debt does raise interest rates and lower current investment, passing the burden of the debt on into the future through lower present capital formation. This conclusion is supported by some economists[10] but opposed by others.[11]

Even while recognizing the logic of the equivalence theorem, it seems reasonable to

---

[9]R. G. Holcombe, John D. Jackson, and Asghar Zardkoohi, "The National Debt Controversy," *Kyklos* 34 (1981), pp. 186–202.

[10]See Martin Feldstein, "Government Deficits and Aggregate Demand," *Journal of Monetary Economics* 9 (1982), pp. 1–20.

[11]See, for example, Roger C. Kormendi, "Government Debt, Government Spending, and Private Sector Behavior," *American Economic Review* 73, no. 5 (Dec. 1983), pp. 994–1010.

assume that if taxes are cut and debt used to finance the tax cut, taxpayers will not save the entire tax cut. In other words the stringent assumptions behind the equivalence theorem are not likely to be satisfied. However, keep in mind that economists at present disagree about the issue and that research in the area is ongoing.

Money Creation and Public Finance

As noted, government spending can be financed through taxation, debt, or money creation; the latter can be thought of as a tool of public finance. Money creation would be a painless way to raise government revenues if it did not cause inflation. The government can, in essence, print up new money to pay for its expenditures, but the printing of new money causes the price level to rise as well. Because inflation is generally viewed as undesirable, it can legitimately be asked why the government would even resort to money creation as a method of public finance. One answer is that inflation generates revenue for the government over and above the amount of money created. Inflation also has some macroeconomic effects, which will be discussed later. This section focuses on the pure revenue-generating capabilities of inflation.

Money Creation as a Way of Raising Revenue

Because of the effects of debt on interest rates and investment, policymakers might prefer to create money to finance government expenditures simply to minimize the effects of debt finance on the economy, that is, to substitute additional money for additional debt. This is the first reason for money creation. If the government does not want to increase taxes or the debt, money creation is the only option left. However, the inflation caused by money creation can interact with taxation and debt finance, thus enhancing the revenue-generating capabilities of printing new money. The rest of this section will deal with these interactions.

Inflation and Bracket Creep

First, with a progressive tax system higher nominal incomes are taxed at higher tax rates. For a given real income one way to raise taxes is to pass a law mandating higher rates. However, higher tax rates are politically unpopular, so Congress rarely wants to legislate tax increases. Another way to increase tax revenues is to create inflation, which raises nominal incomes and pushes taxpayers into higher tax brackets. This phenomenon is known as *bracket creep*. People are pushed into higher tax brackets because inflation causes an increase in peoples' nominal incomes over and above their increase in real income. In this way higher tax rates will be in effect without having to pass a bill mandating an increase in taxes. The government actually has an incentive to create inflation in order to push taxpayers into higher tax brackets, thus increasing tax revenues.

Phantom Capital Gains

Second, inflation allows the taxation of phantom capital gains, that is, nominal capital gains that are due solely to inflation. Inflation causes the nominal value of real assets to rise along with the inflation, so if an asset is purchased in one year and sold many years later, tax will be owed on the nominal capital gain, even though no gain in real dollars may have been realized.

Phantom capital gains due to inflation were discussed in Chapter 13, so there is no need to review the issue in detail here, but note that in this case too the government could benefit from creating inflation. Both the effects of bracket creep and the taxation of phantom capital gains could be eliminated by the complete indexation of taxes for inflation. Indexation of personal tax rates was approved in President Reagan's 1981 tax package, but phantom capital gains are still taxed.

The Government as a Debtor

Another factor to consider is that inflation benefits debtors at the expense of creditors. If one has a loan that requires a fixed nominal payment, inflation lowers the real value of money and therefore the value of the fixed nominal payment, which is to the advantage of the debtor. Keep in mind that the largest single debtor in the economy is the federal government, and also that one way to lower the burden of national debt is to create inflation, which lowers the real value of the debt. Therefore, in real terms the interest payments and repayment of the principal (if that ever happens) will have a lower real value. Of course, the people who hold the government bonds will be made worse off because of the declining value of their assets, but the government will benefit because the real value of its liability will decline due to inflation.

Table 16.2 illustrates this point by comparing, for years beginning in 1970, the nominal debt to the real debt, deflated by the Consumer Price Index. In every year the government ran a deficit, the nominal debt continued to increase, though the real debt

Table 16.2 Real and Nominal Government Debt for Selected Years*

YEAR	NOMINAL FEDERAL DEBT (BILLION $)	REAL FEDERAL DEBT (1970 BILLION $)
1970	382.6	382.6
1971	409.5	392.6
1972	437.3	405.9
1973	468.4	409.3
1974	486.2	382.8[†]
1975	544.1	392.6
1976	631.9	431.0
1977	709.1	454.4
1978	780.4	464.5
1979	833.8	446.1[†]
1980	914.3	430.8[†]
1981	1,003.9	428.6[†]
1982	1,147.0	461.4
1983	1,381.9	538.5
1984	1,576.7	589.4
1985	1,827.5	659.7

*Based on figures in Table 16.1.

[†]Years in which there was a decrease in real debt but an increase in nominal debt. Real debt has been deflated by the Consumer Price Index to compute nominal debt.

increased at a considerably slower rate. The increase in nominal debt over the period was 478 percent, but adjusting for inflation the real debt increased by only 172 percent. Clearly, the government has been retiring a part of the debt by inflating it away. Furthermore, while the government ran a deficit every year, in four of the years shown—1974, 1979, 1980, and 1982—the real value of the debt actually decreased, meaning that inflation in those years more than offset the deficit.

Note that the implications for debt finance differ considerably during inflationary and noninflationary times. In inflationary periods the real value of government debt decreases, so the government can run a deficit equal to the debt times the inflation rate without increasing the government's real indebtedness. Consider the following example, which uses small numbers for the sake of simplicity. If the government's total debt is $100 and there is 10 percent inflation, the government can run a deficit of $100 × .10 = $10 and not increase the government's real indebtedness. Any deficit less than $10 in this example will actually leave the government with a lower indebtedness in real terms.[12]

During the 1970s the United States experienced relatively high inflation rates, so inflation compensated for some of the impact of the relatively large deficits during the 1970s. During the first half of the 1980s, increasing deficits coupled with declining inflation have caused the real impact of the deficits to be more significant. As noted earlier, there is some disagreement among economists about what the true effects of deficit finance are, but from a practical standpoint the issue is more important in the 1980s than it was in the 1970s.

In effect, inflation helps to repay the debt by lowering its real value. Those who do the repaying are the owners of the government bonds who suffer a decline in the real value of their assets. Of course, inflation helps to repay all loans, not just those made to the government. Homeowners during the 1960s and 1970s with large home mortgages were big beneficiaries of the unanticipated inflation that occurred during those decades.[13]

In summary, money creation represents one of the three ways the government can finance its expenditures. In addition to the revenues raised directly by the newly created money, money creation also causes inflation, which has effects on public finance. Through bracket creep and the taxation of capital gains, money creation increases tax revenues and, by lowering the real value of debt, helps to finance the government's deficit. Note that the federal government benefits directly in a number of ways from inflation, which gives those in government an incentive to cause inflation. In addition to inflation's effects on taxation and debt, however, there are still other reasons why it may be politically advantageous to create inflation.

The Political Business Cycle

Both money creation and government borrowing have short-run effects on the performance of the economy. Assuming that taxpayers do not fully capitalize the present value of future tax liabilities, that is, that the equivalence theorem does not hold, an increase in government spending or a reduction in taxes will increase output and lower unemployment in the short run. The same is true of an increase in the growth rate of the money supply,

[12]This theme is explored further in Robert J. Barro, "On the Determination of the Public Debt," *Journal of Political Economy* 87, no. 5, part 1 (Oct. 1979), pp. 940–971.

[13]Although it is true that interest rates will rise to reflect higher anticipated inflation rates, this is somewhat beyond the scope of the discussion here. Besides, the main point—that inflation lowers the real value of debts and benefits the borrower at the expense of the lender—remains valid.

which will provide the economy with more purchasing power than expected. These short-run effects are the foundation of Keynesian economic policy which advocates the use of monetary and fiscal policy to stabilize the economy. Unfortunately, in the long run these effects will disappear.

The macroeconomic details of the effects of monetary and fiscal policy will not be discussed here, as they are really more appropriate to a course in macroeconomics. However, the implications of the possibilities for political manipulation of the economy are directly relevant to the types of public finance decisions made by policymakers.

Political Success and Economic Performance

Some observers have pointed out that the success of politicians is often judged by the current performance of the economy. When the economy is doing well, voters are inclined to reelect politicians to office, but when the economy is performing poorly, incumbents are more likely to be unseated. Therefore, politicians have an incentive to stimulate the economy through monetary and fiscal policy to help ensure reelection.[14]

A stylized political business cycle is depicted in Figure 16.3, in which U^* represents the economy's natural rate of unemployment. Starting from, say, point A, politicians have an incentive to stimulate the economy, reducing

unemployment but causing some inflation; this is shown by a move from A to B. After the election the economy naturally moves back to point C, but at a higher rate of inflation. Perhaps the government will want to fight inflation at this point, thereby increasing unemployment as the economy moves to point D, but keep in mind that the negative effects of higher unemployment make politicians understandably more reluctant to fight inflation than to cause it in the first place. The economy thus returns to the normal rate of unemployment at point E. From there the process begins again, and the economy continues to spiral up to higher rates of inflation due to the political manipulation of monetary and fiscal policy.

Cyclical Behavior Since 1960

How well does this theory describe reality? Figure 16.4 shows the actual data on inflation and unemployment from 1960 to 1986. Although the turns do not correspond perfectly to election years, the same general spiraling effect described in the political business cycle theory is evident. Some details are also of interest. Note that the high inflation and unemployment in 1980 coincides with the end of President Carter's term, where Carter was defeated by a landslide. Also note the declining inflation and unemployment leading up to President Reagan's landslide reelection in 1984.

The theory of the political business cycle must be taken seriously to the extent that it is possible to use monetary and fiscal policy to manipulate the economy. Economic theory is founded on the premise that people respond to incentives, and it is only reasonable to expect that politicians who want to be reelected will respond to the incentives they have to use monetary and fiscal policy to that end. There

---

[14]See William D. Nordhaus, "The Political Business Cycle," *Review of Economic Studies* 42 (April 1975), pp. 169–190, C. Duncan McRae, "A Political Model of the Business Cycle," *Journal of Political Economy* 85 (April 1977), pp. 239–263, and Richard E. Wagner, "Economic Manipulation for Political Profit: Macroeconomic Consequences and Constitutional Implications," *Kyklos* 30, fasc. 3 (1977), pp. 395–410, for discussion of the political business cycle.

Figure 16.3 A Political Business Cycle Before elections the government has an incentive to stimulate the economy, which causes movements like that from *A* to *B*. Later, the economy moves to a long-run equilibrium at *C*. The government might try to fight inflation, causing the moves from *C* to *D* to *E*, but it has less of an incentive to pursue anti-inflationary policies that produce undesirable results in the short run. From point *E* the process begins again, causing ever-increasing spirals upward in the diagram.

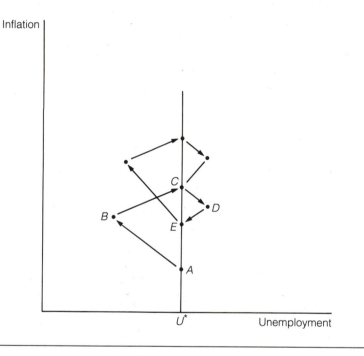

appears to be a significant relationship between the probability of reelection and the performance of the economy, but even if there is not, the belief that there may be still provides the political incentives to use economic policy for political benefit. Perhaps the most important difference between ideal macroeconomic policy and policy in the real world is that in the real world politicians determine the course of public policy. Clearly, politicians have the incentive to use economic policy for their own political ends if at all possible.

Milton Friedman has frequently proposed that, rather than allow discretionary monetary policy, the money supply be mandated to grow at a certain low rate each year (say, 3 to 5 percent). By requiring a steady rate of growth of the money supply, monetary policy could not be used to manipulate the economy. Although monetary policy might indeed have the potential to smooth out fluctuations in the economy, a number of uncertainties are involved. Furthermore, in light of the incentives for political manipulation, a steady rate of

Figure 16.4 Inflation and Unemployment: 1960–1986 The actual inflation and unemployment data from 1960 to 1986 show the clockwise spiraling phenomenon depicted in a stylized way in Figure 16.3, which lends some support to the notion of a political business cycle.

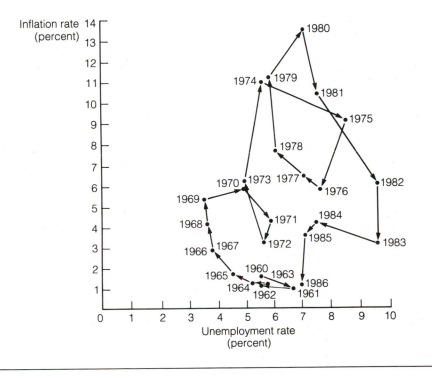

growth of the money supply is likely to be more stabilizing than discretionary monetary policy. Another proposal aimed at curbing manipulative economic behavior is the balanced budget amendment, which we will now examine.

The Balanced Budget Amendment

One of the major economic issues of the 1980s has been the chronic government budget deficit. An oft-proposed solution to the problem has been a constitutional amendment requiring a balanced budget; in fact, such an amendment was actually proposed before Congress in 1982. On the surface a balanced budget amendment is straightforward—it simply requires that the federal government not spend more than it raises in tax revenues for a given fiscal year—though most such proposals also contain some type of escape clause. For example, in the 1982 proposal a vote of three-fifths of Congress or a declaration of war would have been needed for Congress to approve spending in excess of tax revenues. However, a balanced budget amendment actually encompasses a number of complex issues and raises many unanswered questions. For instance, if a balanced budget amendment were in place, how would one make sure that Congress did not spend more than tax revenues? If a deficit were run, would there be any penalties?

What Counts as Government Spending?

Another question involves what should count as government spending. Currently, a number of "off-budget" programs, such as the Postal Service, are not included in government spending, though proponents of a balanced budget amendment think they should be. The off-budget issue is relatively easy to deal with, but there may be other ways to spend without raising revenues from the current budget.

One way is to buy something now but pay for it later. Government retirement programs fall into this category, because part of the compensation for an employee is the deferred compensation of the retirement benefits. The social security program is a prime example of this. Should the accrued liabilities of social security be counted in the government budget? If this answer is easy, consider a military procurement contract that stipulates payment when the items are delivered. The contract could be signed now, without any current expenditure, and payment deferred to the fu-

ture. In the future Congress could argue with some justification that the budget could not be balanced because of commitments made by previous congresses.

Another question arises with the government guarantee of loans, an area that will be familiar to many students. There is no out-of-pocket expense when the government guarantees loans, but in the event that the borrower defaults (as often happens with government guaranteed loans), then the government must repay the loan. Here is another instance where the government can obligate itself to future expenditures without incurring any current expense.[15]

There is yet another important factor to consider. In the face of a balanced budget constraint, the government could reduce its spending by eliminating spending programs and passing legislation requiring individuals to accomplish the same results without, or at reduced, compensation. The military draft provides a good example. The dollar expense of procuring military manpower could be reduced by drafting personnel and paying them low wages. In this way some of the cost of military manpower would be borne directly by the draftees, but less tax revenue would be required. Similarly, federal dollars could be spent on environmental programs or regulations could force individuals and businesses to accomplish the same results without compensation. Chapter 18 discusses in more detail how regulation can be used as a form of taxation. Within the context of a discussion on bal-

---

[15] The reader might again want to consider the issue of whether the government runs a deficit if the real value of the debt does not increase, as for example when inflation erodes the real value of the debt. That issue, as well as some others discussed here, are considered in Robert Eisner and Paul J. Pieper, "A New View of Federal Debt and Budget Deficits," *American Economic Review* 74, no. 1 (March 1984), pp. 11–29.

ancing the federal budget, though, it should be apparent that the government can produce a budget that appears to be closer to balance by passing regulations that replace government spending programs.

Political Realities

Thus, opponents of the balanced budget amendment see potential problems both in enforcing it and in measuring what should count in the budget. As with anything as complex as the federal budget, potential loopholes will always exist. Opponents argue that the amendment cannot be adequately enforced and that it is better not to burden the Constitution with an unenforceable provision.

However, some arguments in favor of a balanced budget amendment can be made as well. Proponents see the amendment as an opportunity to legally mandate fiscal responsibility. In response to popular demand, Congress has shown at least some willingness to consider the measure, which raises several interesting questions. Why would Congress agree to a measure that would constrain them in this way? Why do they not balance the budget without the amendment if they want a balanced budget?

For one thing individual representatives might agree to the amendment now because it would not come into force for a number of years. By supporting the measure now, they can give the appearance of fiscal responsibility while still spending as usual. This is an example of the political shortsightedness that was discussed in Chapter 7. For another, the budget is not balanced now because of the budgeting procedures that make spending popular but taxation unpopular. Politicians simply respond to the demands of their constituents, and they could agree to a balanced budget amendment that would constrain future congresses if they heard a demand for it.

Indeed, proponents of the amendment see the realities of the political process as a potential selling point of a balanced budget amendment. The current political structure almost guarantees continued deficits, but the situation could be turned around by shortsighted politicians who, though not willing to slow government spending now, would be willing to constrain future congresses.

The Gramm-Rudman Act

In late 1985 Congress passed a law that would require the budget deficit to be reduced by equal increments each year, producing a balanced budget by 1991. The law is named the Gramm-Rudman Act after its sponsors, Senators Phil Gramm and Warren Rudman. Although the Gramm-Rudman Act is not a constitutional amendment, it is intended to have the same effect as a balanced budget amendment. Before the act was a year old, its enforcement provisions were declared illegal. Nevertheless, its sponsors continue to claim that it would be effective in producing a balanced budget, though this remains to be seen. Note that if the provisions of the act were carried out, it would become more constraining over time.

The Gramm-Rudman Act mandates that if budget targets are not met, spending on certain programs must automatically be cut to meet the deficit target. Entitlement programs (social security, most income transfer programs) are exempt from the cuts, making the automatic cuts fall most heavily on national defense and nontransfer spending programs. Gramm-Rudman will provide an interesting test of congressional resolve to balance the budget.

Congress can meet its targets either by cutting whatever programs it wants or by raising taxes, so the provisions of the act will be invoked only if Congress is unable to meet its budget-balancing targets. The idea behind the act is that with the threat of across-the-board cuts, Congress will take the initiative to meet the targets to avoid the automatic cuts. Other options are also open to Congress, how-ever, the most obvious being to amend or re-peal the act. Indeed, the first step in this direc-tion was taken in 1986 when the courts declared the enforcement provisions of the act to be unconstitutional.

Conclusion

The government can finance its expenditures in three ways: taxation, debt, and money cre-ation. Having analyzed taxation extensively in previous chapters, we focused here on debt finance and money creation. The key question with regard to debt finance is whether taxa-tion and debt are equivalent in their real ef-fects. They would be if individuals saved in order to offset their future tax liabilities due to debt, but it is probably unrealistic to expect taxpayers to behave in this way. In other words the equivalence theorem does not hold, which means the burden of debt finance is passed on into the future. This happens be-cause government borrowing causes lower private investment at the time of the borrow-ing, thus lowering the amount of capital goods available in the future. Government borrowing not only crowds out private invest-ment, it also has the effect of raising inter-est rates.

Money creation has secondary effects in ad-dition to substituting for debt or taxation. The creation of money to finance the govern-ment's expenditures causes inflation, and in-flation raises tax revenues through bracket creep and through the taxation of phantom capital gains. Inflation also helps pay off the government debt by reducing its real value. Therefore, the government has an incentive to create new money as a form of public fi-nance, not only because the money can be used to pay the government's bills but also be-cause the resulting inflation helps to raise taxes and service the debt. Complete index-ation of the tax system is one way to eliminate the effects of money creation on taxation, but the effects on debt will remain.

In the short run both debt and money cre-ation have effects on real economic activity. Keynesian economic policy is built on the premise that monetary and fiscal policy can be used to help stabilize the economy. If this is true, however, one can expect for politicians to stimulate the economy through the use of monetary and fiscal policy to help the econ-omy look good before elections. This idea forms the foundation of the political business cycle. The political business cycle suggests that economic instability may be caused by political manipulation of the economy to further the private ends of politicians. At the least, it must be recognized that the growing inflation in the 1970s and the resulting recession in the early 1980s, when inflation was slowed, resulted from political decisions, and that this instabil-ity can be more properly called a government cycle than a business cycle.

A number of proposals aimed at limiting the potential for political manipulation of the economy have been advanced, including a balanced budget amendment to the Constitu-tion and a requirement for a fixed rate of growth of the money supply. The balanced budget amendment would eliminate the pos-sibility of debt finance, and the fixed money growth rule would (if fixed at a low rate) eliminate the inflationary consequences of money creation. In 1985 Congress passed the Gramm-Rudman Act in an attempt to balance the budget; the act, though not a constitutional amendment, was viewed as a legally binding method of achieving a balanced budget at the time it was passed. These ideas all represent methods of limiting the ability of government policies to create instability, but we must also acknowledge the potential for political manipulation of economic policy.

Questions

1. What are the three ways by which the government can finance its expenditures? Explain the process through which the government makes its financing decisions.

2. Is the Federal Reserve a government organization or an institution independent of government? Give arguments on both sides of the question.

3. It has sometimes been argued that the national debt is not a burden because "we owe it to ourselves." Assess the validity of this argument. What did Adam Smith have to say about this argument?

4. What is the Ricardian equivalence theorem? Give arguments that support and that oppose the validity of the theorem. Do you think that the equivalence theorem holds?

5. Explain three reasons why the government has an incentive to finance its expenditures through money creation.

6. Explain the political business cycle. Why do those in government have an incentive to create such a cycle? How could it be prevented?

7. Considering the possibility for political manipulation of public financing decisions, would a balanced budget amendment be desirable? How about a constitutional amendment requiring a fixed rate of growth of the money supply? Discuss the advantages and disadvantages of each.

8. What was the objective of the Gramm-Rudman Act? Compare the stated intentions of the act with its actual consequences.

CHAPTER SEVENTEEN

The Government Budgeting Process

*T*his chapter focuses on the procedures by which the federal government determines its levels of spending and taxing. In examining how the federal budget is proposed and approved, we discuss not only the actual steps taken to produce a budget but also the decision-making criteria that contribute to ultimate spending levels for various programs. A section is also devoted to benefit-cost analysis, which is a method for determining whether a public spending program will generate net benefits for the population. Programs seldom live or die based on the results of benefit-cost analysis, but the analysis is frequently undertaken anyway. In this chapter we also examine some of the differences between taxing and spending proposals in the federal budget.

Where many of the earlier chapters provided some theoretical background on the way in which government decisions are made and the impacts of those decisions, this chapter relates theory to the reality of the budgeting process. The chapter, while describing some tools that can be used to try to effectively allocate resources, also recognizes the real world political and informational constraints that sometimes prevent such tools from working as smoothly as theoretical models suggest they should.

From a normative standpoint the role of the budgeting process is to allocate scarce resources to their most highly valued uses. To accomplish this, the government must first assess the relative worth of various programs, that is, whether they should be produced in the public sector. Then the government must decide if the resources are available for the programs, and to what extent. Some programs that appear worthwhile in isolation may not be feasible within the context of the overall budget if the revenue cannot be generated. The soaring budget deficit has become a major economic issue in the 1980s, which implies that certain worthy programs may lose some or all of their funding so the budget can be reduced. As in private finance, possible areas of spending must be weighed against each other in light of the opportunity cost of raising resources to pay for the programs.

This chapter examines the process by which this is done.

The Federal Budgeting Process

The federal budgeting process has undergone some significant changes in this century. Before 1921 federal agencies would submit their budgetary requests to the Treasury Department, which would then forward the requests to Congress; the president was not directly involved. In view of the relatively low level of government expenditures before World War I, this system made some sense—agency requests were relatively small, and the federal government was able to run a surplus during normal times. In 1913 federal government expenditures were 2.5 percent of *GNP*, but by 1921 they had doubled to 5.1 percent of *GNP*, and a new budgetary system was implemented.[1]

Budgetary Reform in the Twentieth Century

The Budget and Accounting Act of 1921 directly involved the president in the budgetary process by requiring the president to submit a budget to Congress, and it established the Bureau of the Budget to assist the president in drawing up a budget. The act also created the General Accounting Office, the congressional agency that audits the government's activities.

The budgetary process has undergone some reform since 1921. The Bureau of the Budget was moved to the newly created Executive Office of the President in 1939, and in 1970 was reorganized and named the Office of Management and Budget (OMB). However, the basic process of presidential preparation of a budget with the assistance of OMB and the submitting of the budget to Congress for approval remains unchanged. The executive branch of government has the primary responsibility for developing the government's budget, especially in its early stages.[2]

The federal government's fiscal year begins on October 1 of the preceding calendar year, so that, for example, October 1, 1987, would be the first day of fiscal year 1988. The federal budgeting process begins well over a year in advance of the beginning of the fiscal year with the development of budget requests by government agencies. These requests are submitted to the OMB for the development of the president's proposed budget.

The President's Budget

OMB is responsible for developing the president's budget, which is submitted to Congress fifteen days after Congress meets, usually in February. To draw up the budget, OMB solicits requests from federal agencies for funding in the year in question. Based on our study of

---

[1] See Thomas D. Lynch, *Public Budgeting in America* (Englewood Cliffs, N.J.: Prentice-Hall, 1979), ch. 1, for a discussion of the evolution of the budgetary process.

[2] Lance LeLoup, *The Fiscal Congress* (Westport, Conn.: Greenwood Press, 1980), gives an account of budget reform.

public sector supply in Chapter 8, we would expect for budget-maximizing agencies to request budgets that are inefficiently large. Recall the strong correlation between budget size and salaries, power, prestige, and work environment. Furthermore, because it is difficult to calculate anything remotely similar to profits and losses for government agencies, a measure of the agency's success is often taken to be the size of the agency's budget.

With all agencies facing the same incentives, the sum of the agencies' requests will be unacceptably large, which means that most agencies can count on the OMB budget allocating the agency less than its request. This suggests that agencies will also request excessive budgets based on the knowledge that their final budgets will be smaller than requested.

The request for excessively large budgets is not necessarily a negative element in the budgeting process, however. OMB, the president, and the Congress cannot possibly be as aware of all of the agencies' possibilities as the agencies themselves will be. Therefore, the budget request from the agency really is a method for the agency to put its best foot forward to show those who must approve the budget what might be accomplished with full funding. In a sense the budget requests can be viewed as a menu of choices for those determining the budget. Obviously, everything on the menu cannot be selected. The agencies are acting as advocates for their programs, thus making it easier for the president and Congress to evaluate the budget alternatives.[3]

To review, OMB is an executive agency, which means it reports to the President. OMB evaluates agency proposals, makes spending and revenue forecasts, and is responsible for drawing up the president's budget. The budget is a political as well as an economic document, and it is drawn up after consultation with and advice from the Treasury Department, members of Congress, and the Council of Economic Advisors. Ultimately, the president uses all of this input to develop the budget that is presented to Congress.

The Congressional Budget

Congress then evaluates the president's budget with the assistance of the Congressional Budget Office (CBO), which was established in 1974 to provide budgetary analysis to Congress. CBO submits a report to congressional budget committees by April 1, and after an evaluation process that runs through April 15, budget resolutions are presented to both houses for the first time. These initial resolutions provide estimates and are scheduled for approval by May 15.

After approval of the initial budget resolution, the House Ways and Means Committee and the Senate Finance Committee hold hearings on specific appropriations bills. Action on all of the bills should be completed before any of them are brought to the floor for consideration. Then another budget resolution is brought before Congress by September 15, and if reconciliation between the House and Senate bills is needed, it must be done by September 25. Considering the new fiscal year begins on October 1, this schedule leaves little leeway.

However, Congress does not always stick to this timetable. For example, Congress was two months late in passing their second budget resolution in 1981, and it never did pass the resolution in 1982. Without a budget agencies have to rely on a continuing resolution for financing, which in essence continues the

---

[3]See Aaron Wildavsky, *The Politics of the Budgetary Process* (Boston: Little, Brown, 1979), for a discussion of budgetary strategy.

agency's existing rate of spending into the next fiscal year. And even when a budget is passed, Congress may pass additional appropriations bills at any time it desires, which means Congress is not constrained by the budget that it passes at the beginning of a fiscal year.

Incrementalism

The previous section outlined the institutional process by which the federal budget is determined, but this really offers little insight into how public sector production decisions are actually made. For example, by what criteria does the government decide how much more resources to allocate to flood control, or that farm subsidies should be reduced but national defense increased?

Davis, Dempster, and Wildavsky have suggested that an agency's budget for one year will tend to be its last year's budget plus some additional increment.[4] This budgetary theory is known as *incrementalism*. Taken at face value, the theory of incrementalism suggests that Congress and the president exert relatively little control over the budgetary process. The federal budget is complex, to be sure, and with so many agencies demanding, and receiving, appropriations, it is difficult to carefully review each, especially when the agencies produce nothing related to profits and losses by which spending can be evaluated.

The Effects of Special Interests

In addition to the difficulty of determining how effective various budgetary appropriations are, the influence of special interests, including the agencies themselves, must be considered. Each program has a set of constituents who benefit from the program and who will therefore be very knowledgeable about it. To eliminate or reduce the program will harm these special interests while benefiting the general public, but recall that the general public tends to be rationally ignorant of most of what the government does. This means that individuals will probably be unaware of the benefits of reducing the expenditure. As a result, political pressure tends to work toward the expansion rather than reduction of existing programs. This is a direct implication of the special interest theory of government discussed in Chapter 7.

Incrementalism and Efficiency

Incrementalism can be easily understood from two different perspectives. It makes sense within the framework of the special interest theory of government. Whereas special interests want to see appropriations to the programs that benefit them increased, the general public has little incentive to lobby for a cut in a program, because the benefits from

---

[4]Otto A. Davis, M.A.H. Dempster, and Aaron Wildavsky, "On the Process of Budgeting: An Empirical Study of Congressional Appropriation," *Public Choice* 1 (Fall 1966), pp. 63–132, and "A Theory of the Budgetary Process," *American Political Science Review* 60 (Sept. 1966), pp. 529–547.

a cut will be disbursed throughout the nation rather than going to a concentrated group. Incrementalism also makes sense when the complexity of government spending is considered, and keeping in mind that there is no profit and loss indicator to suggest where federal dollars are being best spent.[5] In the absence of a clear-cut indicator of the success of a government program, a legislature may be able to do no better than to increase program budgets by approximately the same amount. Obviously successful programs might be increased a little more while less successful programs are increased a little less, but budgets tend to increase at about the same rate because legislators do not have enough information to budget more precisely than this. In this light incrementalism becomes a rule of thumb for making budgetary decisions.

Davis, Dempster, and Wildavsky, who studied incrementalism in public finance, also observed that the actual increments by which agency budgets were being increased varied both for different agencies and for the same agency over time. This suggests that incrementalism cannot be a complete theory of the government budgeting process. Reflecting on the difficulty of determining the effectiveness of government expenditures, incrementalism may make some sense. Programs that are popular or that show increasing demands will be increased by larger increments, while those that were less in demand will receive smaller budgetary increments.

This view of incrementalism shows it to be a rational economic policy, given the limited knowledge about the efficacy of particular government programs. If a program does not appear to be cost-effective at the margin, the solution is to reduce its budget (or increase it by a smaller increment than the budget as a whole) until the program provides a satisfactory return. Likewise, a program that appears to be a good value for the money should rationally be increased by a larger increment until the additional increments no longer appear so worthwhile. And although it is difficult to evaluate the benefits—and often the costs—of government programs, this should not deter us from trying. Indeed, certain principles and techniques can be applied to the evaluation process.

Program Budgets Versus Line Item Budgets

In general budgets can be organized either by program or by line item. A program budget groups expenditures by the program goals they are intended to achieve, whereas a line item budget groups expenditures by the types of items that are purchased. For example, a university's budget might be organized according to line item, including expenditures for faculty salaries, utilities, office supplies, building maintenance, and so on. This would be a line item budget. Alternatively, the budget could be composed of expenditures on business education, arts and sciences, engineering, and so on. Here the budget is composed of programs, so it is a program budget. Each of these budgets could be broken down further, of course. In the line item budget of-

---

[5] Along these lines see Friedrich A. Hayek's insightful essay, "The Use of Knowledge in Society," *American Economic Review* 35, no. 4 (Sept. 1945), pp. 519–530.

fice supplies would include paper, pencils, and typewriter ribbons; in the program budget business education could be broken down into economics, accounting, finance, and so on. In short, the line item budget enumerates by items purchased, whereas the program budget enumerates by objectives sought.

Line item budgets can be useful at times, but they do not give much insight into whether the budgeted expenditures are being effectively spent. How would one evaluate, for example, whether $200 is too much to spend on pencils? The answer lies in the value of the output that the pencils produce. Combined with other resources, the pencils are intended to produce a certain output, and the effectiveness of the expenditures can best be measured by comparing the level of expenditures on a program with the benefits that the program produces. Thus, in order to evaluate the effectiveness of government expenditures, they should be grouped by program wherever possible, so that the costs of attaining certain objectives can be compared to the benefits.

The Planning-Programming-Budgeting System

When President Kennedy took office in 1961, he instituted a reform in the procedure by which the Bureau of the Budget evaluated projects. He instituted a system called Planning-Programming-Budgeting (PPBS), in which government expenditures were grouped by objective in order to facilitate benefit-cost analyses. Under PPBS the government first defined the objectives sought by government activity, then considered alternatives for achieving the objectives, and finally evaluated the costs and benefits of each alternative. President Johnson was so impressed

with the system that in 1965 he required all executive agencies in the federal government to participate in a PPBS system. The requirement was dropped by President Nixon in 1971, but that decade of experience firmly established benefit-cost analysis as a tool for evaluating federal programs.

In some instances such a system may work well, but in other cases it is not well suited to the types of decisions the government must make. PPBS often indicates the need for either a major overhaul of a government program or no action at all. The more realistic option of merely adjusting the growth rate of a program does not fit into the PPBS mold.[6] Even though PPBS is no longer an integral part of the budgetary process, the concept of budgeting for programs rather than line items remains a viable tool, and the benefit-cost analyses that went along with PPBS are still done for many government programs.

In short, budgets should be organized along program lines rather than as line item budgets to facilitate an evaluation of the effectiveness of government spending in particular areas. Although such analysis is not done for every program every year, it is an important part of the process by which new programs are considered for adoption. The principle of benefit-cost analysis is fairly straightforward—one simply compares the costs and benefits of programs and produces the programs that generate net benefits—but a number of difficult questions arise in actually carrying out such an analysis.

---

[6]See Aaron Wildavsky, *The Politics of the Budgetary Process* (Boston: Little, Brown, 1979), ch. 6, for a critique of the PPBS process.

Benefit-Cost Analysis

Benefit-cost analysis is intended to compare the benefits and costs of a program and will typically be performed when a program is in its planning stages to indicate whether the program should be enacted. This requires that both the benefits and the costs of a project be weighed, which means that they must first be estimated. The various steps involved in a complete benefit-cost analysis will be outlined here.

Enumerating the Options

The first step is to enumerate the options available. Sometimes the only option will be to undertake or not to undertake a project, but often other options will present themselves. For example, if a bridge is being considered, a number of potential sites may exist, several types of bridge may be possible, and even the number of lanes can vary. In order to pick the best option, all must be evaluated. This step may seem almost too elementary to mention, but keep in mind that the best option can never be selected unless it is considered. Frequently, a benefit-cost analysis will only compare the proposed program to the status quo, leaving open the possibility of overlooking an option better than the one being considered.

Enumerating the Costs and Benefits

The next step is to enumerate the costs and benefits of each option, thus allowing the analyst to see what costs have to be compared to what benefits. Enumeration of the benefits is not always easy—not only might some benefits or costs be overlooked, but some might also be counted twice. In addition, there may be secondary effects that should be included in the analysis. Some examples can help illustrate the process of enumerating costs and benefits.

In examining the benefits of building a bridge that could be used for shipping in an agricultural region, one will want to consider the lower shipping costs of farmers near the bridge as a benefit. However, even though the value of agricultural land will also rise as a result of the bridge, the increased value of land should not be included as a benefit, because the higher value of the land merely reflects the capitalization of the lower shipping costs. The land will be more valuable because it will be cheaper to ship the products grown on it, which means the increase in the value of the land should be equal to the present value of the lower shipping costs from the land. Thus, either one or the other should be included, but not both. That is, one must be careful not to double count the benefits (or costs) in a benefit-cost analysis.

The mistake of double counting is most easily made when both a stock and the flow that creates that stock are counted. In the chapters on taxation, income was shown to be a flow that emanates from a stock of wealth, so that an increase in the present value of the stock results from an increase in the value of the flow; the two are inseparable. This is clear in the bridge-building example, where an increase in the flow of income that can be produced from the property results in an increase in the value of the property. Both should not be counted as benefits because they are really only different ways of measuring the same thing.

In addition, any type of improvement is likely to have secondary effects. For example, the construction of an interstate highway will allow more inexpensive transportation through an area as a primary benefit. However, secondary benefits will also be realized as automobile service stations and motels built around highway interchanges give rise to additional wealth in the area. And because the people who work in the service stations and motels will have more income, they will spend that income in local towns, providing even more benefits through a multiplier process.

However, secondary costs as well as secondary benefits must be considered. For example, highways that were heavily traveled before the construction of an interstate highway will now be less traveled, causing service stations and motels on those highways to lose business and decreasing overall spending in those areas. Furthermore, increased shipping by truck on the highway might lower rail shipments, harming the rail industry. Thus, the secondary effects, both positive and negative, will be very real, but quite difficult to measure accurately.

Unless the effects are overwhelming, it is often advisable to concentrate the benefit-cost analysis on the primary effects rather than to attempt to include some secondary effects, which, of necessity, will represent only a fraction of the total possible secondary effects. When a benefit-cost analysis includes secondary effects as a large proportion of the benefits generated from a project, this may indicate that the analysis has been slanted to support the project. Secondary benefits can be dreamed up almost without end, as can secondary costs, so one should be suspicious of a project that would not be cost-effective if the secondary effects were not included.

Converting the Costs and Benefits to Dollar Terms

Once the costs and benefits are enumerated, they must be converted into dollar terms so that they can be compared. The costs are usually easier to estimate than the benefits be-

cause they tend to be expressed in the form of dollar costs. By contrast, the benefits of government programs usually do not accrue as money. For example, if a dam is to be built, the cost of purchasing the land to be flooded, in addition to the construction costs of the dam, must be evaluated. Other costs are relevant as well. For example, some roads may be diverted, increasing the travel time of some individuals. Also, the land to be used typically will be condemned, forcing some individuals to sell when they would rather stay. And possible environmental damage must be factored into the analysis, even though it is often difficult to place a dollar figure on environmental damage. All in all, the costs may not be as easy to total as it first appears.

The benefit side of the equation is even more difficult to convert into dollar terms. A dam may produce some hydroelectric power, which can be evaluated at the market rate for electricity, but even this is speculative, because energy prices have been known to change over time. The lake that results from the dam may have recreational uses such as fishing and boating, but these types of benefits are not easily measured in dollar terms. Nevertheless, a successful benefit-cost analysis must attempt not only to enumerate but also to attach dollar figures to the costs and benefits of a project, so that they can be compared on the same terms.

Benefit-Cost Analysis as a Decision-Making Tool

Once the results of a benefit-cost study are in, they can be used as a guideline for whether a particular program should be initiated. We should note, however, that a favorable benefit-cost ratio does not necessarily imply that a program should be undertaken, nor does an unfavorable ratio necessarily mean that a program should not be undertaken. For example, all redistributive programs have dollar costs in excess of their dollar benefits, because the money is collected from some people and given to others, minus the government's administrative costs. Yet, given the government's goals for redistribution, this cannot be helped. Furthermore, as noted in Chapter 14, cash transfers per dollar of expenditure confer the greatest benefit to the recipient, but often the goals of a program call for in-kind payments instead.

Benefits in excess of costs do not necessarily imply the desirability of a program either. For one thing another option might be even more beneficial. A ferry, for example, might show benefits in excess of costs, but a bridge might show even higher benefits for the same cost, in which case the ferry should not be produced. Again, though it seems obvious to state it, all possible options must be examined to ensure that the benefit-cost analysis points to the best option.

One frequently available option is to produce the project on a different scale. For example, the U.S. government has a stockpile of oil stored underground in salt domes in Texas and Louisiana called the Strategic Petroleum Reserve (SPR). Before the reserve was built, a benefit-cost analysis was completed to determine, among other things, how much oil should be stored. The program was begun in the middle 1970s in the aftermath of the 1973–74 OPEC oil embargo, and the oil was intended to be used in the event of another embargo. The results of the benefit-cost analysis indicated that the optimal size of the reserve was 500 million barrels of oil at an estimated price of $13.40 per barrel of oil. On the basis of that study, the SPR was constructed.[7]

Since the original study, several events occurred that placed the desirability of the SPR in doubt. First, President Carter decided that he wanted the reserve to be at least a billion barrels, so despite the benefit-cost analysis the size of the reserve was increased. Second, the cost of oil increased, so that some of the SPR oil was bought at prices as high as $36 per barrel. By substituting the new price of oil into the original benefit-cost analysis, the SPR was demonstrably not cost-effective. Third, oil discoveries in the North Sea, Mexico, and elsewhere made it less likely that an interruption in oil imports would take place. Still, the SPR was built.

This brief case study illustrates several things about benefit-cost analysis. First, an option for any given project is to vary the size of that project. The benefit-cost analysis considered sizes from 500 million to 1 billion barrels before deciding on the optimal size. Second, although the benefit-cost analysis is one factor to be considered, projects, once started, take on a life of their own. The SPR was impossible to stop even though it was designed simply as a cost-effective insurance scheme to guard against oil embargoes and even though new information revealed that the project ceased to be cost-effective almost as soon as it was started.

Benefit-Cost Analysis and the Public Interest

Finally, note that benefit-cost analysis weighs the dollar costs against the dollar benefits regardless of who pays the costs and benefits. In this sense benefit-cost analysis is utilitarian; ultimately, the dollar value of the benefits to the beneficiaries must exceed the dollar value of the costs to those who pay. In Chapter 2 we suggested that the Pareto criteria offer a better guide to what is in the public interest, so any benefit-cost analysis can be opposed on

---

[7] The study for this project is *Strategic Petroleum Reserve Plan* (Public Law 94-163, Section 154), Federal Energy Administration, Strategic Petroleum Reserve Office, December 15, 1976.

normative terms by arguing that the welfare of the beneficiaries (or those who pay the costs) should be weighted more heavily to determine the final outcome. Redistribution programs have already been advanced as an example of when the value of the benefits should be weighted more heavily than the costs to the taxpayers.

Keep in mind that any determination of public interest is necessarily normative. Benefit-cost analysis makes one judgment under the guise of some formal analytic technique, but the results should only be used as an input into the final decision. Benefit-cost analysis provides information to help evaluate the pros and cons of a program, but it is only a guide toward making what ultimately is a normative decision.[8]

The Discount Rate

One problem that affects most benefit-cost analyses is determining the proper *discount rate*, the interest rate at which future benefits are discounted to compute their present value. Typically, the costs and benefits of a program do not occur at the same time, so to provide some mechanism for comparison over time, the future costs and benefits must be discounted back to some common time. For example, at a 10 percent interest rate $100 today is worth the same as $110 a year from now. Thus, if one program will produce $100 in benefits today and another will produce $115 a year from now at the same cost, the second program will provide the greatest benefit for the given cost. If the appropriate discount rate is 15 percent, though, both programs will appear to be equal in value, and any discount rate over 15 percent will make the first program look better.

Selecting the appropriate discount rate becomes especially significant when benefits extend well into the future. For example, a bridge could be built, and could incur most of its costs, before any benefits were produced, but then at relatively low cost it could go on producing benefits for perhaps fifty years. The lower the discount rate, the higher the present value of the project, so it is important to select the right discount rate if the benefit-cost analysis is to provide an accurate representation of the costs and benefits.

Present Value Measurement of Costs and Benefits

According to that line of reasoning, the present value of any stream of costs and benefits can be calculated. Because the present value of benefits due one year from now must be reduced by the rate of interest, or discount rate, the present value of a benefit stream is calculated by the formula

$$PV = B_1/(1 + r)$$

where PV is the present value of benefit B_1 that is produced a year from now and the project is discounted at rate r. If the flow of benefits lasts over two years, the present value of the benefits in the second year will have to be reduced again to reflect the discount rate,

[8]See Edward M. Gramlich, *Benefit-Cost Analysis of Government Programs* (Englewood Cliffs, N.J.: Prentice-Hall, 1981), for additional discussion of the problems involved in estimating costs and benefits.

so that the present value of two years of benefits is calculated as

$$PV = B_1/(1 + r) + B_2/[(1 + r)(1 + r)]$$

The benefits after the second year will be worth $B_2/(1 + r)$ after the first year, which will again have to be divided by $(1 + r)$ to give the benefits at the present time. The same principle applies for benefits in any future year; thus, the benefits in year 2 are divided by $(1 + r)$ times 2, or $(1 + r)^2$, and the benefits in year t are divided by $(1 + r)^t$. Therefore, the general formula for the present value of benefits stretching T years into the future is

$$PV = \sum_{t=0}^{T} [B_t/(1 + r)^t]$$

If the benefits in each year, or B_t, can be estimated, and if the appropriate discount rate is known, then it is possible to calculate the present value of the stream of benefits to the project.

The calculation of the present value of the costs is done in the same way, so that if the cost in each year is substituted for B_t in this equation, PV will be the present value of the costs. In this way it is possible to compare the present value of the benefits with the present value of the costs.

Choosing the Right Discount Rate

Choosing the appropriate discount rate is crucial to a benefit-cost analysis, because it can have a significant effect on the estimate of the present value of the project. Recall that the higher the discount rate chosen, the lower the present value of the project. Furthermore, the longer the time horizon of the project, the more important the discount rate becomes. In the extreme case of an infinite horizon, a doubling of the discount rate halves the present value.

Economists are not in general agreement as to how a discount rate should be chosen. One option is to apply the rate on government bonds of the same maturity as the project; another is to use the market rate of interest as a starting point. However, not only are there many rates of interest in the market but a market rate reflects inflationary expectations. There is also the problem of how to treat the taxes that would have been paid on income taken out of the private sector and spent on a public sector project, as well as the question of risk premiums inherent in interest rates.

The simplest way to deal with inflation in a benefit-cost analysis is just to leave it out and compute all benefits and costs in constant dollars. The main difficulty in trying to abstract from inflation is in finding an inflation-adjusted interest rate. Because all market rates include a real rate of interest plus an inflation premium (plus a risk premium, to be discussed later), ideally the inflation premium should be subtracted from the interest rate to leave only the real rate of interest. The inflation premium is difficult to calculate, though, because the expected future rate of inflation at any point in time is unknown.

If a project is undertaken in the public sector rather than in the private sector, no taxes are paid on the profits. Because the discount rate should reflect the fact that resources are taken out of the private sector for the public sector project, the appropriate public sector discount rate must take into account the opportunity cost of foregone tax revenues to the government. The appropriate discount rate will equal the before-tax return on a private sector investment, reflecting both the public and private benefits of the private sector alternative.

The discount rate in a benefit-cost analysis should be a risk-free rate that will calculate the present value of benefits and costs in the absence of any uncertainty about what those benefits and costs might be. In the private sector a risky undertaking might warrant the addition of a risk premium to the interest rate charged to borrow for the project, but this could have perverse consequences in a benefit-cost analysis, where both the benefits and costs are being considered. For example, assume that a dam is being considered and that in fifteen years there is a 10 percent chance that $1 million in repairs will be needed on the dam but a 90 percent chance that no repairs will be needed. Therefore, the expected value of the future repairs is $100,000. Without taking account of risk aversion, this $100,000 would be discounted back to the present to compute the present value of this future expected cost. But because the costly repairs are not certain, a risk premium might be added to the analysis, leading to a higher discount rate. Note, however, that if the discount rate were raised, the present value of that possible future cost would be lower, because the discount rate would be greater. In fact, the risk should raise, not lower, the present value of the costs.

The correct way to take account of this risk is to compute a certainty equivalent to the uncertain future state of affairs. For example, the analysts might decide that the 10 percent risk of the $1 million future cost was equivalent to a certain cost of $150,000, in which case the $150,000 would be discounted back to the present at the risk-free discount rate. In short, the discount rate in a benefit-cost analysis should be a risk-free rate, and risk should be factored into the analysis using certainty equivalents.

The issues in selecting the appropriate discount rate in a benefit-cost analysis are complex. Keep in mind also that in actual benefit-cost analyses the analysts do not always pay close attention to the discount rate. Often, a discount rate of 10 percent is chosen arbitrarily—or rather, because it has been used in the past—and sometimes studies will be done in which several discount rates are examined.

Average and Marginal Benefits

Sometimes, noneconomists will select the project that has the highest ratio of benefits to costs as the most cost-effective project, though to do so confuses the concepts of average and marginal benefits. The optimal project is the one that produces the highest net benefits.

Consider a case in which two dams of different sizes are being considered. The small dam can be built at a present cost of $1000 and will yield benefits with a present value of $5000, so the ratio of benefits to costs is 5:1. The larger dam will cost $10,000 and yield benefits with a present value of $20,000, for a benefit-cost ratio of 2:1. The benefit-cost ratio of the larger dam is less than the smaller dam, but the marginal cost of the larger dam over the smaller one is $9000 and the marginal benefit is $15,000. In other words, $15,000 in benefits can be acquired for a cost of only $9000, which means the larger project produces the greater net benefits, even though its overall benefit-cost ratio is not as high.

Note that the benefit-cost ratio is the ratio of average costs to average benefits, but the optimal output in the public sector or the private sector is the level that equates marginal costs with marginal benefits. One would never want to undertake a project with a benefit-cost ratio of less than one, but the optimal project among many is not necessarily the one with the greatest benefit-cost ratio. Rather, it is the one with the greatest net benefit, and that cannot be determined from the benefit-cost ratio alone.

Benefit-cost analysis is a good tool for evaluating government projects, but it has a number of inherent limitations. It is difficult actually to measure benefits and costs, and when benefits and costs accrue over time, it is difficult to know how they should be discounted. In addition, the benefit-cost ratio by itself does not provide sufficient information about whether a project should be undertaken. Other issues must be considered as well. Fo example, some projects, such as highway projects, involve decisions that can affect driver safety. How wide should medians be? What types of guard rails should be used? In

a benefit-cost analysis of such a project, the value of human life would have to be entered into the equation. Needless to say, placing a dollar value on a human life is a controversial area, but it must be done if a benefit-cost analysis is to be undertaken. Although benefit-cost analysis can be a useful tool in assessing the relative merits of a given project, the state of the art is not advanced enough to permit decisions about public projects to be made solely on the basis of benefit-cost analysis.

Government Contracts

In our discussion of benefit-cost analysis, we noted that the government must estimate the costs of its programs. This is true not only when the government itself undertakes the project but also when it contracts the work out to private contractors. In such cases the costs still must be estimated, but different types of contracts have different implications for the costs of programs. By looking at some of the various types of contracts, we can illustrate some of the potential problems involved in government contracting.

Fixed Fee

The simplest type of contract is a fixed fee contract, under which the government contracts to buy something at a specific price. Fixed fee contracts are desirable when what is being purchased can be clearly specified ahead of time and when there is little uncertainty about construction methods, feasibility, and so on. For example, if the government wants to buy filing cabinets or electric typewriters, it is easy to specify the characteristics of the product to be purchased and to solicit

bids. Because these types of products are already being produced in the marketplace, bidders have an incentive to bid low enough to win the contract while still covering the costs of production. Thus, the fixed fee contract is the most desirable way to let government contracts.

However, many large government contracts, especially in the military area, do not lend themselves to fixed fee contracting because the product that is being contracted for has never been built and may use technology that has not yet been developed. The contractor, therefore, is not in a good position to estimate development or production costs. On these types of contracts, a company would be risking its survival to promise to produce output on a fixed fee basis, unless the fixed fee was prohibitively high.

Consider, for example, the development of a new military aircraft. Because the builder will have to develop some of the technology as a part of the contract, there will be uncertainty about both how well the aircraft will perform and how much it will cost to build. In an effort to try to get the most advanced product, and to save money, the government will study the qualifications and past work of the company and assess what the company claims it can do in an uncertain environment. In short, when product specifications cannot be identified ahead of time, when costs are uncertain, and when there are no similar products currently being produced, fixed fee contracts may not be the best way to go.

Cost plus Fixed Fee

Another type of contract is cost plus fixed fee, under which the government pays the cost of the project plus a fixed fee to the contractor. This type of contract solves some of the problems of a fixed fee contract in an uncertain situation by ensuring that the costs will be covered by the government and a profit realized by the contractor.

Contractors may not like this type of contract, however, because if the project costs more than anticipated, the fixed fee can end up being a very low rate of return on the assets it employs. Nevertheless, the contractor is at least assured of not taking a loss. Another problem with this type of contract is that the contractor has little incentive to try to control costs, because any cost overruns will be borne by the government. This can lead to inefficient management or even fraud if the contractor attempts to include questionable items in the cost base.

For example, some contractors have tried to include such items as country club dues in the cost of a contract. At first glance this seems inappropriate, but remember that many companies routinely pay for country club memberships, football tickets, and so on for their employees. Perhaps the item should be considered as a part of the fee rather than the cost, though. Note also that such items become irrelevant under a fixed fee contract.

The government simply buys the best product for the price and does not care what the firm does with the income. A major drawback to cost plus fee contracts that does not exist with fixed fee contracts is that the government must monitor and audit the firm's costs.

Cost plus Percentage Fee

Under a cost plus percentage fee contract the government pays for the contractor's cost plus a percentage of the cost as profit to the contracting firm. This type of contract might be used when the costs and final output of a product are quite uncertain. The cost plus percentage fee guarantees the contractor a mutually agreeable rate of return on the investment in the contract. However, this type of contract has an undesirable built-in incentive—the more the contractor spends, the more profit the contractor will make. Cost plus percentage fee clearly minimizes the risk of the contractor and, even more than cost plus fixed fee, provides little incentive to control costs.

Cost plus Incentive Fee

A cost plus incentive fee pays a fixed fee to the contractor in any event and a larger fee the lower the total cost is. This provides an incentive for the contractor to produce output for the government at the minimum possible cost and increases the profits of the contractor for doing so. Although this type of contract may be appealing, its applicability is limited to situations in which a clearly defined output is contracted for. If the output is not well defined, then the contractor may produce a less effective product for less money and receive a higher payment as a result.

To review, when the output the government desires is well defined and can be produced with existing technology, a fixed fee contract is the easiest and most effective way for the government to buy. But when uncertainties arise, other types of contracts may be more appropriate, although all have the disadvantage of requiring the government to monitor the activities of the firm more closely to ensure that the costs declared by the contractor are actually legitimate and necessary costs of performing the contract.

Taxing and Spending

The government's budget comprises two different types of activities—spending and revenue generation. In this chapter we concentrated mainly on the spending side of the government's budget, but there are some important differences between the way in which political decisions on spending and political decisions on revenue generation are made. As pointed out in Chapter 8, special interests can exert an undue influence on government spending programs. The same is true with tax programs, but to a lesser extent.

Much of this is due to the way in which taxes are collected. Spending programs have the potential to focus on a particular area of the country, for example, irrigation projects in the west, waterway projects in states with navigable waterways, tobacco supports in tobacco-growing regions, and so on. Taxes are not allocated on a geographical basis, however. The tax structure raises revenue by taxing people not according to where they live but rather according to how much income they have. Because congressional districts tend to contain people from all income groups, there is less potential for a representative to benefit his or her constituents specifically through favorable tax treatment. Taxes cannot be raised in one area and lowered in others.

There are exceptions, of course. Favorable tax treatment has been given to the oil and gas industry, for example, and realtors as a national group have been successful in retaining the home mortgage interest deduction. Taxes are harder to target to particular special interest groups, however, so the revenue-generating side of the budget is not as prone to political manipulation as the spending side. Special interests will seek political benefits wherever they can find them, but with a nationwide general income tax, it is more difficult to target tax breaks for a particular representative's constituents than it is to target spending benefits.

Another significant factor is that spending programs are politically popular, whereas tax increases are not. The result is that a representative concerned about political popularity has more of an incentive to work for changes on the spending side of the budget than the taxing side. A major contributing factor to the budget deficit is that Congress has been willing to pass spending programs without raising taxes as well. People like government spending, but they do not like taxes, yet another contributing factor to the asymmetry between taxes and spending programs.

Conclusion

We began this chapter by outlining the government's budgeting process. The way in which the government budget is determined is indicative of the system of checks and balances originally built into the Constitution. The president, with the assistance of the Office of Management and Budget, has the initial responsibility for drawing up a budget. This budget is submitted to Congress, where it is modified and finally approved.

It is not always easy to evaluate when the government's money is being effectively spent. In the private sector of the economy, the market gives a clear indication through profits and losses. A firm that makes profits is transforming its inputs into outputs of higher value, whereas a firm taking losses is using valuable inputs and transforming them into resources that are less valuable than the inputs used. Most of the output that the government produces cannot be measured this way, and much output is produced by the government because the market does not provide a good alternative.

A benefit-cost analysis can be undertaken to try to evaluate the effectiveness of potential government programs. These types of studies can contribute much to the evaluation process, but they cannot substitute for more subjective types of evaluation. Any redistributional program, for example, will have a benefit-cost ratio of less than one but still might conform to the overall goals of the society. There is also a tendency to believe that the program with the highest benefit-cost ratio is the best program, but even if all benefits and costs could be enumerated, this would not necessarily be true. The ratio of benefits to costs is an average figure, but the optimal output in either the public or private sector equates marginal costs and marginal benefits.

There are several different types of contracts that the government might use for procurement. A fixed fee contract is the simplest type of contract, and it contains the best incentive structure, but fixed fee contracts are not always feasible, for several reasons. All of the alternatives to fixed fee contracts have some problems with their incentive structures, though, and require close government monitoring to avoid excessive cost overruns and, perhaps, products of inferior quality.

Another factor relevant to the government budgeting process is the different ways in which taxation and spending activities are determined. Spending programs can be strongly influenced by special interests due to the procedures by which spending bills are introduced into Congress; recall that the logrolling and vote trading that take place in Congress tend to produce many special interest programs. This is true to some extent for taxation as well, but taxation is spread more uniformly throughout the nation, so a tax placed on one representative's district will also apply to most other districts. The same is true of tax breaks, which tend to be more national in scope. As a result there is less special interest activity in the taxing side of the budget than the spending side.

Government budgeting is a complex process, and this chapter has only scratched the surface in introducing the subject. An understanding of the process, when combined with material in earlier chapters on the incentives built into public sector decision making, can provide some insight into how the government produces what it does.

Questions

1. Review the method by which the federal budget is proposed and eventually approved. Relate this procedure to the system of checks and balances built into the Constitution.

2. Explain the differences between the current budgetary procedure and the procedure used before 1921. Is there a justification for the change in procedure?

3. What is meant by incrementalism? What prompted this theory of the budgetary process? Is there any way that the incremental increases in government budgets can be rationalized, given the nature of the budgetary process?

4. What is the difference between a program budget and a line item budget? Explain the advantages of program budgets that have caused the government to view its budget more in this way.

5. How is a benefit-cost analysis undertaken? What are the strong points and weak points of such an analysis? Explain why a benefit-cost analysis is potentially valuable for any major government project, and also why it is unwise to rely solely on the results of a benefit-cost analysis to decide whether the project should be undertaken.

6. Why is there the possibility of double counting costs or benefits in a benefit-cost analysis? Explain the potential pitfall of counting stocks and flows, and give examples on both the cost and benefit sides to illustrate this potential problem.

7. Why is the discount rate important to a benefit-cost analysis? What factors determine the appropriate discount rate for such an analysis?

8. Assume that two similar projects are being considered and both are evaluated using a benefit-cost analysis. Should one project be favored over the other because it has a higher ratio of benefits to costs? Explain the issue involved here.

9. Discuss the different types of government contracts that could be used for procurement from the private sector. What are the advantages and disadvantages of each? When would it be appropriate to use each type of contract?

10. Explain the differences in the ways in which spending decisions and taxing decisions are made in Congress. What are the implications of these differences with regard to the types of spending versus taxing programs that are produced?

CHAPTER EIGHTEEN

Regulation

The economic functions of government have been characterized primarily as either public spending programs or revenue-generating activities to pay for public spending. Another area in which the government has a profound influence on the economy is regulation. Regulation, like other governmental activities, can be analyzed within both a positive and a normative framework. Both will be applied in this chapter. We begin by outlining the reasons why the government might want to regulate certain aspects of the economy. Then we analyze regulation according to positive principles. In general, a case for government regulation can be made in instances where the private sector of the economy could be expected to operate with less than optimal results. Such areas were introduced in Chapter 3 and will be examined again here.

The line of reasoning used to justify government regulation is that in many cases the market does a less-than-perfect job of allocating resources. In these instances one might hope to improve on the market's results through regulation. Sometimes, as with national defense and highways, the government is the producer of the good in question; other times market allocation may be aided by regulation, leaving actual production to take place in the private sector. Keep in mind throughout the chapter that just because the market may not perfectly allocate resources does not mean that the government can necessarily improve matters through regulation.

Poorly Defined Property Rights

In Chapters 3 and 4 we discussed the problems that arise when poorly defined property rights cause externalities or create collective consumption goods. In such cases it is theoretically possible, through some set of taxes or subsidies, to provide the incentive for the efficient allocation of all resources. Recall that automobiles produce air pollution as an externality in the process of yielding the services of transportation. Because the cost of the pollution is external to the market, those who drive have little incentive to reduce the amount of pollution that they create. The result is the overutilization of clean air and the resulting production of too much pollution. The same analysis applies to manufacturing plants, trash burners, and anything else that dirties the air as a by-product of other activities.

Regulation as a Substitute for Corrective Taxes

In theory, the optimal solution can be produced by monitoring the amount of pollution caused by each polluter and charging the individual a price equal to the cost of the externality. This provides an incentive to reduce the pollution to its optimal level, as was explained in Chapter 3. In practice, monitoring each individual can be very difficult, as can calculating the cost of pollution and apportioning the cost to its various sources. In this sense corrective taxes work better in theory than in reality.

Another way to handle the problem is to estimate the cost of the pollution using a benefit-cost analysis and then examine the alternative ways that the pollution might be reduced. For example, if automobile drivers were charged for the actual amounts of pollution coming from their cars, they might voluntarily purchase catalytic converters to reduce their pollution and therefore reduce the pollution tax they would have to pay. However, as noted, this would be difficult to monitor. But a benefit-cost analysis might show that the benefits of lower pollution exceeded the costs of requiring cars to have catalytic converters, and a regulation requiring the pollution control devices could be instituted. Presumably, the effect of the regulation would be approximately the same as the effect of a corrective tax if it were feasible to levy the tax. Likewise, industrial polluters are required to

have pollution abatement equipment. For example, coal-burning utilities must install smokestack scrubbers to reduce their emissions. Again, if they could be charged per unit of pollution, they would presumably opt for the pollution reduction equipment as a method of lowering the tax. And some types of activities, such as burning leaves within the city limits, might be outlawed because of the externality involved.

Zoning Laws and Property Rights

Zoning laws can also be viewed within this same framework. For example, a gas station built in a residential neighborhood could create a negative externality, and all of those negatively affected might offer to pay the gas station enough that it would be willing to locate in another area. However, it is difficult to foresee all of the possible undesirable uses of the land. Furthermore, the transactions costs in getting a large number of people to agree on a payment tend to be excessively high. Recall that with large numbers of people, an optimal agreement can potentially be reached if no costs are associated with reaching an agreement, but because of the transactions costs involved, the optimal agreement may never be reached. Zoning laws can be used to address a problem like this by outlawing certain uses of land in certain areas, thus reducing transactions costs and perhaps ensuring a more orderly use of the land.[1]

This is especially true in natural areas such as beaches. People will travel many miles to enjoy a beach, but a developer on the shoreline can lessen the enjoyment available to those people, a majority of whom might live

---

[1]See, however, the discussion in Chapter 4 on zoning laws and especially on land use in Houston, where there are no zoning laws.

in other political jurisdictions. The result is that, due to high transactions costs, the beach area might be overdeveloped, even though in the absence of transactions costs an agreement could in theory be made to keep the beach area undeveloped. Regulation can deal with this by passing zoning laws requiring only certain types of buildings near the beach. A good example of the externality created on a public beach is the effect of tall buildings on eastern beaches. The tall building can cast shadows on the beach in the afternoon, which may be sufficient reason to restrict the height of buildings.

Environmental laws and zoning regulations are good examples of cases where poorly defined property rights can make the passage of regulations desirable. If all property rights were perfectly defined, and if transactions costs were nonexistent, people could bargain to reach the optimal allocation of resources. This conclusion comes from the Coase theorem, discussed in Chapter 4. Because the assumptions of the Coase theorem are not always satisfied, regulations represent a method of requiring that people not impose undue costs on others through their behavior. In this sense poorly defined property rights are one justification for government regulation.

Natural Monopoly

Another reason why regulation might be desired is that without it certain industries can naturally develop into monopolies. Consider, for example, an electric utility. A major cost of providing electricity is the cost of establishing a network of utility poles and wires throughout the area to be served. If several companies are competing, the one with the most customers can spread the cost of the network over a larger number of consumers and thus supply electricity at a lower price. In this case customers shopping for the lowest price will buy electricity from the largest utility, which will increase the customers of the largest utility and decrease the customers of the others. Eventually, only one utility will be left as the monopoly producer of electricity. Because market forces naturally lead to the establishment of a monopoly, this type of case is called a *natural monopoly*. Another example is the local phone company. If there are many local phone companies, a customer desiring service will probably choose the largest company in order to be able to call as many other people as possible. This will result in the largest company growing larger while the other companies become smaller; eventually, only one phone company will remain as a natural monopoly.

The Theory of Regulation

This discussion of natural monopoly has suggested two distinct reasons why one firm might emerge as a single seller out of a competitive situation. First, there may be economies of scale, so that larger firms can produce at a lower average cost, meaning the largest firm can sell at the lowest price in order to eliminate other firms from the industry. Second, individuals might desire to buy from the largest firm, regardless of whether it has a cost advantage, because of the benefits of dealing with the firm that has the greatest number of other customers.

Telephone service may fit into this latter category (although there may be economies of scale as well), because people want to be able to call as many other people as possible, thus giving an advantage to a large firm. Money production could be another example, because people would only be willing to accept a medium of exchange from a large, established institution whose money was readily accepted by most others with whom the individual dealt. In fact, most nations now deal with the money industry by issuing their own currency rather than allowing it to be produced by private firms.[2] Nationalization of the industry is but one possible way of dealing with the natural monopoly problem, however.

Another possible solution to this problem would be to grant one firm a monopoly as a producer of the good or service and then regulate the monopolist to try to get the firm to act as if it were a competitive industry. This type of regulation is depicted in Figure 18.1, which illustrates a simple case in which a monopolist is regulated where there are not economies of scale due to declining average cost. A profit-maximizing monopolist restricts output to Q_m and sells at higher price P_m. The supply curve of the industry is the monopolist's marginal cost curve, so the monopolist is maximizing profits at the point where marginal cost equals marginal revenue. By contrast, a competitive industry will produce Q^*, selling at price P^*.

Many states grant certain firms, such as electric utilities, natural gas suppliers, and phone companies, monopolies over certain areas and then establish a public service commission to regulate the monopolist in an attempt to get the monopolist to produce as if it

were a competitive industry. The commission does this by trying to estimate the costs of the monopolist, usually from cost figures supplied by the firm itself, and then deciding what a fair profit would be for the firm. The commission sets the monopolist's price at P^* and requires it to serve all individuals in the area over which the monopoly is granted. At price P^* the quantity demanded is Q^*, so the regulated monopolist produces the same quantity at the same price a competitive industry would. The idea of regulating a monopoly, then, is to get a monopolistic producer to act in the same way as a competitive industry would.

Decreasing Costs

A natural monopoly is often said to arise when the monopolist has a decreasing average cost over the range of production. This slightly more complex situation is depicted in Figure 18.2. Here it is very apparent that the largest firm in the industry has a cost advantage because cost decreases as the quantity of output rises. If the monopolist were to be regulated in the manner just described, the commission would allow the firm to charge its costs of production, including a normal profit, and would set the price at P', thus making Q' the quantity produced in the market. Although this might be an improvement over no regulation, the optimal amount of output is Q^*, where the marginal benefit of the last unit produced, measured by the demand curve, equals the marginal cost. This amount could be produced by setting the price at Q^*, but at price Q^* the monopolist would be losing money, so could not continue in business.

One way to deal with this problem is to allow the monopolist to charge different prices to different customers. For example, residential users of electricity typically have a more in-

---

[2]Before the Civil War individual banks in the United States were allowed to issue their own bank notes, which circulated as money, so private production of money is not only possible, but also took place in this country.

Figure 18.1 Regulation of Monopoly In the simplest case a regulatory agency regulates a monopolist by requiring the monopolist to sell its output at the competitive price P^* to anyone who wishes to buy. Quantity Q^* is sold, making the regulated monopoly act like a competitive industry.

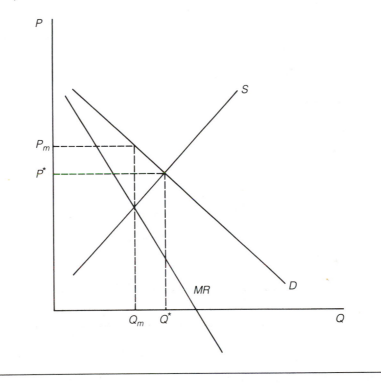

elastic demand than industrial users because industrial users have a wider range of alternative energy sources available. Therefore, the lowest rate Q^* can be charged to industrial users, with residential users paying a higher rate to allow the firm to avoid a loss. Indeed, regulated monopolists typically charge different prices to different types of customers. One justification for this is that the average cost of supplying output is declining, so the different prices allow the monopolist to produce the optimal amount without losing money. The charging of different prices to different customers in this manner is called *price discrimination*.

Another way of dealing with the problem is to charge customers a certain fee just for being able to use electricity and then charging them price P^* for any electricity they actually consume. This method is sometimes used in electricity pricing, and it is applied to the pricing of other goods as well. For example, country clubs often charge a set membership fee and then a greens fee every time a member

Figure 18.2 The Case of Decreasing Average Cost When a monopolist has decreasing average cost, a requirement that the monopolist sell at the point where the demand curve intersects *MC* will result in losses for the monopoly, so some other pricing system must be used.

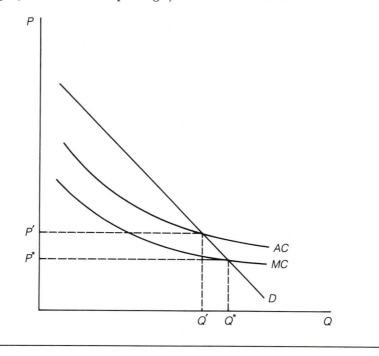

wants to play golf. To play, both the membership fee and the greens fee must be paid. A golf course is likely to have a declining average cost because it is expensive to own and maintain the grounds, but once established it is relatively inexpensive to allow people to play. Thus, the price is set at *P** and the membership fee is charged to make up for the loss that would be incurred if no other revenues were collected. Pricing in this manner is called *multipart pricing,* because in order to use the good the user must pay one price for access and another price for actual use.

The Regulation of Utilities

One can hardly object to allowing a private country club to set its prices as it sees fit, but because the regulation of utilities and the granting of the privileges of monopoly are done through the government, it is worthwhile to examine whether the justifications for regulation just provided hold up to close scrutiny.

The Origins of Utility Regulation

Electric utilities have been regulated virtually since they were established because the distribution of electricity uses public thoroughfares for utility poles and wires. But in their earliest days utilities were regulated by municipalities rather than by states, as is now typically done, and often municipalities granted duplicative franchises. For example, in 1905 Chicago granted 45 franchises for the distribution of electric power.[3] The situation was similar in other large cities, meaning that electric utilities operated in a relatively competitive environment instead of evolving into a natural monopoly.

One would think that if the industry actually were a natural monopoly, then a single producer would emerge that could exploit the public and the public would demand additional regulation. Jarrell has convincingly demonstrated, though, that it was the producers of electricity that were demanding state regulation of the industry and that regulation created the monopoly rather than being a response to it.[4]

In this view state regulation was demanded by the utilities as a method of creating monopoly profits for themselves.[5] Using the justification of natural monopoly causing ruinous competition, the utilities asked to be granted monopolies and then be regulated by the state. Once regulated, the utilities were able to convince the regulators to raise rates and provide monopoly profits to the regulated monopolists; this process will be discussed in the next section. The lesson here is that the natural monopoly model examined in the previous section may not have a counterpart in the real world. At least in the case of electric utilities, there were many competing utilities before state regulation, and apparently the state was the grantor of the monopoly.

This discussion certainly does not prove that contemporary utilities do not have decreasing average costs. It does suggest, however, that when producers were allowed to compete there were many competitors and that it was the utilities themselves rather than the general public that wanted the regulation.[6]

Bidding for the Monopoly Right

Whether the public granting of monopolies is necessary or even desirable will be discussed shortly. At this point we want to examine a proposal by Harold Demsetz that introduces an alternative to regulation of natural monopolies.[7] Consider a typical governmentally granted monopoly, such as a power company, a phone company, a cable TV company, or a gas company, for which the government must evaluate the monopolist's operation to decide what rates the monopolist should be allowed

---

[3]See Gregg A. Jarrell, "The Demand for State Regulation of the Electric Utility Industry," *Journal of Law & Economics* 21, no. 3 (Oct. 1978), pp. 269–295, for a good discussion of these issues.

[4]Jarrell, "The Demand for State Regulation of the Electric Utility Industry," cited previously.

[5]In George J. Stigler and Claire Friedland, "What Can Regulators Regulate? The Case of Electricity," *Journal of Law & Economics* 5 (Oct. 1962), pp. 1–16, the authors examine rates in states that have state regulation of electric utilities with those that do not and conclude that regulation makes no difference in the rates charged.

[6]See Paul L. Joskow, "Mixing Regulatory and Antitrust Policies in the Electric Power Industry: The Price Squeeze and Retail Market Competition," in Franklin M. Fisher, ed., *Antitrust and Regulation* (Cambridge, Mass.: MIT Press, 1985), for a discussion of competition in electric power generation today.

[7]Harold Demsetz, "Why Regulate Utilities?" *Journal of Law & Economics* 11 (Oct. 1968), pp. 55–65.

to charge. Ideally, the regulators will choose the rate that would have been produced in a competitive situation, but Demsetz offers the alternative of allowing competition for the right to be the monopolist, with competitors bidding on the basis of service to be supplied and rates to be charged. The competition for the right to be the monopoly supplier would then yield the competitive price, as revealed by the winning bid.

Consider, for example, the regulator trying to determine what price per kilowatt hour an electric utility should be allowed to charge. If many electric companies competed for the right to be the monopoly supplier by submitting bids on the prices they would charge, consumers could receive the lowest price without the requirement that a regulatory agency set rates. Complications could arise, to be sure. Such a situation might best be handled by having the power distribution network be publicly owned and having firms submit bids to operate the network to facilitate an easy tran-

sition in the event that the lowest bidder in the last period did not win the bid again this period. However, when a single supplier of a good or service is for some reason deemed desirable, a competitive process to select the supplier can substitute for regulation of the monopoly supplier after the fact.

When one thinks of monopolies, it is difficult to name one that either was not granted by the government or is actually run by the government. The natural monopoly theory creates the impression that monopolies will exist without government interference, yet little evidence supports this view. There is, on the other hand, an abundance of evidence suggesting that the government creates monopolies. In this light one must examine closely whether the granting and regulating of monopolies is indeed in the public interest. The next section explains why regulation, even when well intended, may end up serving private interests rather than the general public interest.

The Capture Theory of Regulation

The *capture theory* of regulation, which states that regulatory agencies are "captured" by the industries they are supposed to regulate, builds on some of the material discussed in Chapters 7 and 8 on public sector supply and demand.[8] The first building block of the theory is the influence of special interests in the

political process; the second is the rational ignorance of the general public regarding most of the activities of government.

Special Interests Versus the General Public

Consider the example of a regulated electric utility monopoly. The regulated firm has a special interest in seeing that the public service commission, when deciding rate cases, sets rates favorable for the utility. After all, the utility's income comes from the rates that it

---

[8]The seminal article in this area is George J. Stigler, "The Theory of Economic Regulation," *Bell Journal of Economics and Management Science* 2 (Spring 1971), pp. 3–21.

charges its customers, and the outcome of a rate case can be worth millions of dollars in income to the regulated firm. As a result, when rate hearings are held, the regulated utility sends representatives who are well informed to argue the utility's case.

On the other side of the transaction is the general public—the utility's customers. The outcome of a rate case that means millions of dollars to the utility will affect an individual's utility bill by maybe a few dollars. An individual could spend much time and effort researching the utility's rates to argue before the public service commission that rates should be lower. The individual would be arguing against employees of the utility whose job is to make an effective case for the utility's rates. As a result, the individual stands little chance of influencing the regulation and, even if successful, will benefit by only a few dollars. No individual has an incentive to become informed in exchange for a small chance to have a minor impact on the individual's bill. Therefore, individuals are rationally ignorant about the regulation, the public service commission, and the commission's activities.

The regulator, then, is regulating a special interest who has an incentive to be informed, and although the regulator is supposed to be acting in the general public interest, the general public will be uninformed about the process. The regulator will know the people in the regulated industry and, in fact, may have employment prospects in that industry after leaving the public sector. The regulator thus has little incentive to act in the public interest but has a large incentive to act in the interest of those who interact with the regulator and who may provide future employment. The result is that regulatory agencies tend to act in the best interests of the regulated industry rather than in the interests of the general public.

Regulatory agencies are, in effect, captured by the industries that they are supposed to regulate. The same general principles hold not only for regulated natural monopolies but for any type of government regulation. Special interests who have an incentive to become informed have an undue influence on regulatory agencies, whereas the rationally ignorant general public has little influence.

The Department of Energy provides an interesting informal example of this capture theory. Although the Department of Energy is more than just a regulatory agency, it was established in the 1970s largely in response to the higher energy prices that followed the OPEC oil embargo. The department's mandate included controlling prices to hold them below the market clearing level and allocating the resulting shortages of petroleum products. These activities clearly were not in the best interests of the energy producers, but in the few years since the department was established, its activities have slanted more toward providing grants and subsidies to energy producers, turning the agency from an adversary to a friend of the industry. The department is being captured by the industry it is supposed to regulate and now is rightly viewed more as an advocate for the industry, in much the same way as the Department of Agriculture is viewed as an ally to farmers.

The Interstate Commerce Commission and the now defunct Civil Aeronautics Board represent two other cases in which the regulatory agency clearly worked in favor of the regulated industry. The Interstate Commerce Commission and the Civil Aeronautics Board both regulated their industries by assigning routes for trucks and for commercial airlines, respectively, that carriers could serve, and by setting rates. The agencies would not let one carrier compete on another's routes unless the carrier could demonstrate a need, thus restricting the output of the industry. In addition, rate cutting was almost never approved, whereas higher rates were, which meant that the regulatory agencies effectively kept prices above what they would have been in the absence of regulation, supposedly to stem the effects of ruinous competition.

The Regulatory Agency as a Cartel

Unlike a competitive industry the monopolist restricts output and charges higher prices. This is exactly what both the Interstate Commerce Commission and the Civil Aeronautics Board did in their respective industries. Clearly, the agencies functioned like cartels, allowing the producers in the industry to act as monopolists even though there were many competitors. Keep in mind it is unlikely that the firms in the industry themselves would have been able to band together to form a monopoly. First, it would have been illegal. Second, with a large number of firms in the industry and low barriers to entry, the market would have acted as policeman to enforce competition, even if the firms had wanted to collude. In these cases just discussed, the regulatory agency provided the opportunity for the firms to band together to act as a cartel, and to enforce the cartel the agency made the cartel's rules carry the force of law. The lower air fares offered after the elimination of the Civil Aeronautics Board are evidence of the excessively high prices of the past, and the same reduction in trucking rates would result from the elimination of the Interstate Commerce Commission.

The point is not that regulation is never desirable. Rather, we want to point out that because the general public is rationally ignorant of much of what the government does, whereas special interests tend to be well informed about the issues that concern them directly, regulatory agencies will tend, over time, to favor the industries they are supposed to regulate. The market may not always work perfectly, but neither does the government. Because we choose our political institutions, we should be aware of their potential shortcomings rather than just assume they will function in our best interest.

The Equilibrium Level of Regulation

Regulation often does benefit special interests at the expense of the general public, but vote-maximizing legislators typically do not find it in their interest to provide all of the regulatory benefits that the special interest desires. As with any type of maximizing decision, the legislature weighs the marginal benefits of regulation against the marginal costs, and the resulting equilibrium is seldom the outcome most desired by the special interest.

Because regulation benefits some at the expense of others, the legislature must weigh the marginal political gains from benefiting the special interest against the marginal political costs, which may include, for example, higher prices and less output by the regulated industry. If these costs are borne by the general public, they will be unaware of much of the cost, but some marginal political costs associated with acting against one group will remain. From the legislature's point of view, the optimal amount of regulation is the amount where the marginal costs equal the marginal benefits.

The special interest, however, prefers that regulatory benefits be extended until the marginal benefits to them of additional regulation are zero. As a result, the amount of regulatory protection desired by the special interest exceeds the amount that the legislature will grant, so special interests typically have an interest in lobbying for even greater benefits

Figure 18.3 The Equilibrium Quantity of Regulatory Benefits to Special Interests Legislators weigh the marginal costs against the marginal benefits of decisions, just like anyone else. As a result, the benefits granted to a special interest, Q', will be less than the benefits that the special interest would like to have, Q''. The reason is that special interests would like to receive benefits as long as their marginal value is above zero, whereas the legislature will grant them only up to the point where the marginal political value of granting the benefits equals the marginal political costs.

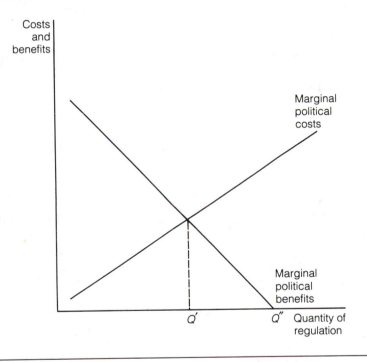

from the legislature. This idea is depicted in Figure 18.3, which shows the political costs and benefits of regulation to the legislature.[9]

The political costs and benefits to the legislature from additional regulatory protection are measured on the vertical axis of the graph, and the quantity of regulatory protection granted is measured on the horizontal axis. The legislature can receive political benefits from additional regulation as long as the regulation has some value to that special interest. In Figure 18.3 regulation up to quantity Q''

[9]This idea is explored more fully in Sam Peltzman, "Toward a More General Theory of Regulation," *Journal of Law & Economics* 19, no. 2 (August 1976), pp. 211–240.

provides benefits to the special interest, so the special interest is willing to provide political support to the legislature for regulation up to that amount. The marginal political benefits that the legislature can expect to receive are shown on the marginal political benefits curve.

But the legislature must also weigh the marginal political costs that result from the regulatory costs imposed on other groups. The marginal political costs curve shows the political costs to the legislature from additional regulatory benefits to the special interest. The legislature maximizes its political benefits from regulation by approving regulation up to quantity Q', where the marginal political costs equal the marginal political benefits.

Note that the special interest prefers regulation up to Q'', but the legislature only produces regulations to Q', so the amount of regulatory benefits given to the special interest is less than the special interest would prefer. In this sense the legislature can act as an agent for special interests, but not as a perfect agent. Thus, whereas the special interest prefers additional benefits as long as they have any positive value, the legislature will weigh the marginal benefits to the marginal costs, usually producing somewhat fewer benefits for the special interest.

The Transitional Gains Trap

The transitional gains trap is a by-product of some types of regulation. Although regulation can benefit the regulated industry in some ways, competition for those benefits can actually negate the gains that the regulation originally conferred, so that eventually the regulation provides no gains. However, if the regulation is removed, the regulated industry experiences transitional losses.[10] Some examples can illustrate the transitional gains trap.

Consider again the case of airline regulation. The Civil Aeronautics Board limited the routes that an airline could fly, thus lessening competition. In addition, the board set the rates that could be charged and would not let rates fall below a level in excess of the rates that would have been charged in a competitive industry. The result was excess profits for the firms in the industry. However, because firms were not allowed to compete on the basis of price, and because there was some overlapping of routes, the airlines found other ways to compete besides offering low fares—they bought new aircraft, they started flying the routes more often, and they usually flew with many empty seats. By offering more convenient schedules, newer aircraft, better meals, and less crowded flights, the airlines competed away their profits. In other words, the initial gain from regulation was transitional, and it ended up being absorbed by nonprice competition. Even though fares were excessively high, the excess profits were eventually competed away, leaving the airlines with only a normal level of profit.

When the regulation was removed and the airlines were allowed to compete by offering lower fares, air fares, as expected, declined. However, the airlines had been using their high fares to pay for newer aircraft, less congested flights, and so on, so the removal of the

---

[10]This section is based on Gordon Tullock, "The Transitional Gains Trap," *Bell Journal of Economics* 6 (Autumn 1975), pp. 671–678.

regulation resulted in lower fares, which caused the airlines to take transitional losses. After deregulation many new airlines were created and new routes were flown, but some of the old airlines suffered losses and were even driven out of business because they could not afford the type of nonprice competition that had occurred before deregulation. In short, the firms suffered transitional losses.

Another good example of transitional gains is the taxicab medallions required to operate a cab in New York City. The number of medallions is fixed, and any cab operating in the city must have one displayed on its hood. The medallions can be bought and sold, so to get into the cab business in New York, a person has to buy a medallion from an existing owner. When the medallions were established, it had the effect of freezing the number of cabs operating in the city. But as demand for cab services increased, cab fares rose above the level that would have existed if more cabs had been allowed to operate. This provided a transitional gain to the owner of a medallion worth the difference between the existing price of cab rides and the price that would have existed if there were no barrier to entry. In recent years the medallions have sold for more than $100,000.

What this means is that the present value in terms of higher fares to a cab operator due to the medallion is over $100,000, but if one wants to own a New York City cab, one must pay that amount for the medallion. The purchaser of the medallion will not receive any financial benefit from the restricted entry into the market, because the additional revenues received will be offset by the price of the medallion. The transitional gain to the original owners of the medallions simply becomes a cost of doing business to the current owner of the medallion.[11] Even though the regulation confers no gain to the current operators, however, to eliminate it and allow free entry into the industry would result in a transitional loss to the owners of medallions because the medallion would become worthless. This is the transitional gains trap.

Rent Seeking

The transitional gains trap is a result of what has sometimes been called *rent seeking*.[12] The term *rent* as used here refers to income that is the result of activities that do not add to the total output of the economy. Ricardo argued that rent on land is this type of income because the landlord collects the rent without engaging in any productive activity.

The case of New York City taxicab medallions fits into this framework. If existing cab owners can establish a regulation to grant themselves medallions and then restrict entry to those who own medallions, then they will

---

[12]Three key articles about rent seeking are Gordon Tullock, "The Welfare Costs of Tariffs, Monopolies, and Theft," *Western Economic Journal* 4 (June 1967), pp. 224–232, Anne O. Kreuger, "The Political Economy of the Rent-Seeking Society," *American Economic Review* 64 (June 1974), pp. 291–303, and Richard A. Posner, "The Social Costs of Monopoly and Regulation," *Journal of Political Economy* 83 (August 1975), pp. 807–827.

[11]This will be true even if the original owner still owns the medallion. Because the medallion can be sold, no monopoly profit results from driving the cab rather than selling the medallion.

benefit by the value of the medallion. If medallions sell for in excess of $100,000, then the rent going to the original owner of a medallion is more than $100,000. Likewise, if airlines or truckers can restrict entry, they will receive rents.

A common type of rent seeking is the pursuit of measures to restrict competition. Tariffs provide a good example. If domestic textile manufacturers can get a law passed to impose a tariff on imported textiles, then imported textiles will cost more, thus providing a competitive advantage to the domestic textile manufacturers. The additional income that accrues to the domestic textile manufacturers is a return to them from an activity that does not add to the total output of the economy, so it is a rent.

Indeed, any activity that limits competition provides rents to those still in the market. For example, the right to be the monopoly supplier of a service in an area confers a rent to the monopolist. Licensing requirements and other restrictions on entry into certain professions also provide rents to those already in the field. Likewise, the establishment of import quotas confers rents to those who are able to sell on the domestic market.

The Costs of Rent Seeking

The true cost of rent-seeking activity can be illustrated in the case of a monopoly to be granted by the government in a particular market. This is depicted in Figure 18.4, where the supply curve is shown as perfectly elastic to represent conditions in the long run in a competitive market. Without a quota $Q*$ is produced and sold at price $P*$. When a monopoly is granted, however, the profit-maximizing monopolist restricts output to Q' and raises the price to P', leaving the producer with a monopoly profit of $P' - P*$ per unit. In the traditional analysis of monopoly,

the welfare loss that results from the monopoly is equal to shaded area A. This area is the consumer surplus lost due to the output being restricted from $Q*$ to Q'.

The monopoly profits that go to the monopolist are equal to $P' - P*$ per unit times Q' units being sold, or the shaded rectangle B. Because the monopolist receives that amount in profits, if the government is going to grant a monopoly, it will pay a potential monopolist to compete for the right to be the monopolist. If the government has not yet decided to whom the monopoly right will be granted, it will pay the potential monopolist to invest as much as the present value of the future monopoly profits times the probability of receiving the monopoly to compete for the privilege. This means that the welfare loss from the monopoly will include not only the shaded triangle A but also the shaded rectangle B as the loss that results from competition to receive the monopoly rights.

The same analysis could apply to the granting of import quotas on certain goods. If the government restricts imports from $Q*$ to Q' for some good, as in Figure 18.4, then potential importers have an incentive to compete for import licenses to be able to import the good. The resulting welfare loss is area A, due to the restricted output, plus area B, equal to the amount that potential importers will invest to try to receive import licenses.

The Real World Costs of Rent Seeking

What are the real world costs that constitute area B? They are all types of lobbying activities that people engage in to try to get the government to grant them favors. Dairy price supports, for example, are costly because they restrict the consumption of dairy products and raise their prices—that is the loss represented by area A. But they are also costly because the dairy industry hires lobbyists to try

Figure 18.4 The Costs of Rent Seeking Triangle *A* is the welfare loss due to monopoly, but if the monopoly can be granted as a political favor, rent seekers will compete for the monopoly profits in rectangle *B*. This rent seeking is a waste of resources that adds to the welfare cost of politically granted monopolies.

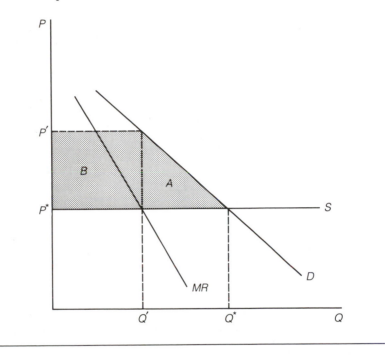

to convince those in government to continue the program (and perhaps expand its coverage)—that lobbying effort is the loss represented by area *B*. The costs also include the lobbyists from other industries who have not (yet) been successful in securing rents for their employers. Because they see rents going to others, they recognize the possibility of using political influence to try to receive rents themselves. Furthermore, potentially productive resources in the form of lobbyists, who are generally very competent individuals, are being wasted in the scramble to secure rents. Lobbyists are producing something for the dairy farmers in the form of price supports, but their efforts do not add to the net output of the economy. Productive resources are being used unproductively.

When the government is willing to grant special interest benefits, rent-seeking activities add to the total social cost of the government programs. In addition to the cost of the programs, valuable resources are being used to try to capture those rents, and the rent-seeking activity, though potentially profitable for the rent seeker, does not add anything to the total output of the economy. Regulation is but one type of special interest benefit that might lead to rent seeking.

Regulation of Product Quality

Thus far, economic regulation has been justified primarily as a means for overcoming problems of monopoly or poorly defined property rights. Regulation is also demanded to assure consumers of goods and services that their purchases meet some minimum level of product quality. For example, medical doctors must be licensed to practice, homes must be built according to local building codes, and restaurants must pass health inspections to be allowed to operate. These are but a few instances in which regulation is designed to ensure product quality.

There can be little doubt that consumers do want assurances of product quality, but this type of regulation is subject to abuse in the same way as any other regulation. For example, some have argued that because the American Medical Association (AMA) has virtual control over the licensing procedures for doctors and over the enrollment in American medical schools, it has, in effect, acted as a monopolist, restricting entry into medical schools in order to limit the supply of doctors and raise their incomes. The relatively high income of doctors lends some credence to this view. Likewise, building codes have sometimes been seen as a way to keep manufactured homes out of an area and provide jobs to local construction workers. Regardless of the beneficial effects of product quality regulation, its potential for lessening competition in a market must be recognized.

Private Sector Alternatives

One alternative to government regulation that is not often considered is private sector regulatory agencies. A good example is Best Western Motels. Best Western owns no mo-

tels, but it allows motels to display the Best Western logo if they meet a detailed list of specifications on motel quality, including the soundproofing of rooms, the width of hallways, the quality of furniture, the number of waste baskets in a room, the temperature in the bathrooms, the number of parking spaces per room, and so on. In short, members of Best Western Motels are willing to pay to be regulated in exchange for displaying a sign that assures potential customers of the quality of their product.

If states no longer required medical doctors to be certified, could the same thing happen there? The AMA already serves as a regulatory agency, and it would continue to exist if medical care were deregulated. Thus, persons wanting to be assured of the same quality of medical care that they now receive could always choose to visit only AMA-certified doctors. But people who wanted less expensive medical care, perhaps because they were only mildly ill and would not seek any treatment at today's prices, would have an alternative to self-treatment.

Consider the possibilities here. The AMA could continue to operate as an association of medical doctors, and people could be guaranteed the same quality of treatment that they now receive by just visiting an AMA doctor. But competing medical associations might also arise, and large, nationwide medical firms might become prevalent. Just as one can choose to stay at a local motel, a Best Western motel, or a Holiday Inn, one could also choose a doctor from an association, a large firm, or even an unregulated physician if one felt that the unregulated doctor could serve better. (Chiropractors, for example, currently fall outside of the regulatory bounds of the AMA, yet they still attract a following of patients.) The question of whether deregulation of med-

ical care—and other areas of product quality—works is certainly worth consideration.[13]

Regulation as a Type of Taxation

Regulation can be viewed as a type of taxation because the effects of regulation can be duplicated by a combination of taxes and subsidies or government programs.[14] For example, environmental regulations require strip miners to reclaim their land after finishing mining operations, but the same effect could be accomplished by taxation. The government could tax strip miners on the output they produce and use the tax revenues to fund a government program that would reclaim exhausted strip mines. Thus, the regulation is equivalent to a tax on the miner to finance an environmental program.

The Use of Regulation to Produce Monopoly Profits

In many professions, including barbers, medical doctors, lawyers, electricians, and real estate agents, regulations require the practitioners to be licensed. In each of these cases, the practitioner cannot simply apply for a license but must pass a test. Some specific education may be required as well. These licenses serve the role of restricting the number of people who practice in those professions and thus raise the income of the practitioners. The regulation, in effect, provides excess profits

to licensed sellers by taxing the sellers' consumers.

For example, one cannot simply take a job as a real estate agent in the same way that one can take a job as a car sales person or bank loan officer, although it is not clear that one job requires any more skill than any of the others. To sell real estate, the practitioner must pass a test, which keeps some potential sales people out of the profession and raises the income of those in the field. The same result could have been accomplished by placing a tax on home sales and paying a subsidy to real estate agents. Of course, the requirement that a test be taken also determines to whom the subsidy will be paid.

Regulation Instead of Taxes and Subsidies

Regulation of monopolies also provides a good example of this type of subsidizing through regulation. For example, utilities and

---

[14]See Richard Posner, "Taxation by Regulation," *Bell Journal of Economics and Management Science* 2 (Spring 1971), pp. 22–50.

[13]The use of brand names is another way to ensure product quality, because an owner of a brand that has its quality called into question stands to lose wealth as a result. A dramatic example is discussed in Andrew Chalk, "Market Forces and Aircraft Safety: The Case of the DC-10," *Economic Inquiry* 24, no. 1 (Jan. 1986), pp. 43–60. In 1979 a DC-10 crashed in Chicago as a result of a defective engine mounting, and Chalk calculates that the stockholders of McDonnell Douglas, the manufacturer of the plane, lost $200 million as a result. Because damage to the reputation of a brand name can be costly, owners of the brand name have an incentive to ensure product quality, even if the odds of low-quality products being manufactured are slim.

common carriers are required to serve all of those who demand service at the approved rates of the regulator. Although this can be viewed within the framework of natural monopoly, this represents more than just the regulation of a monopolist. Because some customers will be more costly to provide service to than others, the regulation really provides a subsidy from low-cost customers to high-cost customers. Similarly, common carriers such as railroads are often prevented by regulation from abandoning unprofitable routes. Because the overall rate structure allows the carrier a profit, this is a clear case of a subsidy from low-cost customers to high-cost customers.

In conclusion, regulation can be viewed as a type of taxation. Regulation requires one group of people to incur costs to do something that benefits another group of people. In this sense the regulation is a tax on the first group to finance a transfer to the second group. Regulation does not appear as government spending in the government's budget, though, so in reality the government's influence on the economy is proportionally greater than the government budget would indicate.

Conclusion

Regulation is a significant activity of government, and one that extends the economic influence of government well beyond revenue generation and public spending. Government regulation might be demanded for a number of legitimate reasons—from correcting problems caused by externalities and collective consumption goods resulting from poorly defined property rights to ensuring that goods and services in the market meet some minimum standards of product quality. Government regulation has the potential to produce benefits for the general public, but it also has the potential to be abused and to produce benefits for special interests to the detriment of the general public interest.

In general terms the danger of regulation, even when the goals of regulation are well thought out, is that the general public is rationally ignorant of most of the government's activities, whereas special interests constantly lobby to alter the government's activities to provide themselves with special interest benefits. As a result, even programs that start with good intentions can end up favoring special interests over the general public.

This does not mean that regulation should never be used; rather, it means that one must take a realistic view of what regulation can hope to accomplish in light of the incentive structure of the public sector. Presumably, regulation is demanded because of some defect in the private sector incentive structure, but it would be naive to think that the public sector will be able to operate flawlessly. Rather, the private sector incentive problems that were examined in Chapters 3 and 4 must be balanced against the public sector incentive problems that are sure to arise. In the real world things rarely work as smoothly as theoretical models predict.

Regulation can be viewed as a type of taxation, because its intention is to impose some cost on one group of people in order to produce a benefit for another group. This transfer can be effected with direct taxation and government spending or through regulation. In light of the conceptual link between taxation and regulation, the government's influence on the economy extends far beyond the amount of public spending that takes place. Regulation has an equivalent effect on the economy and so needs to be considered just as seriously when evaluating the economic activities of government.

Questions

1. In theory externalities can be corrected by applying an optimal tax to the generator of the externality. If this is so, why would regulation ever be desirable as a method of correcting an externality?

2. What is a natural monopoly? Explain the role that decreasing costs can play in producing a natural monopoly. What is the justification for having the government grant a monopoly and then regulate it?

3. Explain the theory behind how the government can regulate a monopoly to get it to act like a competitive industry.

4. Some amusement parks (such as Disneyland) charge an admission fee for entry into the park and then another fee to ride individual rides. Can this be justified from an efficiency standpoint? For what other reasons besides economic efficiency might such a pricing scheme be used?

5. Explain Harold Demsetz's plan that would substitute for the regulation of utilities. Would this plan work? Why or why not?

6. What is the capture theory of regulation? Explain the economic forces behind the theory.

7. What is the transitional gains trap? Why is there an incentive for industries to be lured into this trap? Who gains and who loses in this type of situation?

8. What is meant by the term *rent seeking*? Why does rent-seeking activity result in a social loss?

9. Many regulations exist for the purpose of ensuring product quality for the consumer. Explain the market alternative to regulation of product quality. Would it be feasible (or desirable) to eliminate the government regulation of medical care?

10. Explain the parallel between taxation and regulation. Why can regulation be viewed as just another form of taxation?

CHAPTER NINETEEN

The Federal System of Government

The government of the United States was originally established as a federation of the governments of the original thirteen states, which is why it was called the federal government. Today, a federal system of government refers to a government made up of many levels, and what we refer to as the federal government is the top level of government in the federal system. Under the federal government are the state governments, and states contain city, county, municipal, and other types of governments. This chapter examines the economics of a federal system of government from two different perspectives.[1] First, we consider the question of why a federal system of government might be more desirable than, say, one level of government to provide all public sector output. Second, we examine the economic interactions among the many different governments that coexist in a federal system.

The issue of whether many levels of government are preferable involves an analysis of both the trade-offs that exist between larger and smaller units of government and the effects of competition among governmental units. Competition can aid efficiency in government. Furthermore, some activities are better pursued by smaller governments, and others by large governments. We begin the chapter by looking at the theoretical foundations underlying the federal system of government, and then we examine the roles of the various levels of government in the United States.

The Theoretical Foundations of Federalism

Multiple levels of government are desirable for a number of reasons, though they can be summarized by observing that various governmental activities are best undertaken by governments of different sizes. In addition to the question about the optimal scale of governments, there is also a persuasive reason for wanting governmental activities to be per-

---

[1]See Wallace E. Oates, *Fiscal Federalism* (New York: Harcourt Brace Jovanovich, 1972) for a good discussion of the economics of a federal system of government.

formed at the lowest level of government possible. Many small governments will allow for the possibility of intergovernmental competition.

Intergovernmental competition helps to satisfy the demands of voters and taxpayers in a number of ways, and we will consider it in more detail shortly. For now, note that if intergovernmental competition were the only factor to be considered, the optimal government structure would be a large number of small governments. This section concentrates on reasons why different-sized governments will be best suited for different governmental activities. Recall that in Chapter 5, in analyzing the demand for governmental activity, a government was compared to a club. The rationale was that some goods and services are not easily produced through market transactions, so people get together and produce the goods through collective decisions. This implies that public sector output, by its very nature, is made to be consumed by more than just a few individuals. A number of factors can affect the size of the optimal sharing group.

Economies of Scale

Even in view of the advantages of intergovernmental competition, there are still a number of reasons why larger governments might be preferred to smaller ones. The first has to do with economies of scale in production, though this factor is hardly limited to the public sector; firms in the private sector become large to take advantage of economies of scale as well. For example, a school district will be overseen by a school board, but if school districts are too small, the cost of maintaining the many school boards needed to oversee the districts will raise the price of public education. Economies of scale become even more evident with higher education. Every community could have its own college, but the result would be a large number of colleges with small enrollment—perhaps too small to have a wide variety in the curriculum—and costly duplication of such facilities as libraries and computers would occur. Indeed, economies of scale can be found in any number of public enterprises. Thus, one reason for larger governments is to take advantage of the economies of large-scale operation.

Coordination of Large Programs

Sometimes, larger governments are desirable simply because coordination over a large area is needed. Public roads are a good example in that they are provided at all levels of government. Local governments produce roads to service the local area, but to travel from one area to another, some coordination of highway services is beneficial. Therefore, states have highway departments to coordinate, build, and maintain public roads between localities. But even state highway departments may not coordinate road services enough for people who want to travel from one state to another. In the 1930s the federal government coordinated the U.S. highway system—not by producing highways but by providing a coordinated route structure and a consistent numbering system to lend coherence to the national roads. In the 1950s the mere federal coordination of state-produced highways was deemed insufficient, so the federal government designed and built the interstate highway system. Some of the construction money and all of the maintenance money came from the states, but the interstate highway system was a federal project because states proved to be inefficiently small in providing an effective national highway system.

Collective Consumption Goods

In Chapters 3 and 4 governmental activity was justified as a necessary response to poorly defined property rights that resulted in externalities and collective consumption goods. These motivations for governmental activity may also be important in determining the most efficient size of government to produce the goods. Consider the case of collective consumption goods, which additional consumers can consume at no additional cost. Logically, the good should be produced at the level of government large enough to include everyone who could be accommodated at no extra cost.

In some cases this may require only a small government. For example, a public swimming pool on every block would be inefficient because it would probably be underutilized, but there is certainly no reason for the state to provide swimming pools. With other goods, such as scientific research, the whole nation (and, perhaps, the whole world) can share in the results, so it makes sense to produce these types of goods on a national and even international level if they are demanded. The space program, mainly produced at the national level, also has some programs that are the result of international cooperation.

Externalities

Externalities are sometimes called *spillovers*, a very descriptive term when considering a federal system of government. Sometimes, a program produced in one area has spillover benefits into an adjoining area. For example, a mosquito control program focused in one locale may reduce the mosquito population in another locale. In this light there is some justification for a mosquito control district that covers the entire population, who all benefit from the program.

Often, special districts are set up for just this reason—to coordinate these types of programs among local governments. Another example of spillover benefits might be a regional airport, which could benefit many surrounding municipalities. All the municipalities might contribute to the support of an airport authority that will be jointly run. Such a venture can internalize the externalities produced by the spillovers from one governmental jurisdiction to another.

The Optimal Sharing Group

The optimal sharing group for any given type of public sector output depends on a number of factors, but in general the production of different types of goods is suited to different levels of government. For example, because of travel time, fire departments can cover only a limited area, so the optimal sharing group for a fire department is relatively small. This argues for producing fire departments through local governments. National defense, on the other hand, protects everyone in the nation; in fact, the national defense of the United States even offers some protection to individuals in many other nations of the world. Here, a strong argument can be made for producing defense at the national, and even at the international, level. This is the economic rationale behind international defense organizations such as NATO.

The government produces many different types of goods; some of them are better produced by smaller units of government, others by larger units. This is the economic justification for having a federal system of government. The many different sizes of governmental units, some of them with overlapping jurisdictions, can be justified in light of the various types of goods that these governments produce. Ideally, every good or service is produced at its most efficient level of government.

Intergovernmental Competition

The concept of intergovernmental competition mentioned earlier is examined in more detail here. Although as a general principle every good or service should be produced at the most efficient level of government, intergovernmental competition is a good reason for producing governmental output at the lowest level of government possible. The first of several aspects of intergovernmental competition to be considered is that different governments can supply various types of publicly provided goods and services that potentially can better satisfy the demands of the many types of people in a nation.[2]

Intergovernmental Competition and Consumer Choice

In view of the wide variety of goods demanded in the private sector—different types of automobiles, soft drinks, restaurants, and so on—it stands to reason that people would also have different demands for public sector output such as parks, roads, and schools. One problem with public sector output is that the characteristics of government output tend to be what the median voter demands rather than being tailored to the demands of individual consumers. If there are many different local governments, however, each can produce a mix of goods and services that satisfies the demands of the people in that community better than one government producing only one type of output can.

The concept of intergovernmental competition is depicted in Figure 19.1. Assume that there are three types of people living in an area, with demand curves for public sector output D_1, D_2, and D_3, respectively. If each group contains an approximately equal number of people, then the collective demand for public sector output is the demand curve of the median voter, so Q_2 will tend to be produced. This satisfies individuals with demand D_2, but people with demand D_1 will prefer less output, and people with demand D_3 will prefer more.

If this area were split into three communities, each with their own local governments, then one government could produce Q_1, the second could produce Q_2, and the third could produce Q_3. People with low demands for government output would tend to settle in the community producing Q_1, while those demanding more government output would settle in the community producing Q_3. The resulting public sector output would provide greater utility to individuals preferring something other than what the median voter would most like to consume. In this sense a larger number of local governments can better satisfy a variety of preferences than one big government, which is the first advantage of producing government output through smaller rather than larger governments.

Of course, with a limited number of local governments, everybody's demands cannot be fully addressed. The point is that with a larger number of governments, most people can find one that more closely reflects their individual preferences. Indeed, intergovernmental competition works to provide government output that satisfies the demands of voters as long as the government's leaders compete to retain office by providing the type of output that their constituents want.

---

[2]The classic article on intergovernmental competition is Charles Tiebout, "A Pure Theory of Local Expenditures," *Journal of Political Economy* 64 (Oct. 1956), pp. 416–424.

Figure 19.1 Intergovernmental Competition If a large government contained many individuals with demands such as D_1, D_2, and D_3, the governmental output most preferred by the median voter, Q_2, would tend to be produced. But if there were many small governments producing different levels of output, people could choose among output levels Q_1, Q_2, and Q_3 to receive the amount of governmental output they most preferred.

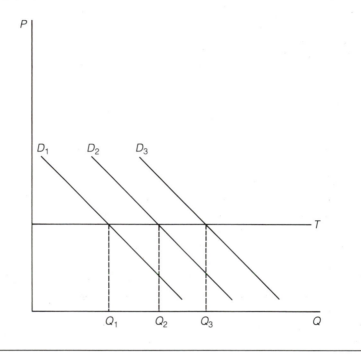

Mobility and Intergovernmental Competition

When many governments exist in an area, people can choose the one that best meets their desires. If they do not like the government where they live, they are free to "vote with their feet," that is, they are free to move to another jurisdiction if one is available. By voting with their feet, they establish a pattern of public sector demands that will result in a variety of types of output from various governments.

Other Governments as a Basis for Comparison

Mobility helps to promote intergovernmental competition, but it is not the only factor. Keep in mind that governmental officials must satisfy their constituents to be reelected. With many different governments in an area, citizens of one government can compare the activities and costs of their government with other, nearby governments. If their government compares favorably, they are more likely to reelect their officials than if it compares unfavorably. In the latter case new elected officials might improve the situation. Therefore, even if the citizens are not mobile, the fact that they can compare their government with others gives them a method by which to evaluate their elected officials and make their preferences known at the ballot box.

The ability to use other governments as a basis for comparison is not a trivial issue, because in light of the limited incentives for governmental efficiency, legitimate questions about the effectiveness of intergovernmental competition can be raised. For example, we argued that with many different local governments available, individuals can seek out the one that provides the public sector output they demand. This presupposes that governmental officials have the incentive to produce the type of governmental output that residents demand. In the private sector the profit motive provides the incentives for suppliers to produce what consumers desire. In the public sector some incentives along these lines are provided because governmental officials in one locality can be compared with officials in other areas.

The incentives may not be perfect, so the point is not to argue that the same incentives for efficiency exist with state and local governments as exist in the private market. However, the lower the level of governmental production, the better voters will be able to compare their governments with other, similar governments. Therefore, there are efficiency reasons for producing public sector output at the lowest level of government possible.

In short, intergovernmental competition has a number of efficiency-generating aspects to it. It allows a greater variety of government goods and services to be made available to people, thereby better satisfying heterogeneous demands for government goods and services. Individuals can "vote with their feet" to register their demands for the different goods and services offered by different communities. In addition, nearby governments can serve as yardsticks against which voters can measure their local government. If their government looks good compared to surrounding governments, they are likely to re-elect their officials, but if it looks bad, they can express their feelings at the ballot box. This provides the elected officials in a community with the incentive to produce government goods and services that satisfy the demands of their constituents.

The Roles of Different Levels of Government

In theory, as previously noted, different levels of government are better suited for different types of public sector output. In this section we examine how that division takes place in the United States. The data in Chapter 1 showed that state and local governments combined spend about as much as the federal government, and that state and local government spending has been growing more rapidly than federal spending since World War II. Table 19.1 provides more information about the spending activities of state and local governments.

Note that education is responsible for by far the largest amount of state and local government spending, followed by public welfare. Recall from Chapter 1 the tremendous increase in importance of government transfer

Table 19.1 State and Local Government Spending for Selected Years

CATEGORY	1970		1980		1983	
	Billion $	Percent	Billion $	Percent	Billion $	Percent
Education	52.7	40.4	133.2	36.1	163.9	33.6
Highways	16.4	12.6	33.3	9.0	36.7	7.5
Public welfare	14.7	11.3	47.3	12.8	60.9	12.5
Health and hospitals	9.7	7.4	32.2	8.7	44.1	9.0
Natural resources	4.6	3.6	12.0	3.3	15.1	3.1
Housing and urban renewal	2.1	1.6	6.1	1.7	8.5	1.7
Interest*	4.4	3.4	14.7	4.0	24.1	4.9
Other	25.8	19.8	90.3	24.5	135.0	27.7

*Includes interest on general debt only.

Source: *Statistical Abstract of the United States*, 1985 edition, p. 263; 1986 edition, p. 264; and author's calculations.

programs. The data in Table 19.1 indicates a similar pattern in state and local spending, though total public welfare spending at that level of government is still less than half of spending on education. If health and hospitals are added to this category as another type of human service, the total increases dramatically, but it still does not equal the amount spent on education. Clearly, education remains the most important governmental function of state and local governments.

In 1970 highways were the second most important category of state and local government spending, behind education. Note that the relative importance of highways has fallen significantly, with highway expenditures in 1983 comprising little more than half of the budget share that they comprised in 1970.

Another category that may warrant comment is interest payments. The figures in the table represent payments on general debt, so they would not include interest payments by a university for buildings, for example, because

that would be a part of education. The figure has risen since 1970, but that reflects higher interest rates more than an increase in indebtedness. Per capita indebtedness increased from $706 in 1970 to $1763 in 1982, but the price level more than doubled during that time, and per capita spending of state and local governments increased from $728 to $2300 during the same time period.

The activities undertaken by state and local governments vary from state to state. For example, elementary and secondary education typically is undertaken at the local level, and states provide educational institutions beyond the secondary level. Even here, variation occurs; some states provide education through city or county governments, and others have separate school districts. Variety in arrangements is also greater than it first appears here because of differing financing for education from state to state. Some states raise educational revenues primarily at the local level, and others have considerable state funding even though the local government provides the education.

Thus, whereas the primary role of the federal government is income redistribution and national defense, state and local governments primarily produce education. State and local governments do provide a variety of other services, such as police protection and fire protection, but these services are a minor part of the overall budgets. As was noted earlier, there are sound theoretical reasons for production of output at different levels of government. These reasons do not tell the whole story, though, because in any government activity political influences also play a role in determining the government's actions. We now turn our attention to some of the political factors.

Special Interests and Government Size

One of the factors that determines the types of goods and services produced by governments is the influence of special interests. As has been discussed at length previously, the government tends to produce programs that benefit special interests rather than programs that are in the general public interest. Legislators, who must be reelected, have an incentive to cater to the special interest groups who can promise the legislators votes and campaign contributions. The general public, however, tends to be unaware of most of what the legislature does, which creates a bias in favor of special interest programs. Although each program does not cost the taxpayer much, the sum of all of the special interest programs ends up being a large burden. But lobbyists always have an incentive to lobby for more concentrated special interest benefits for their groups than to argue for a reduction in the general level of government programs.

Federalism and Special Interests

One possible way to deal with this problem, at least partially, is to produce all government programs at the lowest governmental level possible. For example, the government's tobacco program that provides benefits to

North Carolina tobacco farmers does so by collecting a few dollars from each taxpayer across the nation and redistributing the money in concentrated form to the tobacco farmers. If the program were transferred to the state government, then the concentrated benefits to the farmers would be paid for by taxpayers of the state rather than the nation, and the costs to each taxpayer for the program would be about fifty times as great. This would certainly provide more of an incentive for the taxpayers to become informed about the program, and it is likely that fewer special interest programs could be enacted.

Unfortunately, this type of solution would be unacceptable to many current special interest programs. During President Reagan's first term in office in 1981, he advocated "a new federalism" in which many federal programs would be turned over to the states. Predictably, the states and the special interests protested because they recognized the disadvantages to them, but nobody had an incentive to lobby for the general public interest. It is not surprising that little has been heard about "the new federalism" since then.

Ideally, programs should be produced at the lowest level of government possible to minimize the effects of special interests on the programs and to allow intergovernmental competition to enhance the efficiency of the government. Perhaps it would be possible to move some current programs to lower levels of government despite the political obstacles. Certainly, such possibilities could be advanced when new government programs are being considered. New programs are proposed frequently, especially at the federal level, and sometimes the programs are evaluated on the basis of whether the intended effects are desirable. These programs could also be evaluated in terms of the appropriate level of government at which production should take place.

Indeed, some programs that are produced at the national level probably could be produced at the state level, and some programs produced at the state level probably could be produced at the local level. By producing at the lowest level of government possible, the influence of special interests is minimized, and the benefits of intergovernmental competition maximized. When evaluating the merits of a government program, we must ask whether the program could be produced at a lower level of government.

Centralization and the Cartelization of Governments

In the private sector of the economy the government has a policy, backed by law, of enforcing competition. The most spectacular recent example of that was the breaking up of AT&T in 1983, but the Federal Trade Commission and the Justice Department routinely take action against what they view as anticompetitive behavior, not only by breaking up large firms, as in the case of AT&T, but also by preventing the merger of small firms. Keep in mind, however, that what is viewed as competition in the private sector of the economy is often regarded as duplication of effort in the government. If two agencies or departments have overlapping functions, a move may be made to eliminate the duplication of effort.

Competition in the Public Sector

Competition can be as beneficial in the public sector as in the private sector, and maybe even more so. In the market a price system provides market signals about the efficiency of a firm's production, so in a sense every firm can be compared to every other firm. In the public sector a price system for the government's output usually does not exist, so there is no clear way to judge when a government is producing efficiently, though clues can be provided by comparing the efficiency of one governmental unit with another producing the same type of output.

Cartelizing behavior in government often occurs under the justification of enforcing some types of standards on government programs, and it is more common than generally thought. For example, in recent years state boards of education have been exerting more influence over the educational process when compared to local school districts, and the federal government itself has become more involved, having established the Department of Education under President Carter's administration. The result is that with less power being wielded by smaller governments, and more power by larger ones, intergovernmental competition is lessened.

If the states collect more education taxes

Table 19.2 Number of Governmental Units in the United States

TYPE OF GOVERNMENT	YEAR				
	1942	*1952*	*1962*	*1972*	*1982*
Federal government	1	1	1	1	1
State government	48	48	50	50	50
Local governments	155,067	116,694	91,186	78,218	82,290
County	3,050	3,049	3,043	3,044	3,041
Municipal	16,220	16,778	18,000	18,517	19,076
Township and town	18,919	17,202	17,142	16,991	16,734
School district	108,579	67,346	34,678	15,781	14,851
Special district	8,299	12,379	18,323	23,885	28,588
Totals	155,116	116,743	91,237	78,269	82,341

Source: *Statistical Abstract of the United States*, 1986 edition, p. 261.

(compared to localities), and if the states wield more power and control in enforcing standardized educational programs, this lessens the chances for individuals to take advantage of the intergovernmental competition provided by variety in local government programs.[3] In effect, formerly localized educational programs are evolving into state programs, with the resulting lessening in the amount of intergovernmental competition.

The Number of Governments

Another factor to consider with regard to intergovernmental competition is the number of governments available to compete. Table 19.2 presents some interesting information in this regard. For example, note that from 1942

to 1982, the number of governmental units in the United States fell almost by half, with most of that decrease accounted for by the drastic reduction in the number of school districts. Because education is the largest single function of state and local governments, this is another example of how intergovernmental competition, under the guise of reducing duplication of effort, has been lessened.

Table 19.2 also reveals that the number of special districts has increased by more than three times from 1942 to 1982. Often, the creation of a special district is also a sign of reduced intergovernmental competition, because special districts are frequently formed by groups of governments to pursue activities such as flood and mosquito control and harbor maintenance. Although there may be good reasons for groups of governments to work together in this way, such cooperative efforts still have the undesirable by-product of lessening intergovernmental competition.

[3]See R. G. Holcombe, "The Florida System: A Bowen Equilibrium Referendum System," *National Tax Journal* 30 (March 1977), pp. 77–84, for a discussion of the centralizing tendency in education in Florida.

Regulations and Grants

Regulations also provide a method for centralizing governmental activity and, in effect, cartelizing government. The case of schools was mentioned earlier, but the same process applies to all types of regulation by which a higher government oversees a lower one. Many programs run by lower governments must abide by regulations handed down by higher governments. For example, state governments impose rules on local educational institutions, which limits the amount of variety, innovation, and intergovernmental competition that can occur at the local level, in effect making local governments into cartel members rather than competitors.

Regulation and Competition

State governments are free to impose regulations on localities within their states, but the Constitution limits the federal government's ability to regulate the states. Because of its financial power, however, the federal government often imposes rules as a condition to qualify for certain governmental grants. For example, states must abide by the federal 55 mile per hour speed limit in order to qualify for federal highway funds, and educational institutions have a host of reporting requirements related to affirmative action as a condition of receiving federal aid. In this sense the federal government budget allows the federal government to buy some regulatory control over programs run by states and localities.

Grants and Competition

Direct grants can provide even more direct control and further lessen intergovernmental competition. For example, many major airport improvements are paid for by federal government funding, with the local governments assuming perhaps 10 percent of the total cost. This means that local governments can often buy airport improvements and have their taxpayers pay only 10 percent of the true cost, with the rest of the cost shared over the rest of the nation. Grants of this type give local governments little incentive to evaluate the cost effectiveness of these projects. If a $1 million airport improvement project would be worth only $100,000 to the local taxpayers, it would still be worthwhile for the airport manager to obtain the federal grant and improve the airport. These types of projects would be much less likely to be undertaken if the locality that was reaping the benefits was required to finance 100 percent of the project.

In short, government regulations and grants from larger to smaller governments have the effect of making the smaller governments more homogeneous and therefore lessening the effects of intergovernmental competition. Certainly, there are valid reasons for producing some goods and services at the federal level. By the same token there are valid reasons for keeping production of public sector output at the lowest level of government possible.

Intergovernmental Revenue

Intergovernmental revenue is a significant source of funds for lower level governments. Table 19.3 gives an indication of the extent to which intergovernmental revenues are used to finance expenditures at various levels of government. The federal government re-

Table 19.3 Intergovernmental Revenue, 1982

GOVERNMENT LEVEL	REVENUES FROM OWN SOURCES (MILLION $)	INTERGOVERNMENTAL REVENUE (MILLION $)	INTERGOVERNMENTAL AS A PERCENT OF TOTAL
Federal	685,835	1,812	2.6
State	261,784	69,166	20.9
Local	197,168	115,693	36.9

Source: *Statistical Abstract of the United States*, 1985 edition, p. 264.

ceives a relatively small amount of its revenues from other governments, but state governments rely on other governments—primarily the federal government—for over 20 percent of their financing, and local governments receive over a third of their revenues from other governments.

Intergovernmental transfers of revenue occur for some good reasons. For example, a higher-level government may finance a project that a lower-level government does not have the incentive (or funds) to undertake itself. However, such reasons must be balanced against the alternative of lowering taxes collected at higher levels of governments in order to allow lower levels to tax more. We will consider whether a shift in patterns of taxation is desirable later in the chapter, but first we need to outline why such intergovernmental revenue transfers may have undesirable effects. Two important reasons have already been noted—intergovernmental grants lessen both intergovernmental competition and the incentive for the lower level government to realistically assess the costs and benefits of the project funded by a grant.

Another factor to consider is that the federal tax system allows state and local taxes to be deducted from income to figure income taxable at the federal level. Because of this, intergovernmental grants increase the tax base. If state and local programs are paid for by state and local taxes, those taxes are deducted from the federal income tax base. But if revenue-sharing dollars are used instead, then the taxes are collected at the federal level and the income remains in the tax base. Therefore, using federal taxes rather than state taxes enlarges the tax base and enables the government to raise more revenue.

Intergovernmental revenue transfers can also lead to effective cartelization in lower levels of government.[4] State governments compete with each other for tax bases; this is especially relevant in cases in which industrial location decisions are being made. States can increase their tax rates to try to collect more revenue, but this will lead to an erosion of the tax base as businesses relocate in states with lower tax rates, all other things held equal. Intergovernmental grants can be a way to lessen this intergovernmental competition by making local taxes and expenditures more homogeneous.

There are a number of different types of intergovernmental grant programs, but they can be divided into two distinct groups. First,

---

[4]See Richard B. McKenzie and Robert J. Staaf, "Revenue Sharing and Monopoly Government," *Public Choice* 33, no. 3 (1978), pp. 93–97.

with general revenue sharing, one government—in this case the federal government—gives money to other governments to spend as they choose. Second, with categorical grants the grant money is intended to be spent for some specific purpose. Categorical grants comprise about 95 percent of the intergovernmental revenue received by lower-level governments.

Revenue Sharing

Revenue sharing was established in 1972 as a method by which the federal government could share its revenues with states and localities. Under revenue sharing the federal government distributes funds to smaller governments according to a formula; note that the tax efforts of the states and localities are an important factor in that formula. As a result of this incentive system, even though more revenues come to states and localities, they have a disincentive to reduce their taxes, because this results in a reduction in shared revenue as well. Indeed, revenue sharing can cause state and local taxes to increase, because the higher those taxes are, the more revenue the federal government will disperse to them. In this context revenue sharing has the effect of subsidizing state and local government growth.

When revenue sharing was originally proposed in the early 1960s, many economists believed that federal revenues would grow faster than federal expenditures, leaving the federal government with a surplus to be distributed as revenue sharing. By the time revenue sharing was implemented in 1972, the government had run budget deficits in all but one of the previous twelve years, and the deficit situation in the 1980s suggests that the original economic justification for revenue sharing has disappeared. Nevertheless, the political incentives for revenue sharing as a means of lessening intergovernmental competition remain.

Categorical Grants

Categorical grants are made for some specific purpose, and though the terms of different grants may vary, they share similar effects. Sometimes, a grant pays for an entire project; other times, as in the airport improvement example, the smaller government assumes a portion of the cost. Categorical grants typically are made in order to ensure that the money is spent for the purpose stated in the grant, but this may or may not actually occur. It depends on how much the government would have spent without the grant.

Consider, for example, a local government that is given a federal grant for wastewater treatment. An economic justification for the grant might be that the community would spend less than the optimal amount without the grant because of the negative externality associated with insufficiently treated wastewater. Therefore, a grant is given to the community to assist in the construction of the wastewater plant. This is illustrated in Figure 19.2, where the community's indifference curve and budget constraint are tangent at point A. Presumably, this indifference curve is the indifference curve of the median voter, assuming that the community responds to the median voter's preferences, as suggested in Chapter 7. Without a grant the community would spend W_1 on wastewater treatment and G_1 on all other items in the community budget. The federal government deems that W_1 is a less-than-optimal spending level and therefore grants W_2, which can be spent only on wastewater treatment, to the community. The community's budget constraint now shifts out to the line passing through point B and parallel to the original budget constraint. The new budget constraint shows that the

Figure 19.2 A Categorical Grant That Differs from a General Grant Without a grant a community locates at point A and produces amount W_1 of wastewater treatment. A grant giving the community W_2 to spend on wastewater treatment increases the amount they spend by giving the community the incentive to locate at point B. If a general grant were given, the community would rather locate at point C and spend less on wastewater treatment.

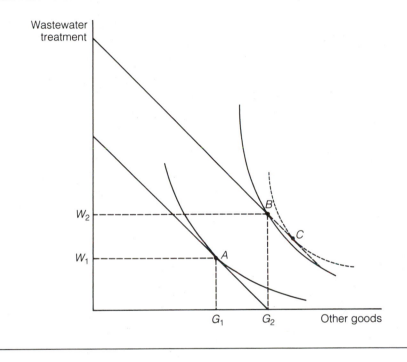

community must spend at least W_2 on wastewater treatment to receive the grant but can allocate the rest of the budget as they please. The community chooses to locate at point B, spending only the grant money on the treatment plant, and spending the rest of the budget on other items.

Two things are worthy of note here. First, the community did spend more in wastewater treatment as a result of the grant. Second, if it had been a general rather than a categorical grant specifically for wastewater treatment, the community would have preferred to lo-

cate at point C on the new budget constraint. Therefore, the categorical grant served its purpose of getting the community to spend more on wastewater treatment than if the community had simply been given an unrestricted grant.

In this example the community spent the grant on the wastewater treatment facility but none of their other discretionary funds. If they had, this would have indicated that the community had treated the categorical grant the same as a general grant. This point is illustrated in Figure 19.3, which resembles Figure

Figure 19.3 A Categorical Grant with the Same Effects as a General Grant

As in Figure 19.2, the community would locate at point *A* without a grant. In receiving a categorical grant of W_2 to spend on wastewater treatment, the community would spend more than this and locate at point *B*. In this case there is no difference between the categorical grant and a general grant of the same amount.

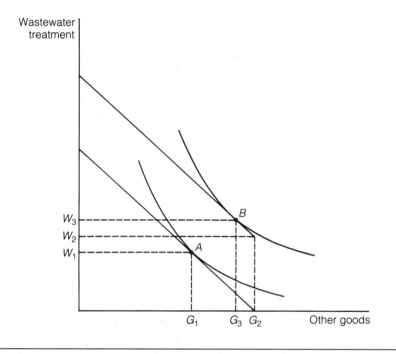

19.2 in that the community starts at point *A* without the grant. However, this time the community locates at point *B* after receiving the grant and spends more than the amount of the grant on the wastewater treatment facility. Although this might be viewed as desirable, note that there is no difference between the categorical grant earmarked for wastewater treatment and a general grant that allows the community to spend the money any way it chooses. In either case W_3 would have been spent on wastewater treatment.

Under these conditions a general grant is preferable because, by allowing unrestricted use of the funds, it reduces both the amount of record keeping that the local government must do and the monitoring that the higher-level government must do to see that the money is spent as the grant requires. In this sense general grants are preferable to categorical grants. However, categorical grants may be desirable in instances where they correct externalities. But again, note that if the community spends any more than the grant requires, the effect is no different from that of a general grant.

When a case like the one depicted in Figure 19.3 arises, it is preferable simply to issue a

Figure 19.4 Matching Grants In this case the local government is required to spend $G_3 - G_2$ on the project in order to receive the grant. This leaves relative prices unchanged but has the effect of preventing the local government from locating in the dashed portion of the budget constraint, where it would rather be.

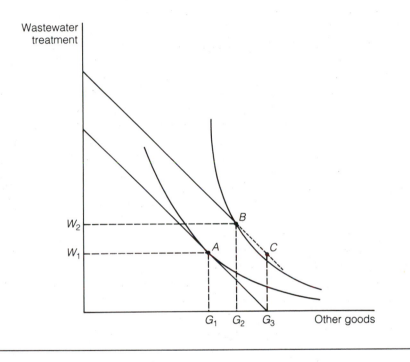

general grant rather than a categorical grant. By contrast, in cases like the one depicted in Figure 19.2, the categorical grant has the effect of getting the local government to spend more on the targeted good than it would have without the categorical grant, which is the grant's intention. Indeed, local governments can be prompted into contributing their own funds to a project such as wastewater treatment through the use of a matching grant. The effects of a matching grant are illustrated in Figure 19.4. Here, the local government must contribute $G_3 - G_2$ in order to receive the grant, after which they can spend W_2, the

combination of the grant plus the local government's contribution. Note that if the same grant had not required the matching contribution, the local government could have located at point C, but because the grant is a matching grant, the local government must end up at point B, or perhaps even further from C on the budget constraint. But again, if the firm were further up on the budget constraint, the matching grant would have the same effect as a general grant.

To this point we have assumed that local governments simply add the amount of the grant to what already would have been spent to increase the local government's level of spending. Another alternative, however, is to use the money to cut taxes. This could be depicted in the diagrams by including tax cuts as one of the other goods purchased with the government's budget. Some tax issues that apply specifically to local governments are examined in the next section.

Tax Issues and Local Governments

The concept of intergovernmental competition is important to local government finance in terms of both tax issues and spending issues. If individuals are dissatisfied with their local government's tax structure, they can leave. Likewise, businesses are sensitive to the tax policies of various local governments, which, in order to attract commercial activity, must remain competitive with alternative locations. Indeed, the mobility of factors of production has significant implications for local government tax policy, because if a factor is being taxed heavily in one area, it can move somewhere else. This mobility is quite relevant to the types of taxes used by local governments. Furthermore, within this competitive framework it makes sense that localities would cut taxes in response to intergovernmental grants. Tax cuts are one of the benefits that can be purchased with the grants. Although this provides some motivation for categorical grants, it cannot stop governments from taking money that would have been spent in the area covered by the grant and converting it into a tax cut.

Taxes Paid by Immobile Factors

Recall from the discussion of property taxes in Chapter 13 that when factors of production that are being heavily taxed in one locality migrate to another, the burden of the tax is shifted to factors that cannot move, which ultimately means land. For example, if a high income tax causes capital to move away from

a particular area, the ratio of capital to land falls, lowering the marginal product of land and its value. Owners of land receive less, and owners of capital more, before-tax income in order to compensate for the tax differentials, and the tax burden eventually is capitalized into the value of the land. This explains why local governments rely relatively more heavily on property taxes than income taxes. Income earners can migrate to another area, but land obviously cannot. Ultimately, all taxes are borne by factors that cannot migrate away from them.

Capitalization of Debt

The same argument applies to the use of debt rather than taxes to finance local public goods. Current taxpayers can avoid taxation by issuing bonds, perhaps intending to move away from the area before the bonds are paid off. But the bonds will be paid off by future taxpayers who might move into the area, which means that the value of moving into the area will be less by the amount of the debt that must be paid off. Therefore, the value of land in the area will fall by the amount of debt that is associated with the property.

Capitalization of Public Goods

Taxes and public debt may lower the value of property in an area if the revenues are not productively spent. However, if the revenues are used productively, perhaps to build parks, roads, and schools and to hire police and fire protection, then the value of these public goods and services will increase the value of the property. In other words increased taxes in an area can be associated with higher property values when tax revenues are spent in a way that enhances the value of residing in that area.

Deductibility of State and Local Taxes

Currently, state and local taxes are deductible from income for purposes of computing the federal income tax.[5] The effect of this deduction is to reduce the marginal cost to the taxpayer of paying state and local taxes. For example, a person in the 25 percent marginal tax bracket for federal taxes who pays $1000 in state and local taxes reduces federal taxable income by $1000 and federal tax liability by $250. Therefore, the person pays $1000 in state and local taxes but suffers a loss of only $750 in income to do so.

As this example suggests, the deductibility of state and local taxes from income provides a subsidy to states and localities, making it less expensive for the state and local taxpayers to pay their state and local taxes. This provides a benefit to those who live in high-tax states at the expense of those who live in low-tax states. An equity argument, however, states that people should not have to pay taxes on the income that they use to pay taxes, that is, that money used to pay state and local taxes should not be taxed again in the income tax. This argument is most persuasive if taxes are viewed as tribute paid to the government. But within the fiscal exchange model of taxation, taxes are viewed as the price one pays for government goods and services. In this light it seems just as fair to pay taxes on the money one uses to buy roads as to pay taxes on the money one uses to buy cars. Regardless of how one views the equity argument, the fact that state and local taxes are deductible for purposes of federal income tax lowers the cost to the taxpayer of paying these taxes and therefore gives the state and local governments an incentive to tax and spend more.

Conclusion

A federal system of government makes sense from an economic standpoint because different sizes of sharing groups are optimal for different types of goods. For some goods, such as swimming pools and garbage collection, small units of government can exhaust all of the economies of scale, and no significant spillovers across government boundaries will occur. In these cases small units of government are well suited to the production of public sector output. For other types of goods, such as national defense, the economies of scale and spillovers suggest that production should take place at the national and even international level of government. For example, NATO can be viewed as an organization that produces public sector output on an international scale.

Although valid reasons can be advanced in support of large units of government, strong arguments can also be made for producing governmental output at the lowest level possible. These arguments center around the

---

[5] This applies only to income taxes. Sales taxes, which were deductible before the 1986 tax reform act, are no longer deductible.

virtues of intergovernmental competition, which allows individuals to move to the local jurisdictions that best suit their preferences for public sector output. If individuals do not like their current local government, they can "vote with their feet" by moving to a locality whose government suits them better. There are two aspects to this. First, individuals can move from inefficient governments to more efficient ones. Second, because people have different preferences for governments (as well as cars, soft drinks, and other goods), a greater diversity of local governments from which to choose enhances the opportunity for individuals to find the one that most closely satisfies their demands.

Even if individuals do not move, simply by having other, nearby governments against which to compare theirs can indicate how their local officials are performing. Elected officials in governments that compare favorably to surrounding governments can expect to be reelected, whereas those in governments that compare unfavorably can expect to be voted out of office. The ability to compare the performance of governments fosters intergovernmental competition regardless of the mobility of residents.

When production of public sector output takes place at larger levels of government than necessary, this enhances the ability of special interests to manipulate the political process to their favor. Special interests can get special interest programs passed because they have an incentive to lobby the government for concentrated benefits. Because the benefits are paid for by tax payments diluted over the entire nation, the general public has little incentive to become informed about the program. But if programs are produced at lower governmental levels, the costs of the programs become far more concentrated, which provides an incentive to keep governmental programs under control.

Often, regulations and grants from larger governmental units to smaller ones have the effect of cartelizing the smaller units of government. Without the influence of larger levels of government, intergovernmental competition will take place, but regulations and grants tend to make smaller governmental units more homogeneous, which lessens the competition among them.

Different types of grants can have different effects under some circumstances. Categorical grants, which make up the bulk of intergovernmental grants, force the recipient to spend the grant in a particular way. When the recipient spends nothing more than the grant requires in that area, the grant increases the amount the government spends. However, the local government can reallocate funds not covered by the grant, so if the local government spends more than the amount required by the categorical grant, the effect on the spending mix of the recipient is no different than that of a general grant.

Issues regarding local taxation are as important to local governments as spending issues. Because factors of production can move away from areas where they are being taxed heavily, the burden of local taxes ultimately is borne by immobile factors, which means land. This explains why local governments rely more heavily on property taxes than on income taxes and other tax bases for revenue.

In conclusion, some government programs are better suited to smaller governments, whereas others are better suited to larger ones. Therefore, a federal system of government stands on a strong economic foundation. However, there are many reasons why governmental programs are most effectively produced at the smallest level of government possible. In evaluating government programs, it is not enough simply to decide whether the program is desirable in and of itself; it is also important to determine at what level of government the program would be most appropriately produced.

Questions

1. What are the most important areas of economic activity for state and local governments? How have these areas been changing over the years?

2. Explain the benefits of intergovernmental competition. Are there benefits to intergovernmental competition even if it is not feasible for individuals to move to different governmental jurisdictions? Explain.

3. What does it mean to say that with many competing governments people can "vote with their feet"? Use a graph to show the benefits that can accrue from individuals locating in governments that best suit their personal preferences for governmental output.

4. What are the advantages and disadvantages of larger governments? Use your answer as a foundation to explain why it is desirable to have different levels of government in an economy.

5. Governments have a tendency to favor special interests. Are special interests more likely to get a better deal from a higher level of government or a lower level of government? Explain the factors that enter into your answer.

6. Governmental programs (and even governments) are often combined, supposedly to eliminate a duplication of effort. Critically examine this assertion. Discuss the role of competition and the incentives facing those in government.

7. Discuss some factors that enable governments to limit intergovernmental competition by acting, in effect, like cartels. Give some examples of cartelizing activities pursued by governments.

8. What is revenue sharing? What was the original justification for the revenue-sharing program? Why, if the original justification no longer applies, is the revenue-sharing program continued? Discuss the political factors involved.

9. Explain the differences between categorical grants and general grants. What will cause the effects to be similar, and what will cause them to be different?

10. Should state and local taxes be deducted from income for purposes of computing federal income tax liability? Discuss the issues on both sides.

CHAPTER TWENTY

Alternatives to Government Production

*I*n the preceding nineteen chapters we have surveyed the activities of governments. Clearly, some persuasive arguments can be advanced in favor of government production of some goods and services that cannot be produced efficiently in the private sector of the economy. Collective consumption goods, positive and negative externalities, and poorly defined property rights in general would lead to inefficient allocation of resources in private sector production, if the goods were produced in the private sector at all. For these reasons the option of having the government step in and produce some output must be considered.

Just as there are impediments to perfect efficiency in the private sector, so there are impediments to perfect efficiency in the public sector as well. Therefore, the recognition that a problem may exist with the market's allocation of a good or service does not necessarily imply that the government can produce the good or service any better. We have discussed these issues throughout the text in an effort to identify not only why government might be desired but also why well-intended government actions can have less-than-optimal re-

sults. We choose the type of government we have, and so we need to be aware of the government's strengths and weaknesses in assessing what types of activities we want the government to pursue. Unlike so much else in life, the government we end up with is the one that we have chosen collectively. Understanding the process of selection, and the implications of those choices, are vitally important— it is what sets public sector economics apart from other branches of economics, which do not produce such direct policy implications.

In this, the final chapter, we want to examine a middle ground between public sector and private sector production. There may be good reasons why the private sector alone cannot produce a good efficiently when measured against some ideal standard, but this does not necessarily mean that all production should be turned over to the public sector. Indeed, some combination of private sector and public sector activity may be more effective.

Several such alternative solutions have appeared throughout the text. Recall, for example, that when a negative externality is produced, the government need not automatically take over production of the good generating the externality. Rather, a corrective tax, a regulation, or perhaps a combination of both can effectively internalize the externality while leaving production of the good primarily in the private sector of the economy. In Chapter 8, which focused on public sector supply, we presented some examples in which the government contracted with private sector organizations for goods and services. Likewise, in Chapter 18 we suggested that the rights to a natural monopoly could be auctioned off, approximating the results of a competitive market. Even competition among governments in a federal system is an alternative to having the central government be responsible for production of a good or service. This chapter will examine in more detail some of these possible alternatives to public sector production.

Note that the material in this chapter represents an application of principles covered in previous chapters and is not, strictly speaking, new material. In Part Two of the text, which covered the idea of economic efficiency, we demonstrated that the market does not always allocate resources as efficiently as in an ideal model. There is a tendency when confronted with inefficient allocation by the market to argue that the government should become involved to remedy the inefficiency. The same

argument might be made with perceived inequities—if the market is inequitable, then the government should step in to provide a remedy.

This argument falls short on two counts. First, it is inappropriate to compare the real world operation of the market with a hypothetical, idealized government. Governments do not allocate resources perfectly either, so market allocation should be measured against the real world operation of government.[1] In Part Three we analyzed governmental decision making to try to provide a framework for making this type of comparison. Keep in mind that one is bound to be disappointed if one expects the government to solve all of one's problems. This is not a criticism of government but simply a recognition of the fact that there are limits to what the government can accomplish.

Even in cases in which the government could be involved beneficially, the simple argument that the government should provide a remedy is incomplete—the government is not a monolithic entity that solves problems, but rather a large number of organizations that have the capability of addressing issues in many different ways. The primary purpose of this chapter is to examine potential alternatives when government action is suggested.

Government Contracts to Private Organizations

Often, government involvement in an economic activity is viewed as desirable because of a failure of the private sector to demand the optimal amount of the good or service in question. The problems of collective consumption goods and positive externalities fall into this category. One frequently used solution to this problem is to have the government

pay for the output but contract with private sector firms for production. For example, national defense is one of those activities in

---

[1] This is the central theme in James M. Buchanan, "Public Finance and Public Choice," *National Tax Journal* 28 (Dec. 1975), pp. 383–394.

which the potential for free riding suggests that not enough defense would be produced through the private sector alone. The Defense Department spends a tremendous amount of money on weapons procurement, but the actual production of the equipment is almost always undertaken by private sector firms under contract to the Department of Defense.

Private Versus Public Production

Admittedly, there can be problems with government contracts to private organizations. Cost overruns and abuses often make the news; some of these problems were outlined in Chapter 17. However, when production by private firms is compared to production by the government, study after study has shown that the private sector firm can produce the output at less expense.[2] Although for many activities undertaken in the public sector, there are no clear private sector counterparts, when direct comparisons can be made, the results are illuminating.

Several studies have compared private sector and public sector health care. For example, Kenneth Clarkson found that proprietary hospitals—hospitals that are privately owned and profit-seeking—were managed more efficiently than public hospitals, with managers in proprietary hospitals spending more time on unpleasant tasks such as working night shifts and supervising employees.[3] Clarkson

also found that wages in government hospitals were higher than wages in private hospitals. Clarkson's explanation for these discrepancies is a direct implication of the differing system of property rights in public and private institutions. Because the managers of public institutions have no claim to any profits generated through efficient operations, they tend to utilize hospital revenues to make management of the hospital less burdensome.

Cotton M. Lindsay compared the lengths of patient stays in Veterans Administration (VA) hospitals with the lengths of stays in proprietary hospitals.[4] One measure of output used by VA hospitals (where veterans are treated at government expense) is the number of patient-days generated by the hospital. As should be expected under this type of system, Lindsay found that for the same illness, patients tended to spend roughly twice as much time in the VA hospital. For example, the average hospital stay for appendicitis was 12.1 days in a VA hospital versus 6.9 days in a proprietary hospital, for kidney stones 18.6 days versus 8.2 days, and for gallstones 26.5 days versus 11.9 days. Lindsay's documentations of inefficiencies in the form of excessively long patient stays for particular illnesses support the hypotheses made about public sector supply throughout the text. They also support Niskanen's hypothesis that bureaucracies tend to maximize their budgets, as discussed in Chapter 8.

Along the same lines H. E. Frech examined Medicare claims processing in government and proprietary hospitals.[5] Frech found

---

[2] A number of these types of studies are reviewed in James T. Bennett and Manuel H. Johnson, "Tax Reduction Without Sacrifice: Private Sector Production of Public Services," *Public Finance Quarterly* 8, no. 4 (Oct. 1980), pp. 363–396. Another relevant set of studies is found in Thomas E. Borcherding, ed., *Budgets and Bureaucrats* (Durham, N.C.: Duke University Press, 1977).

[3] Kenneth W. Clarkson, "Some Implications of Property Rights in Hospital Management," *Journal of Law & Economics* 15, no. 2 (Oct. 1972), pp. 363–384.

[4] Cotton M. Lindsay, "A Theory of Government Enterprise," *Journal of Political Economy* 84 (Oct. 1976), pp. 1061–1077.

[5] H. E. Frech III, "The Property Rights Theory of the Firm: Empirical Results from a Natural Experiment," *Journal of Political Economy* 84, no. 1 (Feb. 1976), pp. 143–152.

higher processing costs, higher processing time, and greater error rates in processing for government hospitals. This finding is supported by Blair, Ginsberg, and Vogel,[6] who found nonprofit health insurers to be less efficient than proprietary health insurers. In short, there is ample evidence that health care and related activities are more efficiently carried out in the private sector of the economy.

A most interesting study by David Davies compared a privately run airline in Australia with a governmentally run airline.[7] Davies notes that the government controls most economic variables for the two firms, including routes serviced, mail carried, and terminal facilities made available. The airlines have similar wage structures and equipment, yet according to several measures of productivity, Davies found the private firm to be uniformly more productive.

The studies cited up to this point have suggested that firms in the private sector produce more efficiently than firms in the public sector. It does not necessarily follow that the government should contract out its productive activities, because it may be that the government is even less efficient at overseeing the work of contractors than in producing the goods and services themselves, in which case the inefficiencies would remain. However, other studies of services performed by the government as compared to having the same services contracted out suggest that the government can save money by contracting out services when possible.

For example, Crain and Zardkoohi compared publicly owned utilities to privately operated utilities in the United States.[8] In some localities the government produces the water supply for the area, whereas in others the government contracts with a private supplier to provide water. Crain and Zardkoohi found the costs of production to be significantly lower for the privately operated firms. In another study Roger Ahlbrandt compared a private proprietary fire department that served Scottsdale, Arizona, to governmentally operated fire departments and found that fire protection in Scottsdale cost about half as much.[9]

Scottsdale is a community outside Phoenix. Before the city was incorporated, the private company provided fire protection to members of the community on a subscription basis. After incorporation the city of Scottsdale agreed to retain the firm for fire protection, and the firm was regulated to allow it to earn a specified return on its investment. The city specified the fire services it wanted, including the number and location of fire stations and the type of equipment and personnel used by the fire department. Although the city contracted to provide a specified return on investment, the fire department still had an incentive to keep costs as low as possible because the city contracted for the fire services for four years at a time. If the city was not satisfied with the service or the cost of service at the end of the contract, it would be free to contract with someone else or to provide its own fire services, as do most municipalities.

---

[6]Roger D. Blair, Paul B. Ginsberg, and Ronald J. Vogel, "Blue Cross-Blue Shield Administration Costs: A Study of Non-Profit Health Insurers," *Economic Inquiry* 13 (June 1975), pp. 237–251.

[7]David G. Davies, "The Efficiency of Public versus Private Firms, The Case of Australia's Two Airlines," *Journal of Law & Economics* 14, no. 1 (April 1971), pp. 149–165. See also David G. Davies, "Property Rights and Economic Efficiency—The Australian Airlines Revisited," *Journal of Law & Economics* 20, no. 1 (April 1977), pp. 223–226.

[8]W. Mark Crain and Asghar Zardkoohi, "A Test of the Property-Rights Theory of the Firm: Water Utilities in the United States," *Journal of Law & Economics* 21, no. 2, (Oct. 1978), pp. 395–408.

[9]Roger Ahlbrandt, "Efficiency in the Provision of Fire Services," *Public Choice* 16 (Fall 1973), pp. 1–15.

Fire insurance costs in Scottsdale are comparable to surrounding areas, and Ahlbrandt concludes that protection provided to residents of Scottsdale is of equal quality to a governmentally operated fire department, but at about half the cost. These findings support the argument on the benefits of having the government contract out for services it wants to provide rather than produce the services itself.

Method of Production

Indeed, the government frequently contracts out for the production of goods and services, but it could do even more. Bennett and Johnson[10] demonstrate for a number of different types of output, including refuse collection, fire protection, debt collection, health care, and ship repair, that efficiency gains could be realized by contracting with private sector firms to produce the output. They cite some of the studies mentioned in this section as well as other studies in arguing that the government tends to be more labor intensive and less productive than private sector firms engaging in the same activities.

Along these lines it is interesting to note that most states contract out the highway construction in the state but use a governmental agency to repair highways. Is there any reason why highway repair could not be contracted out? The U.S. Postal Service has a governmentally granted monopoly on the delivery of first-class mail. Is there any reason why mail delivery could not be contracted out? Consider the possibilities. The government could abandon the mail delivery business altogether, leaving the service to private firms such as United Parcel Service and Federal Express. This would undoubtedly cause those firms to expand and would also lower the cost of local delivery, though it might raise the cost of longer distance delivery or delivery to isolated areas. If this was viewed as undesirable, the government could continue the Postal Service, but could contract out for mail services rather than have them performed by government employees.[11] In short, it is apparent that government contracts to private organizations are an alternative to government production. The choices are not limited to the private sector and the public sector, but can be publicly financed and privately produced.

Competition and Contracts

The popular press continually relates stories about absurd government expenditures, such as $400 hammers and $6000 coffee makers. Abuses like this can be reduced in several ways. One alternative is careful government oversight, regulation, and auditing of contractors. A more effective alternative, however, is competition among suppliers, an idea

---

[10] James T. Bennett and Manuel H. Johnson, "Tax Reduction Without Sacrifice: Private Sector Production of Public Services," *Public Finance Quarterly* 8, no. 4 (Oct. 1980), pp. 363–396.

[11] The postal service and other government services are discussed in Stuart M. Butler, *Privatizing Federal Spending* (New York: Universe Books, 1985).

that was explored in Chapter 18 and is reviewed here.

Contracts in Place of Regulation

The Scottsdale fire department serves as a good example of the application of Demsetz's idea of regulation.[12] Recall Demsetz's proposal that rather than set a price for a utility through regulation, the right to become the monopoly supplier of the service should be subject to competitive bidding. In Scottsdale, where the city has the option of terminating the contract every four years, there is a built-in incentive for the fire company to provide efficient low-cost service. The same could be true of other goods and services. Rather than examine the books of a company to see whether the company was spending government revenues for country club dues and the like, the government could merely choose the lowest bid. It would be irrelevant what the firms spent the money on, as long as the output was produced. Purchasers in the private sector do not know or care whether companies they buy from spend company income on vacation travel and country club dues.

Competitive Bidding

Likewise, when competitive bidding is used in the public sector—for example, when the government purchases office furniture and supplies—the government simply shops for the best deal and does not care what the supplier does with its revenues from sales. Problems can arise, however, when the government buys unique items, such as some military

hardware, where only one supplier is used. There are benefits to competitive bidding, though competitive bidding is not always possible. Indeed, as noted in the previous chapter, benefits can be realized from production of goods and services at the lowest level of government for just this reason. Where competition is possible among various governments, it is easier for each government to evaluate the efficiency of a supplier for any particular government. The lesson here is one repeated throughout the text: There are benefits from competition.

Competition in the Public and Private Sectors

It is thus interesting to note that although the government enforces competition in the private sector through the antitrust laws, competition is often deliberately eliminated in the public sector. Competing government services are often combined under the rationale of eliminating duplication of effort. However, unless there are obvious economies of scale, duplication of effort is a form of competition that has potentially beneficial side effects. Even if there is no actual competition for customers—for example, if each office uses its own typing pool—the duplication of effort means that each office can compare its production efficiency with the efficiency of other, similar organizations. In this sense duplication of effort is a form of competition, and unless strong economies of scale dictate otherwise, it should be encouraged as a way of reaping some of the benefits of competition in a bureaucratic environment.

---

[12]This idea, discussed in Chapter 18, is built on the discussion of Harold Demsetz, "Why Regulate Utilities?" *Journal of Law & Economics* 11 (1968), pp. 55–65.

The Voucher System

In this section we review a proposal by Milton Friedman on how public education can be produced so that it retains the characteristics of public finance but takes advantage of the efficiency gains of private production.[13] Friedman's proposal is commonly known as the *voucher system*, and it provides a good illustration of the principle of public finance with private production advanced earlier in this chapter.

Although one might argue that positive externalities can result from receiving an education, most of the benefits go to the educated individual. This supports the argument that education, like other personal services, should be produced in the private sector of the economy. Even so, there are equity reasons why people might view the public provision of education as desirable. Consistent with the notion of equality of opportunity, it might seem inequitable for the children of wealthy parents to receive better educational opportunities than children of poor parents. Note, however, that this is an argument for the public financing of education, not necessarily for the public production of education.

Public Finance but Private Production

The voucher system retains the public financing characteristic of education but allows the freedom to choose where the student will go to school—the educational institution could be either a public or a private school. Under the voucher system taxes for public education

are collected in the same way as they are now, but the money collected is then used to finance an education voucher for each school-age child. The child's family is allowed to spend the vouchers at the school of their choice. The family turns over the voucher to the school and the school then redeems the voucher with the government to receive payment for the child's education.

The voucher system has many advantages over the current system of public education. Currently, parents can decide to send their children to private schools, but if they do, they must pay taxes for public schools in addition to the tuition for the private school. This means that under the current system private schools are much more available to wealthy families than poor ones. Under the voucher system any family would be allowed to elect to spend their voucher at a private school, making private schools more accessible to every student.

One big advantage of this system would be that with more people able to afford alternatives to public education, the number of private schools would increase. Education today is very standardized because most students are educated in public schools; often, no viable alternatives exist. Just as individual families choose automobiles with different characteristics, so families would demand schools with a variety of different characteristics if they were available. Many more alternatives would be available if public schools did not have such a competitive advantage in being able to offer education without tuition payments.

Under the voucher system public schools could still exist, being funded, like all other schools, by the vouchers of students who

---

[13]Milton Friedman, "The Role of Government in Education," *Capitalism and Freedom* (Chicago: University of Chicago Press, 1962), ch. 6.

chose to enroll in them. Those people who found public schools to be the best alternative would still be able to avail themselves of the public schools. Again, there is every reason to believe that the quality of education would increase. Keep in mind that under the voucher system the only way that schools can continue to exist is to attract vouchers from students who choose to enroll there. In education, as with any other type of service, competition would tend to force producers to offer the highest quality product that they could for the money.

In short, the voucher system offers a number of advantages over the current system of public education. It would allow individuals freedom of choice in educational institutions and would increase competition, thereby increasing educational quality. At the same time it would retain the public financing of education, making alternatives to public education more available to every student.

Some Criticisms

The voucher system has its critics as well. One criticism is that the government would still have to decide what constitutes a school for the purpose of issuing a voucher. Without some criteria schools might be little more than organized babysitting services, and they might even use money collected from vouchers for the entertainment of parents rather than the education of students. Indeed, one can imagine the types of bizarre institutions that might call themselves schools and collect vouchers. Thus, some government guidelines would be needed to prevent abuses of the voucher system, but such guidelines would effectively stifle some of the variety in education that the voucher system could provide. Furthermore, one of the functions of public education is to socialize individuals so that they can get along

as adults in American society. The fact that most people in public education share common backgrounds aids the process. A wide variety of educational institutions could be counterproductive to the national unity fostered by a common educational system.

Another criticism is that under the voucher system some schools might offer extra services but levy a charge on top of the voucher tuition to pay for those services. Many exclusive private schools already do this, but the voucher system would encourage the establishment of more exclusive schools of this type, thus promoting more of a class system in education and subverting the goal of equality of opportunity. Indeed, some private schools might refuse to take some students, leaving the public schools with all of the educational problems. This could be avoided, though, by requiring schools that receive voucher payments to take all applicants.

Politics and the Voucher System

Another factor to consider when looking at the voucher system is the potential political problem of getting the system approved. This is simply an application of a special interest going up against a rationally ignorant general public. The special interest in this case consists of the individuals who work in the current public school system. As it stands, public schools have a great deal of monopoly power by virtue of their state support. Freed from the constraints of competition, it is likely that those working in public schools, including teachers and administrators, do not have to work as hard, do not have to be as concerned about quality, and perhaps can earn above-market wages for the quality of output they produce. Faced with competition and the prospect that many public school students would choose private schools if the cost were the same, educators have a strong economic incentive to retain the current public education system.

Furthermore, those with a vested interest in the continuance of the current system will argue that the voucher system would harm the quality of education, and the rationally ignorant general public might tend to believe the "experts." The current system shelters educators from competition, so in light of the economic incentives involved, one should not be surprised that many educators oppose the institution of the voucher system.

To summarize, the voucher system is a method for retaining the public finance of ed-ucation but allowing educational institutions to exhibit more variety in response to market demands and to provide the efficiency benefits of competition among schools. Criticisms of the voucher system center on this variety that its proponents view as an asset. Critics view standardized education as beneficial to the society as a whole and see the potential for abuse of the system if a voucher system is instituted. Nevertheless, considering the potential for freedom of choice for consumers and the benefits to education in general of increased competition, the voucher system represents an interesting alternative to the current system of public education.

Privatization

In general terms the subject of this chapter is *privatization*, the shifting of productive activity from the public sector to the private sector. The material presented thus far illustrates that privatization can take many different forms. At the two extremes are government production and private sector production, but a number of intermediate alternatives can be categorized and evaluated. In a federal system production can take place at many different levels of government, and by contracting to private organizations, it is possible to combine public finance with private production. Many of these alternatives have been discussed before, so the main purpose of this section is to examine and compare them in a more organized way.[14]

---

[14]See E. S. Savas, *Privatizing the Public Sector* (Chatham, N.J.: Chatham House, 1982), for a similar type of categorization and a good general discussion of privatization.

Federal Government Production

When someone perceives a problem with the private sector and suggests that the government do something about it, production by the federal government is the solution that frequently comes to mind. The growth of federal nondefense spending, documented in Chapter 1, reflects this tendency. The goal of privatization is to return some of this government production to the private sector, but first we need to review why the federal government might be the most desirable producer for some things.

National defense and international relations represent two areas in which the federal government is widely viewed as the best producer. In fact, the optimal scope for defense may encompass more than just one nation—organizations like NATO provide a degree of international defense against perceived international threats. The government does contract out most defense hardware procurement, though. Could the same be done for military units themselves? Could the government pay a private organization to provide an army, a fleet of ships, or an air squadron? Often, alternatives to the status quo are not even considered because people have become accustomed to the current way of doing things.

Even if the government were to contract out more of its defense effort, sound arguments for federal government (and even international) financing and coordination remain. Defense is a good example of a collective consumption good for which the benefits of production are spread over a large area. Most Americans would agree, for example, that the security of Europe is in the American interest, and Europeans would no doubt agree that they benefit from American security.[15] Clearly, programs of national and international scope are best undertaken by national governments and international organizations.

Other programs, such as the interstate highway system, are undertaken, and produce benefits enjoyed, over a wide scope. States have an incentive to produce roads for travel within their states, but not to produce a coordinated highway system that enables travelers to pass through the state while en route to another location. Again, national coordination is desirable, even though production itself could be (and usually is) contracted out.

Lower-Level Government Production

State and local governments are an alternative to federal government production, and though this still constitutes government rather than private production, recall the various reasons why it is beneficial to produce output at the lowest level of government possible. Indeed, many benefits can be reaped from intergovernmental competition. Individuals can move to areas where the government's output best suits their demands, and even if they do not move, simply by comparing other governments with one's own, voters can evaluate the relative efficiency of their governments.

The increasing involvement of the federal government, even in the form of intergovernmental grants and the like, in effect helps to form a cartel of lower-level governments that reduces intergovernmental competition. Even if it is decided that the government should be involved in some type of activity, it is still important to consider what level of government could best perform the activity.

Government Contracts and Franchises

As has already been suggested, the government can contract out production while still relying on public financing for a project. Public finance with private production is feasible for a wide range of public sector activities. Sometimes, when the market would fail to provide the optimal output, the government can involve itself only to the extent of granting a franchise to a private sector firm. Utilities are the best example of this. According to one school of thought, certain industries, especially utilities, are natural monopolies. Thus, utilities such as electricity, gas, and telephone service should be provided by regulated monopolists. The government grants a supplier the right to be the monopoly supplier and then, typically, regulates the supplier.

---

[15] For a persuasive (and disturbing) argument on the other side of the issue, see Earl C. Ravenal, "The Price and Perils of NATO," in David Boaz and Edward H. Crane, eds., *Beyond the Status Quo* (Washington, D.C.: Cato Institute, 1985).

However, there is no particular reason why the government has to grant a monopoly franchise. In some areas more than one cable television company has a government-granted franchise, and taxicab service in New York City is provided by cabs that are given the right to provide service as a government franchise.

Note that if competition is possible, the need for regulation is reduced, but this also may weaken the argument for a government franchise at all. In the New York City cab case the franchise is granted presumably to prevent the streets from being overcongested with cabs. In this context an argument for franchising can be made in view of the externality that would be produced by overuse of the public roads. Keep in mind, however, that private benefits are going to the license holders, which raises questions about whether the regulation was passed in the public interest or to further private interests.

Note the difference between a franchise and a government contract to a private firm. The government is the purchaser in the case of the contract, but with a franchise the supplier sells directly to the consumer, producing more of a market-oriented system. Franchises would work well in operating a toll road, for example. The government could operate the road itself, or it could contract to a private firm to operate the road, or it could sell or lease a franchise to a private firm to run the road. With the franchise the toll payments would go directly to the franchise holder, but the government could solicit bids for the franchise, much as Harold Demsetz suggested be done with utilities.[16] Thus, franchises should be considered as an alternative to direct government production and even government contracting.

---

[16]Harold Demsetz, "Why Regulate Utilities?" *Journal of Law & Economics* 11 (1968), pp. 55–65; Demsetz's proposals were discussed at some length in Chapter 18.

Grants and Vouchers

Often, government programs are designed to encourage certain activities or to help individuals obtain certain goods and services. In these cases grants and vouchers can be, and often are, substituted for government production. For example, the government can build low-income housing for individuals to try to provide them with a better living environment, but another alternative is to provide them with a housing grant. Likewise, the government can hire a team to undertake some research, or it can issue a research grant to a private contractor. And as noted previously, vouchers for education could supplement (or replace) the public school system.

Again, the point is that just because there is some perceived public need does not necessarily mean government production is called for. Provision of a government grant for housing, for example, lets the individual decide which housing offers the best accommodations for the money and allows the person receiving the grant to monitor the behavior of the owner of the housing. If the accommodations prove unsatisfactory, the person can move, thus allowing the market rather than a government bureaucracy to police the efficiency of production.

Private Sector Production

A final alternative is no government activity at all. In the real world things are rarely perfect, and just because one perceives a problem does not necessarily mean that the government can improve things. As the economic concept of scarcity implies, everyone cannot have everything they want. It follows that the government can never solve all of everyone's problems.

When considering the possibility of governmental activity, too often people compare the real world of the private sector with some idealized vision of what government can accomplish. One of the goals of this text has been to realistically assess the strengths and limitations of government. Governmental activity is responsible for much of our well-being in today's society, but too often it has also been called on to solve problems for which it is poorly equipped. Government cannot solve all of the imperfections of an imper-fect world, and a study of public sector economics should provide some insight into the activities that the government is poorly equipped to handle, as well as the activities that it handles well. Private sector production without government involvement should always be considered as an alternative.

Tax Considerations for Privatization

The tax structure may have an influence on whether governmentally provided goods and services are produced by the government directly or are contracted out to private sector producers. These tax considerations are primarily the result of provisions in the federal tax code. There are tax advantages for both public and private provision of output, and sometimes they can be combined to yield even greater advantages.

There are two main advantages to public sector production of output. The first is that governments do not pay taxes on their income, whereas private sector firms, if making profits, do. The effects of this advantage are not entirely clear, however. For one thing the difference in efficiency between private and public sector production could have a more significant effect on the cost of producing output than the tax differences. For another, as noted in the chapter on regulation, the behavior of firms might change when they are regulated monopolies. Furthermore, abstracting from differences in private and public production, any profits from private production are retained by the firm, whereas public firms cannot retain profits (recall that this is the source of many of the differences in the incentives in public and private production). Nevertheless, it is worth noting that public producers do not pay taxes and private producers do.

The second advantage of public production is that interest on state and local bonds is often deductible from income for purposes of federal income taxation. Because taxes are not paid on interest from these bonds, the interest rate that must be offered to sell the bonds is lower. Therefore, considering the interest charges, it will be cheaper to borrow money for a publicly financed project than a privately financed project.

Although private firms would be liable for income taxes on any privatized undertaking, certain tax provisions give advantages for private as opposed to public investment. For example, accelerated depreciation allows a firm to show accounting losses while a project develops a positive cash flow.

State and local governments have sometimes tried to combine the tax benefits of public and private provision by having the government raise the funds for a project and turning the money over to a private firm for production of the good or service. Wastewater treatment is but one area in which this has been attempted, on a limited basis. The local government floats a bond issue to raise money for the facility, taking advantage of the tax-exempt status of the bonds to offer a lower interest rate than could be offered by a private firm. Having received this financing advantage, the government then turns the money over to a private firm, which produces the wastewater treatment plant under contract to the government. The private firm is then able to take advantage of tax write-offs that would not be available to the government.

Although such financing techniques are not now widespread, they have the potential to grow as the movement toward privatization in wastewater treatment gains momentum. Thus, it is important to recognize that the tax structure affects the revenue-generating potential of privatized projects and therefore the cost of the facilities to taxpayers and users.

Regulation

In Chapter 18 regulation was presented as an alternative to taxation. The government can collect taxes to pay for government programs that attempt to produce certain ends, or it can pass regulations that require individuals and firms in the private sector to engage in activities to produce those ends. The regulation is, in effect, a tax on those who are regulated. In this sense regulation is an alternative to government production.

For example, if industry is polluting a river, the government can undertake a program, financed by taxation, to clean up the waterway. Alternatively, the government can pass regulations requiring the polluters to engage in cleanup activities. This keeps the activity in the private sector rather than in the public sector by substituting regulation for government spending. In short, any regulation can be the equivalent of a spending program, financed by taxation, to force the regulated entity to do what the regulation requires without payment. The regulation serves to same function as a tax because the regulated entity must undertake the action the government desires, but without compensation.

Because regulation rather than public spending can privatize government activities, we must recognize that the economic effects of government extend far beyond the government budget. Total government spending is slightly more than a third of GNP, but because regulation is the equivalent of taxation, a better measure of the government's economic impact would add the costs of regulation to the government's budget. Nevertheless, when government involvement is contemplated in the economy, regulation should be considered as an alternative to government production.

Market and Government Production

As the data listed in Chapter 1 illustrated, governmental involvement in economic activity has steadily increased throughout this century. Most people would agree that some governmental activity is necessary for producing a free and productive society.[17] Around the

---

[17] Not everyone would agree, though. Murray Rothbard, *For a New Liberty* (New York: Macmillan, 1973), argues

turn of the century, government spending at all levels of government was less than 8 percent of *GNP*, and an analysis of government at that time did not really require a complete inquiry into the economic effects of governmental activity. For one thing there was not much government activity. For another, what the government was doing was perceived by most people as necessary government functions.

Today the situation is different. The government is called on to solve many economic problems, and one must have a thorough understanding of the way in which both the market and the government allocate resources to be able to evaluate proposals for government involvement in the economy. In an ideal situation the market allocates resources with perfect efficiency; two features of the price system enable this to happen.

Market Prices and Economic Information

First, market prices provide individuals in an economy with all of the information they need concerning resources in an economy, and prices provide that information in a very economical way. For example, consumers making socially optimal decisions about the amount of coffee to drink must take into account the weather in coffee-growing countries, the costs of shipping coffee, and the demands of other consumers for the product. But they do not need to know this information directly. Instead, all of these effects relevant to the consumer's coffee-consuming decisions are summarized in the price of coffee. Indeed, market prices do an excellent job of summarizing and transmitting economic information.

Market Prices and Incentives

Second, market prices provide an incentive to allocate resources efficiently because economic agents get to keep the difference between the prices they are paid for goods and services and the prices they pay for their purchases. This profit motive allows individuals to reap the rewards for efficient resource allocation. Thus, the market provides not only the information necessary for the efficient allocation of resources but also the incentive for individuals to act on that information to allocate resources efficiently.

Problems arise when property rights are poorly defined or transactions costs are high enough that efficient trades cannot take place. These situations give rise to inefficient allocations of resources and often prompt a call for government action. The realities of market allocation of resources must be compared to the realities of government allocation, though, because individuals in government do not always have the incentive to allocate resources efficiently either.

Information and Incentives in the Public Sector

Public sector output typically is not sold on the market, unlike output in the private sector. Indeed, in a market-oriented economy such as in the United States, government action in economic affairs is often the result of an inefficient market. But without market prices, the two functions performed by the price system are absent from government production. First, there is not good information about the efficiency of government resource allocation because market prices are not available to provide signals. Second, the incentives provided by trading at market prices are not available to individuals in government, which means they lack the incentive to allocate resources efficiently.

---

that all activities of government, from courts to national defense, can be better carried out in the private sector.

Niskanen's theory of bureaucracy, discussed in Chapter 8, states that rather than being profit maximizers, government bureaucrats are budget maximizers, which gives rise to larger-than-optimal budgets for government production. Indeed, the studies reviewed earlier in this chapter illustrate that when public enterprise can be compared with private enterprise, production in the public sector is less efficient.

These findings, in both theory and practice, provide the impetus to explore alternatives to government production. Certainly, there are compelling reasons for the government to be involved in many economic activities, but the incentives and information structure that lead to efficiency in the market are absent in the public sector, so one must weigh the alternatives carefully. We have suggested in this chapter that the choices are not merely to allow the unfettered market to operate or to have the government produce output. Rather, a range of options should be considered, from regulation to franchising to government contracting to actual government production. In light of the incentives and information provided through the market, there is good reason to try to retain as much of those market characteristics as possible while addressing perceived problems with the market.

Conclusion

Public sector economics analyzes, from an economic standpoint, the activities of government. As government involvement in the economy has increased, it has become more important to understand not only why it might be desirable to have the government participate in economic activities but also what the limitations of government involvement might be. Examining the weaknesses of government involvement in economic activities is not meant as a critique of the government, any more than looking at the problems that may arise in the market's allocation of resources is a critique of the market system. But by recognizing the principles of market and government allocation of resources—including both strengths and weaknesses—we can make informed choices about the type, and extent, of governmental economic activity.

This chapter has drawn heavily on the analysis from the rest of the text in examining a number of alternative economic structures.

One alternative is to fully utilize the various levels of government in a federal system at which production can take place. Although technically not an alternative to government production, it is an option that merits consideration in any debate about public sector resource allocation.

Another alternative is to contract out production to private firms. The government can finance the production when problems with positive externalities and nonexcludable goods make private financing difficult, but it can leave the production of output to the private sector. In the many studies reviewed here, the private sector appeared to be significantly more efficient than the public sector in the actual production of goods and services. Another alternative is franchising, by which the government can grant, either on an exclusive or a nonexclusive basis, the rights for private sector production.

Grants and vouchers also provide an alternative when public finance would be desirable but there are no impediments to private production. Milton Friedman's voucher system for education is one example of how vouchers might work. The government would provide each student with a voucher that could be used to purchase output from any seller of education. This would provide market incentives for efficient production and would allow much greater variety than is now available. Currently, the government uses housing vouchers in much the same way. Low-income individuals are given housing vouchers that can be applied to their rents at privately owned apartments.

An examination of the available alternatives represents more than just an idle academic exercise, because in a democratic society the citizens ultimately choose what type of government they want, what they want their government to do, and how they want their

government to do it. A clear understanding of the process through which collective decisions are made and the way in which the public sector can be expected to allocate resources is essential for making an informed choice. Much of economics is a study of the market system, which is a result of human action but not of human design.[18] Public sector economics, however, focuses on that part of the economy that is the result of human design and that is constantly being redesigned. The better we understand how a government works, the more effectively we will be able to design government activities to enhance our well-being.

---

[18]This is a recurring theme in the work of Freidrich A. Hayek. See, for example, *Studies in Philosophy, Politics, and Economics* (Chicago: University of Chicago Press, 1969), ch. 6.

Questions

1. Currently, the government contracts with private sector firms for most national defense hardware. Would it be feasible for the government to do the same thing with armies? The government could simply contract with a private firm to provide an army of so many men with certain characteristics and abilities and with certain military hardware. The government could further require that they be able to pass certain tests on military maneuvers and exercises to be compensated. What would be the advantages of this alternative to the current system? What would be the disadvantages? Overall, how do you think the system would work?

2. Explain the dual roles that the price system plays in enabling resources to be efficiently allocated in the market. What types of problems can prevent this efficient allocation from taking place?

3. Explain the operation of Milton Friedman's proposed voucher system. What are its advantages and disadvantages? Overall, would you prefer this system to the current system of public education? What are the political barriers to its implementation?

4. Review some evidence regarding the relative efficiencies of public sector production versus private sector production. What conclusions do you draw from this evidence? Do you think that efficiency considerations alone should dictate whether the private sector or public sector is used to produce goods and services? What other factors might be relevant?

5. What differences would you expect to find in postal service if it were a private sector activity rather than a service of a government-owned monopoly? Discuss some advantages and disadvantages of each type of system. How would your answer be different if the government contracted out the actual mail delivery activities while retaining the current service and fee structure?

6. Critically evaluate the notion that government organizations should be consolidated to eliminate duplication of effort.

7. Explain how the government could use franchises for production rather than directly produce output itself. Give some examples of franchises. Are there situations in which an exclusive franchise would be preferable to a nonexclusive franchise? How could the government use competitive bidding to substitute for regulation of franchise holders?

8. Explain why there can sometimes be tax advantages for privatization of governmentally provided output. What are the implications of these tax advantages for economic efficiency?

9. In general, what activities do you think the government should undertake? At what levels of government should they be undertaken? Considering the realities of political decision making, are your ideas feasible? How could your ideas be implemented through the existing political process?

Index